Avatar–Based Control, Estimation, Communications, and Development of Neuron Multi–Functional Technology Platforms

Vardan Mkrttchian
HHH University, Australia

Ekaterina Aleshina
Penza State University, Russia

Leyla Gamidullaeva
Penza State University, Russia

A volume in the Advances in
Computational Intelligence and
Robotics (ACIR) Book Series

Published in the United States of America by
IGI Global
Engineering Science Reference (an imprint of IGI Global)
701 E. Chocolate Avenue
Hershey PA, USA 17033
Tel: 717-533-8845
Fax: 717-533-8661
E-mail: cust@igi-global.com
Web site: http://www.igi-global.com

Library of Congress Cataloging-in-Publication Data

Names: Mkrttchian, Vardan, 1950- editor. | Aleshina, Ekaterina, 1978-
   editor. | Gamidullaeva, Leyla, 1985- editor.
Title: Avatar-based control, estimation, communications, and development of
   neuron multi-functional technology platforms / Vardan Mkrttchian,
   Ekaterina Aleshina, Leyla Gamidullaeva, editors.
Description: Hershey, PA : Engineering Science Reference, [2020] | Includes
   bibliographical references and index. | Summary: "This book presents
   techniques, case studies, and methodologies that combine the use of
   intelligent artificial and natural approaches with optimization
   techniques for facing problems and combines many types of hardware and
   software with a variety of communication technologies to enable the
   development of innovative applications"-- Provided by publisher.
Identifiers: LCCN 2019031655 (print) | LCCN 2019031656 (ebook) | ISBN
   9781799815815 (h/c) | ISBN 9781799815822 (s/c) | ISBN 9781799815839
   (ebook)
Subjects: LCSH: Avatars (Virtual reality) | Artificial intelligence. |
   Information technology--Social aspects. | Shared virtual environments.
Classification: LCC QA76.76.I59 A984 2020 (print) | LCC QA76.76.I59
   (ebook) | DDC 006.8--dc23
LC record available at https://lccn.loc.gov/2019031655
LC ebook record available at https://lccn.loc.gov/2019031656

This book is published in the IGI Global book series Advances in Computational Intelligence and Robotics (ACIR) (ISSN: 2327-0411; eISSN: 2327-042X)

British Cataloguing in Publication Data
A Cataloguing in Publication record for this book is available from the British Library.

All work contributed to this book is new, previously-unpublished material.
The views expressed in this book are those of the authors, but not necessarily of the publisher.

For electronic access to this publication, please contact: eresources@igi-global.com.

Advances in Computational Intelligence and Robotics (ACIR) Book Series

ISSN:2327-0411
EISSN:2327-042X

Editor-in-Chief: *Ivan Giannoccaro* University of Salento, Italy

MISSION

While intelligence is traditionally a term applied to humans and human cognition, technology has progressed in such a way to allow for the development of intelligent systems able to simulate many human traits. With this new era of simulated and artificial intelligence, much research is needed in order to continue to advance the field and also to evaluate the ethical and societal concerns of the existence of artificial life and machine learning.

The **Advances in Computational Intelligence and Robotics (ACIR) Book Series** encourages scholarly discourse on all topics pertaining to evolutionary computing, artificial life, computational intelligence, machine learning, and robotics. ACIR presents the latest research being conducted on diverse topics in intelligence technologies with the goal of advancing knowledge and applications in this rapidly evolving field.

COVERAGE

- Computational Logic
- Computer Vision
- Evolutionary Computing
- Agent technologies
- Brain Simulation
- Natural Language Processing
- Fuzzy Systems
- Computational Intelligence
- Robotics
- Neural Networks

IGI Global is currently accepting manuscripts for publication within this series. To submit a proposal for a volume in this series, please contact our Acquisition Editors at Acquisitions@igi-global.com or visit: http://www.igi-global.com/publish/.

Titles in this Series

701 East Chocolate Avenue, Hershey, PA 17033, USA
Tel: 717-533-8845 x100 • Fax: 717-533-8661
E-Mail: cust@igi-global.com • www.igi-global.com

Table of Contents

Detailed Table of Contents

Chapter 1

    Vsevolod Chernyshenko, Financial University Under the Government of
        the Russian Federation, Russia
    Vladimir Soloviev, Financial University Under the Government of the
        Russian Federation, Russia
    Vadim Feklin, Financial University Under the Government of the
        Russian Federation, Russia
    Mikhail Koroteev, Financial University Under the Government of the
        Russian Federation, Russia
    Nikita Titov, Financial University Under the Government of the Russian
        Federation, Russia

The chapter formalizes the financial task for the definitions and properties of financial indicators under study. A wide range of traditional approaches used for predicting economic time series were reviewed. Investigated as well were the advanced algorithms for predicting moments of reversals of market trends based on machine learning tools. The chapter discusses the effectiveness of different kinds of approaches, which is illustrated with related examples. Described is an original securities price dynamics trend classification algorithm, based on the use of the sliding window methodology and financial agents. General scheme of the classification algorithm to identify market phases is analyzed and results of computer modeling are presented. Selection of initial and resulting metrics is grounded.

Chapter 2

Anara Kizabekova, Institute of Eurasian Integration, Kazakhstan
Vsevolod Chernyshenko, Financial University Under the Government of
*   the Russian Federation, Russia*

The chapter provides a critical analysis by researchers of Kazakh, Russian and foreign authors in the field of open government. Analysis of state indicators of Kazakhstan, international frameworks regarding ICT development, open data, open government, and budget transparency and ways of their improvement are also presented. Results of an investigation of open government's role from the scope of view of official resolutions and national strategic planning of the Republic of Kazakhstan are shown. Most remarkable international initiatives in the field of Open Government are reviewed. The chapter proves the lack of strategic vision of the open government institutions and necessity to study the best world practices by Kazakhstan's strategic bodies to develop citizen-oriented e-Government platform. Critical analysis of challenges arousing at early stages of open data introduction and proper sustainable solutions is presented.

Chapter 3

Vladimir Gorbachenko, Penza State University, Russia

Digital models are needed in medicine for diagnosis and prediction. Such models are especially needed in personalized medicine. In this area, it is necessary to evaluate and predict the patient's condition from a priori knowledge obtained from other patients. Therefore, a new direction of predictive medicine appeared. Predictive medicine, or "in silicon medicine" is the use of computer modeling and intelligent technologies in the diagnosis, treatment, and prevention of diseases. Using predictive medicine, the doctor can determine the likelihood of the development of certain diseases and choose the optimal treatment. Predictive medicine begins to be applied in surgery. The prognosis in surgery consists in the preoperative evaluation of various surgical interventions and in the evaluation of possible outcomes of surgical interventions.

Chapter 4

Vladimir Gorbachenko, Penza State University, Russia
Konstantin Savenkov, Penza State University, Russia

Digital twins are widely used in modern industry. A digital twin is a computer model that copies the behavior of a physical object. Digital twins of objects with distributed parameters are mathematically boundary value problems for partial differential equation. Traditionally, such problems are solved by finite difference and finite element methods, which require a complex grid construction procedure. The numerical solution of boundary value problems employs mesh less methods that do not require grid construction. Among mesh fewer methods, projection methods that use radial basis functions (RBFs) as basic functions are popular. Methods using RBF allow us to obtain a differentiable solution at any point in the solution domain, applicable to problems of arbitrary dimension with complex computational domains. When solving the problem, the parameters of the basic functions are selected, and the weights are calculated so that the residuals obtained after the substitution of the approximate solution at the test points in the equation are zero.

Chapter 5

>   *Vladimir Soloviev, Financial University Under the Government of the Russian Federation, Russia*
>   *Vsevolod Chernyshenko, Financial University Under the Government of the Russian Federation, Russia*
>   *Vadim Feklin, Financial University Under the Government of the Russian Federation, Russia*
>   *Ekaterina Zolotareva, Financial University Under the Government of the Russian Federation, Russia*
>   *Nikita Titov, Financial University Under the Government of the Russian Federation, Russia*

The chapter is devoted to the problem of analytical analysis of implementation of generative-competitive neural networks in predicting the state of financial markets (particularly to predict future moments of changing market conditions) based on the use of convolutional and generative neural networks, as well as reinforcement training. An algorithm for predicting future moments of trend change under concrete market conditions based on generative adversarial networks was developed. Special software that realizes algorithms for predicting future moments of changing market conditions, based on the algorithms mentioned above was designed.

*Serge V. Chernyshenko, Open University for the Humanities and
Economics, Russia*

The chapter is devoted to the analysis of possibilities in designing dynamic properties of avatars in multi-agent systems. It is shown that determination of "differential logic" of avatars, based on the use of differential equations, gives sufficient flexibility in describing their behavior over time. At the same time, the differential description usually involves a smooth response of the object to external or internal influences, which for avatars is usually not correct. To eliminate this weak point, it is proposed to use the technology of internal bifurcations, which allows to simulate discontinues effects in the avatar dynamics. It is shown that even when using relatively simple quadratic models of the Lotka-Volterra type, the technique allows to describe rather complex information interactions in the multi-agent systems.

*Andrey Tuskov, Penza State University, Russia
Anna Goldina, Penza State University, Russia
Olga Luzgina, Penza State University, Russia
Olga Salnikova, Penza State University, Russia*

One of the determining factors for ensuring regional food security is the sectoral structure of production. It determines the specialization and combination of industries, on which the degree of tension, balance, and economic efficiency of the production program of peasant farming depends. This is achieved subject to the proportionality of the elements of the sectoral complex. For this, it is necessary to coordinate production volumes with available resources, the level of intensification of crop production and animal husbandry, the size of crops, individual crops, and livestock, etc. The size of peasant farms and their structure (the composition and area of land, the combination and size of main and additional industries, the structure of crops) depend on many natural and economic factors. There are various options for the organization of production and territory for the same farming with certain resources of land, labor, and capital. The main task is to choose the optimal one that corresponds to the interests of the farmer and gives the maximum economic effect.

The authors propose a general formulation of the economic and mathematical model of the problem of optimizing the size of the newly created peasant farms and Industrial Development, taking into account the chosen specialization of activity, as well as determining the optimal parameters for the already-known size of farms. The developed mathematical model differs from the classical one by the presence of additional blocks, which prescribe the sales channels of manufactured products and determine the necessary financial resources. The proposed methodological approach should be used for planning the development of regional economies, taking into account the existing specifics.

This chapter discusses digital mechanisms for optimizing the management system in the forest industry, which includes organizational, legal, socio-economic, and environmental aspects. Efficient forest management is considered as an integral part of efficient nature management and includes the use of forest resources, their protection, and reproduction of forests. Digital management mechanisms in forest management in general and in the forest industry in particular are based on platform solutions. Platform solutions are based on the formation and processing of data on the basis of a single automated information system, which acts as the foundation for the development of digitalization in forestry. Such a digital platform is designed to provide informational, analytical, consulting, and other support to the activities of all subjects of relations in the field of use, conservation, protection, and reproduction of forest resources.

Chapter 10
New Perspectives on Cluster Model of Enterprise Development in the

Yulia Vertakova, Financial University, Government of the Russian
Federation, Russia
Galina Surovitskaya, Penza State University, Russia
Lubov Semerkova, Penza State University, Russia
Eugene Leontyev, Southwest State University, Russia
Irina Izmalkova, Financial University Under the Government of the
Russian Federation, Lipetsk Branch, Russia
Potapova Irina, Astrakhan SAS University, Russia
Maksim Kireev, K. G. Razumovsky Moscow State University of
Technologies and Management (FCU), Russia

This chapter presents the author's views about new perspectives on cluster model of enterprise development in the context of risk management. Ensuring the efficiency and risk tolerance of enterprises is possible through the use of network organizational structures. Modern business conditions have created a significant variety of network forms, due to the peculiarities of the functioning of the industries and territories where they are used, the level of availability of information and communication technologies, the development of market infrastructure and social environment. One of the traditional and common forms of networks is the integration of enterprises into a cluster.

Chapter 11
Avatar-Based and Automated Testing System for Quality Control of Student
Training: Using Neuron Natural and Artificial Technology Platform Triple H.212

Mikhail Kataev, Tomsk State University of Control Systems and
Radioelectronics, Russia
Vardan Mkrttchian, HHH University, Australia
Larisa Bulysheva, Old Dominion University, USA
Anatoly Korikov, Tomsk State University of Control Systems and
Radioelectronics, Russia

The chapter covers avatar-based control for neuron natural and artificial technology platform used in automated testing system for quality control of student training. The chapter proposes the concept of creating an automated software system for monitoring student knowledge in the learning process. It is proven that for successful students to learn remotely, it is necessary to develop a knowledge assessment system that takes into account various learning features, as well as the individual characteristics of the student. The block structure of an automated software system is presented and its elements are discussed in relation to the educational process. The role of the teacher in the virtual learning system is discussed and an algorithm of the learning process in this system is presented.

Chapter 12
Avatar-Based Control and Development of Neuron Multi-Functional
Platforms for Transformation Processes in the Digital Economy 231

Vardan Mkrttchian, HHH University, Australia
Serge Chernyshenko, Open University for the Humanities and
*   Economics, Russia*
Ekaterina Aleshina, Penza State University, Russia

The diverse sectors of the economy are subject to transformational processes in the digital economy. The reason for the rapid digital progress based on a functioning mechanism and the great attention to this transformation are the only economic reasons for reducing the costs of the transformation elements that are present in every product and, along with the transformation, affect mainly all sectors of the economy. For example, in the European Union there is a Permanent Forum on the digital teaching of environmental disciplines. In authors' opinion, the existing transformation models are extremely useful in connection with the decision of Russia and the EAEU member countries on the transformation of Digital Economy. This chapter sets the task of managing on the basis of avatars and developing neural multifunctional technological platforms for transformation processes in Digital Economy as based on the analysis of world experience in the use of digital technologies in teaching environmental disciplines and Triple H Avatar.

Chapter 13
Intellectual Property Institute as a Means of Regional Economic Integration
in the Digital Framework: Searching for Ways to Increase Efficiency 248

Leyla Gamidullaeva, Penza State University, Russia
Saniyat Agamagomedova, Penza State University, Russia
Oleg Koshevoy, Penza State University, Russia
Valentina Smagina, Derzhavin Tambov State University, Russia
Natalia Rasskazova, Penza State University, Russia

The effectiveness of intellectual property management in the context of Eurasian economic integration is positioned as a factor in reducing business costs in the EAEU. One of the basic conditions for effective economic development is competition in the field of intellectual property. In the context of globalization and digital transformation, intellectual property management reaches a qualitatively new level of organizational and legal regulation and determines the freedom of movement of goods and services in the single economic territory of interstate integration entities. The authors of the chapter concluded that an effective intellectual property management mechanism in the EAEU is a factor of reducing the costs of foreign trade business. Inequality in the protection of intellectual property in the EAEU impedes the formation and development of competitive relations, and impedes the freedom of movement of goods as the basic goal of economic integration of the EAEU states.

Chapter 14

    Leyla Gamidullaeva, Penza State University, Russia
    Sergey Vasin, Penza State University, Russia
    Nadezhda Chernetsova, Penza State University, Russia
    Elena Shkarupeta, Voronezh State Technical University, Russia
    Dina Kharicheva, Moscow Pedagogical State University, Russia
    Maria Gerasimenko, K. G. Razumovsky Moscow State University of
        Technologies and Management, Russia

This chapter shows that statistics collection methods are the same for various types of websites. Often, a simple "counter" is used for both unique visitors to the site and the total number of hits to the site from unique and previously registered users. Speaking of a "digital" or "smart" economy, authors distinguish different categories (levels) of development: analysis, content of business intelligence, large data warehouses. Business analytics can be divided into a number of parts: modeling and analysis of system dynamics, expert systems and databases; knowledge and technology; geographic information (geo location); system analysis and design. The various methods and forms of information (statistical models) used to identify non-trivial patterns and propose solutions are often associated today with the concept of data mining. Intelligent data analysis involves the use of knowledge from a complex of data (databases). According to experts, data mining is one of the elements that is part of the process (database management system), which includes the analysis and cleaning of data.

Chapter 15

    Rinat Galiautdinov, Independent Researcher, Italy
    Vardan Mkrttchian, HHH University, Australia

The research describes the mathematical modeling of a neuron and the possibility of its technical implementation. Unlike existing technical devices for implementing a neuron based on classical nodes oriented to binary processing, the proposed path is based on bit-parallel processing of numerical data (synapses) for obtaining result. The proposed approach of implementing a neuron can serve as a new elementary basis for the construction of neuron-based computers with a higher processing speed of biological information and good survivability. The research demonstrates the developed nervous circuit constructor and its usage in building of the nervous circuits of biological creatures and simulation of their work.

Chapter 16
Brain Machine Interface for Avatar Control and Estimation for Educational Purposes Based on Neural AI Plugs: Theoretical and Methodological Aspects294
Rinat Galiautdinov, Independent Researcher, Italy
Vardan Mkrttchian, HHH University, Australia

In the future education process where Avatar will be used, it is critically important to have a layer which is responsible for transferring the knowledge from a Student's Avatar to Student. In this research, authors show the method and high-level architecture of how it could be done. And although the suggested approach works, the current level of technology does not allow creating a mobile set which could implement this approach. The general high-level schema of the Avatar methodology used in the education process is enclosed in the following. There are 4 layers which interact with each other. On the first layer there is a professor, who is an expert in some domain. The professor transfers their knowledge to the second layer which is a computer program, performing the role of the Professor's Avatar. The knowledge gets transferred to a Student's Avatar, which is the 3rd layer, and eventually the Student's Avatar transfers the newly received knowledge to the Student, the 4th layer in this schema. So, the most difficult part here is to transfer the knowledge from machine to human.

Preface

INTRODUCTION: AVATAR-BASED CONTROL, ESTIMATION, AND DEVELOPMENT TECHNOLOGY

Avatar-Based Control, Estimation, Communications, and Development (A-BCEC&D) Technology is a global phenomenon similarly to Blockchain. From the computer science and technological perspective A-BCEC&D Technology is a type of distributed computing and database systems with the idea of decentralization realized on modern global data networks for knowledge discovering. From the angle of social science, on the other hand, the Avatar-Based Control, Estimation, Communications, and Development Technology is an evolution that has been revolutionary changing or impacting the economics and, becoming strategic practices for industries and whole society. Avatar-Based Control, Estimation, Communications, and Development Technology, indicated as a typical disruptive technology, enables numerous benefits such as data transparency, immutability and traceability that are very critical in building a cohesive cyber infrastructure that facilitates cooperation and collaboration among different organizations. No doubt, such a disruptive technology has tremendous opportunities to detract the power from centralized authorities and, will usher in new models for economies and marketplaces, communications, governance, identification, and more.

OBJECTIVE OF THE BOOK

While Avatar-Based Control, Estimation, Communications, and Development (A-BCEC&D) Technology is still in its nascent stages, there is considerable research that needs to be done to resolve the issues, challenges and even misunderstandings.

This book aims to provide a better understanding of the global phenomenon via presenting collective recent research, focusing on A-BCEC&D architecture and frameworks for developing of Avatar-Based -enabled systems based on both perspectives of computer science and social science. The motivation is that architecture will help people to understand main features and revolution roadmap of A-BCEC&D technology structurally, while frameworks will provide guidelines for organizations to select, assess and design their strategic applications with the technology.

TARGET AUDIENCE AND READERSHIP

This book targets to those audiences, who are working on, intending to, benefiting from, or simply interesting in applying A-BCEC&D technology for organizations' objectives or even themselves, through providing comprehensive knowledge architecture and frameworks contributed by global research.

As this book collects global perspectives from across a broad range of academic and industries, so ultimately, the audiences are consists of (but not limited): researchers who intend to conduct further study for challenges; practitioners from public and private sectors in which A-BCEC&D technology had been applied or will be applied for their business usage; government bodies who are going to set up policies and rules to govern the disruptive technology and related social concerns; and educators who may use the presented finings as teaching materials. It is also good for individual who is just interested in knowing the technology.

Researchers may find there are considerable the challenges and issues to harness the disruptive technology from this book because A-BCEC&D is still in its nascent stages. Huge research efforts, therefore, need to be done to address the issues such as redundancy, complexity, energy and resource consumption, security flaws etc. Moreover, standards and good practices need to be formalized for universal adoption. Practitioners may refer to some workable cases or projects shared in the book, regarding A-BCEC&D technology applications like supplier chain, account information systems, trade finance, price distribution, decentralized system, distributed process, solar energy, paper peer-reviewing, higher education funding, bank data certification, etc. Although there are differences in various areas, people can view those cases and experiences as guidelines in designing and deploying Avatar-Based applications.

THE CHAPTERS

As this book is devoted to a very diverse range of topics contributed by many professionals and academics, it is felt necessary to provide a bird's eye view of the contents of the chapters. The following paragraphs, therefore, provide a briefing into each chapter individually.

Chapter 1 is titled "A Method of Predicting Moments of Market Trend Reversal for Decision-Making Block of Computer-Based Intelligent Financial Agent-Avatar". The chapter formalizes the financial task for the definitions and properties of financial indicators under study. Wide range of traditional approaches used for predicting economic time series were reviewed. Investigated as well were the advanced algorithms for predicting moments of reversals of market trends based on machine learning tools. The chapter discusses the effectiveness of different kinds of approaches, which is illustrated with related examples. Described is an original securities price dynamics trend classification algorithm, based on the use of the sliding window methodology and financial agents. General scheme of the classification algorithm to identify market phases is analyzed and results of computer modeling are presented. Selection of initial and resulting metrics is grounded.

Chapter 2 is titled "Avatar-Based Modeling and Development of E-Government". The chapter provides a critical analysis by researchers of Kazakh, Russian and foreign authors in the field of open government. Analysis of state indicators of Kazakhstan, international frameworks regarding ICT development, open data, open government and budget transparency and ways of their improvement are also presented. Results of an investigation of open government`s role from the scope of view of official resolutions and national strategic planning of the Republic of Kazakhstan are shown. Most remarkable international initiatives in the field of Open Government are reviewed. The chapter proves the lack of strategic vision of the open government institutions and necessity to study the best world practices by Kazakhstan's strategic bodies to develop citizen-oriented e-Government platform. Critical analysis of challenges arousing at early stages of open data introduction and proper sustainable solutions is presented.

Chapter 3 is titled "Deep Neural Networks in the Diagnosis of Postoperative Complications of Acute Appendicitis". Digital models are needed in medicine for diagnosis and prediction. Such models are especially needed in personalized medicine. In this area, it is necessary to evaluate and predict the patient's condition from a priori knowledge obtained from other patients. Therefore, a new direction of predictive medicine appeared. Predictive medicine, or "in silicon medicine" is the use of computer modeling and intelligent technologies in the diagnosis, treatment and prevention of diseases. Using predictive medicine, the doctor can determine the likelihood of the development of certain diseases and choose the optimal treatment.

Predictive medicine begins to be applied in surgery. The prognosis in surgery consists in the preoperative evaluation of various surgical interventions and in the evaluation of possible outcomes of surgical interventions.

Chapter 4 is titled "Improving Algorithms for Learning Radial Basic Functions Networks to Solve the Boundary Value Problems". Digital twins are widely used in modern industry. A digital twin is a computer model that copies the behavior of a physical object. Digital twins of objects with distributed parameters are mathematically boundary value problems for partial differential equation. Traditionally, such problems are solved by finite difference and finite element methods, which require a complex grid construction procedure. The numerical solution of boundary value problems employs mesh less methods that do not require grid construction. Among mesh fewer methods, projection methods that use radial basis functions (RBFs) as basic functions are popular. Methods using RBF allow us to obtain a differentiable solution at any point in the solution domain, applicable to problems of arbitrary dimension with complex computational domains. When solving the problem, the parameters of the basic functions are selected, and the weights are calculated so that the residuals obtained after the substitution of the approximate solution at the test points in the equation are zero.

Chapter 5 is titled "Generative Adversarial Neural Networking of Agents: Avatars as a Tool for Financial Modeling". The chapter is devoted to the problem of analytical analysis of implementation of generative-competitive neural networks in predicting the state of financial markets (particularly to predict future moments of changing market conditions) based on the use of convolutional and generative neural networks, as well as reinforcement training. An algorithm for predicting future moments of trend change under concrete market conditions based on generative adversarial networks was developed. Special software that realizes algorithms for predicting of future moments of market conditions change, based on the mentioned above algorithms was designed.

Chapter 6 is titled "Design of Avatars With 'Differential' Logic: The 'Internal Bifurcation' Approach". The chapter is devoted to the analysis of possibilities in designing dynamic properties of avatars in multi-agent systems. It is shown that determination of "differential logic" of avatars, based on the use of differential equations, gives sufficient flexibility in describing their behavior over time. At the same time, the differential description usually involves a smooth response of the object to external or internal influences, which for avatars is usually not correct. To eliminate this weak point, it is proposed to use the technology of internal bifurcations, which allows to simulate discontinues effects in the avatar dynamics. It is shown that even when using relatively simple quadratic models of the Lotka-Volterra type, the technique allows to describe rather complex information interactions in the multi-agent systems.

Chapter 7 is titled "Optimizing the Production Parameters of Peasant Holdings for Industrial Development in the Digitalization Era". One of the determining factors for ensuring regional food security is the sectorial structure of production, which determines the specialization and combination of industries, on which the degree of tension, balance and economic efficiency of the production program of peasant farming depends, which is achieved subject to the proportionality of the elements of the sectorial complex. For this, it is necessary to coordinate production volumes with available resources, the level of intensification of crop production and animal husbandry, the size of crops individual crops and livestock, etc. The size of peasant farms and their structure (the composition and area of land, the combination and size of main and additional industries, the structure of crops) depends on many natural and economic factors. There are various options for the organization of production and territory for the same farming at quite certain resources of land, labor and capital. The main task is to choose the optimal one that corresponds to the interests of the farmer and gives the maximum economic effect.

Chapter 8 is titled "Peasant Farms and Industrial Development: Mathematical Approach to the Analysis and Planning". The authors propose a General formulation of the economic and mathematical model of the problem of optimizing the size of the newly created peasant farms and Industrial Development, taking into accounts the chosen specialization of activity, as well as determining the optimal parameters for the already known size of farms. The developed mathematical model differs from the classical one by the presence of additional blocks, which prescribe the sales channels of manufactured products and determine the necessary financial resources. The proposed methodological approach should be used for planning the development of regional economies, taking into account the existing specifics.

Chapter 9 is titled "Digital Mechanisms of Management System Optimization in the Forest Industry". This chapter discusses digital mechanisms for optimizing the management system in the forest industry, which includes organizational, legal, socio-economic and environmental aspects. Efficient forest management is considered as an integral part of efficient nature management and includes the use of forest resources, their protection and reproduction of forests. Digital management mechanisms in forest management in general and in the forest industry in particular are based on platform solutions. Platform solutions are based on the formation and processing of data on the basis of a single automated information system, which acts as the foundation for the development of digitalization in forestry. Such a digital platform is designed to provide informational, analytical, consulting and other support to the activities of all subjects of relations in the field of use, conservation, protection and reproduction of forest resources.

Chapter 10 is titled "New Perspectives on Cluster Model of Enterprise Development in the Context of Risk Management". This chapter presents the author's views about new perspectives on cluster model of enterprise development in the context of risk management. Ensuring the efficiency and risk tolerance of enterprises is possible through the use of network organizational structures. Modern business conditions have created a significant variety of network forms, due to the peculiarities of the functioning of the industries and territories where they are used, the level of availability of information and communication technologies, the development of market infrastructure and social environment. One of the traditional and common forms of networks is the integration of enterprises into a cluster.

Chapter 11 is titled "Avatar-Based and Automated Testing System for Quality Control of Student Training: Using Neuron Natural and Artificial Technology Platform Triple H". The chapter covers avatar-based control for neuron natural and artificial technology platform used in automated testing system for quality control of student training. The chapter proposes the concept of creating an automated software system for monitoring student knowledge in the learning process. It is proved that for successful students to learn remotely, it is necessary to develop a knowledge assessment system that takes into account various learning features, as well as the individual characteristics of the student. The block structure of an automated software system is presented and its elements are discussed in relation to the educational process. The role of the teacher in the virtual learning system is discussed and an algorithm of the learning process in this system is presented.

Chapter 12 is titled "Avatar-Based Control and Development of Neuron Multi-Functional Platforms for Transformation Processes in Digital Economy". The diverse sectors of the economy that are subject to transformational processes in the digital economy are no exception. The reason for the rapid digital progress based on a functioning mechanism and the great attention to this transformation are only the economic reasons for reducing the costs of the transformation elements that are present in every product and, along with the transformation, affect mainly all sectors of the economy. For example, in the European Union there is a Permanent Forum on the digital teaching of environmental disciplines. In our opinion, the existing transformation models are extremely useful in connection with the decision of Russia and the EAEU member countries on the transformation of Digital Economy. In this chapter, the authors sets the task of managing on the basis of avatars and developing neural multifunctional technological platforms for transformation processes in Digital Economy as based on the analysis of world experience in the use of digital technologies in teaching environmental disciplines and Triple H Avatar.

Chapter 13 is titled "Intellectual Property Institute as a Means of Regional Economic Integration in the Digital Framework: Searching for Ways of Increasing the Efficiency". The effectiveness of intellectual property management in the context of Eurasian economic integration is positioned as a factor in reducing business costs in the EAEU. One of the basic conditions for effective economic development is competition in the field of intellectual property. In the context of globalization and digital transformation, intellectual property management reaches a qualitatively new level of organizational and legal regulation and determines the freedom of movement of goods and services in the single economic territory of interstate integration entities. The authors of the chapter concluded that an effective intellectual property management mechanism in the EAEU is a factor of reducing the costs of foreign trade business. Inequality in the protection of intellectual property in the EAEU impedes the formation and development of competitive relations, impedes the freedom of movement of goods as the basic goal of economic integration of the EAEU states.

Chapter 14 is titled "Emerging Perspectives on Using Avatar-Based Management Technique for Internet User Investigations: Social Media as an Information Source". This chapter shows that statistics collection methods are the same for other types of websites. Often, a simple "counter" is used for both unique visitors to the site and the total number of hits to the site from unique and previously registered users. Speaking of a "digital" or "smart" economy, we can distinguish four categories (levels) of development: analysis, content of business intelligence, large data warehouses. Business analytics can be divided into a number of parts: modeling and analysis of system dynamics, expert systems and databases; knowledge and technology; geographic information (geo location); system analysis and design. The various methods and forms of information (statistical models) used to identify non-trivial patterns and propose solutions are often associated today with the concept of data mining. Intelligent data analysis involves the use of knowledge from a complex of data (databases). According to experts, data mining is one of the elements that is part of the process (database management system), which includes the analysis and cleaning of data.

Chapter 15 is titled "Math Model of Neuron and Nervous System Research Based on AI Constructor Creating Virtual Neural Circuits". The research describes the mathematical modeling of a neuron and the possibility of its technical implementation. Unlike existing technical devices for implementing a neuron based on classical nodes oriented to binary processing, the proposed path is based on bit-parallel processing of numerical data (synapses) for obtaining result. The proposed approach of implementation a neuron can serve as a new elementary basis for the construction of neuron-based computers with a higher processing speed of biological information and good survivability. The research demonstrates the developed nervous circuit constructor and its usage in building of the nervous circuits of biological creatures and simulation of their work.

Chapter 16 is titled "Brain Machine Interface for Avatar Control and Estimation for Educational Purposes Based on Neural AI Plugs: Theoretical and Methodological Aspects". In the future education process where Avatar will be used, it is critically important to have a layer which is responsible for transferring the knowledge from a Student's Avatar to Student. In this research the authors shows the method and high level architecture of how it could be done. And although the suggested approach works, the current level of technology does not allow creating a mobile set which could implement this approach. The general high level schema of the Avatar-Based methodology used in the education process is enclosed in the following. There are 4 layers which interact with each other. On the first layer we have a professor, who is an expert in some domain. He transfers his knowledge to the second layer which is a computer program, performing the role of the Professor's Avatar. After that the knowledge gets transferred to a Student's Avatar, which is the 3rd layer. And eventually the Student's Avatar transfers the newly received knowledge to the Student, who is the 4th layer in this schema. So the most difficult part here is to transfer the knowledge from machine to human.

CONCLUSION

This book collects 16 chapters, contributed by professionals from worldwide, reporting high-level academic research outcomes for architecture and framework for developing and/or applying Avatar-Based Control, Estimation, Communications, and Development technology strategically in different sectors in the digitalized world, including government body, private company and academic organizations. This book provides evidence-based insights into the technology, architecture, framework, model and security. It appeals to both researchers and practitioners in the field of Avatar-Based Control, Estimation, Communications, and Development technology and application, no matter whether they are working in public or private sectors, like architects, strategists, system developers, and even social workers.

The architecture and frameworks proposed assist the solution best suited the researchers to support their objectives for distributed business processes where there are multiple companies involved.

Although some chapters in this book provide practical insights and models that are instrumental in getting business value from Avatar-Based Control, Estimation, Communications, and Development, the overall conclusion should be no 'silver bullet' in achieving business objectives from Avatar-Based Control, Estimation, Communications, and Development technology. This book, therefore, may not appeal to those seeking 'quick fixes' to the problems since that is not objective of this book, and quick fixes are not always a realistic option. In short, a long-term view is required to deliver short-term solutions.

Vardan Mkrttchian
HHH University, Australia

Ekaterina Aleshina
Penza State University, Russia

Leyla Gamidullaeva
Penza State University, Russia

Chapter 1

A Method of Predicting Moments of Market Trend Reversal for Decision-Making Block of Computer-Based Intelligent Financial Agent-Avatar

Vsevolod Chernyshenko
Financial University Under the Government of the Russian Federation, Russia

Vladimir Soloviev
Financial University Under the Government of the Russian Federation, Russia

Vadim Feklin
 https://orcid.org/0000-0002-1803-6699
Financial University Under the Government of the Russian Federation, Russia

Mikhail Koroteev
 https://orcid.org/0000-0002-8768-6564
Financial University Under the Government of the Russian Federation, Russia

Nikita Titov
Financial University Under the Government of the Russian Federation, Russia

DOI: 10.4018/978-1-7998-1581-5.ch001

ABSTRACT

The chapter formalizes the financial task for the definitions and properties of financial indicators under study. A wide range of traditional approaches used for predicting economic time series were reviewed. Investigated as well were the advanced algorithms for predicting moments of reversals of market trends based on machine learning tools. The chapter discusses the effectiveness of different kinds of approaches, which is illustrated with related examples. Described is an original securities price dynamics trend classification algorithm, based on the use of the sliding window methodology and financial agents. General scheme of the classification algorithm to identify market phases is analyzed and results of computer modeling are presented. Selection of initial and resulting metrics is grounded.

INTRODUCTION

Design of intelligent computer systems capable to lead to effective economic (particularly financial) decisions is a topical problem that is still far from being solved. It encounters a number of difficulties, one of which is a high randomness of the dynamics of economic indicators, immanently inherent in this class of dynamic processes. On the other hand, they nature may not be considered as a completely chaotic: there are, of course, certain patterns that can be recognized by high-intelligent algorithms. It should be mentioned that even a slight increase of the accuracy of a volatility forecast may provide an investor with a quite significant yield.

Obviously, algorithms that make reliable forecasts regarding market trends dynamic cannot be based just on simple mathematical models with fixed properties. Recent trends in this filed – solutions based on machine learning that collect and analyze big statistical data in real time (including data for an evaluation of the quality of these models previous prognoses and the effectiveness of the corresponding recommended solutions). Such solutions may be represented as computer agents or avatars – pieces of a program code, to be separate objects with their inputs and outputs, interacting with/in a common software environment and having access to the relevant databases. Such computer "financial agents" are widely used in a financial sphere and partly determine financial markets dynamics themselves. That fact, for sure, does not contradict the effectiveness of use of such algorithms, since the described approach doesn't link to a particular market model but is able to adapt to any conditions.

Obviously, one of the key quality of an agent (determining its success mostly) is its ability to predict the market trend in relation to a certain indicator (e.g. share quotation of certain companies). In this chapter, one of such an approaches to create an "avatar self-learning" algorithm will be considered, allowing user to effectively predict changes of financial markets` trends.

BACKGROUND

Traditional Models of Machine Learning for Predicting Market Trends

Most of researchers and traders suppose that a reliable prediction of a real price of financial tools is impossible. In the (Hawawini, and Keim, 1995) it is shown that correlations between prices time series are neither economically nor statistically significant. In most of sources related to the price forecasting, authors mention the *efficient market hypothesis* (EMH) proposed in (Fama 1965). According to this hypothesis, all valuable information is immediately and fully reflected in the market prices of assets. In an efficient market, prices are instantly corrected, which turns out fair, leaving the market participants with no arbitrage opportunities. At the same time, market participants are homogeneous in their approaches, so they do homogeneously interpret incoming information, instantly correcting their decisions as new information comes available.

There are three forms of market efficiency:

- a weak form of efficiency: an asset price is fully reflected by information from the past related to this asset (information currently available to the public regarding previous prices and volumes of trade);
- an average form of efficiency: an asset price is reflected not only by past, but also public information (information that is currently available in financial news, company reports, analyst speeches, etc.);
- a strong weak form of efficiency: an asset price is reflected by past, public and internal information (confidential information, known to a narrow circle of persons due to official position or other circumstances).

Mathematically, an efficient market hypothesis means that the corresponding random processes that determine price behavior are Markov processes, i.e. their future values do not depend on the values at previous points in time, and therefore future asset prices cannot be predicted by only using past prices.

Many traders, brokers, financial analysts, individual investors and other market participants are convinced that they can (intuitively or with the help of various methods) predict market trends and get profit through this. Besides of intuitive forecasts, many methods and models have been developed to predict trends.

Traditional approaches to forecasting market prices can be generally divided into two types:

- fundamental analysis based on the assessment of the "internal" value of the emitter company with its financial indicators, as well as macroeconomic indicators (Basu 1977), (Campbell 1987), (Dourra, Siy 2002), (Fama 1991), (Fama, French 1998), (Fama, French 1998), (Fama, Schwert 1977);
- technical analysis: a set of tools that completely ignore the efficient market hypothesis, suggesting that history repeats itself and the market behavior is determined by past price changes in similar circumstances (Edwards et al. 2013), (Epps, Epps 1976), (Plummer 1990), (Smirlock, Starks 1990), (Treynor, Ferguson 1985).

As a rule, fundamental analysis is applied when the forecasting horizon exceed one year. With shorter forecast periods, technical analysis is applied.

For the last years technical analysis indicators and oscillators are used not with standard (recommended) parameters, but with regularly adjusted sliding samples based on the probability of forecast error $P_{B.} = N_{B.} / N$, where $N_{B.}$ is the number of correct trend signals, N is the total number of trend signals.

Let us mention several articles, which illustrate the approach to the technical analysis.

In the paper (Zarrabi et al. 2017) 7 650 trading rules for technical analysis were applied to the data on the dynamics of six currencies for the period from 1994 to 2014: the authors noticed that some of them showed profit on the historical data, some did not, and therefore some rules worked more often than others.

The authors of the paper (Fang et al. 2014) have investigated the predictive ability of 93 popular technical analysis indicators for 54-year extractions of price data on stocks from the S&P 500, and none of the indicators showed significant ability of prediction.

In the paper (Da Costa et al. 2015) a triple screen method (simple and exponential moving averages combined with stop-loss tactics) was applied to the real set of 198 Brazilian stocks, still no significant predictive ability was found.

In recent years quite a lot of researches have aroused, based on the methodology of data mining and machine learning, including those using the apparatus of trees and forest solutions, neural networks, fuzzy logic, genetic algorithms, etc. Some approaches were proposed by the authors (Volkova et al. 2017a), (Volkova et al. 2017b), (Volkova et al. 2017c), (Radosteva et al. 2018), (Elizarov et al. 2017). All relevant researches can be divided into four groups:

- models that predict price values e.g. (Arévalo et al. 2016), (Chiang et al. 2016), (Enke, Mehdiyev 2013), (Patel et al. 2015);
- models that predict the direction of price change: whether or not tomorrow's price will increase, decrease or not change (Niaki, Hoseinzade 2013), (Zhong, Enke 2017);
- models that determine the phase of the market; however, as a rule, the trend direction is being predicted: up or down, side areas and "gray zones" are not considered (Cervello-Royo et al. 2015), (Chen et al. 2016);
- models that predict the profit of the investor (Qiu et al. 2016), (Huang, Lin 2014).

In the paper (Escobar et al. 2013) authors propose a technical analysis indicator based on fuzzy logic and implementation of subjective expert information about the risk level. However, the quality of the model is evaluated not by a real market data, but by using a multi-algorithm simulation model.

In the paper (Putko et al. 2014) a regression model of the Russian foreign exchange market (RUR / USD) volatility is considered, the decomposition of volatility on components characterizing the fractal structure of the financial row is used, and the quasi-cyclicity of one of the components is confirmed by regression analysis. When discussing the possibility of forecasting the dynamics of volatility, including the forecast of market transition to an unstable state, it appears that forecasting for an interval of one and a half times the characteristic scale does not actually differ from "throwing a coin" - memory completely disappears. But when predicted for an interval of no more than 4 –8 weeks (with a specific scale of 32 weeks), the forecast using the proposed model turns out to be significantly better than the martingale, although its reliability is low (the proportion of coincidences of the predicted and actual trends are at the level of 0.500–0.515).

Machine learning is an alternative to classical statistical methods, which shows interesting results of solving problems in which the definitions and properties of objects under study are poorly formalized:

- pattern and speech recognition;
- unmanned driving;
- medical diagnostics;
- fraud detection;
- cross-selling;
- credit scoring;
- client deflux forecasting;
- analysis of financial markets, etc.

The essence of the machine learning methodology is based on relatively large sets of input data that makes up a model that is used for prognosis.

The predictive ability (considered as a proportion of predictions that came true) of models that forecast a direction of price change through machine learning in models of (Doesken et al. 2005), (Fernandez-Rodriguez et al. 2000), (Chong et al. 2017), (Atsalakis, Valavanis 2009), (Nair et al. 2010) is at the level of 56, 58, 62, 68 and 86%, respectively.

In the models that predict profit of an investor, only special cases are known. For example, in work (Huang, Lin 2014) for two Taiwanese shares year-long period, 54% and 128% yield was shown. However, the model quality on large volumes of data concerning prices of different instruments at different times was not tested.

In the works devoted to the definition of the market phase, special cases of profitable strategies have been published as well.

A rather comprehensive, although not entirely new (2009) review of machine learning methods being applied to forecasting price dynamics is given in (Atsalakis, Valavanis et al. 2009).

In general, models based on machine learning prove to be more effective than traditional ones, in particular, than traditional models of technical analysis and auto-regression.

Among the well-known models for predicting price movements and market conditions based on machine learning, the following classes of models have showed the best results:

- enhanced decision trees (with gain ADABoost, XGBoost);
- decision forests;
- multilayered unidirectional neural networks based on the backward propagation algorithm (MLP BPN);
- combined models (neural networks with fuzzy logic and genetic algorithms, combinations of neural networks and decision trees, etc.);
- multi-step models in which, for example, initially relevant factor signs are selected or generated, and the next steps are used to forecast the signs obtained in the previous steps.

In the paper (Soloviev 2017) one may get acquainted with results of applying reinforced trees to prediction of the market condition. Based on the price dynamics data of 100 stocks from the S&P500 index for the period from 2007 to 2017, in which real traders marked the trend periods and side frames, a machine learning model was built (based on enhanced XGBoost decision trees). However, despite the high-quality metrics of the model (AUC = 0.860, Accuracy = 0.788, Precision =

0.812, Recall $= 0.877$, F1 Score $= 0.843$), the results are not applicable practically due to frequent switching signals.

At the same time, the choice of input parameters is important: except data about price and volume, quality can be improved by adding parameters synthesized from source data (for example, technical indicators) either parameters external to price series (e.g. macroeconomic indicators).

It seems that neural networks do not reveal the full potential in the analysis of financial markets so far: in the existing models, neural networks are applied to forecasting and classifying financial time rows, while neural networks show the best results in classification problems of unstructured data, for example, images and texts.

Therefore, in particular, serious progress is possible in the use of unstructured data for forecasting, first of all, for texts: financial news and analytical forecasts. However, so far there are no publications on this topic in which results would be obtained that are better than those obtained using well-known algorithms for analyzing price series and volumes.

ALGORITHM FOR PREDICTING MOMENTS OF REVERSALS OF MARKET TRENDS BASED ON SLIDING WINDOWS

Current section describes an original market states classification algorithm, based on the sliding window methodology.

Input data contain the price values of this stock for each date from a specific time period (at the beginning and end, minimum and maximum), as well as the volume of transactions:

- Date;
- Open - the opening price;
- Close - closing price;
- High - the maximum price;
- Low - the minimum price;
- Volume - trading volume;

These data are marked up by experts using a specially developed tool. During work with them an expert enters his identifier, so after that he is able to see values of all the indicators, as well as their graphical interpretation (Figure. 1).

Time scale (and the corresponding minimum time step) can vary widely during a data marking. It is also possible to display the graph in the arithmetic and logarithmic scale, as well as its enlargement, removal and scrolling.

Figure 1. Trend data marking tool

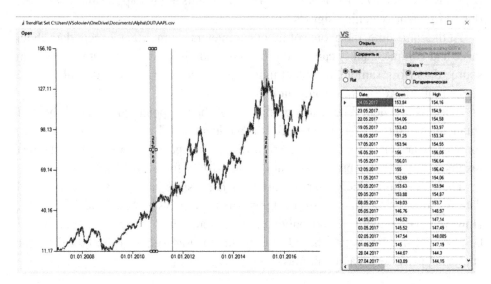

Each marking procedure is a result of determination by an expert on the state of the financial tool market (trend, flat, "gray zone") at each point in time within a specified time period ("markup window"). If this day is defined as part of the trend, the Phase attribute for this day is set to the Trend value. If this day is defined as part of the flat, the Phase attribute for this day is set to Flat. If the day is not identified, it is considered as a part of "Gray zone" and the Phase feature for this day is left blank.

The result of the work of a tool is creation of a metadata file that stores expert assessments of the market condition in CSV format (comma-separated values).

- Expert - expert identifier (categorical attribute);
- Date - the date;
- Open - the opening price;
- Close - closing price;
- High - the maximum price;
- Low - the minimum price;
- Volume - trading volume;
- Phase - market phase (effective categorical attribute).

For an automated collection of marked data, a specialized Python script was used, that allowed you to create automatically a data set for the application of machine learning algorithms. This script creates a file in which data is sorted - first by experts, then by shares, and finally by dates.

Generated file was used to train classification algorithms used to identify market phases, as well as to assess the quality of built up models.

Authors have formed a set of marked data of the state of financial instruments market at various periods of time, including a list of 600 financial instruments approved by customer for the period from 2006 to 2017, rows of daily values, opening and closing prices, maximum and minimum prices and trading volume in which the experts marked out the trend and flat windows.

As a training sample, we used data by dates until October 11, 2014, and as a control sample, after October 11, 2014.

The general scheme of the algorithm for the market state definition, using the slide window methodology, is:

1. first model (Trend or Flat) determines the state of the market on a specific markup between two specified points (trend or flat);
2. second model (Changing Points) determines the critical points at which the identification of one market state is replaced by another;
3. two models are consistently trained on the training sample (first Changing Points, then Trend or Flat);
4. on the tested sample (as well as in the productive model), first day is considered as a critical point, then the Trend or Flat model is being launched daily, which determines what trend is observed from the last critical point to the current day, later - the Changing Points model, that determines if there is a critical point on the current day.

The critical points definition is based on calculation of coefficients of a regression slope for the last 5 days closing price, consequently, the model gives a forecast with a delay of at least five days. In this case, by the sign of the corresponding regression coefficient one may determine the direction of the trend (up or down).

To assess the models quality the following characteristics were used:

- True Negative (TN) - the number of correctly recognized flat panels;
- True Positive (TP) - the number of correctly recognized trends;
- False Negative (FN) - the number of errors of the first kind, i.e., incorrectly recognized flat signals; in the case of using this model in practice, the error of the first kind means that it will be decided to stay in an open position in the flat;
- False Positive (FP) - the number of errors of the second kind, i.e. incorrectly recognized trends; in case of using this model in practice, the error of the second kind means that the trend will be decided to open a position;

$$Accuracy = \frac{TP + TN}{TP + FP + TN + FN}$$

is a proportion of correctly recognized trends and side effects;

$$Precision = \frac{TP}{TP + FP}$$

is a measure of accuracy, describing how much the trends obtained as a result of using the classification model are trends in fact;

$$Recall = \frac{TP}{TP + FN}$$

is a measure of completeness, characterizing the ability of the classifier to "guess" the possible largest number of trends from the expected ones (false trend forecasts do not affect this metric);

$$F1Score = \frac{2\left(Precision \times Recall\right)}{Precision + Recall}$$

is an average harmonic accuracy and completeness;

- ROC (Receiver Operating Characteristic) curve - a line that displays the change in the ratio of the proportion of correctly classified trends in their total number to the percentage of side frames misinterpreted to trends, while varying the threshold of the crucial rule;
- AUC (Area Under ROC Curve) - the area under the ROC curve; the higher the AUC, the better the classifier, the value of 0.5 demonstrates the unsuitability of the chosen classification method (this value corresponds to random fortune-telling based on coin flip), a value less than 0.5 indicates that the classifier acts exactly the opposite: if positive is called negative and vice versa, the classifier will work better.

In addition to the standard machine learning metrics, the following metrics were also calculated:

Figure 2. Forecast trend reversals (BIOX)

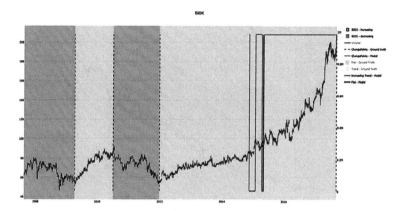

- Freq - switching frequency, which shows how many times the number of real changes in market conditions is greater than the number of predicted changes in market conditions;
- Delay - delay of the prediction, that is the part of the data segment in which the system recognizes the true market state in this area;
- Profit - profitability, which shows how much interest the initial income will increase if you take the appropriate position each time at the beginning and at the end of the trend;
- TimeInPos - time in position, i.e., the total length of the recognized trends.

Results were visualized using Python plotting tools.

On the graph of the initial data on prices and volumes, the initial marking of trends and side panels is highlighted with a green and pink substrate, respectively. Predicted areas of ascending and descending trends are highlighted with bold green and bold red lines, respectively, and the predicted outset lines are marked with bold blue lines.

The value of AUC and Accuracy at 0.58 means that the market condition is correctly recognized for 58% of the test sample days. Considering that the moments of the beginning and end of trends and side effects are not clearly defined, the value of this indicator seems to be generally satisfactory.

The value of the delay indicator (Delay) at the level of 16% means that in order to determine the market state, the system should see its initial segment with a length of 16% on average of the total length of the segment with a constant market phase.

The value of the switching frequency indicator (Freq) at the level of −58% means that the system determines by 58% more switching times than it actually is. A large number of "false positives" is associated with the lack of experts' consensus.

Figure 3. Forecast trend reversals (EUFI)

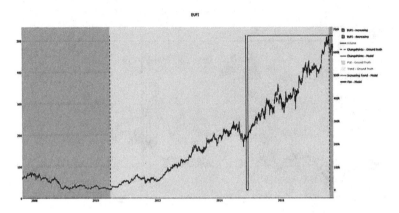

Figure 4. Forecast trend reversals (GEN)

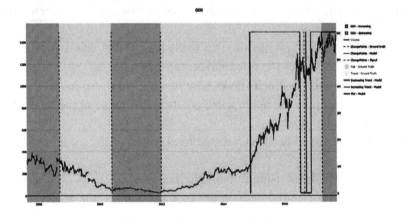

Figure 5. Forecast trend reversals (GLPG)

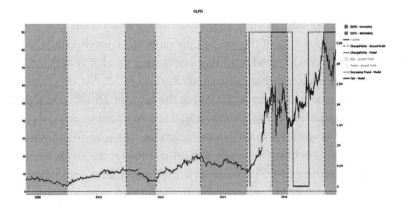

Figure 6. Forecast trend reversals (KSP)

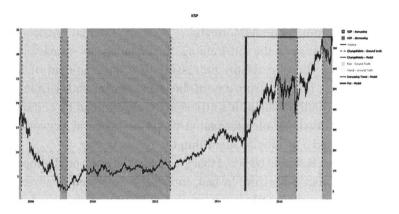

Figure 7. Forecast trend reversals (POLYP)

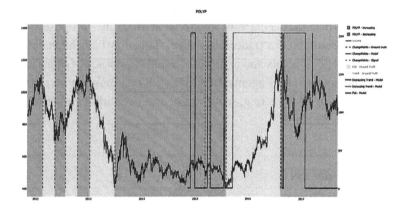

The average profitability of a trading strategy determined by the classifier is 28%, with an average time spent in a position equal to 288 days. Examples of calculation results are presented in Figure 2; Figure 3; Figure 4; Figure 5; Figure 6; Figure 7.

CONCLUSION

As it was shown before, modern information systems in optimal financial decision making are mostly based on the self-training "financial agents -avatar".

Proposed model allows real-time processing of a large amount of numerical and parametric data for an effective portfolio management and defining optimal commercial offers on the market. It`s efficiency is determined by combination of following modern methods of information processing: neural networks, sliding windows method and a qualitative algorithm for agents testing.

At the same time, it should be noted that the uncertainty of a prediction increases as increases the forecast horizon. In fact, to use the described approach for real trading, investor must daily train a new model and make predictions for a period not exceeding a few days. Still, model designed in the course of this chapter, as well as a relevant experimental software, allows to verify the applicability and effectiveness of machine learning and agent-based decision-making for a short or mid-term prognoses.

Practical experience of applying proposed classification in a real time revealed a number of issues in accuracy. That indicates a reason to advance proposed method for advancing strategy suitable for trade automation. This may be achieved in a variety of ways, like redesign of levels and neurons of agents or choice of other methods of initialization and activation of agents. In addition, it can make sense to try various types of deep learning models (e.g. recurrent neural networks) and choose the one that leads to the best results.

ACKNOWLEDGMENT

The reported study was funded by RFBR according to the projects: N° 19-29-07545-мк, 20-010-00326-a.

REFERENCES

Arévalo, A., Niño, J., Hernández, G., & Sandoval, J. (2016). High-frequency trading strategy based on deep neural networks. *Lecture Notes in Computer Science*, *9773*, 424–436. doi:10.1007/978-3-319-42297-8_40

Atsalakis, G. S., & Valavanis, K. P. (2009). Forecasting stock market short-term trends using a neuro-fuzzy based methodology. *Expert Systems with Applications*, *36*(7), 10696–10707. doi:10.1016/j.eswa.2009.02.043

Atsalakis, G. S., & Valavanis, K. P. (2009). Surveying stock market forecasting techniques – Part II: Soft computing methods. *Expert Systems with Applications*, *36*(3), 5932–5941. doi:10.1016/j.eswa.2008.07.006

Basu, S. (1977). The investment performance of common stocks in relation to their price-earnings ratios: A test of the efficient market hypothesis. *The Journal of Finance*, *32*(3), 663–682. doi:10.1111/j.1540-6261.1977.tb01979.x

Campbell, J. (1987). Stock returns and the term structure. *Journal of Financial Economics*, *18*(2), 373–399. doi:10.1016/0304-405X(87)90045-6

Cervello-Royo, R., Guijarro, F., & Michniuk, K. (2015). Stock market trading rule based on pattern recognition and technical analysis: Forecasting the djia index with intraday data. *Expert Systems with Applications*, *42*(14), 5963–5975. doi:10.1016/j.eswa.2015.03.017

Chen, T., & Chen, F.-Y. (2016). An intelligent pattern recognition model for supporting investment decisions in stock market. *Information Sciences*, *346*, 261–274. doi:10.1016/j.ins.2016.01.079

Chiang, W.-C., Enke, D., Wu, T., & Wang, R. (2016). An adaptive stock index trading decision support system. *Expert Systems with Applications*, *59*, 195–207. doi:10.1016/j.eswa.2016.04.025

Chong, E., Han, C., & Park, F. C. (2017). Deep Learning Networks for Stock Market Analysis and Prediction: Methodology, Data Representations, and Case Studies. *Expert Systems with Applications*, *83*, 187–205. doi:10.1016/j.eswa.2017.04.030

Da Costa, T. R. C. C., Nazario, R. T., Bergo, G. S. C., Sobreiro, V. A., & Kumura, H. (2015). Trading system based on the use of technical analysis: A computational experiment. *Journal of Behavioral and Experimental Finance*, *6*, 42–55. doi:10.1016/j.jbef.2015.03.003

Doesken, B., Abraham, A., Thomas, J., & Paprzycki, M. (2005) Real stock trading using soft computing models // International Conference on Information Technology: Coding and Computing (ITCC 05), vol. 2, pp. 162–167.

Dourra, H., & Siy, P. (2002). Investment using technical analysis and fuzzy logic. *Fuzzy Sets and Systems*, *127*(2), 221–240. doi:10.1016/S0165-0114(01)00169-5

Edwards, R., Magee, J., & Bassetti, W. H. C. (2013). *Technical Analysis of Stock Trends*. Boca Raton, FL: CRC Press.

Elizarov, M., Ivanyuk, V., Soloviev, V., & Tsvirkun, A. (2017) Identification of high-frequency traders using fuzzy logic methods // 2017 Tenth International Conference Management of Large-Scale System Development (MLSD). Piscataway, NJ: IEEE. pp. 1-4.

Enke, D., & Mehdiyev, N. (2013). Stock market prediction using a combination of stepwise regression analysis, differential evolution-based fuzzy clustering, and a fuzzy inference neural network. *Intelligent Automation and Soft Computing*, *19*(4), 636–648. doi:10.1080/10798587.2013.839287

Epps, T. W., & Epps, M. (1976). The stochastic dependence of security price changes and transactions volumes: Implications for the mixture of distribution hypothesis. *Econometrica*, *44*(2), 305–321. doi:10.2307/1912726

Escobar, A., Moreno, J., & Munera, S. (2013). A technical analysis indicator. *Electronic Notes in Theoretical Computer Science*, *292*, 27–37. doi:10.1016/j.entcs.2013.02.003

Fama, E. F. (1965). The behavior of stock market price. *The Journal of Business*, *38*(1), 34–105. doi:10.1086/294743

Fama, E. F. (1991). Efficient capital markets. *The Journal of Finance*, *46*(5), 1575–1617. doi:10.1111/j.1540-6261.1991.tb04636.x

Fama, E. F., & French, K. (1998). Dividend yields and expected stock returns. *Journal of Financial Economics*, *22*(1), 3–25. doi:10.1016/0304-405X(88)90020-7

Fama, E. F., & French, K. (1998). Permanent and temporary components of stock prices. *Journal of Political Economy*, *96*(2), 246–273. doi:10.1086/261535

Fama, E. F., & Schwert, W. (1977). Asset returns and inflation. *Journal of Financial Economics*, *5*(2), 115–146. doi:10.1016/0304-405X(77)90014-9

Fang, J., Qin, Y., & Jacobsen, B. (2014). Technical market indicators: An overview. *Journal of Behavioral and Experimental Finance*, *4*, 25–56. doi:10.1016/j. jbef.2014.09.001

Fernandez-Rodriguez, F., Gonzalez-Martel, C., & Sosvilla-Rivebo, S. (2000). On the profitability of technical trading rules based on artificial neural networks: Evidence from the Madrid stock market. *Economics Letters*, *69*(1), 89–94. doi:10.1016/ S0165-1765(00)00270-6

Hawawini, G., & Keim, D. (1995) On the predictability of common stock returns: Worldwide evidence // Handbooks in Operations Research and Management Science, Vol. 9 (Finance) / eds. R. Jarrow et al. Amsterdam: Elsevier Science, pp. 497–544.

Huang, C.-Y., & Lin, P. K. P. (2014). Application of integrated data mining techniques in stock market forecasting. *Cogent Economics and Finance*, *2*(1), 92905–92921. doi:10.1080/23322039.2014.929505

Nair, B. B., Mohandas, V. P., & Sakthivel, N. R. (2010). A Genetic Algorithm Optimized Decision TreeSVM based Stock Market Trend Prediction System. *International Journal on Computer Science and Engineering*, *2*(9), 2981–2988.

Niaki, S. T. A., & Hoseinzade, S. (2013). Forecasting S&P 500 index using artificial neural networks and design of experiments. *Journal of Industrial Engineering International*, *9*(1), 1–9. doi:10.1186/2251-712X-9-1

Patel, J., Shah, S., Thakkar, P., & Kotecha, K. (2015). Predicting stock market index using fusion of machine learning techniques. *Expert Systems with Applications*, *42*(4), 2162–2172. doi:10.1016/j.eswa.2014.10.031

Plummer, T. (1990). *Forecasting Financial Markets: Technical Analysis and the Dynamics of Price*. New York: Wiley.

Putko, B. A., Didenko, A. S., & Dubovikov, M. M. (2014). The volatility model of the RUB / USD exchange rate, built on the basis of the fractal characteristics of the financial series [in Russian]. *Applied Econometrics, No.*, *36*(4), 79–87.

Qiu, M., Song, Y., & Akagi, F. (2016). Application of artificial neural network for the prediction of stock market returns: The case of the Japanese stock market. *Chaos, Solitons, and Fractals*, *85*, 1–7. doi:10.1016/j.chaos.2016.01.004

Radosteva, M., Soloviev, V., Ivanyuk, V., & Tsvirkun, A. (2018). Use of neural network models in market risk management. *Advances in Systems Science and Applications*, *18*(2), 53–58.

Smirlock, M., & Starks, L. (1990). An empirical analysis of the stock price-volume relationship. *Journal of Banking & Finance*, *12*(1), 31–42. doi:10.1016/0378-4266(88)90048-9

Soloviev, V. (2017). Forecasting stock market turnovers with boosted decision trees // 2017 11th International Conference on Application of Information and Communication Technologies (AICT). Piscataway, NJ: IEEE, pp. 140–143.

Treynor, J., & Ferguson, R. (1985). In defense of technical analysis. *The Journal of Finance*, *40*(3), 757–773. doi:10.1111/j.1540-6261.1985.tb05000.x

Volkova, E. S., Gisin, V. B., Soloviev, V. I. (2017). Data mining techniques: Modern approaches to application in credit scoring // Digest Finance, 22(4), (244), pp. 400–412.

Volkova, E. S., Gisin, V. B., Soloviev, V. I. (2017). Methods of the fuzzy sets theory in credit scoring // Finance and Credit, 23(35), (755), pp. 2088–2106. (in Russian)

Volkova, E. S., Gisin V. B., Soloviev V. I. (2017). Modern approaches to application of intelligent analysis methods for the credit scoring problem // Finances & Credit, 23(34), (754), pp. 2044–2060. (in Russian)

Zarrabi, N., Snaith, S., & Coakley, J. (2017). FX technical trading rules can be profitable sometimes! *International Review of Financial Analysis*, *49*, 113–127. doi:10.1016/j.irfa.2016.12.010

Zhong, X., & Enke, D. (2017). Forecasting daily stock market return using dimensionality reduction. *Expert Systems with Applications*, *67*, 126–139. doi:10.1016/j.eswa.2016.09.027

Chapter 2
E-Government Avatar–Based Modeling and Development

Anara Kizabekova
Institute of Eurasian Integration, Kazakhstan

Vsevolod Chernyshenko
Financial University Under the Government of the Russian Federation, Russia

ABSTRACT

The chapter provides a critical analysis by researchers of Kazakh, Russian and foreign authors in the field of open government. Analysis of state indicators of Kazakhstan, international frameworks regarding ICT development, open data, open government, and budget transparency and ways of their improvement are also presented. Results of an investigation of open government's role from the scope of view of official resolutions and national strategic planning of the Republic of Kazakhstan are shown. Most remarkable international initiatives in the field of Open Government are reviewed. The chapter proves the lack of strategic vision of the open government institutions and necessity to study the best world practices by Kazakhstan's strategic bodies to develop citizen-oriented e-Government platform. Critical analysis of challenges arousing at early stages of open data introduction and proper sustainable solutions is presented.

DOI: 10.4018/978-1-7998-1581-5.ch002

INTRODUCTION

Despite a huge variety of researches, frameworks and legal documents devoted to the open government concept and its role, still in most countries we observe an inexistence of informational and analytical basis for the elaboration of development strategy due to the open government and modern IT standards. Same situation we may observe in Kazakhstan, so current paper`s idea is to help in filling this gap.

Gulmira Sheryazdanova and Jim Butterfield (Sheryazdanova G. 2017) have formulated a relation between a line of e-government development and measures of preventing and fighting with corruption. A standardization and transfer of the process of implementation of state services in ICT format is a guarantee of transparency by minimizing the influence of corruption-related factors. At the same time, the narrow focus of this article does not allow to cover a wide range of goals and objectives resolved through e-government and the effects achieved through this institution.

Papers of Kazakh authors are usually a descriptive compilation of state programs, strategic plans of state bodies and other regulatory acts and documents of the state planning system (Kudaykulova K.S. 2007), (Kusherova N.S. 2015), (Muratova G.K. et al. 2017). This fact characterizes these kinds of researchers as works of no scientific novelty or applied value.

At the same time, studies of Russian authors (as Russian Federation proved to implement most advanced ICT solutions in open government sphere among NIS countries) that cover same topics are also inherently descriptive and do not contribute to the creation of a new knowledge (Okolesnova O.A. 2017), (Kuzmina A.V. et al. 2017), (Kamalova G.R. 2014, 2017), (Sulimina A.N. 2015), (Gishko V.Y. et al. 2015).

BACKGROUND

In October 2017 a report of the Center for Legal Policy Studies (CLPS 2017) was published, containing a regulatory and legal educational program in the implementation of the open government model in Kazakhstan, as well as the results of a content analysis of the Open Government Portal. As a result of the study, authors propose a roadmap model of management openness indicators developed (according to their statements) by Transparency International.

At the same time, the Organization for Economic Co-operation and Development (OECD) review of an open government reform in Kazakhstan was published (OECD, 2017). Main conclusions and recommendations in this review may be briefly described as following: guarantee of a systematic approach, strengthening a regulatory framework and its implementation, increasing aa quality and a number of channels of interaction between the state and society, business.

History of open government in Kazakhstan starts in 2006 when first e-Government internet portal has been created as a part of the State program for the formation of an "electronic government" in the Republic of Kazakhstan for 2005-2007 (Decree of the President of the Republic of Kazakhstan No. 1471 2004). Initially, this portal served as a source of information and references, that later transformed into a common provider of public services according to a "one window" principle.

In 2015, the law of the Republic of Kazakhstan "On Access to Information" (No. 401-V ZRK 2015) came into force, that became one of the first stages in the formation of an accountable state, aimed on increasing level of the openness and transparency of government agencies. Previously, in the legal field of Kazakhstan there were no rules on regulating this sphere - rights and obligations of the owner and recipient of information were not structured and decisions to provide or not any information were situational.

In addition, within the framework of the Law of the Republic of Kazakhstan "On Informatization" (No. 418-V ZRK 2015), open data are considered as one of the tools for the development of information technologies in our country.

In addition, the law "On Informatization" obliges ministries, akimats (regional executive bodies in Kazakhstan), judicial authorities and local governments to approve the Open Data Lists, agreed with the Ministry of Information and Communications of the Republic of Kazakhstan. The open data sets indicated in the List are subject to mandatory publication in the appropriate section of the Open Government in machine-readable formats. At the same time, state institutions and quasi-state organizations (national companies, companies with state participation) do not have the obligation to disclose their information, and publish open data on an initiative basis.

In order to protect public interests in the field of access to information, as well as to meet the citizens' needs for access to certain data, a Commission on Access to Information was established at the Ministry of Information and Communications. The Commission is a consultative and advisory body that carries out its work at meetings held as often as necessary (but not more often than once every 6 months).

ANALYSIS OF THE CURRENT STATE OF E-GOVERNMENT IN KAZAKHSTAN

The Open Government of Kazakhstan is one of the modules of the "e-government" that includes 5 independent tools: Open Data, Open NGO-s, Open Budgets and Open Dialogue.

Such a classification is a conditional division of open data into regulatory, budgetary and general lanes; in addition, results of evaluating of the activities of government agencies are part of a separate block. The "Open Dialogue" section is a blog platform of the heads of ministries and akimats, as well as Internet conferences, polls, etc.

Open data is uploaded by government agencies on the basis of approved lists of open information (No. 401-V ZRK 2015) and requests from citizens and representatives of business. At the same time, as it was mentioned above, another criterion is the relevance of open data - the compliance of the information posted by government agencies with needs of stakeholders.

This model of formation of open data has a certain disadvantage. Lists of Open Data are generated directly by government agencies that own this data. In addition, an extension of the Lists of Open Data is possible just by analyzing information flows between government agencies in order to short a time of information transfer.

According to the public statistics of the "Open Data" (URL: https://data.egov. kz/) from 02.07.19, the portal has posted 3,480 data sets. All uploaded data on the portal is available to users in the .XLSX, .DOCX, .JSON and .XML formats. At the same time, open data is categorized both by the organization that is the owner of this dataset, and by industry sector.

For the period from 01/01/2015 to 07/02/19 the total number of views was 973,953 and the number of downloads for the same period was 60,036. Based on the published data sets, 31 mobile applications and web services were developed (URL: https://data.egov.kz/services/sample).

A necessity of the reform to implement model and principles of open government (as a part of "100 steps" Plan of the Nation) is based on the high level of e-Government potential for the state administration system and the national economy of Kazakhstan. It should be noted that the relevance of scientific research in the field of public administration cannot be based on compliance with one or another vector of the current state policy.

Open government is one of the most promising models for the development of the public administration system, based on the principles of open and free interaction of the state with the population, business, research and non-profit organizations.

In the present paper we proceed from the statement according to which, open data is one of the fundamental elements of an open government (Zimmermann H.-D. et al. 2015). The authors argue this statement by the fact that publicly available data of government agencies contribute to ensuring transparency and increasing the involvement of the population in the rule-making, budgetary and other activities of public administration.

According to the definition of the concept of open data open data refers to depersonalized data sets created and/or processed by state or subordinate organizations (Geiger K. et al. 2012). At the same time, the openness of this data implies both the possibility of their free of charge and free use for all comers, and the placement of this data in a machine-readable form (Nizhegorodtsev R.M. 2014), (Nizhegorodtsev R.M. 2016), (Nizhegorodtsev R.M. et al. 2016).

Expanding this definition with a statement on the suitability of open data for subsequent interpretation (reuse), we obtain an extended concept of open data. This formulation correlates to a certain extent with the concept given in the Law of the Republic of Kazakhstan "On Access to Information" (No. 401-V ZRK 2015), according to which open data is "publicly accessible electronic information resources presented in machine-readable form and intended for further use, repeated publication in unchanged form."

In (Bhuiyan S. 2011) referring (De Nardis L. 2010), defines open government as a goal or a final result of evolution of e-government and all Kazakh government system. At the same time, an open government means:

- introduction of interoperable standards for the functioning of the public administration system, providing citizens with free access to government information;
- general strengthening of interaction between the state and citizens based on the principles of accountability, transparency and openness.

Transparency, on the other hand, is defined as a primary component of an open government that provides trust in government and democratic institutions, awareness of decision-making, prevention of corruption, etc.

There are number of challenges facing Kazakhstan in a focus of development of e-government (Sheryazdanova G. et al. 2017):

- technical problems with software and the level of development of computer infrastructure;
- need to improve the computer literacy of the population;
- impossibility of complete elimination of the human factor;
- Limited nature of current e-government model.

As we see, various authors label current limited nature of acting e-government model as a challenge, which is stipulated by the traditional role of a tool for improving quality and minimizing time response of public services, optimizing business and minimizing corruption factors. Buyan Sh. proceeded from the same model, somewhat expanding it due to the prospects of creating socially significant services to ensure and simplify access to medicine, education and other social infrastructure facilities and use e-government as a platform for implementing various business initiatives.

This kind of approach is described both in the framework of recommendations described in the reports of the Center for Legal Policy Studies on the assessment of the promotion of effective public administration standards and the review of proposals for improving the legislation on access to information and in the framework of the above OECD review (OECD, 2017). Both documents contain comments according to which it is necessary to ensure a systematic approach to the development of both e-government and open government and to reconsider the potential of these institutions.

INTERNATIONAL BEST PRACTICES IN OPEN GOVERNMENT. CHALLENGES FOR KAZAKHSTAN

The main drivers of Open Government and open data include (Jansser, M. et al 2012):

1. Open data is critical to ensure transparency and accountability, but this requires the disclosure of operational information on a regular rather than episodic basis. It should also take into account the possibility of using, processing and distributing this data without any restrictions (Gigler, S. et al 2011).
2. Open data and Open Government are designed to enable the general public to participate in certain decision-making processes. Specialized online discussion platforms can be used to provide this capability (Halonen, A. 2012).
3. Open data is a catalyst for innovation and economic growth, because many applications and services can be improved and created on their basis. Also, open data contribute to the strengthening of information and analytical support for decision-making in business and other activities (Yu, H. et al 2012).
4. Open data can also be used by the public sector itself, since publication of data in the public domain will provide easy and quick access to structured information, the use of which may be more efficient by obtaining feedback from citizens and learning from their experience in applying this data. All that allows state agencies to increase the efficiency of their public services and improve their internal understanding of their goals and objectives (Halonen, A. 2012), (Lagace, M. 2010).

These drivers formulations are consistent with the approach of (Hunter M. et al 2007) that proposes to consider open government and open data as e-governance (e-government) tools that use online platforms not only to increase the efficiency of information flows between governments and citizens or between governments and enterprises but also inside the public sector. These tools also have a high potential to promote technological innovation under the leadership of citizen activists focused on the real needs and interests of the society (Lagace M. 2017).

Next, let's consider a number of international initiatives in the field of Open Government. The most ambitious initiative in this area today is the Open Government Partnership, organized by the governments of 8 countries in 2011 (OGP): Brazil, Indonesia, Mexico, Norway, the Philippines, South Africa, the United Kingdom and the United States. Currently, 75 national and 15 local governments are members of the initiative, which together have taken up more than 2,500 commitments to promote openness, transparency and accountability (URL: https://www.opengovpartnership.org).

Obligations are understood as a set of goals and principles publicly adopted by the government to increase the availability of information on government, support civil initiatives, and introduce best practices and new technologies to ensure their openness and accountability (Open Government Declaration 2011).

In 2012, the Open Data Institute was created - an organization that now unites more than 140 organizations, such as Adobe, Thomson Reuters, SAP, and a number of leading universities in the UK (URL: https://directory.theodi.org/members). Open Data Institute implements educational and research projects in the field of open data, its own startup acceleration program and has an extensive network of researchers and analysts around the world.

Another international initiative to promote Open Government is the Open Data Charter, which is a set of principles for the promotion, use and development of open data by all stakeholders, approved in 2015.

The Charter was adopted by 17 national and 35 local (regional, city) governments and supported by 42 organizations, including companies such as the World Bank Group and IBM (Open Data Charter).

It should be noted that not a single Kazakh company or state body, as well as the government of Kazakhstan, are members of any of the initiatives considered. This fact may limit the access of Kazakhstan national experts, politicians, government officials and analysts in the field of open data to international knowledge bases and standards, cases, educational programs, etc.

Referring to the Digital Agenda of the Eurasian Economic Union (hereinafter referred to as the EAEU) (EAEU 2016) as a document governing cooperation of the union members in improving national economies, improving the well-being of their citizens and improving public administration systems, we see that main areas of cooperation are:

- achieving the goals of economic integration of the EAEU Member States, the transition of the economies of the Member States to a new technological order, taking into account their national interests;
- improving the quality of public services;
- creating a favorable environment for the development of innovations;
- creating conditions for increasing the efficiency of economic processes and enhancing the competitiveness of business entities in domestic and global markets;
- Improving the quality of life of citizens of Member States, the level of citizens' involvement in the use of information technology, the protection of the rights and legitimate interests of consumers, the creation of high-tech jobs.

To achieve these goals, members of the EAEU declare support for creating the necessary conditions, including through a set of the following measures:

- development of a regulatory framework for the digital economy of the EAEU Member States;
- preparation of proposals and exchange of experience in the field of protection and enforcement of intellectual property rights;
- building public-private partnerships in the digital economy;
- stimulating and supporting digital initiatives and projects;
- supporting dialogue between all interested organizations and citizens of the EAEU Member States and promoting best practices in the field of the digital economy.

As we see, there is no direct reference to cooperation of e-government and open government in the EAEU Digital Agenda, still there are provisions aimed on improvement of the quality of public services and creating more favorable conditions for the development of information technologies in general.

Meanwhile in the documents relating to the state planning system of Kazakhstan (Decree of the President of the Republic of Kazakhstan No. 840 2014) an open government appears in the text of the state program "Information Kazakhstan - 2020" (Decree of the President of the Republic of Kazakhstan No. 464 2013) within the framework of 2 target indicators:

Table 1. Kazakhstan ranking in international ratings

Rating	2003	2005	2008	2011	2012	2013	2014	2015	2016	2017	2018	+/-
Open Data Barometer						37	49	56	59	-	-	-22
ICT Development Index								52	52	52	-	-
The Networked Readiness Index			73	67	55	43	38	40	39	-	-	+34
The Global Innovation Index			72	84	83	84	79	82	75	78	74	-1
Open budget index			35		48			51	-	53	-	-15
e-Government Development Index	83	65	81		38		28		33	-	39	-44
- e-Participation Index	31	48	106		2		22		67	-	-	-36

- e-Participation Index of Kazakhstan (according to the UN methodology) throughout the implementation of the Program should be kept among the first 5 countries;
- Number of actively used applications based on "open data" services, in 2017 - at least 3, in 2020 - 10.
- Also, an open government appears in the Strategic Plan of the Ministry of Information and Communications of the Republic of Kazakhstan for 2017-21. (MIC 2016) also in the form of the 1st target indicator:
- The relevance of open data sets hosted on the open data portal should be at least 75% in 2017 and at least 98% in 2021.

In this regard, it is possible to make a conclusion that Kazakhstan has no official decree describing expectations, goals and objectives facing an open government either on the national or on the supranational level.

In order to present a more comprehensive picture of the e-government development, open government and information technologies of Kazakhstan as a whole, we consider the dynamics of country indicators in a number of international ratings for the period from 2003 to 2016 (Table 1).

Based on the gathered data (Table 1), the following statement can be made: improvement of Kazakhstan's position in the E-Government Development Index and The Networked Readiness Index, accompanied by a deterioration in performance in the Open Data Barometer, may be a result of insufficiently effective work in terms of using open data in public administration, business and non-profit sector of Kazakhstan. The indicators of The Global Innovation Index have slightly improved, which may indicate the development of creativity in society.

According to the summary table (Table 1) we may state that target indicator of the state program "Digital Kazakhstan" has not been reached; the rate of increase in e-engagement is significantly lower than in other countries. Kazakhstan is not indexed by the Global Open Data Index international rating, that is also an indicator of a low level of Kazakhstan's involvement in international processes in the development of Open Government.

Having considered a number of countries leading in the above ratings, it should be noted that they contain strategic plans and programs for the development of Open Government or open data:

- Canada – Third Biennial Plan to the Open Government Partnership (Treasury Board 2016).
- Great Britain – UK Open Government National Action Plan 2016-18 (Cabinet office 2016).
- Australia – Australia's first Open Government National Action Plan 2018-20 (Department of Prime Minister and Cabinet 2018).
- Finland – Open Government III Action Plan 2017–2019 (Ministry of Finance 2017).

Analysis of objectives, expected results and principles of implementation of these program documents is a subject of a separate study. At the same time, the availability of such documents represents a systematic approach to the implementation of state policy in the field of Open Government.

The McKinsey Global Institute estimates that opportunities and challenges of open data reduce costs and create new products and services that cost between 3 and 5 trillion of dollars annually (Manuika J at al 2013). The presence of long-term development programs ensures the implementation of 3 main elements of value creation through open data: improving the quality of infrastructure planning and management; investment and asset management optimization; and more informed decision making in economic activities (Zimmermann et. al 2015).

Kazakhstan is not the only state that has recently become involved in the process of creating an Open Government and introducing work with open data. Certain problems in the early stages of introducing publicity and working with open data are often associated with the perception of these reforms by government bodies (Lee M. et al 2014). The first stage of work in this area is to convey the value and the need to provide data in user-friendly formats. The adoption of this information by government agencies is in many ways complicated by the work and budget burden on government agencies, the responsibility for other routines, and the creation of new forms of control over their activities in terms of publishing open data. At the same time, the approval of the relevant legislative framework forced government

Table 2.

Challenges	Sustainable Solutions
1. Excessive use of popular data sets. 2. Significant amount of similar applications that solve the same problem (duplication). 3. An absence of value of many newly created applications and services based on open data, either their focusing on a too narrow audience. 4. Publication of data without responses analysis and further improvement of public services. 5. Formal approach to data publication on e-government platform for citizens. 6. Insufficiency of state funds for sustainable development of applications and services. 7. Limited response on requests and initiatives leading to the publication of data. 8. Resistance to data transparency by government agencies.	1. Necessity to involve entrepreneurs and venture investors to evaluate applications and services based on open data. 2. Necessity to introduce enterprise architecture principles on the national level, attracting a full range of stakeholders of e-government platform. 3. Legislative design of requirements for a timely and complete publication of open data. 4. Publication of statements by heads of government agencies regarding a presence of certain problems (challenges) to draw an attention of IT developers and officials. 5. Necessity to provide thorough studies of the work of state bodies by analysts and enterprise architectures for a more comprehensive understanding of duties, achievements and mechanisms of public administration. 6. Strength coordination and monitoring of the government agencies in terms of working with open data. 7. Creation of an open portfolio of applications and services to improve these products and to support sharing relevant experiences.

agencies to work with open data, but the complexity and lack of visual results had a negative effect on their initiative and involvement in this process.

CONCLUSION

Considering the challenges arousing at early stages of open data introduction on the state level by public administration, and the main outcomes identified by 8 cities of the USA and Europe, we may try to formulate both them and sustainable solutions (see Table 2).

Presented ideas as well as strategic resolutions of developed countries (describing development of open government and use of open data) may be taken into account by developing a similar document in Kazakhstan, subject to an analysis of the applicability of this experience in Kazakhstan's realities. Basing on our research, we may formulate following conclusions:

- Open government is a multilateral and very flexible way of development of the public administration system, providing a platform for information and analytical support for the subjects of the national economy of Kazakhstan.
- In order to ensure consistency in the development and maximization of the value created by an open government, the development of fundamental strategic documents is required.
- An extension of the concept of open data in the legal field of Kazakhstan is required, ensuring the openness of all information held by government agencies by default and its timely provision in full.
- It should be possible to compare and compatibility of open data sets, both among themselves and with data published in the framework of state statistics for the purposes of collision detection.
- Consider the experience of developed countries and international organizations in the development of an open government on the subject of cases applicable in Kazakhstan's realities.
- It is necessary to analyze the monitoring tools and the development of applications and services that use open data, as well as study the relevant cases of other countries for their replication.

Conducted analysis made it possible to structure information concerning development of an open government in Kazakhstan in the context of global initiatives and trends and to identify the most critical development directions. Also, a preliminary substantiation of the feasibility of developing a specialized program document in this sphere and the possibility of formulating a common vision of this area of cooperation within the framework of the EAEU Digital Agenda was carried out.

At the same time, reform of introducing an open government in Kazakhstan is only gaining momentum. The first years of the reform showed the need to improve the quality of hosted open data sets and the institutional development of open government tools.

ACKNOWLEDGMENT

The reported study was funded by RFBR according to the projects: № 19-29-07545-мк, 20-010-00326-а.

REFERENCES

Australia's first Open Government National Action Plan 2016-18. [Electronic resource] // URL: https://ogpau.pmc.gov.au/australias-first-open-government-national-action-plan-2016-18

Decree of the President of the Republic of Kazakhstan No. 1471 dated November 10, 2004 "On the State Program of Forming an "Electronic Government" in the Republic of Kazakhstan for 2005-2007". It became invalid by the Decree of the President of the Republic of Kazakhstan No. 829 dated June 18, 2009. Retrieved from http://adilet.zan.kz/rus/docs/U040001471_

Decree of the President of the Republic of Kazakhstan No. 464 dated January 8, 2013 "On the State Program" Information Kazakhstan - 2020 "and amending the Decree of the President of the Republic of Kazakhstan dated March 19, 2010 No. 957" On Approval of the List of State Programs". Retrieved from http://adilet.zan.kz/rus/docs/U1300000464

Decree of the President of the Republic of Kazakhstan No. 840 of June 17, 2014 "On Amendments to the Decrees of the President of the Republic of Kazakhstan of June 18, 2009 No. 827" On the System of State Planning in the Republic of Kazakhstan "and on March 4, 2010 No. 931" On Some Issues further functioning of the State Planning System in the Republic of Kazakhstan". Retrieved from http://adilet.zan.kz/rus/docs/U1400000840

DeNardis, L. E-governance policies for interoperability and open standards // Policy & Internet. 2010. N°2 (3). [Electronic resource] // URL: URL: http://psocommons.org/vol2/iss3/art6

EEU digital agenda. [Electronic resource] // Retrieved from http://www.eurasiancommission.org/ru/act/dmi/workgroup/Pages/default.aspx

Geiger, C., & von Lucke, J. Open Government and (Linked) (Open) (Government) (Data) // JeDEM – eJournal of eDemocracy and Open Government. 2012. N°4 (2). Retrieved from https://www.researchgate.net/publication/271325963_Open_Government_and_Linked_Open_Government_Data

General assessment of the promotion of standards of effective public administration in the Republic of Kazakhstan on the example of implementation and development of the principles of the "Open Government" - Almaty, 2017 - 37 p.

Gigler, S., Custer, S., & Rahemtulla. Realizing the vision of open government data, 2011, [Electronic resource] // Retrieved from https://www.researchgate. net/publication/314237022_Realizing_the_Vision_of_Open_Government_Data_ Opportunities_Challenges_and_Pitfalls

Gishko, V. Ya., Kovalenko, A. S., & Pridyba, O. V. (2015). The "Open Government" Strategy and Some Aspects of Ensuring the Information Security of Russian Society // State and Municipal Management. Scientific notes of SKAGS, 2015, N°3. Retrieved from http://cyberleninka.ru/article/n/strategiya-otkrytogo-pravitelstva-i-nekotorye- aspekty-obespecheniya-informatsionnoy-bezopasnosti-rossiyskogo-obschestva

Glaziev, S. Yu., Nizhegorodtsev, R. M., Kupryashin, G. L., Makogonova, N. V., Sidorov, A. V., & Sukharev, O. S. (2017). Managing the Development of the National Economy at the Federal Level, 2017. N°60 // Public administration. [Electronic resource] // Retrieved from http://cyberleninka.ru/article/n/upravlenie- razvitiem-natsionalnoy-ekonomiki-na-federalnom-urovne-materialy-kruglogo- stola-26-10-2016

Halonen, A. (2012). Being open about data. Analysis of the UK open data policies and applicability of data. 2012. [Electronic resource] // Retrieved from http:// finnishinstitute.org.uk/images/stories/pdf2012/being%20open%20about%20data.pdf

Hunter, M. G., & Tan, F. B. (2007). *Strategic use of information technology for global organizations*. Hershey, PA: IGI Global. doi:10.4018/978-1-59904-292-3

Janssen, M., Charalabidis, Y., & Zuiderwijk, A. (2012). Benefits, Adoption Barriers and Myths of Open Data and Open Government [ISM]. *Information Systems Management, 29*(4), 258–268. doi:10.1080/10580530.2012.716740

Jo, L. M., Esteve, A., & Wareham, J. D. (2014). Open Data & Civic Apps: 1st Generation Failures – 2nd Generation Improvements // ESADE Business School Research Paper. 2014. N°256. [Electronic resource] // Retrieved from https://ssrn. com/abstract=2508358

Kamalova, G. (2017). Public policy in the field of open data: analysis of practices // Economics and Management: A Scientific and Practical Journal, 2017, N°3. [Electronic resource] // Retrieved from https://elibrary.ru/download/ elibrary_29969774_73911263.pdf

Kamalova, G. R. (2014). Open state management: Russian and foreign experience // State and municipal management. Scientific notes of SKAGS, 2014, N°1. [Electronic resource] // Retrieved from http://cyberleninka.ru/article/n/otkrytoe- gosudarstvennoe-upravlenie-rossiyskiy-i-zarubezhnyy-opyt

Kudaykulova, H. Sh. (2007). Electronic government in the Republic of Kazakhstan // State administration, 2007. [Electronic resource] // Retrieved from http://cyberleninka. ru/article/n/elektronnoe-pravitelstvo-v-respublike-kazahstan

Kusherov, N. S. (2015). The development of "e-government" in Kazakhstan // Law and modern states, 2015, N°2. [Electronic resource] // Retrieved from http:// cyberleninka.ru/article/n/razvitie-elektronnogo-pravitelstva-v-kazahstane

Kuzmin, A. V., & Razvozzhaev, D. G. (2017). The development of legal regulation of the processes of openness in the activities of public authorities // Research papers Tambov RuSMU branch. 2017. N°8. [Electronic resource] // Retrieved from http:// cyberleninka.ru/article/n/razvitie-normativno-pravovogo-regulirovaniya-protsessov-otkrytosti-v-deyatelnosti-organov-gosudarstvennoy-vlasti

Lagace, M. (2010). Data.gov: Matching government data with rapid innovation // Harvard Business School Working Knowledge. 2010. [Electronic resource] // URL: http://hbswk.hbs.edu/item/6423.html

Law of the Republic of Kazakhstan dated November 16, 2015 No. 401-V ZRK "On Access to Information". Retrieved from http://adilet.zan.kz/rus/docs/Z1500000401

Law of the Republic of Kazakhstan dated November 24, 2015 No. 418-V ZRK "On informatization". Retrieved from http://adilet.zan.kz/rus/docs/Z1500000418

Manyika, J., Chui, M., Farrell, D., Van Kuiken, S., Groves, P., Van Kuiken, S., & Doshi, E. A. Open data: Unlocking innovation and performance with liquid information. (McKinsey Global Institute, Ed.). [Electronic resource] // Retrieved from http://www. mckinsey.com/insights/business_technology/open_data_unlocking_innovation_ and_performance_with_liquid_information?cid=other-eml-alt-mgi-mck-oth-2910)

Muratova, G. K., & Baisalykova, Sh. A. (2017). E-government in Kazakhstan // Science and education: a new time, 2017, N°1. [Electronic resource] // Retrieved from https://elibrary.ru/download/elibrary_28779613_94050576.pdf

Nizhegorodtsev, R. M. (2016). Import substitution of institutions: the key task of ensuring national security // News of USUE, 2016, N°4 (66). [Electronic resource] // Retrieved from http://cyberleninka.ru/article/n/importozameschenie-institutov-klyuchevaya-zadacha-obespecheniya-natsionalnoy-bezopasnosti

Nizhegorodtsev, R. M. (2014). Stimulation of research and innovation in Russia under the conditions of growth of external threats. Materials of the international scientific-practical conference Innovation management - 2014. pp. 7-14.

Noor, H., & Van Den Broek, T. (2011). Open Data: An International Comparison of Strategies. *European Journal of ePractice.*, *12*(1), 4–16. Retrieved from http://unpan1.un.org/intradoc/groups/public/documents/UN-DPADM/UNPAN046727.pdf

Okolesnova, O. A. Open data as an innovative mechanism for disclosing information // State audit. right. Economy, 2017, N°2. [Electronic resource] // Retrieved from https://elibrary.ru/download/elibrary_29869433_87777383.pdf

Open Government III Action Plan 2017–2019. [Electronic resource] // Retrieved from http://vm.fi/documents/10623/4505456/Open+Government+III+Action+Plan+2017–2019+Finland.pdf/21c926e6-b86b-435f-8d76-d4e9871ef45e

Shahjahan, H. (2011). Bhuiyan. Trajectories of E-Government Implementation for Public Sector Service Delivery in Kazakhstan. *International Journal of Public Administration*, (34), 9.

Sheryazdanova, G., & Butterfield, J. (2017). E-government as an anti-corruption strategy in Kazakhstan. *Journal of Information Technology & Politics*, *14*(1), 83–94. doi:10.1080/19331681.2016.1275998

Strategic Plan of the Ministry of Information and Communications of the Republic of Kazakhstan for 2017 - 2021, approved. by order of the Minister of Information and Communications of the Republic of Kazakhstan No. 310 of December 28, 2016.

Sulimin, A. N. Features of the implementation of the principles of open (electronic) regional management in the Astrakhan region // Bulletin of the expert council, 2015, N°3. [Electronic resource] // Retrieved from http://cyberleninka.ru/article/n/osobennosti-realizatsii-printsipov-otkrytogo-elektronnogo-regionalnogo-upravleniya-v-astrahanskoy-oblasti

Towards an Open Government in Kazakhstan. (2017). Paris, France: OECD Publishing; doi:10.1787/9789264279384-

UK Open Government National Action Plan 2016-18. [Electronic resource] // Retrieved from https://www.gov.uk/government/publications/uk-open-government-national-action-plan-2016-18/uk-open-government-national-action-plan-2016-18

Yu, H., & Robinson, D. The New Ambiguity of "Open Government" // Princeton CITP//Yale ISP Working Paper. 2012. [Electronic resource] // Retrieved from http://papers.ssrn.com/sol3/papers.cfm?abstract_id=2012489

Zimmermann, H.-D., & Pucihar, A. Open Innovation, Open Data and New Business Models, 2015. [Electronic resource] // Retrieved from https://ssrn.com/abstract=2660692

Chapter 3
Deep Neural Networks in the Diagnosis of Postoperative Complications of Acute Appendicitis

Vladimir Gorbachenko
Penza State University, Russia

ABSTRACT

Digital models are needed in medicine for diagnosis and prediction. Such models are especially needed in personalized medicine. In this area, it is necessary to evaluate and predict the patient's condition from a priori knowledge obtained from other patients. Therefore, a new direction of predictive medicine appeared. Predictive medicine, or "in silicon medicine" is the use of computer modeling and intelligent technologies in the diagnosis, treatment, and prevention of diseases. Using predictive medicine, the doctor can determine the likelihood of the development of certain diseases and choose the optimal treatment. Predictive medicine begins to be applied in surgery. The prognosis in surgery consists in the preoperative evaluation of various surgical interventions and in the evaluation of possible outcomes of surgical interventions.

DOI: 10.4018/978-1-7998-1581-5.ch003

INTRODUCTION

Digital models are needed in medicine for diagnosis and prediction. Such models are especially needed in personalized medicine. In this area, it is necessary to evaluate and predict the patient's condition from a priori knowledge obtained from other patients. Therefore, a new direction appeared – predictive medicine *(Brigham and Johns, 2012; Miner, et al., 2014)*. Predictive medicine, or "in silico medicine" is the use of computer modeling and intelligent technologies in the diagnosis, treatment and prevention of diseases. Using predictive medicine, the doctor can determine the likelihood of the development of certain diseases and choose the optimal treatment. Predictive medicine begins to be applied in surgery *(Joskowicz, 2017)*. The prognosis in surgery consists in the preoperative evaluation of various surgical interventions and in the evaluation of possible outcomes of surgical interventions.

This chapter discusses the diagnosis of postoperative complications of acute appendicitis. The problems of early diagnosis, treatment, prevention and prognosis of complications of acute appendicitis are relevant. Among urgent operations, the proportion of appendicitis (appendectomy) removal operations is about 85%. Despite the active use of medical equipment for ultrasound, computer, magnetic resonance, laparoscopic, endoscopic diagnosis of acute appendicitis and its complications, the problem remains unsolved. The solution to this problem is the ability of the doctor to apply diagnostic methods and to objectively interpret them. It is necessary to perform an appendectomy with a clinical analysis of the situation in the abdominal cavity in a timely manner and on the basis of indications: to identify infiltrates, abscesses, local peritonitis. It is necessary to develop treatment tactics that prevent the development of purulent-inflammatory complications. It should be noted that purulent-inflammatory complications after appendectomy occur in 2.7%–39.1% of patients. So far, mortality in acute appendicitis varies from 0.1% to 1.6%. Solving these problems requires the development of methods for predicting postoperative appendicitis complications. In *(Prabhudesai, et al., 2008; Park and Kim, 2015)*, artificial neural networks that diagnose the presence of acute appendicitis were developed. In *(Juliano, et al., 2017)*, a study of risk factors associated with complications of acute appendicitis is conducted, specific types of complications were investigated in *(Bakti, et al., 2011)*. However, mathematical models to predict postoperative appendicitis complications are absent.

Experiments conducted by the authors with a three-layer neural networks for the direct distribution of the classical architecture *(Haykin, 2008)* showed that such networks do not provide high diagnostic accuracy. In addition, such networks are prone to overfitting. Currently, neural networks of deep architecture, using specific learning algorithms and activation functions, are very popular *(Goodfellow, et al., 2016; Aggarwal, 2018)*. Such networks are used to solve various problems of image processing, sound sequences, etc. Their main advantage is that they are able to capture very complex non-linear relationships in the data. The tasks of medical diagnostics, as a rule, have a large number of non-linearly interconnected signs characterizing the patient's condition. Moreover, the sets of features that characterize patients with different conditions may differ quite slightly. Therefore, it seems promising to use neural networks of deep architecture for medical diagnostics, in particular, for the diagnosis of postoperative appendicitis complications.

The aim of the work is the study of direct propagation neural networks of deep architecture for the diagnosis of postoperative appendicitis complications.

FEATURE SELECTION AND PROCESSING

Problems of machine learning in the field of medicine have their own characteristics. For example, to solve problems in which the input data are images (computed tomography of the brain, x-rays of the lungs, etc.), apply its class of machine learning algorithms. In the field of medicine, there is another data format - this is tabular data. For example, test results, assessments of the patient's condition, and so on. For tabular data, you need to use very different approaches. Data of this kind have their own characteristics, in particular, a large number of gaps in the data. Absences occur when a standard set of tests is enough for a doctor to make a diagnosis. And for other patients, it was necessary to clarify the diagnosis by making additional tests. There is also the problem of a small amount of data, and a sufficient amount of data is needed to identify patterns in the data by the machine learning algorithm. But, this is a common problem of machine learning tasks, and not just tasks in the field of medicine.

The solution to the problem of machine learning begins with the engineering and the selecting of features. The task of feature engineering is not formalized and is a kind of art. In the case of medical diagnosis should be guided by well-known guidelines and regulations. To diagnose complications of appendicitis, we will be guided by a set of features of a registered database of acute appendicitis (*Vaschenko, et al., 2014*).

In many problems solved by machine learning methods, there are a large number of features in the training examples. That is, there is a high dimension of features. As the number of features grows, the complexity of learning the model (in our case, the neural network), as a rule, increases rapidly. It should also be borne in mind that features are formed as a result of various measurements, often quite complex and expensive. For example, in the diagnosis of diseases, the features are the values of various tests, the preparation of which is often an expensive procedure. Some features may be informational noise and degrade the result. Therefore, it is necessary to reduce the number of features by selecting the features that have the greatest impact on the result. The procedure for reducing the number of features is called decreasing the dimensionality, since as a result of this procedure, the dimension of the input vectors decreases. The dimension of features can be reduced in two ways:

- feature selection, which have the greatest predictive ability;
- projecting data with a high dimensionality into a space with a smaller dimensionality.

For the features selection, it is advisable to apply formalized methods *(Zheng and Casari, 2018; Chandrashekar and Sahin, 2014)*. In machine learning, filtering methods are often used, based on statistical methods, for example, on the correlation dependence *(Wackerly, et al., 2008; Bruce P. and Bruce F., 2017)* of network output on various attributes. But filtering methods are independent of the model, and therefore do not take into account the features of the model. For example, the neural network model is non-linear, and the correlation is linear. Therefore, the statistical selection of features requires experimental verification on the model used.

The essence of the wrapper methods *(Zheng and Casari, 2018; Chandrashekar and Sahin, 2014)* is that the selection procedure for features is "wrapped" by the procedure that implements the model. The model is trained on different sets of features that are selected by the selection procedure. The selection procedure selects a set of featureы that provides the best model quality score. Three approaches are known in this class of methods — forward selection methods, feature backwards selection, and step wise. Inclusion methods start from an empty subset, where various features are gradually added. Exclusion methods start from a subset equal to the original feature set, and features are gradually removed from it. In the step-by-step approach, at each step after adding a variable, the possibility of deleting the variable is checked. Wrap methods take into account the features of the model and the relationship of features. But the number of subsets of the set of features is expressed by exponential dependence. Therefore, it is usually impossible to iterate over all subsets. Most approaches use "greedy" algorithms, at each step of which a subset is chosen best by some criterion, but the previously made choice is never revised.

Embedded methods *(Zheng and Casari, 2018; Chandrashekar and Sahin, 2014)* do not separate feature selection and model training, but make selection within the model's fitting process. These methods are based on regularization, that is, the introduction of restrictions on model parameters. The idea of regularization is to build an algorithm that minimizes not only the model error, but also the number of variables used. The fact is that machine learning models can be overfitting. Overfitting means that the model loses its ability to generalize. Ability to generalize means that the network trained on the training set produces the correct results when the network supplies data related to the original set, but on which the network has not been trained. For example, the network is trained to diagnose certain diseases in a variety of examples representing the results of medical tests with a known patient condition. After training, the network must correctly diagnose this disease according to tests for which it has not been trained. Overfitting means increased network sensitivity to small changes in input data. Such sensitivity usually means large weights *(Pattanayak, 2017)*. The idea of regularization is to change the error functional, which does not allow the absolute values of weights to grow. To do this, a regularizer equal to the norm of the weights vector is added to the error functional. When using a regularizer, model parameters that have received small values can be excluded.

Principal component analysis (PCA) is a popular and powerful means of decreasing the dimension of the input data. This method finds in correlated data of a high dimensionality of direction with maximum data dispersion and projects data onto a part of these directions, that is, projects data with a high dimensionality into a space with a smaller dimensionality *(Chandrashekar and Sahin, 2014)*. There is a compression of information with the loss of the least significant information. But, for medical applications, the main component method does not allow to reduce the number of tests required for diagnosis.

A promising direction for changing the number of features is the use of auto-encoders *(Goodfellow, et al., 2016; Aggarwal, 2018, Geron, 2017)*. Usually autoencoders are used to reduce the number of signs. The simplest structure of the autoencoder contains an input layer, an intermediate layer that is smaller in dimension than the input one, and an output layer that contains as many neurons as the input layer. Autoencoders are trained without a teacher. Teaching without a teacher means that the same data should come out at the input and output of the autoencoder. Then the output of the intermediate layer will be compressed input.

When building a neural network for the diagnosis of postoperative appendicitis complications, an approach based on the wrapper method is proposed. The model is trained on different sets of features that are selected by the selection procedure. The following approach is proposed for the selection of significant features. A table of size $N \times M$, where N — is the number of combinations of features that need to be checked, and M — is the number of experiments for one combination. We use M experiments, because the learning process of the machine learning model is random: for the initial initialization of the weights, as a rule, a random algorithm is used, also, during the training, the training sample is randomly mixed. Experiments are conducted to avoid the influence of these random events. During the feature selection process, each model is trained once in each combination of features. The results of the trained model, presented as the value of a quality metric, are recorded in a table. We used the F-score (or F-measure) *(Bruce and Bruce, 2017; Geron,*

Table 1. An example of a generated table of F-score metric values

E_1	E_2	E_3	E_4	E_5	E_6	E_7	E_8	E_9	E_{10}
0.57	0.53	0.60	0.60	0.29	0.83	0.83	0.00	0.22	0.33
0.80	0.86	0.57	0.91	0.82	0.92	0.80	0.86	0.67	0.67
0.67	0.25	0.88	0.71	0.78	0.60	0.91	0.57	0.33	0.71

Table 2. Computed table of quantiles and arithmetic mean

Nº	A	Q_1	Q_2	Q_3	Q_4
1	0.48	0.20	0.30	0.60	0.83
2	0.79	0.66	0.70	0.86	0.91
3	0.64	0.32	0.58	0.76	0.88

2017). This metric is an average of harmonic precision and recall. An example for three combinations of features and 10 experiments is presented in Table 1 (measure F1 values are denoted as $E_i, i = 1, 2, \ldots, 10$).

After forming a table of values for each row, quantiles should be calculated *(Bruce and Bruce, 2017)*. For example, such: 0.10 quantile (Q_1); 0.25 quantile (Q_2); 0.75 quantile (Q_3); 0.90 quantile (Q_4) and arithmetic average (A) of F-score metric. At the end you need to create a new table (Table 2).

Using Table 2, it is possible to analyze models using the interquartile range. This approach is based on the ability to get a high and stable result. The metric of the arithmetic mean is unstable - it strongly depends on the limiting values of the sample, if there are very bad results, the arithmetic mean will be lower *(Bruce and Bruce, 2017)*. This metric allows to evaluate the stability of the results obtained. For example, in table 2, in line 2, the value of this metric is maximum (0.79), which means that this combination of features allows to obtain an average value of the quality metric of 0.79. However, quantile values Q_i are also important. If the value of the upper quantile (in this case Q_4) is large, for example, greater than 0.80, then this combination of features theoretically allows obtaining a good quality model. Compare 0.75 quantile Q_3 for the three feature combinations. For the 2 combination, it is maximum, however, for the first and second combination it varies greatly $0.76 - 0.60 = 0.16$, while quantile Q_4 for the first and third combination differs less $0.88 - 0.83 = 0.05$.

This suggests that although theoretically their best results are almost similar, but practically, using the first combination of signs, the chances of getting a good result are lower than when using the third combination. However, the value of quantile Q_1 for the second combination of features is greater than Q_4 of the first combination and Q_2 of the third combination. So the second combination of features allows you to get not only a good result, but also much more stable than other combinations.

After selecting the features, it is necessary to perform data conversion: filling gaps in the training data, encoding and scaling of data. To scale numerical features, we use min-max scaling, or normalization *(Geron, 2017)* — bringing variables to the same range. Input variables are normalized so that the features vary in the range [0, 1]. Each input variable is normalized independently of other variables. The scales of the input and output variables are not related. Use linear normalization

$$p_{ij} = \frac{\left(x_{ij} - x_{j\min}\right)\left(b - a\right)}{x_{j\max} - x_{j\min}} + a \, ,$$

where p_{ij} — normalized value of the j feature in i example, x_{ij} — initial value of the j feature in i example, $[a,b]$ — allowable range of variation of the normalized features $[0,1]$, $[x_{j\min}, x_{j\max}]$ — is the range of the initial values of the j feature.

Neural networks work only with numbers. Therefore, binary and categorical (qualitative) features and target values must be encoded. When encoding binary features, "false" will be encoded as "0", and "true" — as "1". Categorical variables (both attributes and target values) are not recommended to be encoded with integers, for example, "white" — 1, "black" — 2, etc., since encoding categorical variables by numbers introduces the distance between the values of the variables. And there is no such thing for categorical variables. For encoding qualitative variables, a technique known in modern machine learning as One-Hot Encoding (unitary code) is used (Brownlee, 2017). For example, if a quality attribute takes values, it is replaced by n features. In the source data table, the corresponding column is replaced by columns. In the rows of the table, the feature being considered is replaced by features, all of which are zero except for one. The position corresponding to the number of the feature is placed 1.

The training data set (*Vaschenko, et al., 2014*) is presented in the form of a table with 30 features with blood tests, before and after the operation, and 12 common features, such as age, blood type, etc. The following are common features:

- *Gender;*
- *Age;*
- *Bed-day;*
- *Blood type and Rh factor;*
- *Basic diagnosis;*
- *Concomitant diagnosis;*
- *Complications;*
- *Surgical interventions;*
- *The duration of surgical intervention;*
- *ECG;*
- *Clinical assessment of the patient;*
- *Presence of complications.*

Gender is presented in the form of a string that has 2 categories ('male', 'female'). *Age* is an integer, is continuous. *Bed-day* is an integer that determines the total number of days in the hospital. *Blood type and Rh factor* are presented as string. *Basic diagnosis* describes in verbal form the diagnosis of the patient. *Concomitant diagnosis* in a verbal form describes an additional diagnosis. *Complications* are type of complications, empty if *presence of complications is 'no'*. The column will be useful if it is required that the system can determine not only the presence of the complication itself, but also its appearance. *Surgical interventions* in the form of a string describe the type of surgery (eg, 'appendectomy'). So, as it is necessary to predict the presence of complications before the operation, this feature will be suitable only for general analysis of the data set. *The duration of surgical intervention* is the data recorded as a string. *ECG* is a string symptom, a description of the ECG results. *Clinical assessment of the patient* describes in a string form the opinion of the doctor about the patient's condition before the operation. *Presence of complications* is a string with two options ('yes', 'no'). If there were complications (the patient has 'yes' in the row), then the *complications* column describes the type of complication.

Blood tests are presented as real values before and after surgery. Since it is necessary to predict complications before surgery, post-surgery analyzes will be suitable only for general analysis of the data set. The name of the features is presented below:

- *Hemoglobin;*
- *Erythrocytes;*
- *Color indicator;*
- *Leukocytes;*
- *Neutrophil stabs;*
- *Segmented neuthrophils;*
- *Lymphocytes;*
- *Monocytes;*
- *Erythrocyte sedimentation rate;*
- *Common bilirubin;*
- *Total protein;*
- *Amylase;*
- *Urea;*
- *Creatinine;*
- *Glucose.*

All blood test data is presented in the form of real numbers. To facilitate the work with a large amount of data, the Pandas library was used *(Heydt, 2017)*. Using the *info()* method built into the pandas library, you can get a brief summary of the data. This approach is often used to identify features with gaps.

- *Gender;*
- *Age;*
- *Bed-day;*
- *Basic diagnosis;*
- *Surgical interventions;*
- *Hemoglobin (before surgery);*
- *Hemoglobin (after surgery);*
- *Erythrocytes (before surgery);*
- *Erythrocytes (after surgery);*
- *Leukocytes (before surgery);*
- *Leukocytes (after surgery);*
- *Neutrophil stabs (before surgery);*
- *Lymphocytes (before surgery);*
- *Presence of complications.*

Some of the features can be dropped. For example, blood tests after surgery will not be needed, because prediction of future complications must be made before surgery. Also, data on the number of days in the hospital "bed-days" will not be necessary, because on what day the surgery occurred is unknown. The last features that can be dropped is a type of surgical intervention, since only the presence of the complication is predicted, not its appearance. Dropping some of the features will get a new set of features:

- *Gender;*
- *Age;*
- *Basic diagnosis;*
- *Hemoglobin (before surgery);*
- *Erythrocytes (before surgery);*
- *Leukocytes (before surgery);*
- *Neutrophil stabs (before surgery);*
- *Lymphocytes (before surgery);*

and 1 target feature:

- *Presence of complications.*

Pay attention to the types of the remaining columns. Blood tests must be scaled to between 0 and 1. Gender is a categorical feature and can be encoded in two different ways:

- In the form of vector [0, 1] – male gender, [1, 0] – female gender or vice versa.
- In the form of a binary variable 0 – male gender, 1 – female gender.

It was decided to scale this feature in the form of a vector of two elements. Encoding in the form of a binary variable is usually used to encode Boolean variables (for example, the presence of some diseases).

Basic diagnosis is a string. This feature contains 8 unique values:

1. Acute phlegmonous appendicitis
2. Acute appendicitis
3. Acute catarrhal appendicitis
4. Acute catarrhal appendicitis. Typhlitis
5. Acute gangrenous appendicitis
6. Acute gangrenous perforated appendicitis
7. Acute catarrhal appendicitis. Acute pancreatitis
8. Acute destructive appendicitis

Table 3. Encoded values of the presence of complications feature

Text Value	Encoded Vector
Acute phlegmonous appendicitis	[1, 0, 0, 0, 0, 0, 0, 0]
Acute appendicitis	[0, 1, 0, 0, 0, 0, 0, 0]
Acute catarrhal appendicitis	[0, 0, 1, 0, 0, 0, 0, 0]
Acute catarrhal appendicitis. Typhlitis	[0, 0, 1, 1, 0, 0, 0, 0]
Acute gangrenous appendicitis	[0, 0, 0, 0, 1, 0, 0, 0]
Acute gangrenous perforated appendicitis	[0, 0, 0, 0, 0, 1, 0, 0]
Acute catarrhal appendicitis. Acute pancreatitis	[0, 0, 1, 0, 0, 0, 1, 0]
Acute destructive appendicitis	[0, 0, 0, 0, 0, 0, 0, 1]

Target feature *presence of complications* should be coded 1 – yes, 0 – no.

It is noticed that some patients have two diagnoses at the same time. Need to decide how to encode such feature. A primitive approach is to create a feature vector, the length of which is equal to the number of unique values. After analyzing the data, a method of encoding categorical features was proposed, which differs from the generally accepted approach. You may notice that some of the diagnoses are composite, consist of more simple ones. It is proposed to make a vector whose dimension is equal to the dimension of the space of simple diagnoses. Then, if there is a specific patient diagnosis, set the value of this coordinate to 1, otherwise 0. In this case, there are 8 elementary diagnoses:

1. Acute phlegmonous appendicitis;
2. Acute appendicitis;
3. Acute catarrhal appendicitis;
4. Typhlitis;
5. Acute gangrenous appendicitis;
6. Acute gangrenous perforated appendicitis;
7. Acute destructive appendicitis;
8. Acute pancreatitis.

We compose a vector of length 8 of them and encode each of the values.

After determining the method of encoding and scaling of features, the preprocessing should be performed. A library for working with large data Scikit-Learn (Geron, 2017; Scikit-Learn, 2019) was used to perform the preprocessing of features. The library contains built-in classes for performing various kinds of data processing. Inheritance from base classes is also possible, which allows you to implement your own processing methods. This approach allows the flexibility to customize the

Figure 1. Image of the neural network layer: a) compressed view; b) extended view

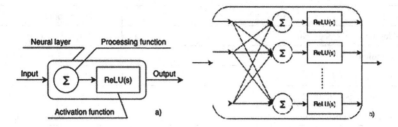

entire process of processing large amounts of data. With the help of the Scikit-Learn library, the features were encoded and scaled.

Using the previously proposed method, a selection of significant features was made. The table was built 8×10 for selection of the main feature, to which the others were added. The main features were taken from the list:

- *Gender;*
- *Age;*
- *Basic diagnosis;*
- *Hemoglobin (before surgery);*
- *Erythrocytes (before surgery);*
- *Leukocytes (before surgery);*
- *Neutrophil stabs (before surgery);*
- *Lymphocytes (before surgery);*

As a metric, evaluating the quality of the selected feature, the F-score metric was chosen. According to the results of the experiment, the *basic diagnosis* was chosen as the main feature. Then, by exhaustively combining the combinations, the most significant for the machine learning model, the following feature combinations were selected:

1. *Basic diagnosis, Gender, Age (categorical), Erythrocytes (before surgery);*
2. *Basic diagnosis, Hemoglobin (before surgery), Erythrocytes (before surgery), Leukocytes (before surgery);*
3. *Basic diagnosis, Gender, Age (categorical), Hemoglobin (before surgery), Leukocytes (before surgery), Neutrophils stabs (before surgery);*
4. *Basic diagnosis, Gender, Age (categorical), Hemoglobin (before surgery), Neutrophil stabs (before surgery), Lymphocytes (before surgery).*

Figure 2. Network architecture based on the MLPClassifier model

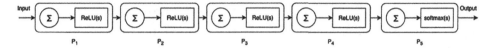

TOOLS, ARCHITECTURE AND NETWORK FITTING

Currently, there are a large number of libraries and machine learning frameworks. Many of them facilitate the development of a proprietary neural network architecture or data preprocessing (Kharkovyna, 2019). The Keras library was chosen as a library for implementing the neural network architecture *(Gulli and Pal, 2017; Chollet, 2017)*. The Keras library is a "wrapper" over the TensorFlow framework *(Geron, 2017)* and greatly facilitates the use of such a complex tool.

After processing the raw data, you need to decide on the neural network architecture, which will perform the task of determining the presence of complications after the operation. To solve such problems, neural network architectures are used, having several layers connected in series with each other.

In figure 1a shows an image of a neural network layer in a compressed form, with a description of its component parts. Neuron is understood as a certain function that performs processing, in this case, it is the summation of input values with weights. The input and output data of the layer are represented as a vector of numbers. A more detailed image is shown in figure 1b. It can be seen from the figure that the layer of the neural network contains, as a rule, more than one neuron. Also, you can see how the layer functions from the inside.

As a basic model, for the initial assessment of the quality of the processed data, a feedforward network was chosen by the type of multilayer perceptron that implements the classification problem. The Scikit-Learn library has an implementation of this model, called the MLPClassifier (Perceptron classifier) *(sklearn.neural_network .MLPClassifier, 2019)*. After selecting the number of layers and neurons in the layers, the network architecture had the following form (Figure. 2). The selection of the best architecture was carried out using a grid search of parameters implemented in the Scikit-Learn library *(Tuning the hyper-parameters of an estimator, 2019)*. A search in the grid of parameters means the search of the specified hyperparameters (the number of layers and neurons in the layers) and the modeling of the neural network at each parameter set.

In fig. 2 layers are numbered: P_1, P_2, P_3, P_4 и P_5. Layers have the following number of neurons: P_1 — 14 neurons, P_2 — 28 neurons, P_3 — 14 neurons, P_4 — 7 neurons, P_5 — 2 neurons. In all layers, as a processing function, an adder is used that calculates a weighted sum

$$s = \sum_i w_i x_i ,$$

where w_i and x_i — i-th components, respectively, the weights vector and the input vector. The activation functions of the layers are different. As the activation functions of hidden layers, the function *Rectified Linear Unit (ReLU)* is used — positive linear activation function, or hard maximum (Glorot, et al., 2011)

$$f(s) = \max(0, s) = \begin{cases} 0, s < 0, \\ s, s \geq 0, \end{cases}$$

where s — weighted sum.

Compared to sigmoidal activation functions, the ReLU function is easily calculated, which is very important for large networks. The derivative of this function is either 1 or 0, which eliminates the "paralysis" of the network.

A competing activation function with a *softmax* is used in the output layer (Neural network models, 2019)

$$f(s_i) = \frac{\exp(s_i)}{\sum\limits_{j=1}^{n} \exp(s_j)} ,$$

where s_i — weighted sum i-th neuron, n — number of neurons in the output layer.

This function provides a sum of layer outputs equal to one for any values of weighted sums of neurons of a given layer. This allows treating network outputs as probabilities of events, the totality of which forms a complete group. When using the *softmax* function, the number of neurons in the output layer is equal to the number of classes to be determined. In our case, the input vector should be assigned to one of two classes: "there is a complication" or "there is no complication".

Figure 3. Architecture of autoencoder

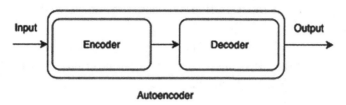

Figure 4. Architecture of autoencoder: a) encoder, b) decoder

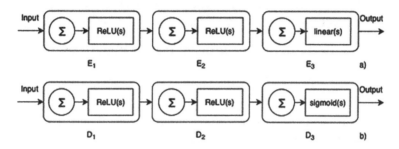

After conducting a series of "fast" experiments, using the architecture of Fig. 2, no good quality classifier was obtained. In medical diagnostics, the features of objects belonging to different classes often differ slightly. It is proposed to apply overcomplete autoencoder to improve classification accuracy. Such autoencoder produces non-linear transformation of the entrance to the space of greater dimension. According to Cover's theorem *(Cover, 1965)*, this increases the probability of a linear separation of features, that is, after such a transformation, the classifier works better. We can assume that the overcomplete autoencoder reveals hidden features.

To solve this problem, a neural network was built, like an overcomplete autoencoder. This neural network will be auxiliary. Before a classification is performed using the MLPClassifier network, the data will be mapped into a larger dimension space, which theoretically increases the probability of successful classification. Then, the converted data will be fed into the input of the classifier, which will be much easier to perform the classification. The autoencoder consists of two parts: an encoder and a decoder. Using the encoder and decoder, you can get an autoencoder (Figure 3).

A good autoencoder at the output produces a vector of values very close to what was received at the input. In figure 4a and 4b are the constituent parts of the auto-encoder.

In fig. 4a presents the encoder. Hidden layers are similar to a neural network built on the basis of the MLPClassifier. The output layer has the same processing functions, however, the activation functions are linear

$$f\left(s\right) = s,$$

where s — weighted sum. This function was used because the result of the operation of the encoder are the new features that it has identified that take real values. In fig. 4a layers numbered: E_1, E_2 and E_3. The number of neurons depends on the dimension of the input features and was calculated by the formula

$$N = k \times n,$$

where k — coefficient, n — dimension of input vector, N — calculated number of neurons. Coefficient k set for each layer:

- for layer E_1 coefficient $k = 1.35$;
- for layer E_2 coefficient $k = 1.75$
- for layer E_3 coefficient $k = 2.00$.

This parameter was chosen experimentally.

In fig. 4b is a decoder. The architecture of hidden layers repeats the architecture of the encoder. The difference lies in the use of asymmetric logistic activation function in the output layer

$$f\left(s\right) = \frac{1}{1 + \exp\left(-s\right)},$$

where s — weighted sum. This function is well suited as an output activation function, since it is distributed from 0 to 1, as is the input feature vector. In fig. 4b layers numbered: D_1, D_2, and D_3. The number of neurons depends on the dimension of the input features, as in the encoder and is calculated by . Coefficient k was experimentally setted for each layer:

Figure 5. Classifier architecture containing dropout layers

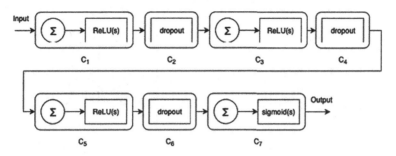

- for layer E_1 coefficient $k = 1.75$;
- for layer E_2 coefficient $k = 1.35$;
- for layer E_3 coefficient $k = 1.00$.

For autoencoder training, algorithms with an adaptive learning rate were used. These algorithms use different learning rates for different components of the parameter vector, since different components can have different effects on network learning. The autoencoder was trained by the Adadelta method *(Zeiler, 2012)*. Another Adam method was also tested *(Kingma and Ba, 2014)*, but the adadelta method was able to achieve the best quality values.

For autoencoder training, the Xavier initialization method *(Glorot and Bengio, 2010)* was used to eliminate the problems of extinction and the explosive growth of the gradient to initialize the weights.

To overcome the overfitting effect, 'early stopping' was used. This approach uses cross-validation: two subsets were selected from the original training data set:

- training set, which is used to configure network parameters;
- validation set, which is used throughout the training to detect the phenomenon of overfitting.

Learning stops when the network error on the validation sample stops decreasing. The training data set was divided into proportions: training sample - 90%, validation sample - 10%.

Autoencoder allowed to improve the results of work, in particular, the quality of the classifier has increased. However, the classifier began to retrain more often. To avoid the problem of retraining, the neuron "dropout" method is used *(Hinton, et al., 2012; Srivastava, et al., 2014)*. The process consists in randomly disconnecting a part of the neurons from the learning process at one iteration. In this method, for

Figure 6. Dropout layer in extended view

Train set (85%)

		Expert decision	
		no	yes
Model decision	no	55	4
	Yes	10	22

Test set (15%)

		Expert decision	
		no	yes
Model decision	no	11	0
	Yes	1	5

each neuron (except for the neurons of the output layer), the probability is established with which the neuron will be excluded from the network. This probability is called the dropout rate. The learning algorithm is constructed as follows: on each new learning example, the probability of deletion is determined for each neuron. If a neuron is removed, its output is assumed to be zero. Zero neuron output means that the neuron does not actually participate in the calculations. When using a trained network, all neurons are involved, but the output of each neuron is multiplied by the probability of conservation, with which the neuron was left during training. Each training example uses a network with its own architecture. The use of a dropout-trained network is equivalent to averaging over an ensemble of networks *(Srivastava, 2014)*, and the use of an ensemble of models is better than the use of a single model.

The Scikit-Learn library does not allow for the flexible design of its network architectures, unlike the Keras library. The use of the dropout approach requires changing the architecture of the classifier, which is not possible using the Scikit-Learn library. In Scikit-Learn, ready-made models are available, the parameters of which can be configured. However, the dropout approach requires a more flexible way to configure the network. This feature is provided by the Keras library. There it is possible to configure networks at the layer level. Modernization of the neural network shown in Figure 2, using the dropout approach, is presented below (see Figure 5).

The architecture of layers C_1, C_3, C_5 and C_7 was introduced earlier. Let us dwell on the dropout layers: C_2, C_4 and C_6. In figure 6 presents the dropout layer in more detail.

The dropout layer performs data transfer by randomly disabling neurons. It does not handle any input values. After adding dropout layers to the model, the quality of the classifier increased. The fact is that not all neurons contribute equally to the work of the entire network. Some more, some less affect the incoming signal. In order that strongly influencing neurons do not "interrupt" the weak signals of other neurons, the dropout approach disables a part of neurons in a random way. The number of neurons in the layers of the classifier was determined by the formula, which was previously used to determine the number of neurons in the layers of the autoencoder. Coefficients k were experimentally selected and equal:

- for layer C_1 coefficient $k = 1.0$;
- for layer C_3 coefficient $k = 0.5$;
- for layer C_5 coefficient $k = 0.2$.

Layer C_7 has one neuron that determines the likelihood of complications. For dropout layers, the threshold of neuron disconnection was set experimentally:

- for layer C_2 threshold parameter is equal to 0.30
- for layer C_4 threshold parameter is equal to 0.15;
- for layer C_6 threshold parameter is equal to 0.05.

The Classifier was trained by the Adam method. This learning method has an adaptive parameter - the rate of convergence. Due to the peculiarities of the method, it is possible to avoid falling into a part of local minima. To initialize the initial parameters of the model, the Xavier method was used. The data set was divided into 3 samples: training - 70%, validation —15% and test - 15%. Using a test sample, you can evaluate the quality of a trained model by calculating the required quality metrics.

When training the classifier, the callback method was used [34]. This approach is used to work with the best model at each iteration and, as a result, to have a good model. If the accuracy of the model has changed for the worse at the current iteration, the model will save the parameters from the previous iteration and not change them to new ones.

ANALYSIS OF RESULTS

When solving problems using neural network models, it is necessary to consider several models or options for building a single model. Therefore, it is important to evaluate the model and choose the best. The task of diagnosing postoperative complications is the task of classification, since the presence or absence of a complication is considered. Consider a metric for evaluating classification models *(Bruce and Bruce, 2017; Geron, 2017)*. Consider the problem of binary classification, in which the labels belong to the set $\{0,1\}$.

Figure 7. Confusion matrix

		Expert decision (actual class)	
		1	0
Model decision	1	T_P	F_N
	0	F_P	T_N

Objects with a label 1 are called positive, and with a label 0 — negative. The machine learning model, in particular, the neural network returns an arbitrary real number. In the case of a sigmoidal activation function in the output layer, this is a number from 0 to 1, in the case of the softmax function, a number from 0 to 1, which is interpreted as the probability of attributing the result to this class. With the help of a cut-off point — the threshold value dividing the classes, the classifier's response is converted to binary. If the output of the neuron exceeds the cut-off threshold, then this means a positive outcome, otherwise it is negative.

Errors made by the model in its practical application can lead to false conclusions, which entail material and, therefore, financial losses from wrong decisions. Such losses are called classification error costs.

In a binary classification, each individual prediction can have four outcomes:

- True Positive, T_P;
- True Negative, T_N;
- False Positive, F_P;
- False Negative, F_N.

A truly positive outcome will be when the actual class of this example is 1 and the output model is 1. The true negative outcome is when the actual observation class is 0 and the model returns 0. A false positive value occurs when the observation class is 0 and the model for it will form output 1. If the output is false negative, the target variable takes the value 1, and the model will return 0 as the output. The results are shown in figure 7 as a confusion matrix.

The concepts considered are associated with the concepts of errors of the first and second kind known in mathematical statistics *(Bruce and Bruce, 2017; Sheshkin, 2003)*. If a binary classification model is built on the basis of a training sample, then all the examples included in it correspond to either positive or negative outcomes. Then in the process of the model, the following errors may occur.

- The example corresponds to a positive outcome, but was recognized as negative: after the operation there will be complications, but the model does not detect them. In other words, the event of interest was not mistakenly detected. Such errors are called type I errors.
- The example corresponds to a negative outcome, but was recognized as positive: there is no complication, but the model determines its presence. In other words, the event of interest did not occur, but was discovered. Such errors are called type II errors.

As the metrics that evaluate the quality of the model, the metrics that were implemented in Scikit-Learn *(Bruce and Bruce, 2017; Geron, 2017)* were chosen:

1. precision or positive predictive value;
2. recall or true positive rate;
3. F1-score or F1-measure;
4. Specificity or true negative rate;
5. ROC curve;
6. ROC AUC;
7. number of type I errors (metrics FP – False Positive);
8. number of type II errors (metrics FN – False Negative);
9. confusion matrix.

The precision score indicates the accuracy of the predicted positive outcome (the patient will have complications). This metric is calculated by the formula

$$PPV = \frac{\sum_i TP_i}{\sum_i TP_i + \sum_i FP_i},$$

where TP — true-positive outcomes, FP — false-positive outcomes, PPV — positive predictive value or precision.

The recall of the model shows the proportion of positive outcomes that the algorithm was able to correctly detect. Calculated by the formula

$$TPR = \frac{\sum_i TP_i}{\sum_i TP_i + \sum_i FN_i},$$

where TP — true-positive outcomes, FN — true-negative outcomes, TPR — true positive rate.

The term 'recall' is often used in machine learning, and 'sensitivity' is often used in medical diagnostics and biostatistics.

The precision and recall of the model can be conveniently combined into a single metric called F-score *(Bruce and Bruce, 2017; Geron, 2017)*. This metric is an average of harmonic precision and recall. Calculated by the formula

$$F_1 = 2 \times \frac{PPV \times TPR}{PPV + TPR}.$$

F-score will be close to zero if at least from its arguments is close to zero. Moreover, precision and completeness have the same effect. The peculiarity of this metric is that the harmonic mean gives a small value more weight. Therefore, a high value of the F-score metric can only be achieved with high values of accuracy and specificity.

The model specificity measures the ability of an algorithm to predict negative outcomes (the proportion of patients without complications). Calculates by the formula

$$FPR = \frac{\sum_i TN_i}{\sum_i TN_i + \sum_i FP_i},$$

where TN — true-negative outcomes, FP — false-positive outcomes, FPR — false-positive rate.

You can minimize the cost of binary classification errors by selecting the cut-off point, a threshold that separates the classes. With a decrease in the cut-off threshold, the probability of false recognition of positive observations (false positive outcomes) increases, and with an increase, the probability of incorrect recognition of negative observations (false negative outcomes) increases. The goal is to find a cut-off

Table 4. The results of experiments on the 1st combination of features

Metric	Metrics Values	
	Train Set (85%)	Test Set (15%)
Precision	0.91	1.00
Recall	0.68	0.90
F-score	0.78	0.95
Specificity	0.97	1.00
ROC AUC	0.82	0.95
Number of type I errors	2	0
Number of type II errors	9	1

Figure 8. Confusion matrices for the first combination of features

value that gives the greatest accuracy in recognizing a given class, and which one is determined by the formulation of the problem.

To select the cut-off point in the binary classification, ROC analysis *(Bruce and Bruce, 2017; Geron, 2017)* is used, based on the construction of the characteristic detection curve (Receiver Operating Characteristic) or the error curve - ROC curve. The ROC curve shows the ratio between the proportion of correctly classified examples (True Positive Rate - TPR), i.e. sensitivity, and the proportion of incorrectly classified examples (False Positive Rate - FPR)

$$R_{FP} = \frac{\sum_i FP_i}{\sum_i FP_i + \sum_i TN_i}.$$

Figure 9. ROC curves of training and test sets

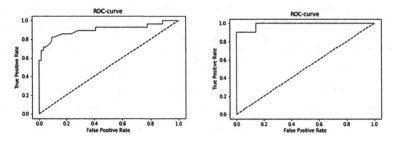

Table 5. The results of experiments on the 2nd combination of features

Metrics	Metrics Values	
	Train Set (85%)	**Test Set (15%)**
Precision	0.85	1.00
Recall	0.69	0.83
F-score	0.76	0.91
Specificity	0.93	1.00
ROC AUC	0.81	0.92
Number of type I errors	4	0
Number of type II errors	10	1

Figure 10. Confusion matrices for the second combination of features

Train set (85%)

		Expert decision	
		no	yes
Model decision	no	55	4
	Yes	10	22

Test set (15%)

		Expert decision	
		no	yes
Model decision	no	11	0
	Yes	1	5

To construct the ROC curve, the cut-off threshold varies from 0 to 1 with a given step. As a result, for each threshold value, the number of correctly and incorrectly recognized examples will change, and accordingly, the sensitivity and proportion of incorrectly classified examples. For each threshold, the sensitivity and fractions of incorrectly classified examples are calculated, and a graph is plotted, along the vertical axis of which the sensitivity is plotted, and on the horizontal axis - the

Figure 11. ROC curves for the second combination of features

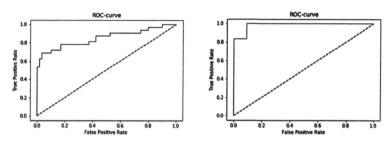

Table 6. The results of experiments on the 3rd combination of features

Metrics	Metrics Values	
	Train Set (85%)	Test Set (15%)
Precision	1.00	1.00
Recall	0.67	1.00
F-score	0.80	1.00
Specificity	1.00	1.00
ROC AUC	0.83	1.00
Number of type I errors	0	0
Number of type II errors	11	0

Figure 12. Confusion matrices for the third combination of features

Train set (85%)

		Expert decision	
		no	yes
Model decision	no	58	0
	Yes	11	22

Test set (15%)

		Expert decision	
		no	yes
Model decision	no	12	0
	Yes	0	5

proportion of fractions of incorrectly classified examples. Since one positive outcome may have several negative outcomes, and vice versa, the real ROC curve is not smooth, but rugged. Each point of the ROC curve corresponds to a certain value of the cutoff threshold. In this case, the value corresponding to the point of the ROC curve with coordinates as close as possible to (0; 1), for which both sensitivity and specificity are equal to 1, that is, both positive and negative examples are correctly

Figure 13. ROC curves for the third combination of features

Train set (85%)

		Expert decision	
		no	yes
Model decision	no	54	4
	Yes	7	26

Test set (15%)

		Оценка эксперта	
		no	Yes
Model decision	no	12	0
	Yes	1	4

Table 7. The results of experiments on the fourth combination of features

Metrics	Metrics Values	
	Train Set (85%)	Test Set (15%)
Precision	0.87	1.00
Recall	0.79	0.80
F-score	0.83	0.89
Specificity	0.93	1.00
ROC AUC	0.86	0.90
Number of type I errors	4	0
Number of type II errors	7	1

Figure 14. ROC curves for the fourth combination of features

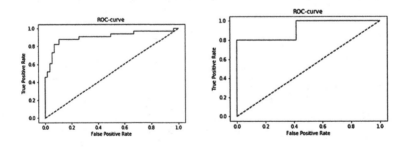

recognized, will be optimal. The diagonal line corresponds to the "useless" classifier when the result is obtained by random guessing. The area under the ROC curve (AUC - Area Under ROC Curve) indicates the predictive power of the model, and AUC = 1 corresponds to the ideal classifier. For real classifiers, the area under the ROC curve is greater than 0.7–0.8, which corresponds to a sufficiently high classification accuracy.

Quality metrics were calculated for various combinations of significant features. In tab. 4 displays the values of the model quality metrics on the 1st combination of signs for the training and test dataset. To select the best model, the data set was divided in the proportions of 85% - a training sample and 15% - a test sample.

In figure 8 shows the error matrix of the 1st combination of features.

Figure 9 shows ROC curves.

Values of metrics for the test set are high (more than 0.90). The error matrix shows that on the test dataset the model was mistaken only 1 time. The model identified the patient without complications as a patient with complications, which is more preferable than skipping complications in a patient.

Analyze the second combination of features (table 5).

In figure 10 shows the confusion matrix.

The ROC curves for the second combination of features are shown in Figure 11.

Indicators of the model trained in the second combination of features do not differ much from those of the model trained in the first combination of features. It is worth noting that on the training set, the model trained on the second set of features allows more errors of the I and II type. Consider the results of the model trained in the third combination of features.

Figure 12 shows the confusion matrices.

ROC curves for the third combination of features are show in Figure 13

This model on the training and test set did not make errors of the I type, in contrast to the 1st and 2nd models. It should be noted that on the test set the machine learning model did not make any errors.

Let us evaluate the results of the fourth combination of features (Table 7).

The ROC curves for the fourth combination of features are presented in Figure 14.

This model showed itself well as a classifier that admits the least error of the II type. The value of the recall metric in this model is more than the rest (0.79). Also, the F-score metric is the largest among the considered combinations of features.

Let us analyze the features of the use of various combinations of features. The first combination of features requires the least analysis (only *erythrocytes (before surgery)*) and shows a good result on the test data set. The second and fourth combinations require more data and allow more false positives. The third combination of features differs from the others in that it did not make any errors on the test dataset, all the values of the model metrics on the test set are maximum.

The experiments were conducted on a computer with a processor Intel Pentium B940 @ 2x 2GHz with 4096MB RAM, running on operating system Ubuntu 18.04.2 LTS (Bionic Beaver) with kernel version x86_64 Linux 4.15.0-45-generic. Python was chosen as the implementation language, with version 3.6.7. Dependencies:

- Scikit-Learn, version 0.19.2;
- TensorFlow, version 1.5.0;
- NumPy, version 1.14.5;
- Keras, version 2.2.4.

The training time of the overcomplete autoencoder was 34 seconds. Classifier trained in 16 seconds.

CONCLUSION

An approach to the selection of features using interquartile range is proposed. The approach allowed us to obtain a high and stable result of the F-measure. A different encoding method for composite categorical features has been proposed. A network of direct deep architecture has been developed and investigated, allowing to diagnose postoperative appendicitis complications. To improve the accuracy of diagnosis, an overcomplete autoencoder is used, projecting features into a space of higher dimension. Network research showed high diagnostic quality indicators.

REFERENCES

Aggarwal, C. C. (2018). *Neural networks and deep learning*. Springer. doi:10.1007/978-3-319-94463-0

Bakti, N., Hussain, A., & El-Hassani, S. (2011). A rare complication of acute appendicitis: Superior mesenteric vein thrombosis. *International Journal of Surgery Case Reports*, 2(8), 250–252. doi:10.1016/j.ijscr.2011.08.003 PMID:22096743

Brigham, K. L., & Johns, M. M. E. (2012). *Predictive health: How we can reinvent medicine to extend our best years*. Basic Books.

Brownlee, J. (2017). *Why One-Hot encode data in machine learning?* Retrieved from https://machinelearningmastery.com/why-one-hot-encode-data-in-machine-learning/

Bruce, P., & Bruce, F. (2017). *Practical statistics for data scientists: 50 essential concepts*. O'Reilly.

Chandrashekar, G., & Sahin, F. (2014). A survey on feature selection methods. *Computers & Electrical Engineering*, 40(1), 16–28. doi:10.1016/j.compeleceng.2013.11.024

Chollet, F. (2017). *Deep learning with Python.* Manning Publications.

Cover, T. M. (1965). Geometrical and statistical properties of systems of linear inequalities with applications in pattern recognition. *IEEE Transactions on Electronic Computers, EC-14*(3), 326–334. doi:10.1109/PGEC.1965.264137

Geron, A. (2017). *Hands-on machine learning with Scikit-Learn and TensorFlow: Concepts, tools, and techniques to build intelligent systems.* O'Reilly.

Glorot, X., & Bengio, Y. (2010). Understanding the difficulty of training deep feedforward neural networks. *International conference on artificial intelligence and statistics,* 249–256.

Glorot, X., Bordes, A., & Bengio, Y. (2011). Deep sparse rectifier neural networks. *Proceedings of the 14th International Conference on Artificial Intelligence and Statistics,* Vol. 15, 315–323.

Goodfellow, I., Bengio, Y., & Courville, A. (2016). *Deep learning.* MIT Press.

Gulli, A., & Pal, S. (2017). *Deep learning with Keras: Implementing deep learning models and neural networks with the power of Python.* Packt Publishing.

Haykin, S. O. (2008). *Neural networks and learning machines.* Pearson.

Heydt, M. (2017). *Learning pandas: High performance data manipulation and analysis using Python.* Packt Publishing.

Hinton, G. E., Srivastava, N., Krizhevsky, A., Sutskever, I., & Salakhutdinov, R. (2012). *Improving neural networks by preventing co-adaptation of feature detectors.* Retrieved from https://arxiv.org/abs/1207.0580

Joskowicz, L. (2017). Computer-aided surgery meets predictive, preventive, and personalized medicine. *The EPMA Journal, 8*(8), 1–4. doi:10.100713167-017-0084-8 PMID:28670350

Keras: The Python deep learning library. Usage of callbacks. (2019). Retrieved from https://keras.io/callbacks/

Kharkovyna, O. (2019). *Top 10 best deep learning frameworks in 2019.* Retrieved from https://towardsdatascience.com/top-10-best-deep-learning-frameworks-in-2019-5ccb90ea6de

Kingma, D. P., & Ba, J. (2014). *Adam: A method for stochastic optimization.* Retrieved from https://arxiv.org/abs/1412.6980

Lamarino, A. P. M., Juliano, Y., Rosa, O. M., Novo, N. F., Favaro, M. L., & Ribeiro, M. A. F. (2017). Risk factors associated with complications of acute appendicitis. *Journal of Brazilian College of Surgeons*, *44*(6), 560–566. PMID:29267552

Miner, L., Bolding, P., Hilbe, J., Goldstein, M., Hill, T., Nisbet, R., ... Miner, G. (2014). *Practical predictive analytics and decisioning systems for medicine: Informatics accuracy and cost-effectiveness for healthcare administration and delivery including medical research*. Academic Press.

Neural network models (supervised). (2019). Retrieved from https://scikitlearn.org/stable/modules/neural_networks_supervised.html

Park, S. Y., & Kim, S. M. (2015). Acute appendicitis diagnosis using artificial neural networks. *Technology and Health Care*, *23*(s2), S559–S565. doi:10.3233/THC-150994 PMID:26410524

Pattanayak, S. (2017). *Pro deep learning with tensorflow: A mathematical approach to advanced artificial intelligence in Python*. Apress. doi:10.1007/978-1-4842-3096-1

Prabhudesai, S. G., Gould, S., Rekhraj, S., Tekkis, P. P., Glazer, G., & Ziprin, P. (2008). Artificial neural networks: Useful aid in diagnosing acute appendicitis. *World Journal of Surgery*, *32*(2), 305–309. doi:10.100700268-007-9298-6 PMID:18043966

Scikit-Learn. Machine learning in Python. (2019). Retrieved from https://scikit-learn.org/stable/

Sheskin, D. J. (2003). *Handbook of parametric and nonparametric statistical procedure*. Chapman and Hall. doi:10.1201/9781420036268

Sklearn.neural_network. MLPClassifier. (2019). Retrieved from https://scikit-learn.org/stable/modules/generated/sklearn.neural_network.MLPClassifier.html/

Srivastava, N., Hinton, G., Krizhevsky, A., Sutskever, I. R., & Salakhutdinov, R. (2014). Dropout: A simple way to prevent neural networks from overfitting. *Journal of Machine Learning Research*, *15*(1), 1929–1958.

Tuning the hyper-parameters of an estimator. (2019). Retrieved from https://scikit-learn.org/stable/modules/grid_search.html

Vaschenko, P. A., Solomakha, A. A., Gorbachenko, V. I., Khazratov, A. A. (2014). *Clinical and laboratory parameters of patients with acute appendicitis*. Certificate of State Registration of Database No. 2014621431. Date of State Registration in the Register of Databases 10 October 2014 (in Russian).

Wackerly, D., Mendenhall, W., & Scheaffer, R. L. (2008). *Mathematical statistics with applicationsition*. Thomson Brooks.

Zeiler, M. D. (2012). *ADADELTA: An adaptive learning rate method*. Retrieved from Shttps://arxiv.org/abs/1212.5701

Zheng, A., & Casari, A. (2018). *Feature engineering for machine learning: Principles and techniques for data scientists*. O'Reilly Media.

Chapter 4
Improving Algorithms for Learning Radial Basic Functions Networks to Solve the Boundary Value Problems

Vladimir Gorbachenko
Penza State University, Russia

Konstantin Savenkov
iD https://orcid.org/0000-0002-8823-7103
Penza State University, Russia

ABSTRACT

Digital twins are widely used in modern industry. A digital twin is a computer model that copies the behavior of a physical object. Digital twins of objects with distributed parameters are mathematically boundary value problems for partial differential equation. Traditionally, such problems are solved by finite difference and finite element methods, which require a complex grid construction procedure. The numerical solution of boundary value problems employs mesh less methods that do not require grid construction. Among mesh fewer methods, projection methods that use radial basis functions (RBFs) as basic functions are popular. Methods using RBF allow us to obtain a differentiable solution at any point in the solution domain, applicable to problems of arbitrary dimension with complex computational domains. When solving the problem, the parameters of the basic functions are selected, and the weights are calculated so that the residuals obtained after the substitution of the approximate solution at the test points in the equation are zero.

DOI: 10.4018/978-1-7998-1581-5.ch004

INTRODUCTION

Digital twins are widely used in modern industry (*Grieves, 2014; Uhlemann, et al., 2017; Madni, et al., 2019*). The digital twin is a dynamic virtual model of a system, process or service. The digital twin continuously learns and updates its parameters, receiving information from a variety of sensors, correctly representing the state of a physical object. When learning, they use current data from sensors, from control devices, from the external environment; it combines actual data with the knowledge gained from specialists in this field. Digital twins allow you to monitor systems and processes in real time and analyze data in a timely manner to prevent problems before they occur, schedule preventive maintenance, reduce downtime, open up new business opportunities and plan future updates and new developments. Digital twins of objects with distributed parameters are mathematically boundary value problems for partial differential equations. (PDE) (*Farlow, 1993*).

When modeling complex technical objects, software packages based on the finite element method or finite differences are usually used (*Mazumder, 2015*). However, modeling a real object with their help runs up against a number of fundamental difficulties (*Vasilyev, et al., 2018*). First, accurate information about differential equations describing the behavior of an object is usually absent due to the complexity of describing the processes occurring in it. Second, to apply the finite element and finite difference methods, one needs to know the initial and boundary conditions, information about which is usually incomplete and inaccurate. Thirdly, during the operation of a real object, its properties and characteristics, the parameters of the processes occurring in it can change. This requires appropriate adaptation of the model, which is difficult to carry out with models built on the basis of finite element methods and finite differences.

An alternative to finite difference and finite element methods is meshless methods (*Belytschko, et al., 1996; Liu, 2003; Griebel and Marc, 2008*), most of which are projection methods. These methods give an approximate analytical solution in the form of a sum of basis functions multiplied by weights. Radial basis functions (RBF) are popular as basic functions (*Kansa, 1999; Buhmann, 2004; Fasshauer, 2007; Chen and Fu, 2014*). Methods using RBF allow to obtain a differentiable solution at an arbitrary point in the solution domain as a function satisfying the required smoothness conditions, are universal, allow working with complex geometry of computational domains, are applicable to solving problems of any dimension. Methods based on RBF require, for the selected parameters of the radial basis functions, finding the weight vector, so that the obtained approximate solution provides, with an admissible error, the equation and boundary conditions on a certain set of sampling points. For example, the sum of the squares of the residuals at the sampling points should be small. The main disadvantage of using RBF is the need for an unformalized selection of parameters of basic functions.

The implementation of meshless methods on neural networks is promising. The solution of boundary value problems for PDE is possible on multilayer perceptrons (*Chen and Fu, 2014; Kumar and Yadav, 2011*). But the most promising is the use of networks of radial basic functions (RBFN) (*Haykin, 2008; Aggarwal, 2018*), since RBFNs contain only two layers, one of which is linear, and the formation of a solution is local, which simplifies the learning of such networks. The use of RBFN allows in the process of learning networks to adjust both the weight and the parameters of RBF. Applications of RBNF for solving boundary value problems are considered in the works of Jianyu L., Siwei L., Yingjian Q., Yaping H., Mai-Duy N., Tran-Cong T., Sarra S., Chen H., Kong L., Leng. W., Kumar M., Yadav N., Vasilyeva A. N., Tarkhova D. A., Gorbachenko V. I. (*Jianyu, et al. 2003; Mai-Duy and Tran-Cong, 2005; Sarra, 2005; Chen, et al., 2011; Vasiliev and Tarkhov, 2009; Tarkhov, 2014; Gorbachenko and Artyukhina, 2010; Gorbachenko and Zhukov, 2017*).

To build digital models of doubles, it is promising to use the ideas of machine learning and neural networks to build models of real objects. This approach allows you to build adaptive models that are refined and rebuilt in accordance with the observations of the object. Therefore, an urgent task is the development of neural network modeling technologies, a more complete account of historical and newly received data, the improvement of methods for automatically adjusting the architecture and model parameters, methods of classification and prediction (*Vasilyev, et al., 2018*). The use of neural network models allows us to develop a unified approach to solving various modeling problems. For example, in (*Gorbachenko, et al., 2016*) a unified approach was proposed for solving direct and inverse boundary value problems described by partial differential equations.

The solution of the problem is formed in the process of learning RBFN. Therefore, it is important to shorten the learning time of networks. But at the present time for learning RBFN, when solving boundary value problems, the simplest gradient methods of the first order are used based on the gradient descent (*Kumar and Yadav, 2011; Yadav, et al., 2015*). Fast methods of the second order are practically not used when solving boundary value problems on RBFN. An exception is the method of confidence regions proposed in (*Gorbachenko and Zhukov, 2017*). But the method is very complicated, since it requires solving the minimization problem at each iteration to solve the conditional minimization problem. The aim of this work is to improve the learning algorithms for networks of radial basic functions when solving boundary value problems, which allow to reduce the time to solve the problem.

ANALYSIS OF THE METHODS FOR SOLVING THE EDGE TASKS BY MEANS OF RADIAL BASIS FUNCTIONS AND NETWORKS OF RADIAL BASIS FUNCTIONS

RBF (*Buhmann, 2004; Fasshauer, 2007*) — these are functions of the distance of a point in space from a parameter of a function, called the center of the function: $\varphi\left(\|x - c\|, p\right)$, where x — point of space, p — function parameter vector, c — center radial basis function, $\|x - c\|$ — Euclidean norm (distance) between point and center. Apply a variety of RBF. In this paper, the well-known Gauss function (Gaussian) is used.

$$\varphi(\| x - c \|, a) = \exp\left(-\frac{\| x - c \|^2}{2a^2}\right),$$

where c — function center position, a — shape parameter, often called width.

Popular also feature — multiquadric (MQ — Multiquadric) Hardy (R. L. Hardy)

$$\varphi(\| x - c \|, a) = \left(1 + -\frac{\|x - c\|}{a^2}\right)^{n/2},$$

where n — whole, usually $n = 1$, then multiquadric looks like

$$\varphi(\| x - c \|, a) = \sqrt{1 + \frac{\| x - c \|^2}{2a^2}}.$$

The considered RBFs are defined for any distance values, that is, are functions with a global carrier, or globally supported functions (Globally-Supported). Functions with compact carrier, or compactly supported functions (Compactly-Supported) are defined at limited distances. For example, for three-dimensional space, one of the compactly supported functions has the form (*Buhmann, 2004*)

$$\varphi(r) = \left(2r^4 \ln(r) - 7\,r^4/2 + 16\,r^3/3 - 2r^2 + 1/6\right)_+,$$

where $r = \| x - c \|$ — distance, $(r)_+$ — cutoff function equal to r, if $0 \leq r \leq 1$ and 0 in other cases.

Although such functions are harder than globally supported ones, their use simplifies calculations.

When using RBF for solving boundary value problems, the type and parameters of RBF are selected before solving the problem. This procedure is informal, requires experimental verification and does not have unambiguous recommendations. Only a few recommendations on the choice of RBF and their parameters are known (*Fasshauer, 2007; Fasshauer and Zhang, 2007*).

The solution of boundary value problems using RBF is based on the approximation of functions. Since when solving boundary value problems, an unknown solution is approximated, the residual minimization at the sampling points is used. E. J. Kansa proposed a method for solving boundary value problems using RBF (*Kansa, 1990a; Kansa, 1990b; Kansa, 1999*), which became the basis for other methods using RBF. Consider the boundary value problem in operator form

$$Lu(x) = f(x), x \in \Omega, \; Bu(x) = p(x), x \in \partial\Omega,$$

where u — the solution of the problem; L — differential operator; operator B — boundary condition operator; Ω — solution area; $\partial\Omega$ — border area; f and p — known functions.

A set of sampling points is set inside the solution area and on the border.

$$\left\{ x_i \, |_{i=1,2,...,N} \subset \Omega \right\} \cup \left\{ x_i \, |_{i=N_1+1,N,...,N+K} \subset \partial\Omega \right\},$$

where N — number of sampling points in the inner area Ω, K — number of sampling points on the border $\partial\Omega$.

The solution to the problem is in the form of a weighted sum of basis functions.

$$u_{RBF}(x) = \sum_{j=1}^{M} w_j \varphi_j(x), x \in \overline{\Omega} = \Omega \cup \partial\Omega$$

where φ_j — RBF; w_j — weights, M — RBF number.

In the number of RBF is taken equal to the number of sampling points: $M = N + K$. RBF parameters are set. Unknown coefficients in are found as a solution to a system of linear algebraic equations, which is obtained from the residuals of the problem in sampling points after substitution in . For this, RBF must be differentiable the necessary number of times. The result is a system of linear algebraic equations.

$$Aw = b,$$

where

$$A = \begin{bmatrix} G_L \\ G_B \end{bmatrix},$$

$$G_L = \begin{bmatrix} L[\varphi_1(x_1)] & L[\varphi_2(x_1)] & L[\varphi_3(x_1)] & \cdots & L[\varphi_N(x_1)] \\ L[\varphi_1(x_2)] & L[\varphi_2(x_2)] & L[\varphi_3(x_2)] & \cdots & L[\varphi_N(x_2)] \\ \cdots & \cdots & \cdots & \cdots & \cdots \\ L[\varphi_1(x_N)] & L[\varphi_2(x_N)] & L[\varphi_3(x_N)] & \cdots & L[\varphi_N(x_N)] \end{bmatrix},$$

$$G_B = \begin{bmatrix} B[\varphi_1(x_{N+1})] & B[\varphi_2(x_{N+1})] & B[\varphi_3(x_{N+1})] & \cdots & B[\varphi_N(x_{N+1})] \\ B[\varphi_1(x_{N+2})] & B[\varphi_2(x_{N+2})] & B[\varphi_3(x_{N+2})] & \cdots & B[\varphi_N(x_{N+2})] \\ \cdots & \cdots & \cdots & \cdots & \cdots \\ B[\varphi_1(x_M)] & B[\varphi_2(x_M)] & B[\varphi_3(x_M)] & \cdots & B[\varphi_N(x_M)] \end{bmatrix},$$

$$b = \begin{bmatrix} f(x_1), f(x_2), & \cdots & f(x_{N_1}), & g(x_{N_1+1}), & g(x_{N_1+2}), & \cdots & g(x_M) \end{bmatrix}^T,$$

$$a = \begin{bmatrix} w(x_1), w(x_2), \ldots, w(x_M) \end{bmatrix}^T.$$

System has a square matrix and its solution is a weight vector w. The Kansa method generates an asymmetric matrix, which makes it difficult to solve the system with a large number of sampling points. With a large number of sampling points, the matrix turns out to be ill-conditioned. When using RBF with a global definition domain, the matrix is dense, which also worsens the conditionality. A serious disadvantage is the non-formalizable selection of the best RBF parameters.

To improve the conditionality of the system various preconditioners are used. The general principle of using preconditioners is to replace system with an equivalent $WAa = Wb$, system that has the best conditionality. The preconditioner W should be close to the inverse matrix of a A^{-1}. Due to the complexity of calculating the inverse matrix, various approximate methods are used. In (*Ling and Kansa, 2005*) a simple method for calculating a preconditioner based on the least squares method was proposed. For each c_i center a small subset of S_i centers of $m \ll N$ size is selected. The W matrix is assumed to be diagonal. The diagonal elements of the w_{jj} matrix must satisfy the condition

$$\sum_{j \in S_i} w_{jj} \psi(x) = \delta_i(x),$$

where

$$\left\{ \psi_i(x) \right\}_{i=1}^{N} = \left\{ \left\{ L\left[\varphi(x - c_i) \right] \right\}_{i=1}^{N_1} \cup \left\{ B\left[\varphi(x - c_i) \right] \right\}_{i=N_1+1}^{N} \right\}, \; \delta_i(x) = 1$$

at the point c_i zero at other points.

Expression — is a system of linear equations with unknowns. To solve it, the least squares method was applied.

Another approach to improving the conditionality of the system — is the Domain Decomposition Method (DDM — Domain Decomposition Method) (*Li and Hon, 2004*). The solution area is calculated by sub-areas, for example, using the Schwartz method. The improvement in conditionality is due to a reduction in the order of the system.

A promising direction of simplification of the system is the use of RBF with a compact carrier, which leads to systems with sparse asymmetric matrices. To solve such systems, effective iterative methods of Krylov subspaces are known (*Saad, 2003; Liesen, 2015*) — he generalized minimum residual method (GMRES - General Minimal Residuals) and the stable algorithm of bi-conjugate gradients (BiCGSTAB - Biconjugate Gradient Stabilized).

In the well-known works, the relationship between the number of RBFs and the number of sampling points is not considered. Usually take the number of sampling points equal to the number of RBF. However, for approximation problems, the relation between the number of RBFs M and the number of sampling points $N + K$ is known: $M \propto (N + K)^{\frac{1}{3}}$, where $\propto$ means proportionality (*Niyogi and Girosi, 1996*). Since the number of sampling points in this case significantly exceeds the number of RBFs, system turns out to be overdetermined. The singular value decomposition method (Singular Value Decomposition) (*Watkins, 2010*) is convenient for solving such systems.

When using RBF, tasks describing processes in homogeneous media are usually considered. Processes in inhomogeneous media are rarely considered (see, for example, (*Wang, et al., 2005*), where a complex algorithm using a fundamental solution was used). For practically the most common case of piecewise homogeneous media, the problem can be significantly simplified. Consider an equation describing a heterogeneous medium.

$$\frac{\partial}{\partial}\left(k\left(x\right)\frac{\partial u}{\partial x}\right) = f\left(x\right),$$

where $k\left(x\right)$ — function describing the properties of the environment.

At sampling points x_i it is necessary to calculate the value of the differential operator

$$\frac{\partial}{\partial}\left(k\left(x\right)\frac{\partial u}{\partial x}\right)\bigg|_{x_i} = \frac{\partial k\left(x_i\right)}{\partial x} \cdot \frac{\partial u}{\partial x}\bigg|_{x_i} + k\left(x_i\right)\frac{\partial^2 u}{\partial x^2}\bigg|_{x_i},$$

approximating the unknown solution u to an approximate solution using RBF. The problem is that the function in real problems is known from experimentally determined values at some points. But in the case of a piecewise homogeneous medium, the first term vanishes and it suffices to know the function $k\left(x\right)$ at the sampling point.

RBF can be used to solve nonlinear boundary value problems (*Sarra and Kansa, 2009*). The application of the Kansa method in this case leads to the solution of a nonlinear algebraic system instead of . For example, in (*Fasshauer, 2002*) the Newton method was applied to solve the obtained nonlinear system.

When solving non-stationary problems, RBF can be used to approximate a differential operator with respect to spatial variables, while maintaining differential operators with respect to time (the method of lines). The result is an ordinary differential equation containing a differential operator approximated by RBF (*Fasshauer, 2002*). Simpler is the technique in which the time derivative is replaced by the bed difference and at each time layer the stationary problem is solved using RBF. For example, the equation

$$\frac{\partial u}{\partial t} = LU$$

after approximation, the time derivative will take the form

$$\frac{u^k - u^{k-1}}{\tau} = Lu^k,$$

where τ — time discretization step, k — number of temporary layer. Then on the time layer k the stationary problem is solved

$$\tau Lu^k - u^k = -u^{k-1}.$$

Thus, the use of RBF allows one to implement meshless methods and obtain a solution in an approximate analytical form. The solution obtained makes it possible to calculate the solution and its derivatives at arbitrary points in the region. But methods using RBF require solving ill-conditioned systems of linear algebraic equations with dense rectangular matrices. There are no formalized methods for determining the position and parameters of the RFB form. The networks of radial basic functions are free from most of these drawbacks, all parameters of which are determined in the process of learning networks.

RBFN includes two layers (*Aggarwal, 2018*). The first layer consists of RBF, producing non-linear transformation of the input vector $x = \begin{bmatrix} x_1, x_2, ..., x_d \end{bmatrix}$ — coordinates of the point at which the approximation to the solution is calculated (d — dimension of space). The second layer of RBFN is a linear weighted adder

$$u(x) = \sum_{m=1}^{M} w_m \varphi_m(x; p_m),$$

where M — number of RBF, w_m — weight RBF φ_m, p_m — vector of parameters.

The RBFN structure is shown in Figure 1.

The process of solving boundary value problems using RBFN will be considered using the example of the problem, defined in the operator form. In the simplest case, it consists of 3 stages:

Figure 1. RBFN structure

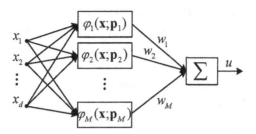

1. From the sets Ω and $\partial\Omega$ select N internal and K boundary sampling points (points at which the error of the solution is controlled). When there is no a priori information about the solution, it is advisable to use random uniform placement of sampling points over the region and at the boundary of the solution. If there is a priori information about the solution of the problem, you can increase the number of sampling points in those areas in which you need to obtain improved solution accuracy. For example, it is advisable to increase the number of trial points in areas in which a change in the characteristics of the solution is expected. Since the properties of solving a problem are a priori difficult to estimate, you can first find a crude solution of the problem using the minimum number of sampling points, and then, determining the areas in which the error functional takes the greatest values, decide on the number of sampling points and their placement. As already noted, the ratio between the number of RBF M and the number of sampling point $N + K$ is known: $M \propto \left(N + K\right)^{\frac{1}{3}}$, where $\propto$ means proportionality (*Niyogi and Girosi, 1996*). However, when approximating solutions of boundary-value problems using RBFN, this dependence gives an excessive number of sampling points, so you have to select the number of sampling points. An increase in the number of sampling points leads to an increase in the computational complexity of the problem. Periodic random regeneration of a limited number of sampling points, used to prevent network relearning, reduces the number of sampling points.

2. Determine the RBFN structure: network type, RBF number, RBF type, set initial values for the weights vector and RBF parameter vectors. Unambiguous recommendations on choosing the type of RBF are absent. When solving a second order PDE, it is necessary to calculate the second derivatives of the network output. Therefore, it is advisable to use the Gauss function, the domain of which is comparable to the domain of its derivatives, which is not the case with multiquadrics, for which there is a large scatter of values. Unlimited multiquadric values also complicate their use when the RBF centers are unevenly distributed.

When selecting preliminary values, you need to set the RBF parameters and the weights vector. The methods for choosing the location of RBF centers are in many ways similar to the methods for selecting sampling points. Centers can be placed in the nodes of a uniform grid or randomly. You can increase the RBF density in areas where a change in the nature of the decision is expected. You can start a solution with a minimum amount of RBF and in the process of learning add RBF in areas with large error values (*Jianyu, 2003*). When placing RBF centers at the nodes of a uniform grid, it is advisable to set the same preliminary widths for all RBFs. The widths in this case are selected depending on the size of the step. If the centers are randomly distributed, the width can be chosen randomly from a certain interval. The boundaries of the interval can be the same for all RBFs, or depend on the distance between the center of the RBF and the centers of its neighbors. Weights are usually initiated by small random numbers.

3. Perform network learning, i.e. select such values of weights and RBF parameters so that the error functional at the sampling points assumes the minimum value. The solution of the boundary value problem on RBFN is an approximation of the unknown solution on the set of sampling points . Since the solution at trial points is unknown, only minimization of residuals on the set of sampling points is possible. To construct the error functional, the least squares method is used. The error functional for finding the weights w and the p RBF parameters that minimize residuals at sampling points has the form

$$J\left(w,p\right) = \sum_{i=1}^{N}\left[Lu_{RBF}\left(x_i;w,p\right) - f(x_i)\right]^2 + \lambda \sum_{i=N+1}^{N+K}\left[Bu_{RBF}\left(x_i;w,p\right) - p(x_i)\right]^2 \to \min,$$

where x_i — sampling points, λ — pick a penalty factor, u_{RBF} — is an approximate solution obtained at RBFN .

The penalty factor λ ensures the fulfillment of the boundary conditions, since in meshless methods the conditions on the boundary are not fixed. As seen from, Using RBFN allows you to optimize not only the weight, but also the RBF parameters (in the case of the Gauss function, the coordinates of the cent and the width). The error functional can include terms with penalty factors, which are also responsible for other conditions of the problem statement, for example, the relations at the interfaces between the media.

RBFN network learning is different from solving the problem of unconditional optimization of the functional . The functional is minimized on a limited set of sampling points. A trained network must have the property of generalization, that is, to ensure the formation of a solution with a given accuracy rate not only at trial points, but also at arbitrary points in the solution domain. When learning a network, relearning is possible: in the sampling points, the accuracy indicator may be small, and in other points - large. The possibility of relearning is reduced by using a large number of trial points. But this approach increases the solution time. The output is a periodic random regeneration of a set of sampling points (*Tarkhov, 2014*). From the modern point of view on learning neural networks, this technique is the implementation of mini packet (stochastic) learning (*Goodfellow, et al., 2016*). When using trial points regeneration, the RBFN learning process is organized as a process of minimizing a set of error functionals, each of which is obtained by a specific choice of trial points. Each error functional is not minimized to the end. Between regenerations of sampling points, only a few steps of the selected method of minimizing the error functional are performed. Such an approach avoids the problem of falling into a local extremum, which is characteristic of most global nonlinear optimization methods.

The absolute majority of RBFN learning algorithms are based on gradient optimization methods (*Gill, et al., 1982*). All gradient methods are methods of local optimization, which in general does not guarantee the achievement of a global minimum of the error functional. At the same time, the search for a global minimum of the error functional, generally speaking, is not necessary, it suffices to find a local minimum with a certain given accuracy. There are known applications of genetic algorithms for learning RBFN networks in solving classification problems (*Jia, et al., 2014*), which are much simpler than solving PDEs. Among the gradient methods, there are three classes: methods of zero order, which use only the values of the optimized function for optimization, but not the values of its derivatives, first-order methods using the first derivatives of the function to be optimized (function gradient), and second-order methods that use the second derivatives (Hesse matrix, Gaussian).

Methods to minimize the error functional can be divided into two groups. The first group includes methods for sequential adjustment of weights and RBF parameters. The first are the weights that have the greatest impact on the error functional, then the RBF parameters are adjusted. Since weights are included linearly in the formula for network output, optimization methods different from those used for learning non-linear RBF parameters in . can be used to train them. For example, learning with sequential adjustment of parameters is performed in (*Jianyu, 2003*) using the algorithm:

Step 1. Fix the RBF parameters and perform several iterations of the gradient descent method for learning weights.

Step 2. Fix the weights and perform several iterations of the gradient descent method for learning the parameters of RBF.

Step 3. If the solution error is less than the required value or the maximum number of iterations is reached, then complete the learning, otherwise proceed to Step 1.

The second group includes methods with simultaneous adjustment of parameters. For this, a single vector of weights and RBF parameters is formed and configured. Sequential tuning allows decreasing the dimension by minimization tasks and using highly efficient, well-developed methods for minimizing linear quadratic functional to tune weights. Simultaneous adjustment of all network parameters makes it necessary to solve problems of a higher dimension and requires the use of highly efficient methods of multiparameter minimization of nonlinear problems. On the other hand, this approach allows is more universal. In the following we consider only the simultaneous setting of parameters.

In the well-known papers devoted to solving PDE on RBFN (*Chen and Fu, 2014; Kumar and Yadav, 2011; Yadav, et al., 2015; Jianyu, 2003; Mai-Duy and Tran-Cong, 2005; Sarra, 2005; Chen, et al., 2011; Vasiliev, 2009*), the simplest first-order method is used — the gradient descent method. Consider the implementation of the method of rapid descent on the example of a two-dimensional problem and the use of Gaussian as RBF. Consider a single vector of parameters RBFN

$$\theta = \left[w_1, w_2, \ldots, w_{n_{RBF}}, c_{11}, c_{21}, \ldots, c_{n_{RBF}1}, c_{12}, c_{22}, \ldots, c_{n_{RBF}2}, a_1, a_2, \ldots, a_{n_{RBF}} \right]^T,$$

where w_j — RBF Weight, $j = 1, 2, 3, \ldots, n_{RBF}$, n_{RBF} — number of RBF, c_{j1} and c_{j2} — coordinates of the centers, a_j — width.

Correction of vector at iteration k in the gradient descent method is performed using the formula

$$\theta^{(k+1)} = \theta^{(k)} + \Delta\theta^{(k+1)},$$

where $\Delta\theta^{(k+1)} = -\eta \nabla J\left(\theta^{(k)}\right)$ — vector correction parameters, η — learning speed, selectable hyperparameter, $\nabla J\left(\theta^{(k)}\right)$ — functional gradient vector by vector components $\theta^{(k)}$ at iteration k.

Calculations from end with a small value of the error functional . The gradient descent method has a low convergence rate, which does not allow solving problems with high accuracy.

Second-order methods are based on quadratic approximation of the error functional. In the vicinity of the next approximation of the parameters of the $\theta^{(k)}$ network, the error functional is approximated by the Taylor formula

$$J\left(\theta^{(k)} + \Delta\theta^{(k+1)}\right) \approx J\left(\theta^{(k)}\right) + \left[\nabla J\left(\theta^{(k)}\right)\right]^T \Delta\theta^{(k+1)} + \frac{1}{2}\left[\Delta\theta^{(k+1)}\right]^T H\left(J\left(\theta^{(k)}\right)\right)\Delta\theta^{(k+1)},$$

where $\nabla J\left(\theta^{(k)}\right)$ — gradient functional, $H\left(J\left(\theta^{(k)}\right)\right)$ — Hesse matrix (matrix of second derivatives of the functional), calculated for $\theta^{(k)}$.

From the condition of the minimum of the functional the vector $\Delta\theta^{(k+1)}$ of the network parameters correction can be obtained, ensuring the reduction of the error functional. Due to the complexity of calculating the Hessian matrix for multilayer perceptrons, various approximations of the Hessian matrix are used. For example, the conjugate gradient method uses the Fletcher-Reeves (Fletcher R., Reeves C.M.) (*Fletcher and Reeves, 1964*) and Polack-Rieber formulas (Polak E., Ribiere G.) (*Polak and Ribiére, 1969*). In quasi-Newtonian methods, the Hessian approximation matrix is calculated at each learning step, for example, using the Broyden-Fletcher-Goldfarb-Shanno formula (Broyden-Fletcher-Goldfarb-Shanno - BFGS) (*Tarkhov, 2014*). In the Levenberg-Marquardt method (*Gill and Murray, 1982*) the Hessian matrix is approximated using the product of the Jacobi matrices of the network error vector.

Second order methods are not common when learning RBFN. Although the presence of only one layer with nonlinear functions and the differentiability of most RBFs make it possible to use second-order optimization methods for learning RBFN. In (*Zhang, et al., 2012*) when solving the approximation problem, the nonlinear layer was studied by the method of conjugate gradients, and weights by the method of orthogonal least squares. In (*Gorbachenko and Artyukhina, 2010*) an algorithm for the method of conjugate gradient adjustment of RBFN weights was proposed, which differs from the known ones by taking into account the specifics of solving boundary value problems. RBF parameters were trained by the gradient descent method. The algorithm takes into account the differentiability of RBF and is based on the matrix-vector representation of the error functional

$$J = (Aw, w) - 2(s, w) + 0,5(f, f) + 0,5\lambda(p, p),$$

where $A = 0,5(M^T M + \lambda N^T N)$, $s = 0,5(M^T f + \lambda N^T p)$, M —matrix $N \times M$, elements of which are the values of the operator $Lu(x_i)$ in internal sampling points; N — matrix $K \times M$, elements of which are the values of the operator $Bu(\mathbf{x}_i)$ at the boundary sampling points; N and K — is the number of internal and boundary sampling points, M — is the number of RB functions; f and p — vectors of values of functions of $f(x_i)$ and $p(x_i)$ at sample points.

Since A — is a symmetric positive definite matrix, the task of adjusting the weights of the RBFN network is reduced to the problem of minimizing a quadratic functional with a symmetric positive definite matrix. This problem is easily solved by the classical conjugate gradient method, which is much simpler than the Polac-Ribiera and Fletcher-Reeves methods used in learning neural networks.

In (*Gorbachenko and Zhukov, 2017*), a fast RBFN learning algorithm was proposed, based on an effective optimization method, the confidence-domain method (TRM) (*Conn, et al., 1987*). In (*Gorbachenko, et al., 2017; Alqezweeni, et al., 2018; Elisov, et al., 2018*), this method was investigated. The method allows you to simultaneously optimize a large number of parameters, has a high rate of convergence, even for ill-conditioned tasks, allows you to overcome local minima. In (*Wild, et al., 2008*), TRM was used to solve the interpolation problem using RBF. In (*Bernal, 2016*), RBF is used to solve nonlinear partial differential equations. The RBF weights are determined by solving a system of nonlinear equations. Solving a system of nonlinear equations reduces to minimizing the functional, and minimization is performed using the method of confidence regions.

Consider the details of the implementation of the algorithm TRM (*Gorbachenko and Zhukov, 2017*). In TRM, at each iteration k the error functional (7) in some confidence region $B_k \subseteq \Omega$ is replaced by the approximating function m_k and the minimum of m_k in B_k, is looked for, which becomes the new minimum of the functional. Depending on how much the decrease predicted by the model is confirmed by the functional, a decision is made to narrow or expand the trust domain. Let us denote the vector of network parameters at the k - iteration as $\theta^{(k)}$. Then the TRM algorithm has the following form. First, the algorithm initializes, consisting in setting the initial value of $\theta^{(0)}$ and the radius of the confidence region Δ_0; the threshold values of the accuracy estimates of the model μ_1 and μ_2 ($0 < \mu_1 \leq \mu_2 < 1$),the transform coefficients of the confidence area γ_1 and γ_2 ($0 < \gamma_1 \leq \gamma_2 < 1$); iteration numbers $k = 0$. At each iteration of the algorithm, there are 5 steps.

Step 1. Constructing an m_k, function approximating the error functional in the B_k domain.

Step 2. The conditional minimization of the m_k — is the finding of the step s_k, such that the point $\theta^{(k)} + s_k$ is the global minimum of the m_k in the B_k area.

Step 3. Evaluation of the accuracy of the model p_k

$$
p_k = \frac{J\left(\theta^{(k)}\right) - J\left(\theta^{(k)} + s_k\right)}{m_k\left(\theta^{(k)}\right) - m_k\left(\theta^{(k)} + s_k\right)}.
$$

if $p_k \geq \mu_1$, then $\theta^{(k+1)} = \theta^{(k)} + s_k$, otherwise $\theta^{(k+1)} = \theta^{(k)}$.

Step 4. Change the radius of the confidence area

$$
\Delta_{k+1} \in \begin{cases} [\Delta_k; \infty), 5A\ 8\ p_k \geq \mu_2, \\ [\gamma_2 \Delta_k; \Delta_k), 5A\ 8\ p_k \in [\mu_1, \mu_2), \\ [\gamma_1 \Delta_k; \gamma_2 \Delta_k), 5A\ 8\ p_k < \mu_1. \end{cases}
$$

Step 5. Checking the process termination condition: if a small value of the error functional is reached, or k is equal to the maximum number of iterations, or the radius of the confidence area is too small, then complete the learning. Otherwise, you need to increase the iteration number $k = k + 1$ и and go to step 1.

To construct the function m_k the expansion of the error functional J using the second-order Taylor formula (10) is used. Then at each iteration of the algorithm it is necessary to solve the problem of minimizing the function (10) while limiting

$$
\left\| \Delta \theta^{(k+1)} \right\| \leq \Delta_k,
$$

i.e. the solution should not go beyond the confidential domain.

The vector $\Delta \theta^{(k+1)}$ is determined from the solution of a system of linear algebraic equations

$$H\left(J\left(\theta^{(k)}\right)\right)\Delta\theta^{(k+1)} = -\nabla J\left(\theta^{(k)}\right)$$

while limiting .

To reduce the computational cost, instead of the exact value of the Hessian matrix, the approximate value $H \approx J^T J$, is used, where the Jacobi matrix of the error vector function is

$$J = \begin{vmatrix} \dfrac{\partial r_1}{\partial q_1} & \dfrac{\partial r_1}{\partial q_2} & \cdots & \dfrac{\partial r_1}{\partial q_{M\cdot(1+d+l)}} \\ \dfrac{\partial r_2}{\partial q_1} & \dfrac{\partial r_2}{\partial q_2} & \cdots & \dfrac{\partial r_2}{\partial q_{M\cdot(1+d+l)}} \\ \vdots & \vdots & \ddots & \vdots \\ \dfrac{\partial r_{N+K}}{\partial q_1} & \dfrac{\partial r_{N+K}}{\partial q_2} & \cdots & \dfrac{\partial r_{N+K}}{\partial q_{M\cdot(1+d+l)}} \end{vmatrix},$$

where

$$r_i(\theta) = \begin{cases} Lu(x_i;\theta) - f(x_i), 1 \le i \le N, \\ \sqrt{\lambda}\left[Bu(x_i;\theta) - p(x_i)\right], N < i \le N+K. \end{cases}$$

The gradient of the functional can be calculated using the $\nabla J = J^T r$. formula. Thus, we arrive at the problem of conditional minimization of a quadratic functional with constraints. For this, the Stayhaug method (*Staihaug, 1983*) is used. It is based on the conjugate gradient method with preconditioned (Preconditioned Conjugate Gradient Method). The preconditioner is the Jacobi preconditioner (*Watkins, 2010*).

The TRM algorithm is rather complicated, since at least it is found in limited areas, which requires, at every step of the optimization process, the solution of the conditional optimization problem. Therefore, it is advisable to investigate the possibility of adaptation for learning RBFN of modern fast first-order methods and the Levenberg Marquardt method. Of particular interest is the Levenberg-Marquardt method, which is simpler to implement than TRM, and, as shown in (*Marquardt, 1963*), is equivalent to TRM.

Thus, RBFNs are a promising means of implementing meshless methods for solving boundary value problems. An important problem in using RBFN is the lack of fast and relatively simple learning algorithms.

DEVELOPMENT OF ALGORITHMS FOR LEARNING NETWORKS OF RADIAL BASIS FUNCTIONS IN SOLVING THE TASKS OF APPROXIMATING FUNCTIONS AND LOCAL TASKS

Since the PDE solution on RBFN is an approximation on the network of the unknown solution of the equation, it is advisable to begin the study of the RBFN learning algorithms by solving simpler problems of approximation of functions for which the target values are known at sampling points. In addition, the use of RBFN for data approximation has an independent meaning. When modeling the relief, reconstruction of surfaces and in many other cases, there is a need to approximate the "scattered" data (*Wendland, 2010*), when the interpolation nodes are arranged in an arbitrary way, and not on a certain grid. Methods of approximation of such data are meshless (meshfree) methods (*Fasshauer, 2007*).

When solving the approximation problems, the input vectors are the vectors of the coordinates of the sampling points, and the target values are the known values of the function at the sampling points. After learning, the network allows you to determine the value of a function at an arbitrary point in the function definition domain. RBFN network learning is a minimization of the error functional.

$$I = \frac{1}{2}\sum_{j=1}^{n} e_j^2 = \frac{1}{2}\sum_{j=1}^{n}\left(u\left(x_j\right) - T_j\right)^2,$$

where n — number of sampling points, e_j — is the residual (error) approximation at the j-*th* sampling point, x_j — is the vector of coordinates of the j-*th* trial point (for approximation of the function of two variables $x_j = \left[x_{j1}, x_{j2}\right]^T$), $u\left(x_j\right)$ — trial point (for approximation of the function of two variables, T_j — the known (target) value of the function at the j-*th* sampling point, the factor $1/2$ is introduced to simplify the calculations.

Let us consider the use of RBFN for learning in approximation of functions of accelerated gradient methods of the first order. Simple accelerated gradient methods (*Goodfellow, et al., 2016; Pattanayak, 2017*) are popular in teaching deep-architecture networks: gradient descent with impulse (*Polyak, 1964*) and the Nesterov Accelerated Gradient accelerated gradient method (*Sutskever, et al., 2013*). The use of these algorithms for learning RBFN was first proposed in (*Alqezweeni and Gorbachenko, 2017*).

In the gradient descent algorithm with a pulse, the correction to the parameter vector is formed as follows.

$$\Delta\theta^{(k+1)} = \alpha\Delta\theta^{(k)} - \eta g_\theta\left(\theta^{(k)}\right),$$

where η — is the learning rate, α — is the moment coefficient taking values in the interval $[0, 1]$, $g_\theta\left(\theta^{(k)}\right) = \nabla J\left(\theta^{(k)}\right)$ — is the gradient vector of the error functional.

Expression (14) contains terms depending on the gradient and not dependent on the gradient. Moreover, the greater the value of the coefficient α, the stronger the effect on the adjustment of the scales is affected by the term independent of the gradient. This effect increases substantially in flat regions of the objective function and near local minima. In these regions, the term independent of the gradient begins to dominate in (14), which leads to an exit from this region. It can be said that the change in weights occurs "by inertia" in the direction of the vector of the amendment of the previous learning step. As a result, the rate of convergence increases and it becomes possible to exit from the regions of the local minimum and flat sections of the error functional, in which the gradient is close to zero.

NAG differs from the gradient descent with a pulse when using the gradient vector of the correction of the parameters of the previous iteration, which significantly increases the rate of convergence.

$$\Delta\theta^{(k+1)} = \alpha\Delta\theta^{(k)} - \eta g_\theta\left(\theta^{(k)} + \alpha\Delta\theta^{(k)}\right).$$

New direction in the gradient learning algorithms of neural networks are algorithms with an adaptive learning rate (*Goodfellow, et al., 2016; Pattanayak, 2017*). The general idea of these algorithms is that at each iteration each component of the gradient vector is normalized to the square of the Euclidean norm of the gradient vector at the last iteration. Such an approach better takes into account the effect on learning of individual features of the examples and increases the rate of convergence in the case of elongated lines of the error functional level (the so-called "gully" effect). It is empirically shown that the effective algorithm of this class is RMSProp (Root Mean Square Propagation) in combination with the NAG (*Goodfellow, et al., 2016*). The algorithm works well in the case of a nonconvex error functional containing local minima and "ravines". The iteration of the RMSProp algorithm is described as follows.

$$g = g_\theta \left(\theta^{(k)} + \alpha \Delta \theta^{(k)} \right), r^{(k+1)} = \rho r^{(k)} + \left(1 - \rho \right) g \bullet g,$$

$$\Delta \theta^{(k+1)} = \alpha \Delta \theta^{(k)} - \frac{\varepsilon}{\sqrt{r^{(k+1)}}} \bullet g, \theta^{(k+1)} = \theta^{(k)} + \Delta \theta^{(k+1)},$$

where $r^{(0)} = 0$, $\bullet$ — means element-wise multiplication, $\sqrt{r^{(k+1)}}$ is also calculated elementwise., $\rho, \alpha, \varepsilon$ — coefficients selected experimentally.

The RBFN structure and RBF differentiability allow analytically calculating the components of the error functional gradient. For example, to approximate a function of two variables, the components of the gradient are

$$\frac{\partial I}{\partial w_i} = \sum_{j=1}^{n} \left(u \left(x_j \right) - T_j \right) \cdot \varphi_i \left(x_j \right), \frac{\partial I}{\partial c_{i1}} = w_i \sum_{j=1}^{n} \left(u \left(x_j \right) - T_j \right) \cdot \varphi_i \left(x_j \right) \cdot \frac{x_{j1} - c_{i1}}{a_i^2},$$

$$\frac{\partial I}{\partial c_{i2}} = w_i \sum_{j=1}^{n} \left(u \left(x_j \right) - T_j \right) \cdot \varphi_i \left(x_j \right) \cdot \frac{x_{j2} - c_{i2}}{a_i^2}, \frac{\partial I}{\partial a_i} = w_i \sum_{.j=1}^{n} \left(u \left(x_j \right) - T_j \right) \cdot \varphi_i \left(x_j \right) \cdot \frac{\left\| x_j - c_i \right\|}{a_i^3},$$

where c_{i1} and c_{i2} — is the coordinates of the center of the i-th RB function, x_{j1} and x_{j2} — is the coordinates of the sampling point x_j, $\left\| x_j - c_i \right\|$ — is the Euclidean norm.

Second-order methods are not common when learning RBFN networks. Only some examples of the application of the Levenberg – Marquardt method are known in areas not related to solving approximation problems and PDE (*Zhang, et al., 2013; Xie, et al., 2012*), (*Markopoulos, et al., 2016*). For RBFN learning, an algorithm based on the method of confidence areas is promising. But this method is quite complicated. To solve the problems of approximation of functions and the solution of PDE, it is proposed to use the Levenberg Marquardt method (*Gill and Murray, 1982*). The Levenberg Marquardt method is popular for teaching direct propagation neural networks (multilayer perceptrons) containing a small number of layers (*Haykin, 2008*), but is not used for teaching RBFN. The Levenberg-Marquardt method is equivalent to the confidence-field method (*Marquardt, 1963*), but simpler, since it does not require a conditional optimization problem to be solved at each iteration. Since RBFN contains only two layers and one of them is linear, the Jacobi matrix used in the Levenberg Marquardt method can be calculated analytically.

Consider the use of the Levenberg-Marquardt method for learning RBFN in approximating functions of two variables. The correction of the vector of parameters Θ in the k-*th* cycle (iteration) of learning is described by formula, in which the vector of the correction $\Delta\Theta^{(k)}$ is a solution of a system of linear algebraic equations

$$\left(J_{k-1}^T J_{k-1} + \mu_k E\right)\Delta\theta^{(k)} = -g_{k-1},$$

where E — is the identity matrix, μ_k — is the regularization parameter, $g = J^T e$ — is the gradient of the error functional according to the vector of parameters θ, $e = \begin{bmatrix} e_1 & e_2 & \dots & e_n \end{bmatrix}^T$ — is the error vector used when calculating the error functional, J_{k-1} — is the Jacobi matrix, which is calculated from the network parameter values in the $k-1$ iteration.

The Jacobi matrix in the bit-wise representation is

$$J = \begin{bmatrix}
\dfrac{\partial e_1}{\partial w_1} & \dots & \dfrac{\partial e_1}{\partial w_{n_{RBF}}} & \dfrac{\partial e_1}{\partial c_{11}} & \dots & \dfrac{\partial e_1}{\partial c_{n_{RBF}1}} & \dfrac{\partial e_1}{\partial c_{12}} & \dots & \dfrac{\partial e_1}{\partial c_{n_{RBF}2}} & \dfrac{\partial e_1}{\partial a_1} & \dots & \dfrac{\partial e_1}{\partial a_{n_{RBF}}} \\
\dfrac{\partial e_2}{\partial w_1} & \dots & \dfrac{\partial e_2}{\partial w_{n_{RBF}}} & \dfrac{\partial e_2}{\partial c_{11}} & \dots & \dfrac{\partial e_2}{\partial c_{n_{RBF}1}} & \dfrac{\partial e_2}{\partial c_{12}} & \dots & \dfrac{\partial e_2}{\partial c_{n_{RBF}2}} & \dfrac{\partial e_2}{\partial a_1} & \dots & \dfrac{\partial e_2}{\partial a_{n_{RBF}}} \\
\dots & \dots & \dots & \dots & \dots & \dots & \dots & \dots & \dots & \dots & \dots & \dots \\
\dfrac{\partial e_n}{\partial w_1} & \dots & \dfrac{\partial e_n}{\partial w_{n_{RBF}}} & \dfrac{\partial e_n}{\partial c_{11}} & \dots & \dfrac{\partial e_n}{\partial c_{n_{RBF}1}} & \dfrac{\partial e_n}{\partial c_{12}} & \dots & \dfrac{\partial e_n}{\partial c_{n_{RBF}2}} & \dfrac{\partial e_n}{\partial a_1} & \dots & \dfrac{\partial e_n}{\partial a_{n_{RBF}}}
\end{bmatrix}.$$

Jacobi matrix is conveniently presented in a block form

$$J = \begin{bmatrix} J_w & J_{c_1} & J_{c_2} & J_a \end{bmatrix},$$

where

$$
J_w = \begin{vmatrix} \dfrac{\partial e_1}{\partial w_1} & \dfrac{\partial e_1}{\partial w_2} & \cdots & \dfrac{\partial e_1}{\partial w_{n_{RBF}}} \\ \dfrac{\partial e_2}{\partial w_1} & \dfrac{\partial e_2}{\partial w_2} & \cdots & \dfrac{\partial e_2}{\partial w_{n_{RBF}}} \\ \cdots & \cdots & \cdots & \cdots \\ \dfrac{\partial e_n}{\partial w_1} & \dfrac{\partial e_n}{\partial w_2} & \cdots & \dfrac{\partial e_n}{\partial w_{n_{RBF}}} \end{vmatrix}, J_{c_1} = \begin{vmatrix} \dfrac{\partial e_1}{\partial c_{11}} & \cdots & \dfrac{\partial e_1}{\partial c_{n_{RBF}1}} \\ \dfrac{\partial e_2}{\partial c_{11}} & \cdots & \dfrac{\partial e_2}{\partial c_{n_{RBF}1}} \\ \cdots & \cdots & \cdots \\ \dfrac{\partial e_n}{\partial c_{11}} & \cdots & \dfrac{\partial e_n}{\partial c_{n_{RBF}1}} \end{vmatrix},
$$

$$
J_{c_2} = \begin{vmatrix} \dfrac{\partial e_1}{\partial c_{12}} & \cdots & \dfrac{\partial e_1}{\partial c_{n_{RBF}2}} \\ \dfrac{\partial e_2}{\partial c_{12}} & \cdots & \dfrac{\partial e_2}{\partial c_{n_{RBF}2}} \\ \cdots & \cdots & \cdots \\ \dfrac{\partial e_n}{\partial c_{12}} & \cdots & \dfrac{\partial e_n}{\partial c_{n_{RBF}2}} \end{vmatrix}, J_a = \begin{vmatrix} \dfrac{\partial e_1}{\partial a_1} & \cdots & \dfrac{\partial e_1}{\partial a_{n_{RBF}}} \\ \dfrac{\partial e_2}{\partial a_1} & \cdots & \dfrac{\partial e_2}{\partial a_{n_{RBF}}} \\ \cdots & \cdots & \cdots \\ \dfrac{\partial e_n}{\partial a_1} & \cdots & \dfrac{\partial e_n}{\partial a_{n_{RBF}}} \end{vmatrix}.
$$

Given the structure of the RBFN and the differentiability of the RBF, the elements of the matrix J are easy to calculate analytically. So the elements of the matrix J_w taking into account and have the form

$$
\frac{\partial e_i}{\partial w_j} = \frac{\partial}{\partial w_j}\left[u(x_i) - T_i\right] = \frac{\partial u(x_i)}{\partial w_j} = \varphi_j(x_i),
$$

where $\varphi_j(x_i)$ — is the value of the j-th radial basis function at the sampling point x_i.

The elements of the matrix J_{c_1} have the form

$$
\frac{\partial e_i}{\partial c_{j1}} = \frac{\partial}{\partial c_{j1}}\left[u(x_i) - T_i\right] = \frac{\partial}{\partial c_{j1}}\left[\sum_{k=1}^{n_{RBF}} w_k \varphi_k(x_i)\right] = w_j \frac{\partial}{\partial c_{j1}}\left[e^{-\frac{(x_{i1}-c_{j1})^2+(x_{i2}-c_{j2})^2}{2a_j^2}}\right]
$$

$$
= w_j e^{-\frac{\|x_i - c_j\|^2}{2a_j^2}} \cdot \frac{\partial}{\partial c_{j1}}\left[-\frac{(x_{i1}-c_{j1})^2+(x_{i2}-c_{j2})^2}{2a_j^2}\right] = w_j \varphi_j(x_i) \cdot \frac{x_{i1}-c_{j1}}{a_j^2}.
$$

87

Similarly for J_{c_2} we get

$$\frac{\partial e_i}{\partial A_{j2}} = w_j \cdot \varphi_j\left(x_i\right) \cdot \frac{x_{i2} - c_{j2}}{a_j^2}.$$

The elements o J_a are calculated by the formula

$$\frac{\partial e_i}{\partial a_j} = \frac{\partial}{\partial a_j}\left[u\left(x_i\right) - T_i\right] = \frac{\partial}{\partial a_j}\left[\sum_{k=1}^{n_{RBF}} w_k \varphi_k\left(x_i\right)\right] = w_j \frac{\partial}{\partial a_j}\left[e^{-\frac{\left\|x_i - c_j\right\|^2}{2a_j^2}}\right]$$

$$= w_j e^{-\frac{\left\|x_i - c_j\right\|^2}{2a_j^2}} \cdot \frac{\partial}{\partial a_j}\left[-\frac{\left\|x_i - c_j\right\|^2}{2a_j^2}\right] = w_j \varphi_j\left(x_i\right) \cdot \frac{\left\|x_i - c_j\right\|^2}{a_j^3}.$$

The matrix $J_{k-1}^T J_{k-1} + \mu_k E$ of system is dense, symmetric and positive definite. Therefore, to solve system it is advisable to use the Cholesky method (*Watkins, 2010*), implemented in mathematical packages, for example, in MATLAB, and in mathematical libraries of popular programming languages. A disadvantage of the Cholesky method is the use of a lengthy square root operation when decomposing matrices. The LDL[T] decomposition method is free from this disadvantage (*Watkins, 2010*), which represents a matrix in the form $A = LDL^T$, where L — is the lower triangular matrix with a unit principal diagonal, D — is a diagonal matrix, and, T — is the matrix transposition operation. The decomposition does not apply the square root operation.

In the process of learning the regularization parameter should change. The process starts with a relatively large value of the parameter. This means that at the beginning of the learning process in $J_{k-1}^T J_{k-1} + \mu_k E \approx \mu_k E$ and the gradient descent method is implemented with a small step. As the error functional decreases, the parameter μ decreases and the method approaches the Newton method with an approximate representation of the Hessian $H \approx J_{k-1}^T J_{k-1}$. This ensures a good convergence rate near the minimum of the error functional. It is recommended to start with a certain μ_0 value and use the $\nu > 1$ coefficient (*Wild, et al., 2008*). The current value of μ is divided by ν, if the error functional is reduced, or multiplied by ν, if the error functional is increased.

The disadvantage of the Levenberg-Marquardt method is the poor conditionality of the system . Conditionality depends on the initial values of the width of the RB functions and increases with increasing accuracy of network learning (*Alqezweeni and Gorbachenko, 2017*). For the Gauss function with increasing width, the values of the RB functions in J_w tend to unity, and the elements of the matrices J_{c_1}, J_{c_2} and J_a tend to zero, the conditionality of the matrix J worsens. In the limit, the matrix becomes special. The deterioration of conditionality is facilitated by the Gauss transformation $J_{k-1}^T J_{k-1}$. The regularization parameter improves conditionality. But with a decrease in the parameter μ with a decrease in the learning error, the conditionality worsens. There are problems with the choice of the regularization parameter: a small value of the parameter leads to a low convergence rate, a large one leads to a non-smooth character of the decrease in error.

Since the PDE solution is, in essence, an approximation of an unknown solution, the algorithms proposed for the function approximation can be applied to solve the PDE. Consider the PDE solution on RBFN using the example of problem. The solution of the problem is reduced to minimizing the error functional. Consider the solution of a model problem described by the Laplace equation with Dirichlet boundary conditions

$$\frac{\partial^2 u}{\partial x_1^2} + \frac{\partial^2 u}{\partial x_2^2} = f\left(x_1, x_2\right), \left(x_1, x_2\right) \in \Omega, \ u = p\left(x_1, x_2\right), \left(x_1, x_2\right) \in \partial\Omega,$$

where $\partial\Omega$ — is the boundary of the area; f and p — are known functions of the coordinates (x, y).

The error functional for the model problem is

$$I = \left[\sum_{i=1}^{N} \left(\Delta u_i - f_i\right)^2 + \lambda \cdot \sum_{j=1}^{K} \left(u_j - p_j\right)^2 \right],$$

where Δu_i — is Laplacian at point i.

Since the components of the gradient vector of the error functional are easy to calculate analytically, the implementation of first order gradient algorithms on RBFN for solving PDE is not fundamentally different from the implementation of these algorithms to solve the function approximation problem, which allows the moments and NAG algorithm not previously used for RBFN to be implemented.

Formulas for the analytical calculation of the gradient vector of the error functional were obtained. The components of the gradient of the weights of the network are calculated by the formula

$$\frac{\partial I}{\partial w_p} = \sum_{i=1}^{N}\left(\Delta v_i - f_i\right) \cdot e^{-\frac{\|x_i - c_p\|^2}{2a_p^2}} \cdot \frac{\|x_i - c_p\|^2 - 2a_p^2}{a_p^4} + \lambda \sum_{j=1}^{K}\left(v_j - p_j\right)w_p e^{-\frac{\|x_i - c_p\|^2}{2a_p^2}}.$$

The components of the gradient in the c_{p1} coordinate of the RBF centers are calculated by the formula

$$\frac{\partial I}{\partial c_{p1}} == w_p \sum_{i=1}^{N}\left(\Delta v_i - f_i\right)e^{-\frac{\|x_i - c_p\|^2}{2a_p^2}}\left(x_{i1} - c_{p1}\right)\frac{\|x_i - c_p\|^2 - 4a_p^2}{a_p^6} + \lambda w_p \sum_{j=1}^{K}\left(v_j - p_j\right)e^{-\frac{\|x_j - c_p\|^2}{2a_p^2}}\frac{\left(x_{j1} - c_{p1}\right)}{a_p^2}.$$

Components of the gradient along the c_{p2} coordinate have a similar appearance. The gradient component is equal to the width

$$\frac{\partial I}{\partial a_p} = w_p \sum_{i=1}^{N}\left(\Delta v_i - f_i\right)\frac{\|x_i - c_p\|^4 - 6a_p\|x_i - c_p\|^2 + 4a_p^4}{a_p^7}e^{-\frac{\|x_i - c_p\|^2}{2a_p^2}}$$

$$+\lambda w_p \sum_{j=1}^{K}\left(v_j - p_j\right)\frac{\|x_j - c_p\|^2}{a_p^3}e^{-\frac{\|x_j - c_p\|^2}{2a_p^2}}.$$

The network learning process ends with a small value of the error functional or the mean square error.

Consider the adaptation of the Levenberg-Marquardt method for learning RBFN on the example of the problem; the errors in the Jacobi matrix are the residuals at the sampling points. The elements of the Jacobi matrix are easy to calculate analytically. The elements of the matrix J_w for internal sampling points are calculated by the formula

$$\frac{\partial r_i}{\partial w_j} = \frac{\partial\left(\Delta v_i - f_i\right)}{\partial w_j} = e^{-\frac{\|x - c_j\|^2}{2a_j^2}} \cdot \frac{\|x - c_j\|^2 - 2a_j^2}{a_j^4}.$$

For boundary sampling points calculations are made according to the formula

$$\frac{\partial r_i}{\partial w_j} = \exp\left(-\frac{\|x - c_j\|^2}{2a_j^2}\right).$$

The elements of the matrix J_{c_1} for internal sample points are

$$\frac{\partial r_i}{\partial c_{j1}} = \frac{w_j}{a_j^4} \cdot e^{-\frac{\|x-c_j\|^2}{2a_j^2}} \cdot \left(x_1 - c_{j1}\right) \cdot \frac{\|x - c_j\|^2 - 4a_j^2}{a_j^2}.$$

For boundary points, the matrix elements are written as

$$\frac{\partial r_i}{\partial c_{j1}} = w_j \cdot e^{-\frac{\|x-c_j\|^2}{2a_j^2}} \cdot \frac{\left(x_1 - c_{j1}\right)}{a_j^2}.$$

Similarly, the elements of the matrix J_{c_2} are calculated. The elements of the matrix J_a for internal sampling points are calculated by the formula

$$\frac{\partial r_i}{\partial a_j} = \frac{w_j}{a_j^5} \cdot e^{-\frac{\|x-c_j\|^2}{2a_j^2}} \cdot \left[\frac{\|x - c_j\|^2}{a_j^2} \cdot \left(\|x - c_j\|^2 - 2a_j^2\right) - 4 \cdot \left(\|x - c_j\|^2 - a_j^2\right)\right].$$

For boundary points, the matrix elements are written as

$$\frac{\partial r_i}{\partial a_j} = w_j \cdot e^{-\frac{\|x-c_j\|^2}{2a_j^2}} \cdot \frac{\|x - c_j\|^2}{a_j^3}.$$

In the above formulas, r — is the discrepancy at the point i. The conditions for completing the learning process using the Levenberg-Marquardt method are the same as in the first-order methods.

Figure 2. First approximated function

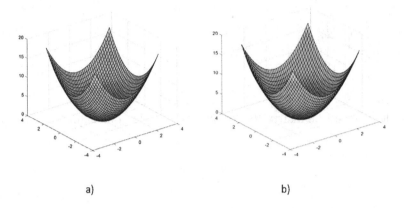

a)   b)

Thus, an adaptation has been made for learning RBFN networks in solving problems of approximation of functions and solving PDE of modern fast first-order gradient algorithms. An algorithm for learning RBFN networks based on the Levenberg Marquardt method has been developed.

EXPERIMENTAL STUDY OF LEARNING ALGORITHMS FOR NETWORKING OF RADIAL BASIC FUNCTIONS

For an experimental study of the developed algorithms, a set of programs was created in the MATLAB R2019a system for solving two-dimensional functions approximation problems and PDE solutions. The program complex includes functions for calculating the error functionals, the components of the gradient vector, the Jacobi matrix, the values of the Gauss function at a given point, the network output at a given sampling point. To solve system, we used the solver (solver) of the systems of linear algebraic equations MATLAB. The main programs allow you to implement network settings, organize network learning, output curves of change of error functionals in the learning process, and output problem solving results. The experiments used a computer with an Intel Core i5 8500 processor, a frequency of 3.0 GHz, and a 16.0 GB RAM.

First, an example of approximation of a simple function $z = x^2 + y^2$ (*Alqezweeni and Gorbachenko, 2017*) in the domain

$$\left(x = -3 \ldots + 3, y = -3 \ldots + 3 \right)$$

Figure 3. Centers and width of RB functions when solving the first approximation problem

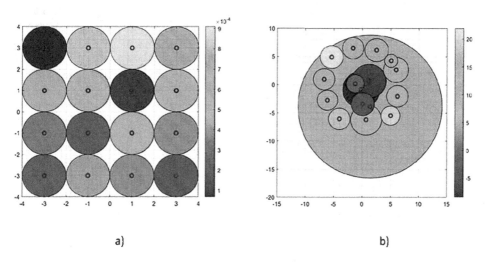

a)   b)

Figure 4. Changes in the root-mean-square error in the process of network learning by the Levenberg Marquardt algorithm when approximating the first function

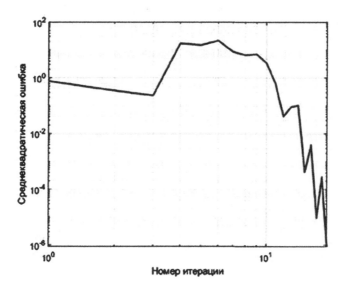

Table 1. Experimental results when solving problem 1

Algorithm	Parameters	Number of Iterations	Decision Time, S
Gradient descent	$\eta_1 = 0.00150$, $\eta_2 = 0.00100$, $\eta_3 = 0.00050$	60000	3500
Gradient descent with impulse	$\eta_1 = 0.00700, \alpha_1 = 0.9$, $\eta_2 = 0.00002, \alpha_2 = 0.9$, $\eta_3 = 0.00020, \alpha_3 = 0.9$	1800	60
NAG	$\eta_1 = 0.00500, \alpha_1 = 0.9$, $\eta_2 = 0.00200, \alpha_2 = 0.5$, $\eta_3 = 0.00100, \alpha_3 = 0.3$	350	20
RMSProp+NAG	$\eta_1 = 0.00100$, $\eta_2 = 0.00200$, $\eta_3 = 0.00100$, $\alpha_1 = 0.90000, \rho_1 = 0.90000$, $\alpha_2 = 0.50000, \rho_2 = 0.90000$, $\alpha_3 = 0.10000, \rho_3 = 0.90000$	9500	300
Levenberg-Marquardt method	$\mu_0 = 0.1, \nu = 10$	8	2

was considered (Fig. 2a). The function is known at 100 interpolation nodes arranged randomly. The number of RBF is 16. In fig. 3a shows the location of the centers, the width symbol (in the form of circles with radii equal to the width) of RBF and the weights using the MATLAB color palette before learning the network using the Levenberg Marquardt algorithm. As initial values, weights were assigned random uniformly distributed numbers from 0 to 0.001 numbers. The initial widths were set equal to 3.0 for the algorithms of descent and NAG and equal to 1.0 for the Levenberg Marquardt algorithm for all RB functions.

The graph of the change in the mean square error for iterations is shown in Figure 4.

Changes in the mean square error are not smooth. The result of the approximation (Fig. 2b) visually coincides with the graph of the analytical function. The final location of the centers and the values of weights and widths after learning the network (Fig. 3b) are radically different from the initial state, which confirms the importance of setting not only the weights, but also the centers and widths.

The results of network learning in solving the first problem using algorithms of the first and second order are shown in the table. The iterative learning process continued until the mean square error of 0.01 was reached. Since the number of iterations and the solution time depend on random initial values of the weights, 10 experiments were carried out for each method. The table for each method presents the average result of 10 experiments. The coefficients for the weights are designated by the index 1, for the centers - by the index 2 and for the width - by the index 3. The values of the coefficients were chosen experimentally.

Accelerated first-order methods have a great advantage over the gradient descent algorithm. The impulse method turned out to be very sensitive to random changes in the initial parameters. For this algorithm, the change in the mean square error has a pronounced non-smooth character. The best and most stable results showed NAG. The RMSProp + NAG algorithm works stably, but showed a significantly lower rate of convergence than NAG. The Levenberg Marquardt method reduces the number of iterations by an order of magnitude compared to the NAG. Methods of the first order practically did not allow learning the network to a smaller standard error, while the Levenberg – Marquardt method allowed, on average, to obtain an average quadratic error of 10–6 in 20 iterations (Fig. 4). The disadvantages of the Levenberg-Marquardt method are the uneven nature of reducing errors and worsening the conditionality of the system (15) as the accuracy of network learning increases.

The proposed algorithms were tested using the Franke function (*Franke, 1982*), popular in approximation (Fig. 5a)

$$f(x,y) = 0,75 \exp\left(-\frac{(9x-2)^2}{4} - \frac{(9y-2)^2}{4}\right) + 0,75 \exp\left(-\frac{(9x+1)^2}{49} - \frac{9y+1}{10}\right)$$

$$+0,5 \exp\left(-\frac{(9x-7)^2}{4} - \frac{(9y-3)^2}{4}\right) - 0,2 \exp\left(-(9x-4)^2 - (9x-7)^2\right).$$

he first-order methods for approximating the Franck function did not allow us to obtain the mean square error of less than 10^{-1}. The Levenberg Marquardt method averaged over 15 iterations made it possible to achieve an average square error equal to 10^{-6}. The approximation was carried out in the field of $(x = 0...1, y = 0...1)$.

Figure 5. Franke function

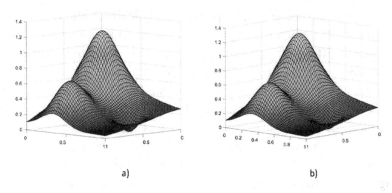

a)   b)

Figure 6. Centers and width of RB functions when approximating Franck function

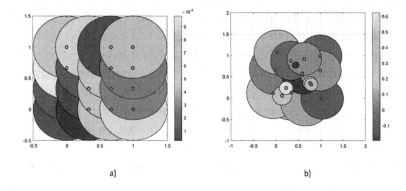

a)   b)

The function is known at 100 interpolation nodes arranged randomly. The number of RB functions is 16. Before learning the network, RBF centers were located at the nodes of the grid (Fig. 6a). As initial values, weights were assigned random uniformly distributed from 0 to 0.001 numbers. The initial width of all RBF is, 5. Best results are obtained when $\mu = 2.0$ and $\nu = 1.5$.

In figure 6 shows the location of the centers, the symbol for the width of the RB functions and the values of weights before learning and after learning the network. Fig. 6 shows a radical change in the coordinates of the centers, widths and weights in the process of learning the network. Therefore, it is important in the process of learning RBFN to adjust not only the weight, but also the parameters of the RBF.

Experiments on the solution of PDE were carried out on the example of solving problem (17) with

Figure 7. PDE solution

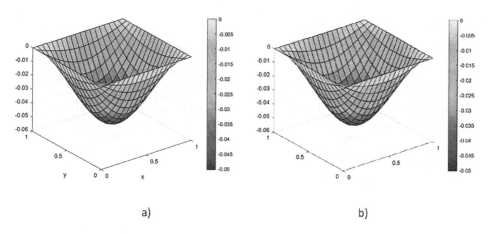

a)　　　　　　　　　　　　　　　　　　b)

$$f\left(x_1, x_2\right) = \sin\left(\pi x_1\right) \cdot \sin\left(\pi x_2\right) \text{ and } p\left(x_1, x_2\right) = 0 .$$

The task has an analytical solution (Fig. 7a)

$$u = -\frac{1}{2\pi^2} \sin \pi x \cdot \sin \pi y .$$

Figure 8. Location of sampling points

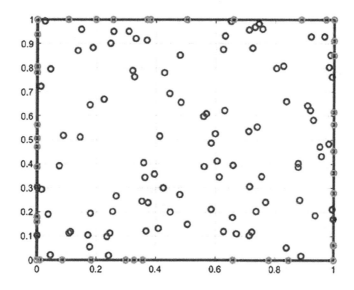

Figure 9. Centers and width of RB functions when solving PDE

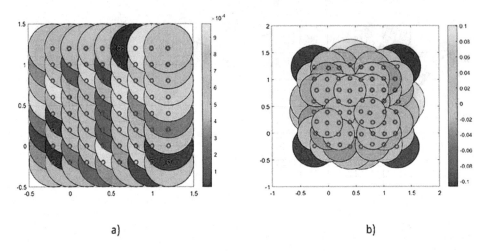

a)   b)

Figure 10. Dependence of the mean square error of various algorithms on the iteration number

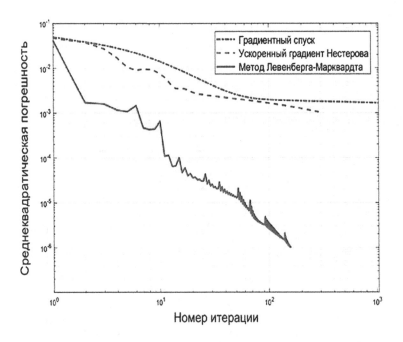

Table 2. Experimental results on PDE solution

Algorithm	Mean Square Error	Number of Iterations	Decision Time, C
Gradient descent	$3*10^{-3}$	1000	1100
NAG	$7*10^{-4}$	1000	1120
Levenberg-Marquardt method	10^{-6}	30	8.5

The problem was solved in a unit square. The number of internal sampling points $N = 100$. The number of boundary sampling points $K = 40$. The penalty coefficient of the error functional on the $\lambda = 10$ boundary.

Sampling points were located randomly in the solution area and on the border of the region (Fig.8).

As initial values, weights were assigned random uniformly distributed numbers from 0 to 0.001 numbers. The initial width of all RBF was constant, equal to 0.2 for all methods. At initialization, the RBF centers were located on a square grid 8×8. he location of the centers, the conditional representation of the width and size of the weights before learning the network (Fig. 9a) and after learning (Fig. 9b) show the importance of setting the RBF parameters.

The result of a numerical solution for learning the RBFN network by the Levenberg Marquardt method is shown in Fig. 7b. The dependence of the mean square error of various algorithms on the iteration number is shown in Fig. 10.

The results of experiments to solve the boundary value problem on RBFN networks, trained by various algorithms, are presented in Table. 2. The gradient descent method allowed solving the model problem with a small accuracy. For a solution with great accuracy, the method is practically inapplicable. Somewhat greater accuracy is provided by the Nesterov method. Only the Levenberg Marquardt method allowed to solve the problem with high accuracy in an acceptable time. The Levenberg Marquardt method showed almost identical results as compared to the confidence domain method (*Gorbachenko and Zhukov, 2017*), but the implementation of the Levenberg Marquardt method is simpler. The disadvantages of the Levenberg-Marquardt method are the poor conditionality of the system, which forms the correction parameters, and the uneven nature of convergence.

Thus, the algorithm of the Levenberg Marquardt method showed a clear advantage over the first-order algorithms and ensured accuracy at the level of known implementations of the algorithm of confidence domains, but simpler than these algorithms.

CONCLUSION

Networks of radial basis functions are a promising tool for solving boundary value problems described by partial differential equations. But the known methods of teaching networks of radial basic functions do not provide fast learning of networks of radial basic functions. As a way to eliminate this drawback, it was proposed to improve the network learning algorithms.

For the first time for learning networks of radial basis functions, modern fast first-order gradient algorithms have been adapted: a gradient descent algorithm with a pulse, an accelerated Nesterov gradient, an algorithm with an adaptive learning rate RMSProp. Adapted algorithms take into account the architecture of networks of radial basis functions. Analytical expressions for calculating the gradient of the error functional are obtained. When solving model problems up to a standard error of 0.01, Nesterov's accelerated algorithm provided a reduction of the number of iterations by more than two orders of magnitude compared with the gradient descent algorithm currently used.

For learning networks of radial basic functions intended for solving problems of approximation of functions and boundary-value problems, a learning algorithm based on the method

Levenberg Marquardt, distinguished by the specifics of the network architecture and analytical calculation of parameters. The method allowed on model problems to reach the mean-square error, which is not achievable by known first-order algorithms. The proposed algorithm achieves a small error for the number of iterations, equal to the number of iterations of the algorithm based on the method of confidence regions, but simpler than this algorithm, since it does not require solving the conditional optimization problem at each iteration.

REFERENCES

Aggarwal, C. C. (2018). *Neural networks and deep learning*. Springer. doi:10.1007/978-3-319-94463-0

Alqezweeni, M. M., Gorbachenko, V. I. (2017). Improvement of the learning algorithms in radial basis functions networks for solving the approximation tasks. *Models, systems, networks in economics, technology, nature and society, 3*(23), 123–138 (in Russian).

Alqezweeni, M. M., Gorbachenko, V. I., Zhukov, M. V., & Jaafar, M. S. (2018). Efficient solving of boundary value problems using radial basis function networks learned by trust region method. *Hindawi. International Journal of Mathematics and Mathematical Sciences*, 9457578.

Belytschko, T., Krongauz, Y., Organ, D., Fleming, M., & Krysl, P. (1996). Meshless methods: An overview and recent developments. Computers Methods in Applied Mechanics and Engineering, 139(1–4). pp. 3–47.

Bernal, F. (2016). Trust-region methods for nonlinear elliptic equations with radial basis functions. *Computers & Mathematics with Applications (Oxford, England), 72*(7), 1743–1763. doi:10.1016/j.camwa.2016.07.014

Buhmann, M. D. (2004). *Radial basis functions: theory and implementations*. Cambridge University Press.

Chen, H., Kong, L., & Leng, W. (2011). Numerical solution of PDEs via integrated radial basis function networks with adaptive learning algorithm. *Applied Soft Computing, 11*(1), 855–860. doi:10.1016/j.asoc.2010.01.005

Chen, W., & Fu, Z.-J. (2014). *Recent advances in radial basis function collocation methods*. Springer. doi:10.1007/978-3-642-39572-7

Conn, A. R., Gould, N. I. M., & Toint, P. L. (1987). *Trust-region methods*. MPS-SIAM.

Elisov, L. N., Gorbachenko, V. I., & Zhukov, M. V. (2018). Learning radial basis function networks with the trust region method for boundary problems. *Automation and Remote Control, 79*(9), 1621–1629. doi:10.1134/S0005117918090072

Farlow, S. J. (1993). *Partial differential equations for scientists and engineers.* Dover Publications.

Fasshauer, G., & Zhang, J. (2007). On choosing "optimal" shape parameters for RBF approximation. *Numerical Algorithms, 45*(1–4), 345–368. doi:10.100711075-007-9072-8

Fasshauer, G. E. (2002). Newton iteration with multiquadrics for the solution of nonlinear PDEs. *Computers & Mathematics with Applications (Oxford, England), 43*(3–5), 423–438. doi:10.1016/S0898-1221(01)00296-6

Fasshauer, G. E. (2007). *Meshfree approximation methods with MATLAB.* World Scientific Publishing Company. doi:10.1142/6437

Fletcher, R., & Reeves, C. M. (1964). Function minimization by conjugate gradients. *The Computer Journal, 7*(2), 149–154. doi:10.1093/comjnl/7.2.149

Franke, R. (1982). Scattered data Interpolation: Tests of some Methods. *Mathematics of Computation, 38*(157), 181–200.

Gill, P. E., Murray, W., & Wright, M. H. (1982). *Practical optimization.* Emerald Group.

Goodfellow, I., Bengio, Y., & Courville, A. (2016). *Deep learning.* MIT Press.

Gorbachenko, V. I., Alqezweeni, M. M., & Jaafar, M. S. (2017). Application of parametric identification method and radial basis function networks for solution of inverse boundary value problems. *2017 Annual Conference on New Trends in Information and Communications Technology Applications, NTICT 2017; Baghdad; Iraq,* 18–21. 10.1109/NTICT.2017.7976151

Gorbachenko, V. I., & Artyukhina, E. V. (2010). Mesh-free methods and their implementation with radial basis neural networks. *Neirokomp'yutory: Razrabotka, Primentnine,* No. 11, 4–10 (in Russian).

Gorbachenko, V. I., Lazovskaya, T. V., Tarkhov, D. A., Vasiljev, A. N., & Zhukov, M. V. (2016). *Neural network technique in some inverse problems of mathematical physics. Advances in Neural Networks - ISNN 2016: 13th International Symposium on Neural Networks, ISNN 2016, St. Petersburg, Russia, July 6-8.* Springer, 310–316. 10.1007/978-3-319-40663-3_36

Gorbachenko, V. I., & Zhukov, M. V. (2017). Solving boundary value problems of mathematical physics using radial basis function networks. *Computational Mathematics and Mathematical Physics*, *57*(1), 145–155. doi:10.1134/S0965542517010079

Griebel, M., & Schweitzer, M. A. (2008). *Meshfree methods for partial differential equations IV*. Springer. doi:10.1007/978-3-540-79994-8

Grieves, M. (2014). Digital Twin: manufacturing excellence through virtual factory replication. *White Paper*, 1–7.

Haykin, S. O. (2008). *Neural networks and learning machines*. Pearson. Retrieved from http://ieeexplore.ieee.org/document/7976151/authors. http://www.scottsarra.org/math/papers/mqMonographSarraKansa.pdf

Jia, W., Zhao, D., Shen, T., Su, C., Hu, C., & Zhao, Y. (2014). *A New optimized GA-RBF neural network algorithm* (p. 982045). Article, ID: Computational Intelligence and Neuroscience.

Jianyu, L., Siwei, L., Yingjian, Q., & Yaping, H. (2003). Numerical solution of elliptic partial differential equation by growing radial basis function neural networks. *Neural Networks*, *16*(5–6), 729–734. doi:10.1016/S0893-6080(03)00083-2 PMID:12850028

Kansa, E. J. (1990a). Multiquadrics — A scattered data approximation scheme with applications to computational fluid-dynamics — I surface approximations and partial derivative estimates. *Comput. Math. Appl., 19*(8–9), 127–145.

Kansa, E. J. (1990b). Multiquadrics — A scattered data approximation scheme with applications to computational fluid-dynamics — II solutions to parabolic, hyperbolic and elliptic partial differential equations. *Comput. Math. Appl., 19*(8–9), 147–161.

Kansa, E. J. (1999) *Motivation for using radial basis function to solve PDEs*. Retrieved from http://www.cityu.edu.hk/rbf-pde/files/overview-pdf.pdf

Kumar, M., & Yadav, N. (2011). Multilayer perceptions and radial basis function neural network methods for the solution of differential equations: A survey. *Computers & Mathematics with Applications (Oxford, England), 62*(10), 3796–3811. doi:10.1016/j.camwa.2011.09.028

Li, J. C., Hon, Y. C. (2004). Domain decomposition for radial basis meshless methods. *Numeric Methods Partial Differ. Eq., 20*(3), 450–462.

Liesen, J. (2015). *Krylov subspace methods: principles and analysis*. Oxford University Press.

Ling, L., & Kansa, E. J. (2005). A least-squares preconditioner for radial basis functions collocation methods. *Advances in Computational Mathematics, 23*(1-2), 31–54. doi:10.100710444-004-1809-5

Liu, G. R. (20013). *Mesh free methods: moving beyond the finite element method.* Boca Raton, FL: CRC Press.

Madni, A. M., Madni, C. C., & Lucero, S. D. (2019). Leveraging digital twin technology in model-based systems engineering. *Systems, 7*(1). *Article-Number,* 7. doi:10.3390ystems7010007

Mai-Duy, N., & Tran-Cong, T. (2005). Solving high order ordinary differential equations with radial basis function networks. *International Journal for Numerical Methods in Engineering, 62*(6), 824–852. doi:10.1002/nme.1220

Markopoulos, A. P., Georgiopoulos, S., & Manolakos, D. E. (2016). On the Use of Back Propagation and Radial Basis Function Neural Networks in Surface Roughness Prediction. *Journal of Industrial Engineering International, 12*(3), 389–400. doi:10.100740092-016-0146-x

Marquardt, D. W. (1963). An algorithm for least-squares estimation of nonlinear parameters. *Journal of the Society for Industrial and Applied Mathematics, 11*(2), 431–441. doi:10.1137/0111030

Mazumder, S. (2015). *Numerical methods for partial differential equations: finite difference and finite volume methods.* Academic Press.

Niyogi, P., & Girosi, F. (1996). On the relationship between generalization error, hypothesis complexity, and sample complexity for radial basis functions. *Neural Computation, 8*(4), 819–842. doi:10.1162/neco.1996.8.4.819

Pattanayak, S. (2017). *Pro deep learning with TensorFlow: a mathematical approach to advanced artificial intelligence in Python.* Apress. doi:10.1007/978-1-4842-3096-1

Polak, E., & Ribiére, G. (1969). Note sur la convergence de méthodes de directions conjuguées. *Revue française d'informatique et de recherche opérationnelle*, série rouge, Tome 3, n° 1, 35–43.

Polyak, B. T. (1964). Some methods of speeding up the convergence of iteration methods. *U.S.S.R. Computational Mathematics and Mathematical Physics, 4*(5), 1–17. doi:10.1016/0041-5553(64)90137-5

Saad, Y. (2003). *Iterative methods for sparse linear systems.* SIAM. doi:10.1137/1.9780898718003

Sarra, S. (2005). Adaptive radial basis function methods for time dependent partial differential equations. *Applied Numerical Mathematics*, *54*(1), 79–94. doi:10.1016/j. apnum.2004.07.004

Sarra, S. A., & Kansa, E. J. (2009). Multiquadric radial basis function approximation methods for the numerical solution of partial differential equations. *Advances in Computational Mechanics, 2*(2).

Staihaug, T. (1983). The conjugate gradient method and trust region in large scale optimization. *SIAM Journal on Numerical Analysis*, *20*(3), 626–637. doi:10.1137/0720042

Sutskever, I., Martens, J., Dahl, G., & Hinton, G. (2013). On the importance of initialization and momentum in deep learning. *ICML'13 Proceedings of the 30th International Conference on International Conference on Machine Learning*, Vol. 28, III-1139-III-1147.

Tarkhov, D. A. (2014). *Neural network models and algorithms. Reference book.* Radiotekhnika. (in Russian)

Uhlemann, T. H.-J., Schock, C., Lehmann, C., Freiberger, S., & Steinhilper, R. (2017). The digital twin: Demonstrating the potential of real time data acquisition in production systems. In *7th Conference on Learning Factories* Procedia Manufacturing, 9, 13–120.

Vasiliev, A. N., & Tarkhov, D. A. (2009). *Neural network modeling: Principles. Algorithms. Applications.* St. Petersburg Polytechnic University Publishing House. (in Russian)

Vasilyev, A., Tarkhov, D., & Malykhina, G. (2018). Methods of creating digital twins based on neural network modeling. *Modern Information Technologies and IT-Education*, *14*(3), 521–532.

Wang, H., Qin, Q.-H., & Kang, Y. L. (2005). A new meshless method for steady-state heat conduction problems in anisotropic and inhomogeneous media. *Archive of Applied Mechanics*, *74*(8), 563–579. doi:10.100700419-005-0375-8

Watkins, D. (2010). *Fundamentals of matrix computations.* Wiley.

Wendland, H. (2010). *Scattered data approximation.* Cambridge University Press.

Wild, S. M., Regis, R. G., & Shoemaker, C. A. (2008). ORBIT: Optimization by radial basis function interpolation in trust-regions. *SIAM Journal on Scientific Computing*, *30*(6), 3197–3219. doi:10.1137/070691814

Xie, T., Yu, H., Hewlett, J., Rozycki, P., & Wilamowski, B. (2012). Fast and Efficient Second-Order Method for Learning Radial Basis Function Networks. *IEEE Transactions on Neural Networks and Learning Systems*, *23*(4), 609–619. doi:10.1109/TNNLS.2012.2185059 PMID:24805044

Yadav, N., Yadav, A., & Kumar, M. (2015). *An introduction to neural network methods for differential equations.* Springer. doi:10.1007/978-94-017-9816-7

Zhang, L., Li, K., He, H., & Irwin, G. W. (2013, November). A New Discrete-Continuous Algorithm for Radial Basis Function Networks Construction. *IEEE Transactions on Neural Networks and Learning Systems*, *24*(11), 1785–1798. doi:10.1109/TNNLS.2013.2264292 PMID:24808612

Zhang, L., Li, K., & Wang, W. (2012). An improved conjugate gradient algorithm for radial basis function (RBF) networks modelling. In *Proceedings of 2012 UKACC International Conference on Control.* pp. 19–23.

Chapter 5
Generative Adversarial Neural Networking of Agents:
Avatars as Tools for Financial Modelling

Vladimir Soloviev
Financial University Under the Government of the Russian Federation, Russia

Vsevolod Chernyshenko
Financial University Under the Government of the Russian Federation, Russia

Vadim Feklin
(iD) https://orcid.org/0000-0002-1803-6699
Financial University Under the Government of the Russian Federation, Russia

Ekaterina Zolotareva
Financial University Under the Government of the Russian Federation, Russia

Nikita Titov
Financial University Under the Government of the Russian Federation, Russia

ABSTRACT

The chapter is devoted to the problem of analytical analysis of implementation of generative-competitive neural networks in predicting the state of financial markets (particularly to predict future moments of changing market conditions) based on the use of convolutional and generative neural networks, as well as reinforcement training. An algorithm for predicting future moments of trend change under concrete market conditions based on generative adversarial networks was developed. Special software that realizes algorithms for predicting future moments of changing market conditions, based on the algorithms mentioned above was designed.

DOI: 10.4018/978-1-7998-1581-5.ch005

INTRODUCTION

Quality of multi-agent (avatar-based) systems depends not only on an algorithm, which define behaviour of their constituent agents, but also on nature of the interaction between the agents. In modern intelligent systems, the agents almost always are based on neural networks that allow them to learn. Nether less, the problem of creating special conditions for the functioning of the agents, aimed at stimulating their learning, are rarely considered. Usually the agents are designed to act independently in conditions, when the possibility of their cooperative self-learning (for example, by a mutual exchange of semantic information - "exchange of experience") is not foreseen.

In this regard, populations of computer agents (avatars) are still inferior to teams of human experts, operating in a certain social environment and interacting each other in many ways. In particular, this situation concerns a modelling of economic and financial processes, when the study of trends is extremely challenging for the reason of chaotic nature of indicators' dynamics. Using agent population not only for reflecting a structure of groups of real actors in the financial market, but also as an expert population with its own special internal structure, is promising being able to significantly increase predictive power of the multi-agent model.

One of features of the classical artificial feed forward neural networks (when agents are considered as separate learning units) is that being universal classifiers, they are unable to generate sample data sets belonging to recognisable classes of objects. Deep multilayer perceptrons, for example, are capable to highlight fairly high-level features of images, which allow them to implement complex classification of images that the network did not see at the training stage. In the same time, generating an image that the network did not see during its training, is a task of another level. The generative models are aimed to solve it; in particular, it corresponds to the generative adversary networks, which have become very popular last years (Palazzo et al. 2018), (Arakaki et al. 2018), (Karras et al. 2017), (Arora et al. 2017), (Arjovsky, Bottou et al. 2017).

Neural generative-competitive network (Goodfellow et al. 2014) is a technology that is inherently focused on the interaction of the network with some parallel process, which can be neural network of another agent. In this paper, results of a few numerical experiments with such "binary" agents, using generative-competitive networks, are presented. The data obtained confirm the assumption that results of the work of a group of agents exceed the simple sum of their individual contributions.

Figure 1. Sketch diagram of a generative adversarial network

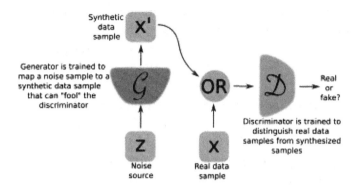

BACKGROUND

The idea of generative-adversarial networks (GANs) was proposed by J. Goodfellow of the University of Montreal (Goodfellow et al. 2014). During literally a couple of years, this method has found its application in the tasks of semantic image segmentation, medical information analysis, material recognition, time series analysis (Luc et al. 2016), (Che et al. 2017), (Erickson et al. 2017), (Esteban et al. 2017), (Chen et al. 2016), (Hinton, Salakhutdinov 2006), (Mescheder et al. 2017), (Dumoulin et al. 2016), (Donahue et al. 2016), (Li et al. 2017), (Reed et al. 2016), (Isola et al. 2016), (Ledig et al. 2016), (Ren et al. 2015), (Lee et al. 2016).

The schematic diagram of generative-adversarial network is presented in the Figure. 1. Here X is the real object of the domain (e.g. a plot); Z – source of a random noise; G – neural network of a generator; X' – artificially generated data that imitate the real one; OR – random selection of one of two inputs; D – neural network of a discriminator.

The main idea of the generative adversarial networks is to train two networks (a generator and a discriminator) simultaneously. The generator accepts a random vector as an input (a source of entropy; sometimes it is interpreted as a one belonging to a "space of hidden variables" or "latent space") and generates a certain image. An artificial image, created by the generator, or an object of a real training sample is forwarded as an input of the discriminator. The last one is to distinguish the artificial image from the real one. In theory, during the learning process, the generator learns a stochastic distribution of the original sample and begins to generate images more and more comparable to the real ones. Discriminator in its turn becomes more and more accurate in recognition of the input images.

GAN is not the first generative model; however, Good fellow and co-authors proposed an original method of competitive training for such models, when two networks "compete" in solving opposite tasks.

Researchers identify several variations of the original idea of generative-adversarial networks:

1. Fully connected GAN – first proposed architecture, where the generator and discriminator are multi-layered feed forward networks (Creswell et al. 2018), (Jost 2018), (Theis, van den Oord, Bethge 2015).
2. Convolutional GAN (deep convolutional GAN, DCGAN) – based on multilayer convolutional networks. They are a logical evolution of the GAN idea applied to image synthesis tasks. The disadvantage of convolutional generative adversarial networks is a rather long-term learning process (Radford et al. 2015).
3. Conditional GAN (CGAN) – an algorithm where both a generator and a discriminator have an additional input that is a vector indicating the class of the object. Such networks can generate a conditional sample distribution, with an indication of a particular class. Thus, they are used for modelling of multimodal distributions (Mirza et al. 2014).
4. Adversarial Auto encoders (AAE) – are networks consisting of two parts, an encoder and a decoder, that learn deterministic mapping from data space to a hidden variable space (regularly with a much smaller dimension) and inverse mapping. Competitive learning is used to optimize, like in case of variation auto encoders, and is used to give the space of hidden variables a meaningful organization in terms of the subject area.
5. GAN with output models (ALI, BiGAN) – extend the functionality of GAN with mechanism for outputting hidden. Regular GANs can generate a verisimilar object from a random vector in the space of hidden variables (latent space). Two independently proposed adversarial learning inference and bi-directional GANs (BAN) provide a mechanism for finding the inverse transform, which can be useful for a task of indicators recognition. However, today, a reliability of such methods is seriously limited.

In Figure 2 a schematic diagram of a bidirectional GAN is presented, in which: E - The encoder's neural network; Z' - representation of a real object in the space of hidden variables; OR - Random choice of a pair (X, Z ') or (X', Z);

A search for new applications of generative-adversarial networks is currently a highly proactive area of research. These networks have proven themselves in such spheres as image classification, image generation by textual description, image conversion, resolution enhancement. Moreover, in 2018, generative-adversarial networks remain an actively developing method of machine learning.

Figure 2. Schematic diagram of the bidirectional GAN

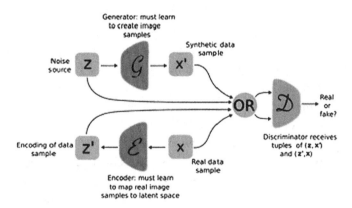

However, during its existence, generative-adversarial networks have shown significant problems in application, e.g. collapse of the model (situation in which the generator produces one object for any input values), instability of learning, lack of generally accepted approaches to evaluating performance.

USE OF GENERATIVE ADVERSARIAL NETWORKS FOR AGENTS' INTERACTION AND ECONOMIC FORECASTING

Artificial neural networks have proven to be effective by solving many kind of tasks, still their efficiency depends on the ability to select the correct network architecture for each specific data analysis task.

While designing network architecture, an expert confronts a necessity to make many decisions, both quantitative and qualitative. The performance of the resulting model directly depends on their implementation. Among them are: a choice of the amount of layers, a number of neurons in each layer, a choice of the activation function, a use of recurrent and convolutional layers. In the process of such a design, the expert's task is to balance between the variability of the model and the propensity to retrain. There are also external factors that need to be taken into account: available computing power, the time frame for solving the problem, etc.

The space of possible neural networks in which a search may be conducted is enormous. By neural networks design, specialists use certain heuristic rules and diagnostic tools, but it is difficult to call such a search a full value methodology, it is rather a creative process.

A very natural direction of research in the field of artificial intelligence is the construction of methods and tools for reducing human participation in the construction of machine learning systems, the automation of this process. Currently, the are two fundamentally different approaches: machine learning automation (AutoML) and neuron evolution (evolutionary artificial neural networks, EANN).

Further research has led to the creation of the NEAT method (neuron evolution through augmenting topologies), that has been significantly optimized for the use of computational resources. More recently, this method has been adapted for the evolutionary search for deep neural network structures.

Today, evolutionary programming makes it possible to create networks that are comparable in performance to those best-in-class with zero human participation in the design and training process for image classification tasks and speech recognition tasks.

Currently, active work of using neuron evolution in such areas as: prediction of time series by ensemble models, prediction of energy consumption by computer clusters, construction of interplanetary trajectories, recognition of the language of speech, prediction of oil prices is under way.

The main disadvantage of the neuron evolutionary approach is very high computational power requirements to support this process to convergence. The development of deep neural networks and the distribution of big data raise this level even higher. Therefore, at present we are witnessing a decline of interest in the evolutionary programming of artificial neural networks: the time of a programmer and data analyst is cheaper now than the required processor time.

However, large corporations with sufficient computing power can experiment with neuron evolution. Apparently, with increasing productivity of computing technology, interest in evolutionary methods in machine learning will return (perhaps iteratively).

The authors have developed an algorithm for predicting future moments of change in market conditions based on a generative-contention neural network.

Diagnostics of learning generative-adversarial networks showed several options for learning dynamics. We illustrate them on typical cases from our pool. The first case can be called successful learning (Figure 3).

Validation accuracy increases and approaches asymptotically to an accuracy on the training set, then begins to decrease due to retraining. We have observed this picture on balanced and not the most variable models. It is worth noting cause, as seen in Figure 1, the accuracy almost approaches the value of 1.0. However, this does not necessarily tell us about the exceptional quality of the model. There's a reason to recall the parameters of the data set. Particularly in this data set 99.84% of all observations are negative cases. This is a classic example of the shifted classes problem, which is expressed in this case by using a primitive model that always predicts 0, we get an accuracy of 99.84%. Naturally, this indicator is not representative.

Figure 3. Layout 10-2, network option 2-2, normal training

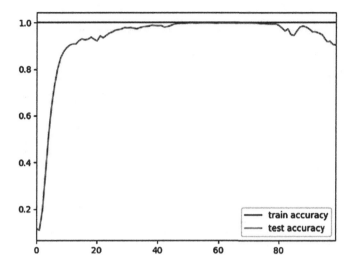

Figure 4. Layout 10-0, network option 0-3, model collapse

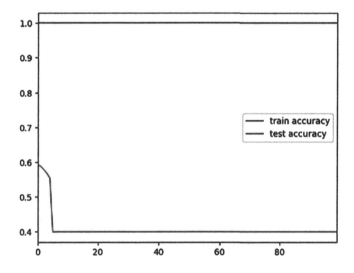

A second case may be observed when the discriminator in variability far exceeds the generator (Figure 4). In this case, despite the competitiveness of training, the weakly variable generator is not able to exert considerable pressure on the discriminator. Owing to this process, the accuracy of recognition of discriminator samples decreases rapidly and is unable to recover, which is clearly seen in the Figure 5.

Figure 5. Dynamics of the remaining parameters during the collapse of the model

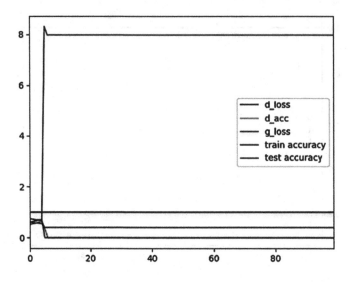

Figure 6. Layout scheme 10-10, network option 1-3, intermittent learning

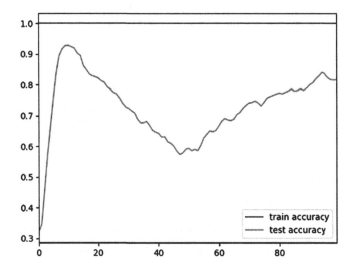

Figure 7. Layout scheme 30-0, network option 0-1, retraining

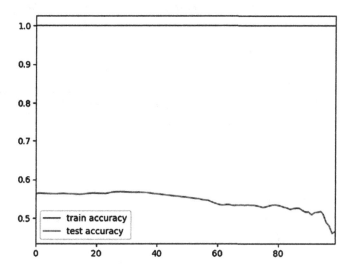

The unstable behavior of the model, characterized by the complex dynamics of the test error (Figure 6), is quite common when, during the training period, the dynamics of the main indicators of the competitive network change their direction several times. This indicates a divergence of the learning process in principle, and the unstable nature of the competition, which does not allow us to expect reliable predictions from such models.

It should be mentioned that, as in many models of machine learning, in GSS there is a tendency towards retraining. However, paradoxically, it is more visible in less variable models (Figure 7). This can be explained by the fact that with a small fraction of the generator variation, the entire network resides in a smaller space of possible samples, which effectively reduces the dimension of the data set, which is detrimental to the dynamics of the predictive ability of the model as a whole.

To analyse results in a more or less acceptable case of learning, consider a plot with a dynamics of the generator and discriminator errors (Figure 8). On this graph, we are interested in two lines - the dynamics of the generator error and the ratio of the discriminator error with a threshold value of 0.5.

In an ideal case, as learning generative adversarial networks, we should observe a smooth decrease in the generator error with a tendency towards zero from above, as well as a discriminator error tendency of 0.5 from below. In the classical approach, we are interested in the final value of the generator error, since competitive training is used to train the generator to play plausible samples.

Figure 8. The error value of the discriminator and generator in each era of learning (discriminator error is shown in blue colour; generator error is shown in orange colour)

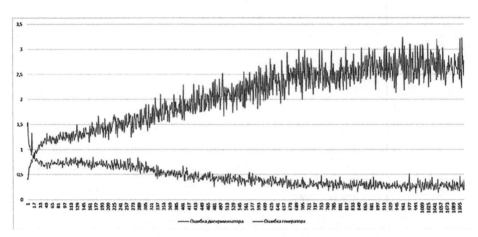

In our case, the problem is the reverse to the classical one; we use a generator to train the discriminator of the ability to recognize a given pattern. Accordingly, we are not satisfied with the classical dynamics of the discriminator's aspiration error to 0.5, that is, the situation of random discrimination with a low generator error. Our task is to try to force the discriminator to reduce the error indefinitely. At the same time, we want to have the generator error as low as possible, since it is impractical to discriminate samples that are far from natural for this task.

According to the schedule of this training, we see that with an increase in the number of steps, the discriminator error smoothly decreases, and at the end of the training passes the threshold value.

It would seem to speak about the success of the training. However, at the same time, the generator error grows indefinitely, that is, the generator training diverges on its own.

In this case, it is not necessary to speak about the effectiveness of training, since the discriminator is trained on implausible patterns.

However, when the discriminator error values are less than 0.5, it puts learning pressure on the generator, which, in fact, is the competition of training.

As a result of such training, the trend is determined very "noisy" - too often the points replace the class from trend to non-trend (Figure 9).

Positive deviations in the quality of the model, if present, are insignificant, which may serve as a basis for concluding that among those tested there is no model capable of giving reliable predictions with a statistically significant accuracy higher than the chance.

Figure 9. CGAN learning outcome

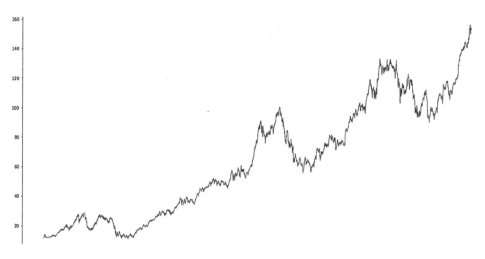

CONCLUSION

Generative-concurrent neural networks algorithms are relatively new technology (it appeared only in 2014, and the first full-scale results appeared in 2016-2017) but already are one of the most promising machine learning algorithms without a teacher. Currently, such neural networks are used to generate photo-realistic images based on the examples provided to it. However, no one yet knows for sure what may be achieved with the help of GAN. In this paper, we studied the current state of research in the use of generative-competitive neural networks. First of all, a very interesting class of GAN generative models used to forecast financial trends was studied.

During the presented research, the classifier network was successfully trained. Based on the trained network, an analysis of plots of financial indicators was used for trend visualization that maximizes the output of internal neurons of the network. At the same time, the diagnostics of teaching generative-competitive networks showed several variants of learning dynamics.

A special generator was designed to teach the discriminator the ability to recognize imported financial indicators pattern. To reach this goal, the following methods were used: a variation of an auto encoder network consisting of successive convolutional and scanning layers, and a generative adversarial network characterized by a discriminatory network. On the studied model data, a long-term dynamics of the discriminator was observed, which can give us a hope that one well-trained discriminator will allow to reduce predicting errors.

ACKNOWLEDGMENT

The reported study was funded by RFBR according to the projects: N° 19-29-07545-мк, 20-010-00326-a.

REFERENCES

Arakaki, T., Barello, G., & Ahmadian, Y. (2017). Capturing the diversity of biological tuning curves using generative adversarial networks, [Electronic resource] Retrieved from (access date: 21.10.2018). doi:10.1101/167916

Arjovsky, M., & Bottou, L. (2017). Towards Principled Methods for Training Generative Adversarial Networks. *arXiv.*

Arora, S., Ge, R., Liang, Y., Ma, T., & Zhang, Y. (2017). Generalization and Equilibrium in Generative Adversarial Nets (GANs). *arXiv.*

Che, Z., Cheng, Y., Zhai, S., Sun, Z., & Liu, Y. (2017). Boosting Deep Learning Risk Prediction with Generative Adversarial Networks for Electronic Health Records. In *Proceedings IEEE International Conference on Data Mining (ICDM).* Piscataway, NJ: IEEE. pp. 787–792.

Chen, X., Duan, Y., Houthooft, R., Schulman, J., Sutskever, I., & Abbeel, P. (2016). InfoGAN: Interpretable Representation Learning by Information Maximizing Generative Adversarial Nets. *Advances in Neural Information Processing Systems. arXiv.*

Creswell, A., White, T., Dumoulin, V., Arulkumaran, K., Sengupta, B., & Bharath, A. A. (2018). Generative Adversarial Networks: An Overview. *IEEE Signal Processing Magazine, 35*(1), 53–65. doi:10.1109/MSP.2017.2765202

Donahue, J., Krähenbühl, P., & Darrell, T. (2016). Adversarial Feature Learning. *arXiv.*

Dumoulin, V., Belghazi, I., Poole, B., Mastropietro, O., Lamb, A., Arjovsky, M., & Courville, A. (2016). Adversarially Learned Inference. *arXiv.*

Erickson, Z., Chernova, S., & Kemp, C. C. (2017). Semi-Supervised Haptic Material Recognition for Robots using Generative Adversarial Networks. *arXiv.*

Esteban, C., Hyland, S. L., & Rätsch, G. (2017). Real-valued (Medical) Time Series Generation with Recurrent Conditional GANs. *arXiv.*

Goodfellow, I. J., Pouget-Abadie, J., Mirza, M., Xu, B., Warde-Farley, D., Ozair, Sh., . . . Bengio, Y. (2014). Generative Adversarial Nets. *arXiv*.

Hinton, G. E., & Salakhutdinov, R. R. (2006). Reducing the dimensionality of data with neural networks. *Science, 313*(5786), 504–507. doi:10.1126cience.1127647 PMID:16873662

Isola, P., Zhu, J.-Y., Zhou, T., & Efros, A. A. (2016). Image-to-Image Translation with Conditional Adversarial Networks. *arXiv*.

Jost, Z. Overview of GANs (Generative Adversarial Networks) – Part I, 2017 [Electronic resourse]. Retrieved from https://www.kdnuggets.com/2017/11/overview-gans-generative-adversarial-networks-part1.html (access date: 21.10.2018).

Karras, T., Aila, T., Laine, S., & Lehtinen, J. (2017). Progressive Growing of GANs for Improved Quality, Stability, and Variation. *arXiv*.

Ledig, C., Theis, L., Huszar, F., Caballero, J., Cunningham, A., Acosta, A., . . . Shi, W. (2016). Photo-Realistic Single Image Super-Resolution Using a Generative Adversarial Network. *arXiv*.

Lee, J. D., Simchowitz, M., Jordan, M. I., & Recht, B. (2016). Gradient Descent Converges to Minimizers. *arXiv*.

Li, C., Liu, H., Chen, C., Pu, Y., Chen, L., Henao, R., & Carin, L. (2017). ALICE: Towards Understanding Adversarial Learning for Joint Distribution Matching. *Advances in Neural Information Processing Systems. arXiv*.

Luc, P., Couprie, C., Chintala, S., & Verbeek, J. (2016). Semantic Segmentation using Adversarial Networks. *arXiv*.

Mescheder, L., Nowozin, S., & Geiger, A. (2017). Adversarial Variational Bayes: Unifying Variational Autoencoders and Generative Adversarial Networks. *arXiv*.

Mirza, M., & Osindero, S. (2014). Conditional Generative Adversarial Nets. *arXiv*.

Palazzo, S., Spampinato, C., Kavasidis, I., Giordano, D., & Shah, M. (2017). Generative Adversarial Networks Conditioned by Brain Signals, [electronic resource]. Retrieved from http://openaccess.thecvf.com/content_ICCV_2017/papers/Palazzo_Generative_Adversarial_Networks_ICCV_2017_paper.pdf (access date: 21.10.2018).

Radford, A., Metz, L., & Chintala, S. (2015). Unsupervised Representation Learning with Deep Convolutional Generative Adversarial Networks. *arXiv*.

Reed, S., Akata, Z., Yan, X., Logeswaran, L., Schiele, B., & Lee, H. (2016). Generative adversarial text to image synthesis. *arXiv*.

Ren, S., He, K., Girshick, R., & Sun, J. (2015). Faster R-CNN: Towards Real-Time Object Detection with Region Proposal Networks. Advances in Neural Information Processing Systems. *arXiv*.

Theis, L., van den Oord, A., & Bethge, M. (2015). A note on the evaluation of generative models. *arXiv*.

Chapter 6
Design of Avatars With "Differential" Logic:
The "Internal Bifurcation" Approach

Serge V. Chernyshenko

iD https://orcid.org/0000-0002-2852-6878

Open University for the Humanities and Economics, Russia

ABSTRACT

The chapter is devoted to the analysis of possibilities in designing dynamic properties of avatars in multi-agent systems. It is shown that determination of "differential logic" of avatars, based on the use of differential equations, gives sufficient flexibility in describing their behavior over time. At the same time, the differential description usually involves a smooth response of the object to external or internal influences, which for avatars is usually not correct. To eliminate this weak point, it is proposed to use the technology of internal bifurcations, which allows to simulate discontinues effects in the avatar dynamics. It is shown that even when using relatively simple quadratic models of the Lotka-Volterra type, the technique allows to describe rather complex information interactions in the multi-agent systems.

INTRODUCTION

The power of avatar-based technologies in many applied fields, such as digital management systems, knowledge bases, big data, decision making systems and so on, is well known. The team from Australia, Armenia, Russia and Ukraine, the author belongs to (Mkrttchian et al., 2016; Mkrttchian et al., 2019), proposed a set of approaches to development of avatar-based management using blockchain technology

DOI: 10.4018/978-1-7998-1581-5.ch006

for implementation of economic solutions on different levels. It is a way to identify a avatar-based model as a tool for policy advice. An empirical basis was collected mainly during realization of the recently completed project "Triple H Avatar an Avatar-based Software Platform for HHH University, Sydney, Australia which was carried out 2008-2018" (Mkrttchian et al., 2016). Elaborated models were based on avatars and unified macro and micro levels of the simulating process. It was an attempt to propose a single platform for solving problems in various areas of the digital economic system. Possibility to scale simulations for a set of economy-involved avatars and to provide graphical user interfaces allows to the digital system to serve researchers, who are not familiar with the technical details of the model realization. It allows also designing special parts of used model for numerical experiments and analysis of modeling results.

In the same time, an optimal internal structure of the used avatars is the open problem. It is clear, that, additionally to ability of synchronization with external actors, the avatars should have an individual characteristics of behavior, including mechanisms of learning (with corresponding learning curve (Acorn, 1985; Chernousenko et al., 1988) and artificial intelligence. Special algorithms of transmission of inputs to outputs have to be proposed. One of possible ways is to use, for determination of these algorithms, a number of well-known models of the decision-making process, based on classical differential equations. It can be models with linear transmission functions, or quadratic ones, like Lotka-Volterra models. A weak point of such approach is a pure continuous character of behaviour of such avatars; particularly, they reactions for small impacts will be also small. It is not a good property for the avatars; they should have in many cases "information reaction", when small, but special impact can produce very intensive reaction of an avatar.

The article is devoted to consideration of mathematical aspects of constructing avatars with logic of behavior, based on differential equations, but, in the same time, demonstrating pseudo-discrete properties (Chernyshenko, 1997). A main used concept is "internal bifurcation" (Chernyshenko, 2006), a tool, which generalizes ideas of the catastrophe theory from models' external properties to internal ones. An example, a system of two interacting avatars can be considered.

BACKGROUND

Effectiveness of computer simulating business processes, particularly, with use of such modern approaches as avatars, big data and so on, is considered in numerous scientific publications. A review of works, devoted to this topic, can be found in the articles ((Natalicchio et al., 2017; el al, 2017; Spender et al, 2017) et al., 2017).. The considered ideas can be used as a basis of the logic of the functioning of avatars; there are interesting approaches, sometimes implemented in the form of ready-made algorithms (Cegarra et al., 2015; Gambal et al.,2018; Sjödin et al., 2018; West, Bogers, 2014).

Computer intelligent agents ("avatars" in the context) are very popular objects in computer science last decades (Dawid & Fagiolo, 2008; Ferber, 1999). Avatar-based approach to decision-making in economy and politics becomes very popular also (Arifovic et al., 2010; Dawid & Fagiolo, 2008; LeBaron & Winker, 2008). A specification of avatar inputs/outputs is in focus of a specific application researches; thus, special "Triple H Avatars" were proposed for the considering problem in (Mkrttchian, 2015).

Process of interaction of avatars each other and with their environment can be used for forming "self-developing" information systems of various profiles (Maiyya et al, 2018; Mohan, 2017). It can be a part of knowledge base technology, which is a separate and also rapidly developing part of the computer science (Krishna, 1992; Natalicchio et al., 2017 el al, 2017).

The intelligent avatar has a mechanism of a trigger switch that allows it to connect inter-organizational processes with web services. The trigger property provides an ability to implement intelligent built-in control at certain points in the digitalized process (Mkrttchian, et al, 2016). The engineering realization of this advance is still nascent. For example, intelligent enforcing the process execution in a trustworthy way can be generated from a special avatar models (Mkrttchian, and Aleshina, 2017).

Multi-agent models are another important trend in computer science researches (Ferber, 1999; Gilbert & Troitzsch, 2005). The technology is useful for forming an "environmental" algorithm, merges the agents into a system, and for organizing an effective computations, including selection of software tools.

Design of avatars with "differential logic" is closely connected not with "internal bifurcation" concept only, but with concept of "logical complexity". Linear behavior has zero complexity; variety of internal bifurcations creates complexity of the avatar.

Interaction of elements of majority of real systems is certainly non-linear and rather complex (Svirezhev, 2001). "Sketch" or "conceptual" (Troitzsch, 1994) models reflect some rather precisely determined laws of interaction of system elements in a form of mathematical relations. A classical example is Lotka-Volterra models (Lotka, 1925; Volterra, 1931], describing interactions of the "predator–prey" or competition types. They can describe quite well dynamics of simple nature systems (Maynard Smith, 1974), and sense of their coefficients is rather transparent. At the same time, such models are not applicable to the description of really complex objects. In the same time, the complexity of big systems can be often "decompose" to a set of interacting less complex "sub-models". There is a view that finally, after such decomposition, one can fix several basic types of relatively simple models. Each the simple model is called as a "model of a universal unit", which reflects corresponding "dynamical stereotype" (Bossel, 1994).

THE CONCEPT OF INTERNAL BIFURCATION

A matter of special interest is investigating internal reorganisations of the avatar, both under influence of changing external parameters and as a result of internal processes. For differential models an appropriate mathematical tool is methods of the theory of bifurcations (or catastrophes) (Thom, 1972). For the investigation of internally initiated bifurcation, a new conception of "internal bifurcation" is proposed in (Chernyshenko. 2015). The bifurcation means the change of phase space topology after passing by an external (maybe, vectorial) "bifurcation parameter" through a critical value or surface. The "internal bifurcation" means a change of topology of some m-dimensional subspace of n-dimensional phase space (originated by m phase coordinates) after passing by other n-m coordinates through some "critical" surface.

In other words, the classical bifurcation concept presumes that one can observe salutatory, irreversible changes in ecosystem behaviour when certain external parameters (for example, aqueous or temperature characteristics) pass through some critical values. The internal bifurcation extends this concept to the case, when *internal* parameters of the system pass through a critical value (for example, size of a first population), and, as a result, other internal parameters (size of a second population) change their steady values.

This generalisation of the bifurcation concept seems useful, because it is not always simple to divide systems parameters into external and internal. If in the focus of investigation there is an internal structure of the ecosystem, connected with mutual non-linear interaction of elements or subsystems, the classical bifurcation concept, strictly speaking, is inapplicable.

Estimation of "complexity" of the dynamic system (Casti, 1979; Davies, 1988) can be based on the number of internal bifurcations in some characteristic area of the phase space. This number depends not only on mathematical complexity of the system model (dimension of the system, its order, degree of polynomials in the polynomial case, etc.), but even on functional relations, existing between numerical parameters of the equations.

INTERNAL BIFURCATIONS IN DIFFERENTIAL MODELS

Quite often the system is described by a set of ordinary differential equations of the first order, represented in the normal Cauchy form:

$$\frac{dx_i}{dt} = f_i\left(x_1, \ldots, x_n\right), i = \overline{1, n}.$$

(1)

For use the model (1) for avatar's description, the variables x_i can be interpreted as a internal characteristics of the avatar's stay.

In the two-dimensional case only one form of the internal bifurcation is possible: the change of topology of a one-dimensional phase space of the first coordinate, when the second coordinate passes through some critical value (or vice versa). For the first equation, considering separately, the standard bifurcation method can be applied, when x_2 is interpreted as an external parameter. The equilibrium points

$$\phi_1\left(x_2\right), \phi_2\left(x_2\right), \ldots, \phi_{m\left(x_2\right)}\left(x_2\right)$$

are sought from the equation

$$f_1\left(\phi_j\left(x_2\right), x_2\right) \equiv 0, j = \overline{1, m\left(x_2\right)}.$$

Then it is necessary to investigate steadiness of the points and to find values of x_2, for which the value $m(x_2)$ changes or the points ϕ_j change their topological properties. Similarly, the consideration of the second equation separately gives the possibility to find the critical values $\left\{\overline{x_1}^{-(i)}; i = \overline{1, k_1}\right\}$ of the first coordinate.

As a quantitative estimation of complexity one can use a pair of numbers (k_1, k_2) or their sum. Restrictions of the values of phase coordinates are typical for most real systems. For instance, in mathematical ecology, the variable x_i usually means biomass or population density, therefore, $x_i \geq 0$. Critical values $\overline{x}_i$ should be determined in this special area only, so the values k_1 and k_2 will appear, probably, smaller. The complexity of the system behaviour is not interesting under unrealistic values of coordinates.

In a multidimensional case, the group of coordinates can be selected by a natural way (for example, it can be the "slowest" coordinates), and they are considered as bifurcation parameters for other coordinates. If the system has a hierarchic nature, the internal bifurcations can be considered as a result of subsystems interaction, etc.

The analysis of critical regimes and singularities of the parametric space can be used to reveal "acupuncture points", where small local perturbations provoke a great large-scale metamorphosis of the object. A spectrum of quasi-stationary solutions is realised as a set of possible forms of morphogenesis. The discarded forms are still within system's reach but remain dormant, unknown to observers in the course of its evolution.

The role of information flows in the functionality of natural and artificial systems is universally recognised. And, at the same time, their special nature is not so clear. Even the term "information" is interpreted in scientific literature in various ways. The consideration has been started from the classical results of C. Shannon (1948) and J. von Neumann (1951), founders of the information theory. Then different directions of the generalisation of the term wewrw developed by different scientists. On the basis of a views about the nature of biological information (Beltrami, 1993) and the "energy criterion" (Bertalanffy, 1973), it is possible to interpret the model (1) with the "internal bifurcations" as a model information processes. Information interaction can be considered as a non-linear process of internal bifurcations. Information exchange inside the avatar (for example, between the program and its host) or between two avatars changes characteristics of its state discontinuously. It is a basic feature of any information interaction.

VOLTERRA-LIKE MODELS OF AVATAR FUNCTIONALITY

The usage of sketch models gives, particularly, a possibility to use different kinds of well-developed methods of qualitative analysis (Starfield et al., 1990). It is reasonable to use on the microlevel, as a "universal unit", a differential model of Volterra type, whose complexity can be regulated by the method of internal bifurcations adequately to real behaviour of an avatar.

For analysis of the two-dimensional Volterra's systems on the basis of the internal bifurcations concept, a special form is proposed

$$
\begin{cases}
\dfrac{dx_1}{dt} = -a_1 x_1 \left(x_1 - B_2 x_2 - K_1 \right), \\[2mm]
\dfrac{dx_2}{dt} = -a_2 x_2 \left(x_2 - B_1 x_1 - K_2 \right).
\end{cases}
\tag{2}
$$

Here for *i*-th avatar's characteristic: x_i is its value, a_i is its scale factor, K_i is its steady size, B_i – coefficient of influence on the other characteristic.

As the order of the right-hand member equals two, each of the equations can have only two equilibrium points: 0 and $B_i x_{3-i} + K_i$. It is shown that in any special case each equation has one critical (internal bifurcation) point, and the system can have four kinds of internal bifurcations: during forward and backward passing of the coordinate x_1 through the bifurcation value $-K_2 / B_2$ and the coordinate x_2 through the value $-K_1 / B_1$. Correspondingly, $k_1 = k_2 = 1$, and the system complexity can be evaluated as $(1,1)$ or 2.

Usually the Volterra's equations are surveyed only in the first quadrant (and, as it follows from the form of the equations right-hand members, the trajectories never cross the coordinate axes). Taking into account this fact, the complexity equals $(1,1)$ only when $K_1 \cdot B_1 < 0, K_2 \cdot B_2 < 0$. If $K_1 \cdot B_1 < 0$, $K_2 \cdot B_2 > 0$, the complexity equals $(1,0)$; if $K_1 \cdot B_1 > 0$, $K_2 \cdot B_2 < 0$ it is $(0,1)$; and, at last, for the case $K_1 \cdot B_1 > 0$, $K_2 \cdot B_2 > 0$ it is $(0,0)$. The comparison of these results with classical analysis of Volterra's equations (2) (Volterra, 1931; Takeuchi, 1996) shows, that the highest level of complexity takes place for the competitive and "predator–prey" relations.

A change in one of the state characteristics of the avatar at some point can cause crossing by another parameter of a critical value, and the behaviour of the corresponding component will get qualitative changes. Since the coordinate change can be very small, and the provoked changes in the state of the system, on the contrary, are significant, the interaction between the components can be attributed as information interaction.

As an example, let us consider the model (1) for the case of two internal bifurcations:

$$\begin{cases} \dfrac{dx_1}{dt} = \Phi_1 \left(x_1 - \phi_1^{(1)}(x_1, x_2) \right) \left(x_1 - \phi_2^{(1)}(x_1, x_2) \right), \\ \dfrac{dx_2}{dt} = \Phi_2 \left(x_2 - \phi_1^{(2)}(x_1, x_2) \right) \left(x_2 - \phi_2^{(2)}(x_1, x_2) \right). \end{cases} \tag{3}$$

If $\varphi_1^{(1)}(x_1, x_2) \equiv 0$; $\varphi_2^{(2)}(x_1, x_2) \equiv 0$ and the function $\varphi_2^{(1)}(x_1, x_2)$ и $\varphi_1^{(2)}(x_1, x_2)$ are linear, the system (3) can be classified as the Volterra's model (2). Thus, it can be used for study of informational interaction in the avatar within the Volterra description. The transition of an avatar characteristic through a critical value "signals" to the other characteristic about the need to change the trend of its dynamics.

There is another, slightly changed comparing with (3), form of the information interaction model with two characteristics:

$$\begin{cases} \dfrac{dx_1}{dt} = \left(x_2 - a_2\right)\Phi_1\left(x_1 - x_1^*\right)\left(x_1 - x_1^{**}\right), \\ \dfrac{dx_2}{dt} = \left(x_1 - a_1\right)\Phi_2\left(x_2 - x_2^*\right)\left(x_2 - x_2^{**}\right). \end{cases} \qquad (4)$$

Although qualitatively similar effects can be obtained for quadratic Volterra's systems, the cubic model (4) more clearly reflects the features of the information interaction. The equations for both x_1 and x_2 have a "trigger" character, since each coordinate can have two stable equilibrium positions - (x_1^*, x_1^{**}) and (x_2^*, x_2^{**}), respectively. After receiving a "message" about the transition of the other characteristic through the critical value a_i, the characteristic changes its equilibrium position. Coefficients ϕ_i evaluate the "reactivity" of the corresponding avatar "coordinate".

It seems that many models of systems dynamics, having a form different from (4), can be reduced to a similar form, which allows distinguishing in their structure links between their elements of informational nature.

CONCLUSION

The analysis of the potential informational properties of avatars, based on the technology of internal bifurcations, showed that the approach provides quite broad possibilities for constructing avatars with nonlinear discrete behaviour. Although the consideration concerned only the case when the state of the avatar is described by two characteristics only, even in this case, the complexity of avatar's behaviour, estimated by the number and structure of internal bifurcations, can be quite high.

The "differential logic" of the avatar is based on the use for determining its dynamic properties of differential equations systems with pseudo-discrete behaviour. The complexity of the behaviour logic cannot be high when using linear systems, however, the use of quadratic Volterra's equations provides enough number of degrees of freedom for choosing proper nonlinear effectors in the avatar behaviour.

ACKNOWLEDGMENT

The reported study was funded by RFBR according to the projects: N° 19-29-07545-мк, 20-010-00326-a.

REFERENCES

Acorn, A. G. (1981). Alternative learning curves for cost estimating. *Aeronautical Journal, 844*, 194–205.

Arifovic, J., Dawid, H., Deissenberg, C., & Kostyshyna, O. (2010). Learning Benevolent Leadership in a Heterogenous Avatars Economy. *Journal of Economic Dynamics & Control, 34*(9), 1768–1790. doi:10.1016/j.jedc.2010.06.023

Beltrami, E. (1993). *Mathematical models in the social and biological sciences.* Boston, MA: Jones & Bartlett.

Bertalanffy, L. (1973). *General system theory (foundation, development, application).* New York: Brazillier.

Bossel, H. (1994). *Modelling and simulation.* Wellesley, MA: A. K. Peters.

Casti, J. L. (1979). *Connectivity, complexity, and catastrophe in large-scale systems.* Chichester, UK: Wiley.

Cegarra, J., Soto-Acosta, P., & Wensley, A. (2015). Structured knowledge processes and firm performance: The role of organizational agility. *Journal of Business Research, 69.* . doi:10.1016/j.jbusres.2015.10.014

Chernousenko, V. M., Chernyshenko, S. V., & Chernenko, I. V. (1988). *Analysis of nonlinear models of distributed learning system.* Nonlinear and turbulent processes in physics. In *Proc. of the 3rd Intern. Workshop.* Kiev, Ukraine: Naukova Dumka. Vol. 1. pp. 239-243.

Chernyshenko, S. V. (1997). Discrete effects in dynamical differential models. Social Science Microsimulation: Tools for Modelling, Parameter Optimisation, and Sensitivity Analysis. Seminar report, Dagstuhl, Germany. pp. 29-30.

Chernyshenko, S. V. (2005). Monograph.

Davies, P. (1988). A new science of complexity. *New Scientist, 120*, 48–50.

Dawid, H., & Fagiolo, G. (2008). Avatar-based models for economic policy design: Introduction to the special issue. *Journal of Economic Behavior & Organization, 67*(2), pp. 351–354. doi:10.1016/j.jebo.2007.06.009

Ferber, J. (1999). *Multi-Agent Systems.* Addison-Wesley.

Gambal, M., Kotlarsky, J., & Asatiani, A. (2018). Enabling Strategic Technological Innovations in IS Outsourcing Relationships: Towards an Innovation-melding Framework. New York.

Gilbert, N., & Troitzsch, K. G. (2005). *Simulation for the Social Scientist* (2nd ed.). Open University Press.

Krishna, S. (1992). *Introduction to Database and Knowledge-base Systems*. Singapore: World Scientific Publishing. doi:10.1142/1374

Le Baron, B., & Winker, P. (2008). Introduction to the Special Issue on Avatar-Based Models for Economic Policy Advice. *Journal of Economics and Statistics, 228*.

Lotka, A. G. (1925). *Elements of physical biology*. Baltimore, MD: Williams and Wilkens.

Maiyya, S., Zakhary, V., Agrawal, D., & El Abbadi, A. (2018). Database and distributed computing fundamentals for scalable, fault-tolerant, and consistent maintenance of blockchains. *Proceedings of the VLDB Endowment*, 11. pp. 2098-2101. 10.14778/3229863.3229877

Maynard Smith, J. (1974). *Models in ecology*. Cambridge, MA: Cambridge University Press.

Mkrttchian, V. (2015). Modeling using of Triple H-Avatar Technology in online Multi-Cloud Platform Lab. In *Encyclopedia of Information Science and Technology* (pp. 4162–4170). Hershey, PA: IGI Global; doi:10.4018/978-1-4666-5888-2.ch409

Mkrttchian, V., & Aleshina, E. (2017). *Sliding Mode in Intellectual Control and Communication: Emerging Research and Opportunities*. Hershey, PA: IGI Global; doi:10.4018/978-1-5225-2292-8

Mkrttchian, V., Bershadsky, A., Bozhday, A., Kataev, M., & Kataev, S. (Eds.). (2016). *Handbook of Research on Estimation and Control Techniques in E-Learning systems*. Hershey, PA: IGI Global; doi:10.4018/978-1-4666-9489-7

Mkrttchian, V., Veretekhina, S., Gavrilova, O., Ioffe, A., Markosyan, S., & Chernyshenko, S. (2019). *The Cross-Cultural Analysis of Australia and Russia: Cultures, Small Businesses, and Crossing the Barriers // Industrial and Urban Growth Policies at the Sub-National, National, and Global Levels* (pp. 229–249). Hershey, PA: IGI Global; doi:10.4018/978-1-5225-7625-9.ch012

Mohan, C. (2017). Tutorial: blockchains and databases. In *Proceedings of the VLDB Endowment*, 10. pp. 2000-2011. 10.14778/3137765.3137830

Natalicchio, A., Ardito, L., Savino, T., & Albino, V. (2017). Managing knowledge assets for open innovation: A systematic literature review. *Journal of Knowledge Management, 21*. . doi:10.1108/JKM-11-2016-0516

Shannon, C. (1948). A mathematical theory of communication. *The Bell System Technical Journal, 27*(4), 379–423. doi:10.1002/j.1538-7305.1948.tb01338.x

Sjödin, D., Frishammar, J., & Thorgren, S. (2018). How Individuals Engage in the Absorption of New External Knowledge: A Process Model of Absorptive Capacity. *Journal of Product Innovation Management, 10.* 1111/jpim.12482.

Spender, J.-C., Corvello, V., Grimaldi, M. & Rippa, P. (2017). Startups and open innovation: a review of the literature. *European Journal of Innovation Management, 20.* pp. 4-30. . doi:10.1108/EJIM-12-2015-0131

Starfield, A. M., Smith, K. A., & Bleloch, A. L. (1990). *How to model it: Problem solving for the computer age.* New York: McGraw-Hill.

Svirezhev, Yu. M. (2001). *Thermodynamics and ecological modelling.* Berlin, Germany: Springer.

Takeuchi, Y. (1996). *Global dynamical properties of Lotka-Volterra systems.* Singapore: World Scientific. doi:10.1142/2942

Thom, R. (1972). *Structural stability and morphogenesis.* New York.

Troitzsch, K. G. (1994). Modelling, simulation, and structuralism. *Poznan Studies in the Philosophy of the Science and the Humanities, 42,* 159–177.

Volterra, V. (1931). *Leçons sur la theorie mathématique de la lutte pour la vie.* Paris, France: Gauthier-Villars.

von Neumann J. (1951). The general and logical theory of automata. Cerebral mechanisms of behavior. *The Hixon Symposium.* pp. 1-31. New York.

West, J., & Bogers, M. (2014). Leveraging external sources of innovation: A review of research on open innovation. *Journal of Product Innovation Management, 31*(4), 814–831. doi:10.1111/jpim.12125

Chapter 7
Optimizing the Production Parameters of Peasant Holdings for Industrial Development in the Digitalization Era

Andrey Tuskov

iD https://orcid.org/0000-0003-1760-2676
Penza State University, Russia

Anna Goldina

iD https://orcid.org/0000-0002-6483-2362
Penza State University, Russia

Olga Luzgina
Penza State University, Russia

Olga Salnikova
Penza State University, Russia

ABSTRACT

One of the determining factors for ensuring regional food security is the sectoral structure of production. It determines the specialization and combination of industries, on which the degree of tension, balance, and economic efficiency of the production program of peasant farming depends. This is achieved subject to the proportionality of the elements of the sectoral complex. For this, it is necessary to coordinate production volumes with available resources, the level of intensification of crop production and animal husbandry, the size of crops, individual crops, and livestock, etc. The size of peasant farms and their structure (the composition and area

DOI: 10.4018/978-1-7998-1581-5.ch007

of land, the combination and size of main and additional industries, the structure of crops) depend on many natural and economic factors. There are various options for the organization of production and territory for the same farming with certain resources of land, labor, and capital. The main task is to choose the optimal one that corresponds to the interests of the farmer and gives the maximum economic effect.

INTRODUCTION

The insufficient pace of overcoming negative processes in regional agriculture, and, consequently, strengthening regional food security, is largely due to the insignificance of direct state support for agriculture, as well as the low level of program-targeted planning and management of the development of the regional agricultural economy. This does not contribute to strengthening regional food security due to the lack of competitiveness of agricultural products in agricultural markets, and also determines the conditions for ensuring unbalanced development of the region.

One of the determining factors for ensuring regional food security is the sectoral structure of production, which determines the specialization and combination of industries, on which the degree of tension, balance and economic efficiency of the production program of peasant farming depends, which is achieved subject to the proportionality of the elements of the sectoral complex. For this, it is necessary to coordinate production volumes with available resources, the level of intensification of crop production and animal husbandry, the size of individual crops and livestock, etc.

The size of peasant farms and their structure (the composition and area of land, the combination and size of main and additional industries, the structure of crops) depends on many natural and economic factors. There are various options for the organization of production and territory for the same farming at quite certain resources of land, labor and capital. The main task is to choose the optimal one that corresponds to the interests of the farmer and gives the maximum economic effect.

LITERATURE REVIEW

Linear programming is methods that solve the problem of distributing limited resources between competing activities in order to maximize or minimize some numerical values, such as marginal profit or expenses. The beginning of modern stage in development of economic and mathematical modeling was laid by the academician A. N. Kolmogorov. He conducted modeling of economic phenomena and processes and developing of data analysis methods in traditions of the Soviet probabilistic and statistical scientific school. In 1946, A. N. Kolmogorov gave a geometric presentation of least squares method (Kolmogorov, 1946).

General problems of mathematical modeling of economic phenomena and systems are considered in the monographs of N.P. Buslenko (Buslenko, 1978), J. Kemeny and J. Snell (Kemeny and Snell, 1970), J. von Neumann and O. Morgenstern (Von Neumann and Morgenstern,1944) and others.

Today linear programming at all and least squares method in particular is popular not only in practical research, it is used to manage and value early or multiple exercise real options. In business, it can be used in areas such as production planning to maximize profits, selecting components to minimize costs, selecting an investment portfolio to maximize profitability, optimizing the transport of goods to reduce distances, distributing staff to maximize work efficiency and scheduling work in in order to save time. But also it can be used in theoretical researches. A. Ahn and M. Haugh have researched using of linear programming in control of diffusion processes (Ahn and Haugh, 2015). S. Nadarajah and N. Secomandi have studied relationship between least squares Monte Carlo and approximate linear programming. Their research in this area has started applying approximate linear programming and its relaxations, which aim at addressing a possible linear programming drawback (Nadarajah and Secomandi, 2017).

Linear programming is used in various areas of economy when make economic and mathematical modeling. So Iranian scientists H. Zohali, B. Naderi and M. Mohammadi use linear programming to build mathematical models at economic lot scheduling problem in limited-buffer flexible flow shops. They developed two new mixed integer linear programming models for the problem. Fruit fly optimization algorithm is developed to effectively solve the large problems and the proposed algorithm is also evaluated by comparing with two well-known algorithms (tabu search and genetic algorithm) in the literature and adaption of three recent algorithms for the flexible flow shop problem (Zohali, Naderi and Mohammadi, 2019).Swedish scientists M. R. Hesamzadeh, O. Gallandand D. R. Biggar used linear programming for modeling short-run economic dispatch. Three stages model the state of power system before, during, and after contingency occurred, because the higher the cost of responding to contingencies ex post the greater the need there is to distort the ex ante operation of the power system (Hesamzadeh, Galland and Biggar, 2014).

Also linear programming is used in agriculture area for designing of optimal decision-making algorithm for fertilization by Chinese scientists J. Wang, J. Dong, Y. Wang, J. He and O. Changgi. Aiming to solve the problem of crop yield forecasting and accurate fertilization, they presented the method based on optimized design ideas about fertilization decision-making (Wang, Dong, Wang, He and Changgi, 2011).

American scientists Zh. Chen, A. Roze, F. Prager and S. Chatterjeein 2017 made economic consequence analysis used computable general equilibrium modeling and linear programming in sphere of aviation system disruptions caused by terrorist attacks. Statistical analysis is applied to the "synthetic data" results in the form of both ordinary least-squares and quantile regression. The analysis yields linear equations that are incorporated into a computerized system and utilized along with Monte Carlo simulation methods for propagating uncertainties in economic consequences(Chen, Rose, Prager and Chatterjee, 2017).

Linear programming is also used in agriculture. Different methods of modeling and linear programming can be used in many spheres of medicine science, for example population-based modeling for analysis of amyotrophic lateral sclerosis as multistep process. Authors regressed the log of age-specific incidence against the log of age with least squares regression and did the analyses within each register, and also did a combined analysis, adjusting for register (Al-Chalabi, Calvo, Chio, Colville and Pearce, 2014). Spanish scientists F.-J. Santonja, E. Sánchez, M. Rubio and J.-L. Morera made mathematical modeling in alcohol consumption in Spain and its economic cost. Predictions about the future behavior of the alcohol consumption in Spain are presented using this model and linear programming (Santonja, Sánchez, Rubio and Morera, 2010). W. Cheng, L. Su, Sh. Chen, T. Li and H. Lin examined the economic burden of diabetes mellitus on medical expenditure among patients with respiratory failure requiring mechanical ventilation during hospitalization. They performed independent t-tests, chi-square tests, and multivariate linear regression analysis to identify factors associated with excess medical expenditure (Cheng, Su, Chen, Li and Lin, 2014).

MAIN FOCUS OF THE CHAPTER

Issues, Controversies, Problems

The developed economic and mathematical models of optimization of the production structure of peasant (farm) holdings are fully adapted to market conditions, have flexibility, as they may be added by new blocks and sub-blocks, depending on the need. Therefore, it is advisable to use them to determine the rational production and economic parameters of peasant (farm) holdings not only in the Penza region, but also in other regions.

SOLUTIONS AND RECOMMENDATIONS

The authors solved five variants of this problem. To select an optimal size of farm, it is necessary to analyze the decision of each variant.

Table 1. Structure of croplands in farms with different sizes

Crop	1 Variant		2 Variant		3 Variant		4 Variant		5 Variant	
	ha	%	ha	%	ha	%	ha	%	ha	%
Winterwheat	11.2	11.2	22.1	11.1	33.6	11.2	44.8	11.2	56	11.2
Winterrye	11.3	11.3	21.4	10.7	33.9	11.3	47	11.75	55	11
Springwheat	4.3	4.3	10.7	5.4	13.3	4.4	6.6	1.65	34	6.8
Barley	0.5	0.5	0.5	0.3	1.2	0.4	1.5	0.37	2.3	0.46
Millet	5.7	5.7	11.3	5.7	17	5.7	22.7	5.68	28	5.6
Oats	0.9	0.9	2.2	1.1	2.48	0.8	1.5	0.37	2.3	0.46
Peas	29	29.0	58	29.0	87	29.0	116	29	145	29
Buckwheat	0	0.0	0	0.0	0	0.0	0	0	0	0
Sugarbeet	9.7	9.7	19.3	9.7	29	9.7	38.8	9.7	39	7.8
Sunflower	9.5	9.5	19	9.5	28.5	9.5	38	9.5	47.5	9.5
Feedcrops	17.9	17.9	35.5	17.8	54	18.0	83.1	20.78	91	18.2
Total	100	100.0	200	100.0	300	100	400	100	500	100

(Source: authors' calculations)

The resulting structure of croplands is as follows.

In the structure of cropland, the share of grain and leguminous crops accounts for almost 60% of total tillage, tilled perennial and annual grasses occupy respectively 20% each. The high proportion of pea crops is mainly due to the fact that it is an excellent predecessor for subsequent crops, since this structure does not provide for the allocation of areas for pure steam. The proposed models of farms provide full plowing of tillage.

Crop focus activities of farms was provided in the models. The volume of feed production was determined in accordance with the scientifically-based norms of their consumption for the structural head and standard diets. Guaranteed supply of livestock needs in feed was achieved as a result of problem solving. In these problem s, it is envisaged that the products of the livestock industry are completely spent on the own needs of the farming family. This is illustrated more clearly inFigure 1

Optimal variants offer the following gross output.

With increase in farms size, volumes of production are also increasing. So if in the first of proposed variants only 1826 centners in bunker weight of grain were produced, then in the fifth one there were already 9548.5 centners or 5.3 times more. A similar situation can be traced with production of sugar beet and sunflower seeds. However, to compare the effectiveness of proposed variants, it is advisable to analyze the gross output per 100 hectares of cropland.

Figure 1. The structure of cropland in the proposed models
(Source: authors' calculations)

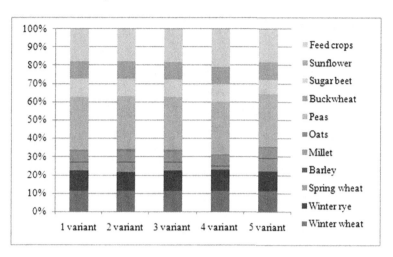

Table 2. Production of gross output, center

Products	1 Variant	2 Variant	3 Variant	4 Variant	5 Variant
Grain in bunker weight, total, including:	1826	3676	5480	7285.5	9548.5
winterwheat	322.5	645.4	968	1290.5	1613.6
winterrye	310.1	586.9	930.3	1290	1517.6
springwheat	179.3	447.8	555.5	735.4	1429.4
barley	18.7	19.7	47.2	63	92.3
millet	213.3	426.6	640	853.2	1066.5
oats	33	50.8	91	56.4	82.7
peas	754	1508	2262	3016	3770
buckwheat	0	0	0	0	0
Sugarbeet	2902.5	5779	8707	11639	11713.5
Sunflower	33.2	66.5	100	133	166

(Source: authors' calculations)

Figure 2. Production of gross output per 100 hectares of cropland
(Source: authors' calculations)

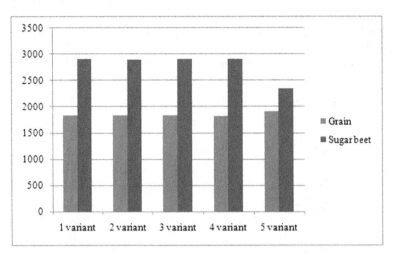

Table 3. Production of commercial products, center

Products	1 Variant	2 Variant	3 Variant	4 Variant	5 Variant
Commercialgrain, total, including:	1454.2	2958	4378	5816	7631.5
winterwheat	275.3	551	826	1101.6	1377.4
winterrye	261.3	494.5	783.8	1086.9	1278.6
springwheat	155	386.8	480	635.2	1234.6
barley	0	0	0	0	0
millet	191.3	382.7	574	765.3	956.7
oats	14.5	29.6	43.8	0	0
peas	556.8	1113.6	1670.4	2227.2	2784
buckwheat	0	0	0	0	0
Sugarbeet	2902.5	5779	8707	11639	11713.5
Sunflower	33.2	66.5	100	133	166

(Source: authors' calculations)

Based on 100 hectares of cropland, the largest amount of grain products was obtained when solving the fifth variant of the proposed task - 1909.7 C. Therefore, given size of farm, production of grain products is the most efficient (the share of winter crops is 32.8% of the total amount of grain produced). The production of

Table 4. The structure of commercial products in the proposed models

Products	1 Variant		2 Variant		3 Variant		4 Variant		5 Variant	
	thousandrubles	%	thousandrubles	%	thousandrubles	%	thousandrubles	%	thousandrubles	%
Winterwheat	54.3	8.4	118.7	9.1	164.8	8.5	211.5	8.1	322	10.7
Winterrye	47.8	7.4	92.6	7.1	143.5	7.4	200.6	7.7	238.1	7.9
Millet	26.6	4.1	53.2	4.1	79.8	4.1	106.4	4.1	133	4.4
Peas	230.5	35.6	461	35.5	691.5	35.5	922.1	35.5	1153	38.1
Sugarbeet	275.7	42.6	549	42.2	827.2	42.5	1105.7	42.6	1113	36.8
Sunflower	12.8	2.0	25.5	2.0	38.4	2.0	51.1	2.0	63.8	2.1
Total	647.7	100.0	1300	100.0	1945.2	100.0	2597.4	100.0	3022.3	100.0

(Source: authors' calculations)

Table 5. Production costs necessary to implement the proposed projects

Resources	1 Variant	2 Variant	3 Variant	4 Variant	5 Variant
Mineral fertilizers, total, c including:	78.2	156.6	234.4	311	404.1
nitric	27.7	55.7	83	109.5	144.1
phosphoric	20.6	40.7	62	83.3	104.1
potash	30.2	60.9	90.6	119.5	157.9
Organicfertilizers, t	63.9	128.1	192	256.2	320.4
Meansofprotection, kg	333.1	671.1	999.4	1325.8	1756.4
Fuel, c	735.5	1465.1	2206.6	2948.5	3011
Laborcosts, man-hours	2011.4	4008.7	6034.5	8062.4	8934.4
Cash, rubles	390280	780560.1	1170840	1561120	1786400

(Source: authors' calculations)

sugar beet per 100 hectares of cropland (or tillage, as the task provides for complete plowing of the land plot) differs sharply from the first four options by an average of 560 C. The maximum gross output of sugar beets is observed in farms with sizes ranging from 301 to 400 hectares. The production of sunflower seeds per 100 hectares of cropland has the same size in all the proposed options - 33.2 C. This is illustrated more clearly in Figure 2.

Comparing the data from the two tables, it can be concluded that the grain is sold by 80%. At the same time the barley is consumed completely for feed purposes. In 4 and 5 variants, oats are used for fodder purposes. Sugar beet and sunflower are sold in full.

Table 6. Structure of products sales through various channels, thousand rubles

	Soldtotal	includingsaleschannels			
		procurementorganizations	on a market	topopulation	onbartertransactions
1 variant	647.7	257.8	340.6	-	49.3
2 variant	1300	515.6	685.8	-	98.6
3 variant	1945.2	773.4	1023.9	-	148.0
4 variant	2597.4	1031.2	1368.9	-	197.3
5 variant	3022.3	1289	1486.7	-	246.6

Source: authors' calculations

Analyzing the structure of commercial products in the proposed variants, it can be concluded that farms retain grain-beet specialization. In the first four variants of the solution, a high proportion of sugar beets in the structure of commercial products is preserved (over 42%). In the last variant received, its share decreased by almost 6%. At the same time, an increase in weight of winter crops occurred by almost 3%, of peas by 2.6%. Also in the latter variant, the highest proportion of commercial sunflower is marked - 2.1%. At this stage of economic development, such specialization is most beneficial for farms. But as the authors have already said above, a certain specialization can be recommended to these types of farms only at this stage of economic development, since at the moment the production and sale of these particular types of products is the most effective direction of production activity.

Part of the need for organic fertilizers in the farm can be met through own production. Fertilizer cost can be reduced by rational organization of agriculture.

Thus, in order to organize an effective farm in the Penza region at present, it is necessary to have available from 390 thousand rubles up to 1786 thousand rubles depending on the size of the farm being created.

In creating the economic-mathematical model, product sales were provided through various channels. As a result of solution, the optimal variant is offered by the following sales structure.

In the proposed variants, the largest number of products sold on a market. The sale channel "population" (or in payment of labor) is inefficient. This is explained by the fact that a farmer is trying to make the whole volume of necessary work on its own, without attracting hired power. For barter transactions from 7.5 to 8% of commercial products is sold. The remaining products are sold through procurement organizations.

Table 7. Economic efficiency in the proposed models

Indicator	1 Variant	2 Variant	3 Variant	4 Variant	5 Variant
Revenue, rubles	647705.8	1300025.8	1945271.7	2597380.2	3022280.9
Productioncosts, rubles	390280	780560.1	1170840	1561120	1786400
Profit, rubles	257425.7	519465.7	774431.7	1036260.2	1235880.9
Profitabilityofproductionactivities, %	66.0	66.6	66.1	66.4	69.2
Profitabilityofsale, %	39.7	40.0	39.8	39.9	40.9

Source: authors' calculations

Figure 3. Dependence of profitability level of production costsvalue
(Source: authors' calculations)

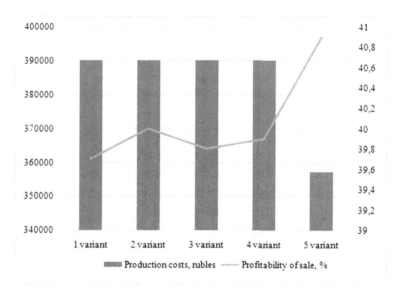

Profitability indicators most fully characterize the efficiency of work as a whole, since their value shows the ratio of the effect to the available or consumed resources.

According to obtained results, the largest mass of profit the farm has with size of land plot on 401-500 ha. The profitability of production activities in this group is on average 3% higher compared to other variants, the profitability of sales is also the highest. The latter indicator has been widely used in a market economy.

Farms with land use sizes of 101–200 hectares are the most efficient compared to other farm types (except for the last variant). The graph below shows the dependence of profitability level on value of production costs. Practically with equal costs per

Figure 4. Dependence of profitability level on total costs and credit amount per 100 hectares of cropland
(Source: authors' calculations)

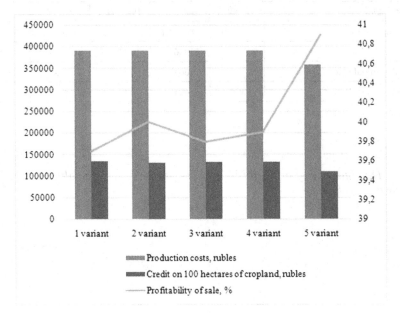

100 hectares in the first four variants, the highest level of profitability is observed in farms with sizes ranging from 101 to 200 hectares. In the last variant of obtained solution, with the lowest expenditure per 100 hectares of cropland, the highest level of profitability was noted. This is illustrated more clearly in Figure 3.

From all the above, following conclusion can be drawn. At the present stage of development, with prevailing market conditions and prices for agricultural products, grain-beet specialization is most effective for the conditions of Penza region. The volume of livestock production is determined by personal needs of farms. If profitability level is taken as criterion of optimal farm size, then the best for Penza region will be farms with sizes from 401 to 500 hectares (with profitability level of 69.2%). On the "second place" are farms with sizes from 101 to 200 hectares (profitability level is 66.6%). If, however, profit is taken as criterion of optimality, then farms with sizes from 401 to 500 hectares should also be considered the most optimal. The general condition for all farms of Penza region, in authors opinion, is to overcome the critical size of 100 hectares.

Because these models provide for an optimal combination of all available resources, they should be proposed for practical application as the basis for formation of optimal production and economic parameters of farms.

Unfortunately, none of the proposed variants of profit is not enough to fully cover of production costs in the next year. In this regard, farmers will need to take credits.

Currently, commercial banks do not show a desire to work with agricultural producers, especially with such small units as farms. In this case, political aspect is manifested not so much economic as.

If conditionally accept that all profits will go to cover the costs in the next year, the farmers of the first group need a credit in amount of 133 thousand rubles, the second - 261 thousand rubles, and the third - 396 thousand rubles, the fourth - 525 thousand rubles and the fifth - 551 thousand rubles. This is illustrated more clearly in Figure 4.The figure shows the relationship of profitability level with amount of funds spent on 1 hectare of cropland.

As the results of decision show, with a decrease in credit value per 100 hectares of cropland, level of profitability increases. Based on the law of diminishing marginal productivity of resource, with increase in this resource, profitability will decrease.

Financial and economic commercial organizations - banks, leasing companies, investment companies, wholesale trade organizations, etc. are inconvenient for small partners. The costs associated with their service, per thousand rubles of credit resources are much more expensive than when working with large partners. Small agricultural producers are also inconvenient for state officials involved in distribution of state support funds. When working with farmers, their paperwork increases many times over compared to large agricultural organizations. Moreover, for civil servants to "feed" from large organizations are simpler and more satisfying than from family farms that are stingy and geographically dispersed.

Political appeals for support of small agribusiness and even relevant laws run into indifference to commercial organizations and officials. Mainly because of this, farmers' quotas for state support are not implemented and prescriptions and rules of regulations and procedures for implementation of state support for peasant family farms do not apply.

It is hardly possible to change situation by improving procedures and instructions. World experience shows that situation can be partially corrected if, at legislative level, banks and other commercial organizations are interested in working with small businesses - creating tax or other benefits for them in economic relations with government. However, the same foreign experience shows that this problem is solved fundamentally when creating a financial-economic and trade-commercial infrastructure specific to small business.

Multidimensional econometric models describe the formation of several economic events and their indicators, with each equation of multidimensional model explaining the behavior of one indicator. Economic events explained by multidimensional model are represented by endogenous variables. Economic events that are not explained by model and are necessary for explaining endogenous variables are represented by exogenous variables. Endogenous variables without a time lag are called jointly interdependent; they are denoted as Y1, Y2, Ym. Endogenous variables with a time lag and exogenous variables are denoted as Z1, Z2, Zm.

The general form of multidimensional model in above notation can be represented as:

$$Y_1 = \sum_{i=2}^{m} \beta_{1i} Y_i + \sum_{j=1}^{k} \gamma_{1j} Z_j + \varepsilon_1$$

$$Y_2 = \sum_{\substack{i=1 \\ i \neq 2}}^{m} \beta_{2i} Y_i + \sum_{j=1}^{k} \gamma_{2j} Z_j + \varepsilon_2 \tag{1}$$

$$\dotfill$$

$$Y_m = \sum_{i=1}^{m-1} \beta_{mi} Y_i + \sum_{j=1}^{k} \gamma_{mj} Z_j + \varepsilon_m$$

where $\varepsilon_1, \varepsilon_2, \ldots \ldots \varepsilon_m$ - random deviations, β_{Ji}, γ_{ij} - model coefficients.

Let's introduce the following multidimensional model of form:

$$I_t = \beta_{13} P_t + \gamma_{11} I_{t-1} + \gamma_1 + \varepsilon_1$$
$$Z_t = \beta_{23} P_t + \gamma_{22} K_t + \gamma_2 + \varepsilon_2 \tag{2}$$
$$P_t = \beta_{32} Z_t + \gamma_{31} I_{t-1} + \gamma_3 + \varepsilon_3$$

based on the analysis of available data, where

I - investment costs for agriculture;
Z - number of employees in agricultural sector;
P - agricultural output;
K - cost of fixed assets.

Denote by X_i a variable that has a single value and is located at the parameters $\gamma_1, \gamma_2, \gamma_3$. Let's analyze and classify variables available in the model.

In the presented model, I, P, Z are endogenous variables, and K, X are exogenous variables. In turn, It, Pt, Zt are mutually interdependent, and It=1, Kt, Xt are predefined variables.

Consider the procedure for constructing a system of simultaneous equations using the two-stage least squares method (TSLS) in the Gretl package.

Table 8. Indicators for small farms of Penza region

T	I(t)	Z(t)	K(t)	P(t)	I(t-1)
2007	69954	5614	105300	27418	65322
2008	79118	5817	112332	29145	68932
2009	89361	5969	115995	28445	79118
2010	170185	10103	218123	144279	89361
2011	311460	14896	774991	399600	170185
2012	251915	15174	360260	362528	311460
2013	240318	16025	480205	315223	251915

(Source: authors' calculations)

The first way to implement TSLS in Gretlis done by selecting the menu item Model\Other Linear Models\Two-Stage Least Squares….

The second way is select Simultaneous Equations item in Model menu.

In the first case, the estimation of each equation there is one step at a time. In the second - the entire system is evaluated in one operation. In addition to TSLS method, Simultaneous Equations also provides other assessment methods, such as 3SLS, etc.

Baseline data set is presented in table 8.

Holding "Ctrl" button, note by click left mouse button variables Pt (production volume), Zt (employment) and It (investment volume), Kt (fixed assets). Then click right mouse button brings up context menu and select Time series plot, click next to OK.

From the graph it is clear that only the change in production volume shows pronounced positive trend for the analyzed period.

Select the Model\Other Linear Models\Two-Stage Least Squares menu item that activates the single equation specification window. In three segments of specification window using buttons Choose and Add for separate equation of model structural form it is necessary to determine:

1. Dependent variable – (endogenous) dependent variable (y) on the left side of equation;
2. Independent variables – all variables on the right side of equation;
3. Instruments – all predefined (exogenous and endogenous lagged) variables of the whole system.

The evaluation results of system using TSLS presented in tables 17.18 and 19 for the first, second and third equations, respectively.

The structural form of system will eventually take the form:

Table 9. Window of simulation results using TSLS for the first equation

Variable	Coefficient	Std. Error	z	P-Value	
const	5564.82	772.945	7.1995	<0.00001	***
P_t_	0.0331936	0.00695034	4.7758	<0.00001	***
K_t_	-0.00402718	0.00467836	-0.8608	0.38934	
Meandependentvar	10514.00		S.D. dependentvar	4799.069	
Sumsquaredresid	5993597		S.E. ofmodel	1224.091	
R-square	0.956627		Adjusted R-square	0.934940	
F(2, 4)	44.11134		P-value (F)	0.001881	
Log-likelihood	-57.74359		Akaikecriterion	121.4872	
Schwarzcriterion	121.3249		Hannan–Quinn	119.4816	
Parameterrho	-0.666511		Durbin–Watson	1.850248	

(Source: authors' calculations)
Model 2: TSLS, used the observations of 2007-2013 (T = 7)
Dependent variable: Z_t_
Instruments: constP_t_ I_t_1_ K_t_

Table 10. Window of simulation results using TSLS for the second equation

Variable	Coefficient	Std. Error	z	P-Value	
const	-160310	41294.8	-3.8821	0.00010	***
K_t_	0.146149	0.133386	1.0957	0.27322	
Z_t_	28.6975	6.7721	4.2376	0.00002	***
Meandependentvar	186662.6		S.D. dependentvar	168225.3	
Sumsquaredresid	5.01e+09		S.E. ofmodel	35379.62	
R-square	0.971039		Adjusted R-square	0.956559	
F(2, 4)	67.46102		P-value (F)	0.000829	
Log-likelihood	-214.0772		Akaikecriterion	434.1544	
Schwarzcriterion	433.9921		Hannan–Quinn	432.1487	
Parameterrho	-0.735095		Durbin–Watson	1.978256	

(Source: authors' calculations)
Model 3: TSLS, used the observations of 2007-2013 (T = 7)
Dependent variable: P_t_
Independent variables: K_t_ Z_t_
Instruments: const I_t_1_ I_t_

Table 11. Window of simulation results using TSLS for the third equation

Variable	Coefficient	Std. Error	z	P-Value	
const	81273	8073.88	10.0662	<0.00001	***
_t_	0.724139	0.0575696	12.5785	<0.00001	***
I_t_1_	-0.292184	0.0949222	-3.0781	0.00208	***
Meandependentvar	173187.3		S.D. dependent var	96924.31	
Sumsquaredresid	4.89e+08		S.E. of model	11055.31	
R-square	0.991604		Adjusted R-square	0.987406	
F(2, 4)	217.8362		P-value (F)	0.000083	
Log-likelihood	-154.7042		Akaike criterion	315.4085	
Schwarzcriterion	315.2462		Hannan–Quinn	313.4028	
Parameterrho	0.045166		Durbin–Watson	1.575028	

(Source: authors' calculations)
Model 4: TSLS, used the observations of 2007-2013 (T = 7)
Dependent variable: I_t_
Independent variables: P_t_
Instruments: const I_t_1_ Z_t_

$$I_t = 0,72 * P_t - 0,29 * I_{t-1} + 81273 + \varepsilon_1$$
$$Z_t = 0,033 * P_t - 0,004 * K_t + 5564,8 + \varepsilon_2$$
$$P_t = 28,7 * Z_t + 0,15 * K_t - 160310 + \varepsilon_3$$

Estimation results of first equation indicate that volume of agricultural production and volume of external borrowings of previous period have significant impact on volume of external borrowings (It), since, according to Student's t-test, parameters for these variables are statistically significant at significance level of 1% (***), because p-value values of 0.046% and 0.001% are less than 1%. In general, the model is adequate at significance level of 1%, since for Fisher's F-test p-value 0.001% is less than 1%.

Estimation results of second and third equations show that volume of production and values of farm assets have a significant impact on number of employees in agricultural sector, and output of farms greatly depends on number of employees and also from value of fixed assets. Volume of foreign borrowings of previous period does not have significant effect on total volume of agricultural production.

In general, the proposed model is adequate and suitable for practical calculations in field of small business.

FUTURE RESEARCH DIRECTIONS

In the transition to the Industry 4.0 paradigm, previously developed methods for optimizing production business processes remain relevant. The use of digitalization technologies will allow the use of such methods optimizations that were previously unavailable due to lack of necessary infrastructure. The choice of specific methods and technologies used remains with the company, as it may have its own strategic priorities and resource constraints. Only optimal the combination of implemented measures and their compliance with existing and future needs will allow companies to make cost-effective and efficient business optimization. Concerning practical applications, evaluation as a concept becomes more important for regional cluster initiatives, in particular, as well as other programs that contribute to the development of entrepreneurship for optimizing the production parameter of peasant holdings.

CONCLUSION

Estimation results of second and third equations show that volume of production and values of farm assets have a significant impact on number of employees in agricultural sector, and output of farms greatly depends on number of employees and also from value of fixed assets. Volume of foreign borrowings of previous period does not have significant effect on total volume of agricultural production. In general, the proposed model is adequate and suitable for practical calculations in field of small business.

Multidimensional econometric models describe the formation of several economic events and their indicators, with each equation of multidimensional model explaining the behavior of one indicator. Economic events explained by multidimensional model are represented by endogenous variables. Economic events that are not explained by model and are necessary for explaining endogenous variables are represented by exogenous variables.

REFERENCES

Ahn, A., & Haugh, M. (2015). Linear programming and the control of diffusion processes. *INFORMS Journal on Computing, 27*(4), 646–657. doi:10.1287/ijoc.2015.0651

Al-Chalabi, A., Calvo, A., Chio, A., Colville, A., & Pearce, N. (2014) Analysis of amyotrophic lateral sclerosis as a multistep process: a population-based modelling study. In The Lancet Neurology, pp. 1108-1113. doi:10.1016/S1474-4422(14)70219-4

Buslenko, N. P. (1978). *Modeling complex systems.* Moscow, USSR: Science.

Chen, Zh., Rose, A., Prager, F., & Chatterjee, S. (2017) Economic consequences of aviation system disruptions: A reduced-form computable general equilibrium analysis. In Transportation Research Part A: Policy and Practice, pp. 207-226. DOI: doi:10.1016/j.tra.2016.09.027

Cheng, W., Su, L., Chen, Sh., Li, T., & Lin, H. (2014) Economic Burden of Diabetes Mellitus on Patients with Respiratory Failure Requiring Mechanical Ventilation during Hospitalizations. In Value in Health Regional Issues, pp. 33-38. DOI: doi:10.1016/j.vhri.2014.02.003

Hesamzadeh, M. R., Galland, O., & Biggar, D. R. (2014). Short-run economic dispatch with mathematical modelling of the adjustment cost. In *International Journal of Electrical Power* (pp. 9–18). Energy Systems; doi:10.1016/j.ijepes.2013.12.020

Kemeny, J., & Snell, J. (1970). *Cybernetic Modeling.* New York: Some Applications.

Kolmogorov, A. N. (1946). Justification of least squares method. In Advances in Mathematical Science. pp. 57–70.

Mkrttchian, V. (2013). Training of Avatar Moderator in Sliding Mode Control Environment for Virtual Project Management. In Enterprise Resource Planning: Concepts, Methodologies, Tools, and Applications. IRMA (pp. 1376–1405). Hershey, PA: IGI Global. doi:10.4018/978-1-4666-4153-2.ch074

Mkrttchian, V. (2015). Modeling using of Triple H-Avatar Technology in online Multi-Cloud Platform Lab. In *Encyclopedia of Information Science and Technology* (pp. 4162–4170). Hershey, PA: IGI Global; doi:10.4018/978-1-4666-5888-2.ch409

Mkrttchian, V., Bershadsky, A., Bozhday, A., Kataev, M., & Kataev, S. (Eds.). (2016). *Handbook of Research on Estimation and Control Techniques in E-Learning Systems*. Hershey, PA: IGI Global; doi:10.4018/978-1-4666-9489-7

Nadarajah, S., & Secomandi, N. (2017) Relationship between least squares Monte Carlo and approximate linear programming. In Operations Research Letters, pp. 409-414. doi:10.1016/j.orl.2017.05.010

Popov, A. V. (2019). Business Process Optimization in the Digitalization Era of Production. In Strategic Decisions and Risk Management. pp. 28–35. DOI: doi:10.17747/2618-947X-2019-1-28-35

Santonja, F.-J., Sánchez, E., Rubio, M., & Morera, J.-L. (2010) Alcohol consumption in Spain and its economic cost: A mathematical modeling approach. In Mathematical and Computer Modelling, pp. 999-1003. doi:10.1016/j.mcm.2010.02.029

Von Neumann, J., & Morgenstern, O. (1944). *Theory of Games and Economic Behavior*. Princeton University Press.

Wang, J., Dong, J., Wang, Y., He, J., & Changqi, O. (2011) The design of an optimal decision-making algorithm for fertilization. In Mathematical and Computer Modelling, pp. 1100-1106. doi:10.1016/j.mcm.2010.11.041

Zohali, H., Naderi, B., & Mohammadi, M. (2019) The economic lot scheduling problem in limited-buffer flexible flow shops: Mathematical models and a discrete fruit fly algorithm. In Applied Soft Computing, pp. 904-919. DOI: doi:10.1016/j.asoc.2019.03.054

KEY TERMS AND DEFINITIONS

Endogenous Variable: A variable in a statistical model that's changed or determined by its relationship with other variables within the model. Endogenous factors are the opposite of exogenous variables, which are independent variables or outside forces.

Exogenous Variable: Is used for setting arbitrary external conditions, and not in achieving a more realistic model behavior. An exogenous variable is a variable that is not affected by other variables in the system.

Multidimensional Data Model: Is designed to solve complex queries in real time. The multidimensional data model is composed of logical cubes, measures, dimensions, hierarchies, levels, and attributes. The simplicity of the model is inherent because it defines objects that represent real-world business entities.

Optimization Methods: Often non-linear, non-convex, multimodal, and multidimensional, and might be expressed by both discrete and continuous variables, which makes this a difficult problem.

Peasant Farming: Refers to a type of small-scale agriculture.

Chapter 8
Peasant Farms and Industrial Development:
Mathematical Approach to Analysis and Planning

Andrey Tuskov

(iD) https://orcid.org/0000-0003-1760-2676
Penza State University, Russia

Viktor Volodin
Penza State University, Russia

Anna Goldina

(iD) https://orcid.org/0000-0002-6483-2362
Penza State University, Russia

Olga Salnikova
Penza State University, Russia

ABSTRACT

The authors propose a general formulation of the economic and mathematical model of the problem of optimizing the size of the newly created peasant farms and Industrial Development, taking into account the chosen specialization of activity, as well as determining the optimal parameters for the already-known size of farms. The developed mathematical model differs from the classical one by the presence of additional blocks, which prescribe the sales channels of manufactured products and determine the necessary financial resources. The proposed methodological approach should be used for planning the development of regional economies, taking into account the existing specifics.

DOI: 10.4018/978-1-7998-1581-5.ch008

INTRODUCTION

The only condition of highly efficient farming in Russia is to choose a rational production structure that takes into account market requirements, natural and economic conditions, providing the maximum realization of its opportunities. Further development of farming assumes creation of economic conditions for its formation: optimization of farms' land-use size; preservation and rational use available production potential (Fadeev, 2001).

The most effective way to determine the rational parameters in the peasant (farmer) holdings is the economic and mathematical modeling of their optimal production structure. Application of such methods allows considering a set of the specific conditions characteristic for a certain production system, to reflect interrelations between the production potential and results of economic activity, to balance the amount of production and volumes of production costs (Fadeev, 2001).

When developing the optimal size of farms is very important to choose its indicators. The main parameter characterizing the actual size of the farm is the volume and cost of gross output. Small farming, while remaining small in terms of land area, can turn into large by the amount of production. Consequently, the amount of land indicates the volume of production only indirectly, and "the value of the products produced by the farming speaks of its size not indirectly, but directly and in all cases'. The indicator will characterize the result of production in terms of the solving its main task – creations of consumer values, satisfactions of the growing needs of the market for products. However, when determining the optimal parameters of peasant farms, the task is to achieve the greatest volume of products at the lowest cost and the most efficient use of all available resources. A generalizing parameter of the effective use of production resources is profitability, which characterizes the profitability of production and is expressed in the presence of profit. It evaluates production in terms of satisfying the interests of the peasant economy itself, activates entrepreneurial activity, encourages the peasant to master new types of resources, machinery, technologies, expand and cheapen production, creates certain guarantees for the continued existence of the farm (Fadeev, 2001).

The size of peasant farms and their structure (the composition and area of land, the combination and size of main and additional industries, the structure of crops) depends on many natural and economic factors. There are various options for the organization of production and territory for the same farming at quite certain resources of land, labor and capital. The main task is to choose the optimal one that corresponds to the interests of the farmer and gives the maximum economic effect.

The task can have two main statements. The first is to determine the structure, composition and area of land, the optimal size of the production of various types of products based on the known area of the farm. The second statement is more complicated. It consists in determining the total area and structure of the farming and at the same time optimizing production, based on the size of the peasant family, its financial possibilities and the specific economic situation. It is possible to choose various development options that are optimal for a given situation with appropriate parameters and expected economic results by varying the resources of the farm, prices, qualitative characteristics of the fixed lands and other conditions (Anfimov, 1961).

BACKGROUND

Today linear programming at all and least squares method in particular is popular not only in practical research, it is used to manage and value early or multiple exercise real options. In business, it can be used in areas such as production planning to maximize profits, selecting components to minimize costs, selecting an investment portfolio to maximize profitability, optimizing the transport of goods to reduce distances, distributing staff to maximize work efficiency and scheduling work in in order to save time. But also it can be used in theoretical researches. A. Ahn and M. Haugh have researched using of linear programming in control of diffusion processes (Ahn and Haugh, 2015). S. Nadarajah and N. Secomandi have studied relationship between least squares Monte Carlo and approximate linear programming. Their research in this area has started applying approximate linear programming and its relaxations, which aim at addressing a possible linear programming drawback (Nadarajah and Secomandi, 2017).

Linear programming is used in various areas of economy when make economic and mathematical modeling. So Iranian scientists H. Zohali, B. Naderi and M. Mohammadi use linear programming to build mathematical models at economic lot scheduling problem in limited-buffer flexible flow shops. They developed two new mixed integer linear programming models for the problem. Fruit fly optimization algorithm is developed to effectively solve the large problems and the proposed algorithm is also evaluated by comparing with two well-known algorithms (tabu search and genetic algorithm) in the literature and adaption of three recent algorithms for the flexible flow shop problem (Zohali, Naderi and Mohammadi, 2019).Swedish scientists M.R.Hesamzadeh, O. Gallandand D.R. Biggar used linear programming for modeling short-run economic dispatch. Three stages model the state of power system before, during, and after contingency occurred, because the higher the cost of responding to contingencies ex post the greater the need there is to distort the ex-ante operation of the power system (Hesamzadeh, Galland and Biggar, 2014).

MAIN FOCUS OF THE CHAPTER

Issues, Controversies, Problems

The optimal number of industries in the farm and their rational combination is determined by the cumulative effect of many factors of specialization, which according to their focus are divided into two groups: some contribute to it, others – interfere.

In difficult market conditions, when farms are practically deprived of state support, farmers have to activate the search of internal reserves and opportunities to improve the efficiency and sustainability of their farms. For example, in terms of local conditions and own resources it is necessary to determine in reasonable way the sectorial structure and size of production, to develop low-cost technologies in accordance with their resource base, to develop economically sustainable models of economic organization. All of these are elements of the internal production structure, the optimization of which must be decided by the owners of the farms themselves.

In this chapter authors proposes economic and mathematical models for optimizing the production structure of peasant (farmer) holdings with the following types of specialization: milk-meat, beet-grain and grain, since they fully correspond to the actual (identified by us) specialization of these farms in the Penza region.

When developing economic and mathematical models, we used the recommendations on the rational combination of agricultural crops in crop rotations, developed by scientists of the Penza State Agricultural Academy for the conditions of the Middle Volga region. The definition of types and kinds of crop rotation, alternation of crops was made on the basis of the principles of cultivated plants' shift, self-compatibility, specialization, and compaction, economic and biological expediency.

It should be noted some features that must be taken into account in the development of economic and mathematical models for peasant (farm) holdings with dairy and meat specialization. The material and monetary costs per 1 hectare of forage lands can be determined either by multiplying the actual cost of feed by their yield or by calculating technological charts for these crops.

The cost of 1 head in livestock can be taken from actual (initial) data for peasant (farmer) holdings. They do not include feed costs, because the structure of feed consumption is determined in the problem through the structure of the acreage of fodder and grain feed crops. Designing the cost per livestock head can be done using process charts or technological maps.

The cost per 1 center of milk can also be taken from the initial data or be designed. They do not include feed costs.

The authors prepared the initial information on the basis of technological maps developed per 100 hectares of agricultural crops, and in livestock production – per 100 structural uterus.

The task was realized by means of the LINO program, developed by specialists of the Penza state agricultural academy. This program allows reproducing a simple method algorithm.

To write a mathematical model aimed at determining the optimal size of peasant (farmer) holdings with beet-grain and grain specialization, we should adopt the following notation:

$X(j)$ – the desired value of the j-th variable, denoting the calculated indicators of the crop area;

$X(j_1)$ - the desired value of the j-th variable denoting the calculated indicators (unknown amounts of resources);

$X(j_2)$ – production volume of the j-th type;

$X(j_3)$ – the volume of sales of the j-th type;

$X(j_4)$ – volume of monetary current assets;

$B(i)$ – volume of land resources of the i-th type;

$V(ij)$ – production costs per 1 ha of cultivation of j-crop;

$A(ij)$ – the cost of land resources of the i-th type per 1 hectare of sowing of the j-th culture;

α_{ij}, α_{ij} – ratios between different cultures;

$W(ij)$ – output of commercial products of i-th type from 1 ha of j-th culture;

N – set of variables, denoting all culture according to the degree of intensity of fertilizer application;

$N_{(1)}$ – set of variables, denoting resource costs;

$N_{(2)}$ – a set of variables, denoting manufactured products;

$N_{(3)}$ – a set of variables, denoting manufactured commercial products sold through various channels;

$N_{(4)}$ – a set of variables, denoting products sold through various channels

N_5 – availability of monetary current assets;

$M(1)$ – group of restrictions by area;

$M_{(2)}$ – group of restrictions by the ratio of grain crops;

$M_{(3)}$ – group of restrictions by the use of production resources;

$M_{(4)}$ – group of restrictions by n the sale of manufactured products;

$M_{(5)}$ – group of restrictions by material and monetary costs;

E_{j3} – the possible volume of sales of product j-th type at the j-th channel realization;

C_{j3} – sales price of the j-th type on the j_3 – channel.

The structural model at the symbols accepted above will have the following form:
Find the values of Xj, at which the objective function reaches an extreme value with the following restrictions:

1. by using of land resources

$$\sum_{j\in N_1} a_{ij} x_j = b_i \left(i \in M_1 \right)$$

2. by implementation the agro technical requirements of crops

$$\sum_{j\in N_1} X_j \begin{bmatrix} \geq \\ = \\ \leq \end{bmatrix} A_{ij} \left(i \in M_1 \right)$$

3. by definition of production costs

$$\sum_{j\in N_1} v_{ij} x_j = X_{j1} \left(i \in M_3 \right)$$

4. by the production of commercial products

$$\sum_{j\in N_2} W_{ij} X_j = X_{j2} \left(i \in M_2 \right)$$

5. by sales of manufactured products

$$\sum_{j\in N_4} X_{j2} = X_{j3} \left(i \in M_4 \right)$$

6. by sales of manufactured products, through various channels, according to demand

$$\sum_{j\in N_4} X_{j4} \leq E_{j4} \left(j \in M_4 \right)$$

7. by material and monetary costs

$$X_{j1} - \sum_{j \in N_5} X_{j4} \leq 0 \left(j \in M_5 \right)$$

8. by no negativity of variables

$$X_{j3} \geq 0, X_{j2} \geq 0, X_{j1} \geq 0, X_{j1} \geq 0, X_{j4} \geq 0,$$

The list of variables used in the task is given below.

The main feature of the developed economic and mathematical model in contrast to the classical model of the optimal combination of industries is its adaptation to market conditions. It provides for the optimization of sales channels of manufactured products, which allows to increase the profit of the peasant (farmer) holding. Also, this model has been supplemented with a block of the balance of current assets, which allows determining the amount of loans and credits

To write a mathematical model aimed at determining the optimal size of peasant (farm) holdings with dairy and meat specialization, the following designations should be adopted.

The economic and mathematical model has a block structure. The main blocks of the model are:

- Feed production block (sub-blocks: sowing areas, nutrient production, green conveyor belt, feed ration structures, ratio between subgroups of animals);
- livestock production block.

The first block covers the balance ratios on production of forages and number of cattle aimed at maximizing the profits of the enterprise. The second block characterizes the possible production and the corresponding costs

The system of variables of model includes:

- acreage of forage crops, land;
- the amount of feed received from commodity industries and purchased on the side;
- animal population by groups;
- the increment of feed by types;
- quantity of raw meat and milk;
- monetary costs.

Table 1. The system of variables used in solving the problem of optimizing the size of peasant (farm) holdings of the Penza region with beet-grain and grain specialization

Cultures, Products, Resources	Unit	Sown Area			Resources, Costs	Production	Selling			
		Commodity	Fodder	Seeds			To Procurement Organizations	On the Market	To People	On Barter Transactions
1	2	3	4	5	6	7	8	9	10	11
Winter wheat		X_1, X_2		X_{14}						
Winter rye		X_3, X_4		X_{15}						
Spring wheat		X_5		X_{16}						
Barley		X_6	X_{11}	X17						
Millet		X_7		X_{18}						
Oats		X_8	X_{12}	X_{19}						
Pea		X_9	X_{13}	X_{20}						
Buckwheat		X_{10}		X_{21}						
Sugar beet		X_{71}								
Cost: Fertilizers, total, including					X_{23}					
nitrogen					X_{24}					
potassium					X_{25}					
phosphate					X_{26}					
organic fertilizers					X_{27}					
Remedies					X_{28}					
Fuels and lubricants					X_{29}					
Labor					X_{30}					
Monetary assets					X31					
Production: Seeds						X22				
Grain in bunker weight, total, including						X32				
winter wheat						X33				
winter rye						X34				
spring wheat						X35				
barley						X36				
millet						X37				
oats						X38				

continued on following page

Table 1. Continued

Cultures, Products, Resources	Unit	Sown Area			Resources, Costs	Production	Selling			
		Commodity	Fodder	Seeds			To Procurement Organizations	On the Market	To People	On Barter Transactions
pea						X39				
buckwheat						X40				
fodder barley						X41				
fodder oats						X42				
fodder peas						X43				
sugar beet						X72				
Commodity grain, total, including						X44				
winter wheat						X45				
winter rye						X46				
spring wheat						X47				
barley						X48				
millet						X49				
oats						X50				
pea						X51				
buckwheat						X52				
Selling: winter rye							X53	X55		X54
wheat							X56	X57	X58	X59
barley								X60	X61	
millet							X62	X63		X64
peas							X65	X66	X67	X68
oats							X69	X70		
buckwheat								X52		
Own funds					X73					
The amount of credit					X74					

The model's restriction system consists of following restriction groups:

- on use of arable land and land grounds;
- on providing animals with nutrients and structure of feed rations;
- on the ratio between the sex and age groups of livestock;
- on the production of livestock products.

The objective function is the difference in revenue from the sale of finished products and the cost of production of finished products.

The mathematics of the model. Introduce the notations.

Indices and sets:

j - type of fodder crops and land (j $\in$ Y);

j 1- type of livestock (j, $\in$ Y1);

j 2- feed increments (j2 $\in$ Y2);

j 3- type of raw material (j3 $\in$ Y3);

j 4-type of costs (j4 $\in$ Y4);

i - index of lands of nutrients, groups of forages, production resources, types of raw materials;

Ai - the total number of i-th land, the permissible limit of individual crops;

Di— the volume of feed received from the commodity sectors;

M- set of land grounds;

M1 - set of nutrients;

M2 – set of various groups and animal types;

M3 - set of different types of raw materials;

Vij - output of i-th nutrient per 1 ha of j-th culture or output of i-th group of feeds per 1 ha of j-th culture;

dij1 - annual rate of feed consumption per head of j-th type of cattle;

aij1- the minimum rate of consumption of the i-th group of feed per 1 centner of the ji-th type of animal products or per 1 head of the j-th species of animals;

βij1 - the difference between the maximum and minimum consumption rates of the j-th feed group per unit of measurement of the j1 -th livestock industry;

Pji1 — the difference between the adopted rate of feed unit costs as a whole and the amount of the minimum allowable rate of feeding of all groups of feed per unit of measurement of the j1-th livestock industry;

vij1 - livestock productivity;

cj cj5, cj6 - sales price per unit of j-th type;

xj- variable indicating the area of cultivation of the j-th culture;

xj1 - the number of goals in the j1-th type;

xj2- the excess of the minimum amount of j1-th feed in the total livestock feeding structure;

xj3— amount of produced milk and meat raw materials;

xj4— monetary costs;

Defining of vector $X\{x; x\}$ under the conditions:

1. On the use of land resources:

$$\sum_{j \in J} x_j \leq A_i \left(i \in M \right)$$

2. On providing livestock with nutrients:

$$-\sum_{j \in J} V_{ij} Xj - \sum_{j1 \in J1} d_{ij1} X_{j1} \leq D_1 \left(i \in M_1 \right)$$

3. On the formation of the structure of feed resources:
    a. On feed balance

$$-\sum_{j \in J} V_{ij} Xj + \sum_{j1 \in J1} d_{ij1} X_{j1} + \sum_{j_2 \in J_2} X_{ij2} \leq 0$$

    b. On feed increment

$$-\beta_{ij_1} X_{j_1} + X_{ij_2} \leq 0$$

$$-\sum_{j1 \in J1} P_{ij1} X_{j1} + \sum_{j_2 \in J_2} X_{ij_2} = 0$$

According to the ratio between the groups of livestock:

$$X_{j1} = \lambda \cdot X_{ji}^1 \left(j_1, j_1^1 \in Y_1 \right)$$

On production:

$$\sum_{j_1 \in J_1} v_{ij_1} X_{j_1} = X_{j_3} \left(i \in M_3 \right)$$

No negativity of variables: $Xj \geq 0$ $Xj1 \geq 0$ $Xj2 \geq 0$ $Xj3 \geq 0$ $Xj4 \geq 0$ $Xj5 \geq 0$ $Xj6 \geq 0$
Target function statement

Table 2. The system of variables used in solving the problem of optimizing the size of peasant (farm) holdings of the Penza region with dairy and meat specialization

Crops, Products, Livestock, Forage	Unit	Acreage	Stern	Resource Costs	Livestock	Production	Selling
1	2	3	4	5	6	7	8
Grain and forage crops	ha	X_1					
Fodder beet	ha	X_2					
Corn for: silage	ha	X_3					
green fodder	ha	X_4					
Annual herbs for:	ha						
hay	ha	X_5					
haylage	ha	X_6					
green fodder	ha	X_7					
Plant "Kosher" (Brómus) for:	ha						
hay	ha	X_8					
green fodder	ha	X_9					
Plant "Kozlyatnik vostochniy" (Galena orientalists) for:	ha						
hay	ha	X_{10}					
haylage	ha	X_{11}					
green fodder	ha	X_{12}					
Silage	ha	X_{13}					
Perennial herbs for seeds	ha	X_{14}					
Winter rape (Barbarea)	ha	X_{15}					
Natural pastures	ha	X_{16}					
Cultivated pastures	ha	X_{17}					
Milk for forage	center		X_{18}				
Skim milk for forage	center		X_{19}				
Straw for forage	center		X_{20}				
Cows	cattle heads				X_{21}		
oung cattle	Cattle heads.				X_{22}		
The increment of forage for cows:	Center feed unit.						
concentrates	center feed unit		X_{23}				
root vegetables	center feed unit		X_{24}				
hay	center feed unit		X_{25}				

continued on following page

Table 1. Continued

Crops, Products, Livestock, Forage	Unit	Acreage	Stern	Resource Costs	Livestock	Production	Selling
haylage	center feed unit		X_{26}				
silage	center feed unit		X_{27}				
green fodder	center feed unit		X_{28}				
The increment of feed for young cattle:							
concentrates	center feed unit		X_{29}				
root vegetables	center feed unit		X_{30}				
hay	center feed unit		X_{31}				
haylage	center feed unit		X_{32}				
silage	center feed unit		X_{33}				
milk	center feed unit		X_{34}				
straw	center feed unit		X_{35}				
green fodder	center feed unit		X_{36}				
Production of: milk	center					X_{37}	
cattle increments	center					X_{38}	
Material and monetary costs	thousand rubles			X_{39}			

$$Z = \sum_{j_7 \in J_7} C_{j_7} x_{j_7} - x_{j_4} \rightarrow \max$$

The formation of a numerical economic and mathematical model of the functioning of the livestock industry is made taking into account the relationships between the blocks and sub-blocks.

Table 3. The structure of the cultivated area of the optimal size of the peasant (farmer) holding with milk and meat specialization

Crop	Cultivated Area, hectare	%
Grain and forage crops	12,6	28,8
Fodder beet	1,0	2,3
Annual herbs	3,9	8,9
Plant "Koster" (Brómus)	9,8	22,4
Plant "Kozlyatnik vostochniy" (Galega orientalis)	0,4	0,9
Natural pastures	6,0	13,7
Cultivated pastures	10,0	22,9
Total	43,7	100,0

Table 4. The structure of the acreage in the peasant (farmer) holdings with beet-grain and grain specialization

Crop	Beet Grain Specialization		Grain Specialization	
	ha	%	ha	%
Winter wheat	5,32	14,0	37,82	14,0
Winter rye	15,09	39,7	127	47,0
Spring wheat	3,35	8,8	22,4	8,3
Barley	3,13	8,2	0,32	0,1
Millet	0	0,0	78,8	29,2
Oats	3,14	8,3	0,33	0,1
Peas	0,38	1,0	3,5	1,3
Sugar beet	7,61	20,0	0	0,0
Total	38,05	100,0	270,17	100,0

Table 5. Production of gross and marketable products, center

Products	Beet Grain Specialization		Grain Specialization	
	Gross Products	Marketable Products	Gross Products	Marketable Products
Grain in bunker weight, total, including	961,1	608,3	8521,7	7397,6
winter wheat	153,4	131,0	1089,1	929,7
winter rye	414,4	349,0	3484	2939,3
spring wheat	140,0	121,0	931,1	804,3
barley	128,4	0,0	0,0	0,0
millet	0,0	0,0	2966,1	2660,8
oats	115,1	0,0	12,3	0,0
peas	9,9	7,3	91,6	67,6
buckwheat	0,0	0,0	0,0	0,0
sugar beet	2283,5	2283,5	0,0	0,0

Table 6. Sales of products through various channels in the peasant (farmer) holdings with grain-beet and grain specialization, center

Product	The Peasant (Farmer) Holdings With Grain-Beet Specialization		The Peasant (Farmer) Holdings With Grain Specialization		
	To Procurement Organizations	Barter	To Procurement Organizations	On the Market	Barter
Winter rye		349,0		2708,8	226,5
Wheat		245,8		1171,0	489,0
Millet			10,8	188,0	2462,0
Peas	7,3		67,6		
Sugar beet	2283,0				

Table 7. Production of gross and marketable products in optimal variants, rubles

Products	The Peasant (Farmer) Holdings With Grain-Beet Specialization	The Peasant (Farmer) Holdings With Grain Specialization	The Peasant (Farmer) Holdings With Dairy and Meat Specialization
Marketable product, total, including	309573,8	1043885,5	284363,0
winter rye	59679,0	466721,9	-
wheat	29987,6	213761,6	-
millet	-	335415,6	-
peas	3022,2	27986,4	-
sugar beet	216885,0	-	-
meat	-	-	46125,0
milk	-	-	238240,0
Gross output	491387,0	1202633,0	297043,0
The output of marketable products per 100 hectares of farmland	814668,0	386624,0	605028,0
Gross output per 100 ha of farmland	1293124,0	445420,0	632006,0

Table 8. Economic efficiency of optimal models of peasant (farm) holdings of Penza region

Indicators	The Peasant (Farmer) Holdings With Grain-Beet Specialization	The Peasant (Farmer) Holdings With Grain Specialization	The Peasant (Farmer) Holdings With Dairy and Meat Specialization
Revenue from product sales, rub.	309573,8	1043885,5	284363,0
Production costs, rub.	209087,5	452000,1	219076,4
Net profit, rub.	94457,1	556372,3	61369,4
Profitability of production activitiy, %	45,2	123,1	28,0
Profitability of sales, %	30,5	53,3	21,6
Actually: net profit, rub.	19200,0	152000,0	4100,0
profitability of sales, %	1,6	2,2	1,0

In accordance with the formulation of the problem, its economic and mathematical model and initial information, the numerical model includes the variables given in table 2.

The developed economic and mathematical models of optimization of the production structure of peasant (farm) holdings are fully adapted to market conditions, have flexibility, as they may be added by new blocks and sub-blocks, depending on the need. Therefore, it is advisable to use them to determine the rational production and economic parameters of peasant (farm) holdings not only in the Penza region, but also in other regions.

Solutions and Recommendations

According to the results of solving the developed economic and mathematical models of problems of optimization of the production structure of peasant (farmer) holdings, their optimal sizes were determined taking into account the specialization.

The first version of the problem was solved for peasant (farmer) holdings with a milk and meat direction. The result was the following.

Almost 30% of the total area of Cultivated area is occupied by grain and forage crops. The area under the Plant "Koster" (Brómus) and cultural pastures differ slightly, but the Plant "Kozlyatnik vostochniy" (Galega orientalis) accounts for only 0.9 percent. Almost 37% of the total area of agricultural land belongs to natural and cultivated pastures.

In accordance with the obtained structure the optimal size of the peasant (farm) holding is 43.7 hectares. This area provides for the cultivation of 13 heads of cows and 10 heads of calves, which ensures 595.6 c of milk and 18.45 c of meat. Income from the sales will be 284363,2 rubles.

To implement this project one need 219076.4 rubles. Profit will be 65286,8 rubles, net profit – 61370 rubles.

Dairy and meat specialization have peasant (farmer) holdings with land size less than 10 hectares. The optimal size of the peasant (farm) holding exceeds the actual more than 4 times. After solving the problem per 1 ha of arable land 1494 rubles of profit were received, which is 2.5 times higher than the actual value

The second and third options provide for the optimization of the size of peasant (farm) holdings with beet-grain and grain specialization.

The largest share in the optimal structure of acreage in peasant (farmer) holdings accounts for winter rye crops, with beet-grain specialization – 39.7%, with grain – 47 percent. In farms with a pronounced grain specialization, crops under sugar beet are completely absent. This structure corresponds to the field specialized crop rotation with rotation duration from 3 to 8 years.

The structure of acreage corresponding to peasant (farmer) holdings with beet-grain specialization meets the requirements of grain-crop rotations, in the structure of which the share of row crops accounts for 15 to 25% of the arable land (in our case, 20 percent).

Comparing the results, we conclude that the largest size of the peasant (farm) holding correspond to farms with a pronounced grain specialization of 270.17 hectares, and the smallest – farms with beet and grain specialization.

The obtained structure of acreage provides the following volumes of gross and marketable products in the farms with beet-grain and grain specialization.

Sugar beet is completely absent in the structure of gross output of peasant (farmer) holdings with grain specialization. Sugar beet is fully implemented in farms with beetroot grain specialization. Grain of fodder crops is spent on production needs.

This task provides for the sale of products through various channels

Peasant (farmer) holdings with beet-grain specialization sell the half of all products through procurement organizations. In fact, in the Penza region, the selling of sugar beet is carried out at a local sugar factory located in the town of Kamenka. The channel of realization "population" is absent in both variants. Farms with grain specialization sell their products through three channels. The largest number of products sold on the market. The sales channel of products "population" is absent in both variants, as it is economically inefficient. The sale of products through this channel will lead to a decrease in the profit of business.

The next point is to consider the production of gross and marketable products, as well as indicators that reflect the output of gross and marketable products per 100 hectares of agricultural land.

The share of sugar beet in the structure of marketable products of peasant (farmer) holdings with beet-grain specialization is 70 percent. In farms with grain specialization in the structure of marketable products there is only grain products. In the structure of marketable production in farms with dairy and meat specialization almost 84% accounted for milk.

The data in table 36 show that the highest output of gross and marketable products per 100 hectares of agricultural land is observed in peasant (farmer) holdings with beet-grain specialization – 1 293 124 rubles and 814 668 rubles respectively. The least of all gross and marketable products per 100 hectares of agricultural land is produced by farms with grain specialization – 445 420 and 386 624 rubles. In general, the trend identified earlier remains here: with the increase in the size of farms there is a decrease in their marketable and gross output per 100 hectares. If this criterion (volume of production per unit area) is taken as the optimal one, then the farms with beet-grain specialization will be the most acceptable for the conditions of the Penza region in the current situation.

Indicators of economic efficiency of optimal models of peasant (farm) holdings are considered in Table 8.

The largest amount of profit was received by peasant (farmer) holdings with grain specialization – 556,4 thousand rubles. The profitability of sales was 53.3 percent. The smallest amount of profit and level of profitability of sales obtained in the farms with dairy and beef specialization 61369,4 rub. and 21.6%, respectively. In each of the proposed options for optimal farm sizes, the project profit is several times higher than the actual one - 5 times in peasant (farmer) holdings with grain-beet specialization, 4 times with grain and 15 times with milk and meat. A similar situation occurs with the profitability level indicator.

Thus, with the current market conditions and prices for agricultural products, the most profitable in the conditions of the Penza region, in terms of maximizing profits, is the grain direction of production activities. Within this specialization, the volume of livestock production is determined at the level necessary to satisfy exclusively personal needs of participants of peasant (farm) holdings.

The proposed models can be used in practice to form the optimal production and economic parameters of peasant (farm) holdings of the Penza region, which can significantly improve the economic efficiency of their activities by establishing the optimal combination of available resources.

Thus, for farms with beet-grain specialization, the optimal farm is 38 hectares in size. The level of profitability will be 30.5%, net profit - 94.5 thousand rubles

Farmers with dairy and meat specialization are recommended to have a farm size of 44 hectares. The level of production profitability is 28%, the level of sales profitability is 21.6 percent. Subject to compliance with all the conditions put in the models, it will be possible to obtain projected profits and specified production volumes.

FUTURE RESEARCH DIRECTIONS

Concerning practical applications, evaluation the presented mathematical approach becomes more important for regional cluster initiatives, in particular, as well as other programs that contribute to the development of entrepreneurship for analysis and planning of the peasant farms development with the use of Avatar-Based Mathematical Approach (Mkrttchian, et al., 2013, 2015,2016,2017) .

CONCLUSION

Estimation results of second and third equations show that volume of production and values of farm assets have a significant impact on number of employees in agricultural sector, and output of farms greatly depends on number of employees and also from value of fixed assets. Volume of foreign borrowings of previous period does not have significant effect on total volume of agricultural production. In general, the proposed model is adequate and suitable for practical calculations in field of small business.

Multidimensional econometric models describes the formation of several economic events and their indicators, with each equation of multidimensional model explaining the behavior of one indicator. Economic events explained by multidimensional model are represented by endogenous variables. Economic events that are not explained by model and are necessary for explaining endogenous variables are represented by exogenous variables.

REFERENCES

Ahn, A., & Haugh, M. (2015). Linear programming and the control of diffusion processes. *INFORMS Journal on Computing*, 27(4), 646–657. doi:10.1287/ijoc.2015.0651

Al-Chalabi, A., Calvo, A., Chio, A., Colville, A., & Pearce, N. (2014) Analysis of amyotrophic lateral sclerosis as a multistep process: a population-based modelling study. In The Lancet Neurology, pp. 1108-1113. doi:10.1016/S1474-4422(14)70219-4

Anfimov, A. M. (1961) Zemel'naya arenda v Rossii v nachale 20 veka. Moskva: Izdatel'stvo Akademii nauk USSR.

Fadeev, V. P. (2001) Fermerskoe hozyajstvo: problemy stanovleniya i razvitiya. Saratov: Saratovskij gosudarstvennyj universitet im. N.I. Vavilova

Hesamzadeh, M. R., Galland, O., & Biggar, D. R. (2014). Short-run economic dispatch with mathematical modelling of the adjustment cost. In *International Journal of Electrical Power* (pp. 9–18). Energy Systems; doi:10.1016/j.ijepes.2013.12.020

Mkrttchian, V. (2013). Training of Avatar Moderator in Sliding Mode Control Environment for Virtual Project Management. In *Enterprise Resource Planning: Concepts, Methodologies, Tools, and Applications. IRMA* (pp. 1376–1405). IGI Global. doi:10.4018/978-1-4666-4153-2.ch074

Mkrttchian, V. (2015). Modeling using of Triple H-Avatar Technology in online Multi-Cloud Platform Lab. In *Encyclopedia of Information Science and Technology* (pp. 4162–4170). Hershey, PA: IGI Global; doi:10.4018/978-1-4666-5888-2.ch409

Mkrttchian, V., & Aleshina, E. (2017). *Sliding Mode in Intellectual Control and Communication: Emerging Research and Opportunities*. Hershey, PA: IGI Global; doi:10.4018/978-1-5225-2292-8

Mkrttchian, V., Bershadsky, A., Bozhday, A., Kataev, M., & Kataev, S. (Eds.). (2016). *Handbook of Research on Estimation and Control Techniques in E-Learning Systems*. Hershey, PA: IGI Global; doi:10.4018/978-1-4666-9489-7

Nadarajah, S., & Secomandi, N. (2017) Relationship between least squares Monte Carlo and approximate linear programming. In Operations Research Letters, pp. 409-414. doi:10.1016/j.orl.2017.05.010

Zohali, H., Naderi, B., & Mohammadi, M. (2019) The economic lot scheduling problem in limited-buffer flexible flow shops: Mathematical models and a discrete fruit fly algorithm. In Applied Soft Computing, pp. 904-919. DOI: doi:10.1016/j.asoc.2019.03.054

KEY TERMS AND DEFINITIONS

Endogenous Variable: A variable in a statistical model that's changed or determined by its relationship with other variables within the model. Endogenous factors are the opposite of exogenous variables, which are independent variables or outside forces.

Exogenous Variable: Is used for setting arbitrary external conditions, and not in achieving a more realistic model behavior. An exogenous variable is a variable that is not affected by other variables in the system.

Linear Programming (LP, also called Linear Optimization): Is a method to achieve the best outcome (such as maximum profit or lowest cost) in a mathematical model whose requirements are represented by linear relationships. Linear programming is a special case of mathematical programming (also known as mathematical optimization).

Multidimensional Data Model: Is designed to solve complex queries in real time. The multidimensional data model is composed of logical cubes, measures, dimensions, hierarchies, levels, and attributes. The simplicity of the model is inherent because it defines objects that represent real-world business entities.

Optimization Methods: Often non-linear, non-convex, multimodal, and multidimensional, and might be expressed by both discrete and continuous variables, which makes this a difficult problem.

Peasant Farming: Refers to a type of small-scale agriculture.

Chapter 9
Digital Mechanisms of Management System Optimization in the Forest Industry

Yulia Vertakova
iD https://orcid.org/0000-0002-1685-2625
South-West State University, Russia

Saniyat Agamagomedova
Penza State University, Russia

Irina Sergeeva
Penza State University, Russia

Andrey Tarasov
Penza State University, Russia

Svetlana Morkovina
Voronezh State Forestry University by G. F. Morozova, Russia

Enric Seedine
Voronezh State Forestry University by G. F. Morozova, Russia

Potapova Irina
Astrakhan SAS University, Russia

ABSTRACT

This chapter discusses digital mechanisms for optimizing the management system in the forest industry, which includes organizational, legal, socio-economic, and environmental aspects. Efficient forest management is considered as an integral part of efficient nature management and includes the use of forest resources, their

DOI: 10.4018/978-1-7998-1581-5.ch009

protection, and reproduction of forests. Digital management mechanisms in forest management in general and in the forest industry in particular are based on platform solutions. Platform solutions are based on the formation and processing of data on the basis of a single automated information system, which acts as the foundation for the development of digitalization in forestry. Such a digital platform is designed to provide informational, analytical, consulting, and other support to the activities of all subjects of relations in the field of use, conservation, protection, and reproduction of forest resources.

INTRODUCTION

The forest complex of modern Russia is a complex economic system, combining two equal components in its composition - forestry and management. Management in the forest complex has significant specificity, which is determined by the fact that it has two subsystems built on different principles: state forest management (in terms of forestry) and management of the production activities of enterprises engaged in logging and wood processing. At the same time, both parts of the forest complex - forestry and forest industry - are equal and closely interconnected. At the same time, forestry ensures the reproduction of resources, the consumer of which is the forest industry. In other words, forestry acts as a resource base for the development of all sectors of the forest complex. Despite significant forest resources, the forest complex of the Russian Federation does not play an appropriate role in the country's economy. The reason for this lies in the imperfection of management, determined in many respects by the permanent reform of the state forest management system. On the territory of Russia is one fourth of the world's forest reserves, which, in addition to logging, provide the most important functions, such as: recreation, tourism, hunting, water and soil protection, the functions of harvesting resin and food forest resources, as well as collecting medicinal plants, being not only a key element of the ecological framework, but also a colossal resource for improving the well-being and strengthening the health of Russian citizens. Reform of forest management, decentralization of powers in practice did not lead to significant changes in the performance of the economy of the forest complex, the contribution of the forest industry to the country's GDP remains at 1.5%, the share of Russian forest in the world goods market does not exceed 5%, an extensive model of forest management is maintained. Unfortunately, Russia's forestry remains a backward, low-tech and investment-unattractive sector of the forest complex. About 200 million cubic meters of wood is harvested annually in the country's forest fund, which is 1.5-2.0 times lower than in the USA, India and China. In the whole country, an imbalance of forest retirement and reproduction remains. In just five years, the area of forest retirement exceeded reforestation by more than 350 thousand ha, despite the fact that annual forest reproduction is carried out on an area of about 800 thousand ha.

BACKGROUND

Forest national wealth has traditionally occupied and still occupies a unique position in the socio-political, economic and cultural activities of people. Forests support life, improve its quality and act as a center of national culture and social structure. Forests are rightfully considered as a special factor of production, without which practically none of human activity is possible.

The underdevelopment of financial and economic relations and the removal of the state from economic activities in the forest industry have increased the imbalance of economic interests and do not allow for the effective interaction of government bodies and business entities in the forestry system. Against the background of these negative trends, the created mechanism of forest management turned out to be ineffective and costly. The incomes of forestry in Russia, unlike most of the "forest powers" in the world, are significantly lower than government spending, and the rental institution continues to stagnate. Not more than 20% of the forest fund lands, concentrated mainly in the European part of the country, were leased. The mechanism of state forest management in Russia that has emerged from the reform results does not fully take into account the multi-purpose nature of the forest. All of the above does not allow us to assume that the forest management system established as a result of the reforms of the last decade is capable of ensuring the social and environmental security of the country, the most important functions of the state in relation to forests and inhibiting the growth of the forest sector of the economy as a whole. It is necessary to develop tools for state forest management, based on effective and mutually beneficial interaction of participants in forest relations (representatives of legislative bodies - federal and regional, representatives of entrepreneurial structures and civil society) and their motivation for quality forest management. Under the current conditions, the role of the analytical, when forming development forecasts, and the control, when assessing the results of forest management, management aspects that create incentives for integrated forest management and efficient use of forest resources is important. In this regard, a system of balanced indicators can become a support for decisions made in the field of forest management and a demanded management tool in terms of both management of forest users and improvement of state forest management.

Forests represent a remnant wilderness of high recreational value in the densely populated industrial societies, a threatened natural resource in some regions of the world and a renewable reservoir of essential raw materials for the wood processing industry (Corona, et al., 2003).

An analysis of the scientific literature on the management system in the forest industry and the problems of its optimization in the context of the digitalization of the economy suggests that, according to the studies of the current state and patterns of development of the forest resources system in modern conditions, scientists propose various mechanisms and models for managing them, taking into account relevant managerial trends.

The supply chain planning methodology in the forest industry is quite common. C. Alayet, N. Lehoux, L. Lebel and M. Bouchard offer (Alayet, et al., 2016) a model for centralized supply chain planning for several forest companies. S. Akhtari and T. Sowlati (2015) also investigate the supply chain of forest products and use hybrid modeling and optimization approaches to solve the problems of such supplies.

The role of digital mechanisms for ensuring sustainability and efficiency in forest products supply chains has motivated several studies in the field of precision forestry. Sensor technologies can collect relevant data in forest supply chains, including all types of activities in forests and the production of wood raw materials for its conversion into marketable forest products.

Optimization of the planning system can help support the decisions of various participants in the supply chain, which include owners of forests and forest products, logging companies, transport companies, timber exporting companies, and representatives of the timber processing industry.

Such mechanisms are designed to cope with the complex relationships between different organizations that can improve the efficiency of forest products supply chains. Improving the sustainability and effectiveness of forest supply chains requires a continuous flow of information to facilitate integrated planning of activities throughout the supply chain. It thereby facilitates the smooth exchange of data between supply chain entities and as well facilitates new forms of cooperation.

In this regard, scientists are considering aspects of data exchange and joint work of several subjects of relations in the field of the forest industry, combined on the basis of advanced planning systems. In addition, we can talk about a certain interdisciplinarity of the prospects of scientific research in the field of forest industry management (Scholz, et al., 2018).

Approaches are quite widespread when all industrial operations with forest products are differentiated and considered as separate management objects. For example, specialists in the management of logging routing have developed and proposed a decision support system (Andersson, et al., 2008). It should be noted that over the past two decades, many decision support systems have been developed in forest management. Among them, methodological approaches such as artificial neural networks, knowledge-based systems, and multicriteria decision-making models are significant (Reynolds, et al., 2008).

M. Rönnqvist considers the problems of planning in the forest industry. Periods of such planning may be different. Planning tasks are formed using linear, integer and non-linear models. The mathematical methods used are time-dependent and include, for example, dynamic programming, branching and linking methods, heuristics, and column generation (Rönnqvist, 2003).

A study of planning and other managerial functions in the forest industry is naturally based on developed classification systems for land use and land cover for using with remote sensor data (Anderson, et al., 1976, 2008). The specifics of goals and planning of forest reserves in modern conditions are considered by M. Köhl, M. Marchetti (2016).

De Moraes Gonçalves J. L., Silva L.D., Behling M. and Alvares C.A. (De Moraes Gonçalves, et al., 2014), who study the problem of developing financially and environmentally sustainable forest stands, use a process approach to forest management. They differentiate management criteria depending on specific climatic and other conditions, formulate principles, goals, strategies and practices of sustainable forest management.

Leary R.A. develops "interaction" as an integrative principle in forestry. He reflects on the profession of a forester and the loss of the image of this unique profession. The latter has been influenced by inefficient logging practices in national forests in the United States and other factors (Leary, 1985).

In the last decade, the so-called urban area of forest research has been developing. Throughout history, cities in Europe and the world have developed close ties with nearby forest areas. In some cases, cities even stimulated a distinct "forest identity" (*Cortner and Moote, 1994*).

Konijnendijk explores the rich heritage of urban forests, presents them as cultural landscapes, and shows that cities and forests can be useful to each other (Konijnendijk, 2018).

Urban forests play an increasingly important role in sustainable development programs of local authorities; they serve as an important guide for those involved in urban planning and decision-making, public relations and administration, communication with sports services, cultural and health care departments.

Urban forests are positioned as sources of livelihood, as a healthy environment for recreation, as places of inspiration and learning, as sources of conflict. The socio-economic and cultural development of cities and forestry is closely related. These relationships show that a better understanding of urban forests as distinct cultural and social phenomena can help strengthen the interaction between cities and forests, between greening and urbanization, between urban society and nature (Konijnendijk, 2018).

The main trends in the development of forest industry organizations in Russia on the basis of a project approach to the management of industry enterprises were considered by S. Fisenko (Fisenko, 2013).

The peculiarity of the forest and forest resources is that this potential cannot have exclusively economic significance. The forest potential of the state is inextricably linked with the economic and environmental security of the country, with social indicators of the quality of a modern person's life.

N. Zhavoronkova and G. Vypkhanova (2018) emphasize the need to use conceptual approaches in the study of managerial mechanisms in the forest industry, ensuring a balance of economic and social guidelines for the forest management along with maintaining the ecological potential of forests.

Other scientists also talk about the environmental focus of forest management and use the concept of «forest ecosystems» as an object of study. Forest ecosystems provide a variety of services, and forest ecosystem management (FEM) is an effective approach to maximize services (Limin, et al., 2006). Due to the complexity of forest ecosystems, their management can be facilitated through decision support systems that recognize and include environmental and socio-economic variables. Moreover, scientists talk about forest ecosystem services through an auction mechanism. The auction mechanism uses cost-effective management models in which stakeholders compete with each other. The competitive advantages of forest ecosystems are recreational properties, aesthetic comfort, water quality and others (Roesch-McNally, et al., 2016).

R. Barrett and H. Salwasser (1982) consider an adaptive management system for wood and wildlife using models of the relationship between DYNAST and wildlife.

Forest management issues for benefits were explored by S. Boyce, who differentiated varieties of such benefits into several benefits (DYNAST-MB), benefits associated with wood (DYNAST-TM), optimal benefits (DYNAST-OB) (Boyce, 1977; Boyce, 1978; Boyce, 1980).

Forest management is inextricably linked with trends and problems in the management of other natural resources - land and water. The traditional paradigm shift model is used to study the changes taking place in the management of all natural resources.

Scientists rightly point out that the previous management theory, which is characterized by stable income, is losing relevance today. The new paradigm proposed by scientists is based on two principles: ecosystem management and joint decision-making. The implementation of these two principles will build new management mechanisms in the use of forest and other natural resources (Cortner and Moote, 1994).

With the rapid development of computing as well as information and communication technologies, decision support systems (DSS) have been implemented in many ways. In China, in the absence of affordable quantitative decision support tools to transform the concept into forest management actions, intelligent modeling mechanisms have been developed. They operate within the framework of a geographic information system (GIS) and forest models. Scientists propose strengthening forest ecosystem management (FEM) with the help of special FORESTAR applications (Limin, et al., 2006).

From the economic point of view, the term "forest resources assessment" is used in scientific studies of forest industry management, which is understood as the "procedure for obtaining information on the quantity and condition of the forest resource, associated vegetation and components, and other characteristics of the land area where the forest is located" (Hush et al. 2003). In addition, the term "forest inventory" is actively used in the study group under consideration, which refers both to the forest information system and to the procedures for measuring and evaluating the data on which this information is based. Forest inventory is the basis of forest planning and forest policy.

The evolution of forest management mechanisms suggests that early sustainable forest management and forest inventory projects were focused on timber production. Modern approaches to efficient forest management are based on environmental, economic and social principles of forest management.

Forest management in the state covers a complex set of public relations, including not only forest management, reproduction, conservation and protection of forests, but also the forest complex, which includes forestry and timber industries for the harvesting and processing of wood. V. Kolesnik, L. Sinyatullina (2017) believe that from the point of view of management, the forest complex is a complex of two interconnected blocks: forestry and timber industry. Consequently, public administration in the field of forest relations should be considered in conjunction with forest management.

Unlike most countries in the world, Russia's forestry is unprofitable (Isaev and Korovin, 2009). Among the reasons for this situation should be called:

- frequent changes in forest legislation over the past decades;
- continuous reform of the structure and functions of state forest management in the country;

- liquidation of state forestries;
- transfer of functions for the protection, protection, reproduction of forests to private companies;
- a significant reduction in forest protection personnel;
- refusal of the state to finance forest management, protection and reproduction of forests;
- transfer of forestry to auctions (Shpakovsky, 2018).

The current state of forest management, focused on increasing the investment attractiveness of forest resources, the intensification of their use along with the prospects for the development of the forest complex, necessitates a review of traditional approaches to public administration in the field of forest relations. In this case, it is important to determine the content and limits of the implementation of public administration in the field of forest management. In this regard, it should be noted that there is a lack of unified terminology in forest management issues. Scientists use such concepts as "state forest management", "forest complex management", "forest management" and many others. Such terminological diversity discourages a common understanding of public administration in this area (Zhavoronkova and Vypkhanova, 2018)

In the science of natural resource law, public administration in the field of forest use and protection (or forest management) is defined as the executive-administrative activity of public authorities based on forestry legislation to organize the rational use and protection of forests (Bykovsky, 2016).

The Forest Code of the Russian Federation, which is the basic regulatory act governing forest relations, includes the entire subject area of regulated relations, including the use, conservation, protection, reproduction of forests (chapter 10 of the Forest Code of the Russian Federation (Forest Code RF, 2006).

Moreover, most types of forest use are entrepreneurial activities carried out by legal entities and individual entrepreneurs working in logging and other sectors of the economy. Thus, state forest management is an integral part of state management in the field of economic relations, and managerial mechanisms in the forest industry are elements of the industrial complex management system as a whole.

When reforming the public administration system in the field of forest management, we must not forget that the effectiveness of public administration should be measured using not only economic, but also social criteria. If exclusively economic indicators are used as a criterion for the effectiveness of public administration in a certain area, this forces management entities to turn to those projects that can give positive results in the short term. Unlike economic indicators, social indicators do not have a similar rate of change (Bartsits, 2008). In relation to the state management of the forest industry, performance criteria should include economic, social, and environmental indicators.

Von Gadow K., Pukkala T. and Tomé M. (Von Gadow, et al., 2000) also offer a holistic approach that includes environmental, socio-political, and economic issues related to wood supply.

Scientists also propose a general theory of tree growth modeling and its application in Europe. It is unique as for the first time it introduces a platform that promotes and implements the theory of tree growth modeling, which is necessary to manage mixed tree species (Hasenauer, 2006).

Environmental problems and public concern, the economic interests of business in the forest sector stimulate interest in finding a more systematic between different modes of forest management. Interestingly, such a choice is seen as a search for a balance between the natural and socio-economic components of ecosystems.

Here, Monserud, Haynes and Johnson (Monserud, et al., 2003) focus on specific management strategies. They represent broad objectives such as biodiversity, wood production, and habitat conservation. Other forest land values that are desirable and interesting to the public are also important.

Scientists believe that marketable products (wood, timber) and other forest values (biodiversity, fish and wildlife) can be simultaneously produced from the same area in a socially acceptable way.

They argue that there are alternatives for managing forest ecosystems that do not contain a mandatory choice between economic, environmental and other interests.

Attention is drawn to two aspects of forest management:

1. a combination of different methods of forest management is associated with a number of related production of goods and services;
2. the impact of different approaches to forest management on large and complex ecosystems.

In the context of a decrease in world forest wealth, the range of goods and services related to forest management is growing rapidly. Appeals for sustainable forest management will not achieve the goal if the legal, political and administrative environment does not oppose the negative practices of forest management and forest protection (Corona, et al., 2003).

MAIN FOCUS OF THE CHAPTER

Issues, Controversies, Problems

The digital revolution in modern society is changing all social institutions, including the public administration system (Talapina, 2015).

Today in Russia, in the context of the new digital reality, the process of transition from the prevailing methods of public administration to the most promising with the use of interactive analytics is unfolding.

Implementation of digital transformation is impossible under the conditions of an endless stream of paper documents, in various departments that create information systems duplicating each other and reduce the effectiveness of the public administration system as a whole. A new management culture should be based on digital skills and knowledge, as well as a true understanding of the opportunities that technology provides. As a result, the approach of digital transformation state and public administration will lead to reforms in the system and a change in personnel policy.

So, the digitalization of public administration will lead to a transition to a digital document and a revision of ineffective processes. In this logic, self-digitization covers the entire spectrum of segments aimed at simplifying interaction and ensuring coordination of the work of departments at various levels, for example, federal and municipal. This in turn will also allow simplifying the relations of business representatives as effective forest users with the state.

Thus, the digitalization of public administration will lead to the search for new information management platforms. This will be possible by building a flexible modern architecture, using the latest methodologies, frameworks, technologies and tools in modern visualization.

The implementation of digital technologies and platform solutions in the areas of public administration and the provision of public services, including in the interests of the population and small and medium-sized enterprises as well as individual entrepreneurs, is planned to be implemented through the following measures:

1. development of a system for the provision of state and municipal services, the introduction of new principles for their provision, focused on the maximum convenience and comfort of citizens and organizations in the process of obtaining services;
2. creating a national data management system in the Russian Federation;

3. creating a unified electronic cartographic framework, ensuring its maintenance and providing access to spatial data, as well as developing services for the exchange and processing of spatial data;
4. creation of a digital services platform for translating activities, document management and mechanisms of interaction between government bodies and local self-government bodies into a digital format, implementing digital mechanisms and strategic planning tools on the basis of a single platform solution, forming a compact set of interconnected strategic planning documents and implementing digital reporting;
5. ensuring digital transformation of the state (municipal) service through the introduction of digital technologies and platform solutions (Unified Plan ...).

With regard to forestry as a field of activity, informatization should develop accounting the specifics of the creation, use and protection of the forest potential of the state as an essential part of the national natural potential. Moreover, not only economic (market) priorities should be put at the forefront, but also the social, environmental goals of forest management, and aspects of national security.

Solutions and Recommendations

The introduction and development of information technologies in the field of forestry complies with the requirements for the implementation of the Digital Economy of the Russian Federation program, approved by decree of the Government of the Russian Federation of July 28, 2017 N 1632-r.

This program defines the goals, objectives, directions and timing of the implementation of the main government policy measures to create the necessary conditions for the development of the digital economy in Russia, in which digital data is a key factor in production in all areas of socio-economic activity.

In Russia, the Development Strategy for the Forestry Complex of the Russian Federation until 2030 was approved (Order of the Government of the Russian Federation of September 20, 2018 N 1989-r) (hereinafter - the Strategy).

According to the Strategy, the development of informatization in forestry envisages both the improvement of existing systems in the field of forestry management and the development of new ones.

It is planned to optimize such existing systems as the federal state information system "Information System for Remote Monitoring of the Federal Forestry Agency" and a unified state automated information system for recording wood and transactions with it.

The state recognizes the need to create such new systems as the departmental spatial data fund; automated system "Control over the authenticity of acts of forest

Figure 1. System of forest management entities

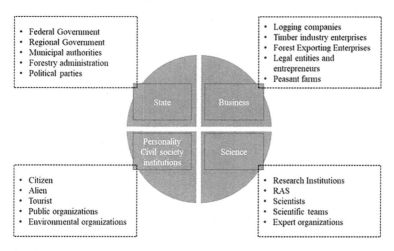

pathological examinations"; situational center of the Federal Forestry Agency; unified automated information system.

The foundation for the development of digitalization in forestry will be the creation of a unified automated information system (hereinafter - UAIS) as a unified platform for providing informational, analytical, consulting and other support to the activities of all subjects of forestry relations. The latter should include all persons who directly or indirectly participate in public relations to create, use and protect forest resources. A special place in the system of these relations is occupied by the state as a whole and state bodies of various levels as carriers of public authority.

The system of forest management entities is a set of participants in public relations for the creation, use and protection of forest resources, interacting within the framework of socio-economic, environmental and other interests and united by common goals and principles of effective forest management.

The structure of the UAIS should include the following structured data:

1. Information for the inventory of forest resources (quantitative and qualitative);
2. Information for passing phytosanitary control;
3. Information for export and customs control;
4. Information for EMERCOM of Russia;

Figure 2. Digital forest management system

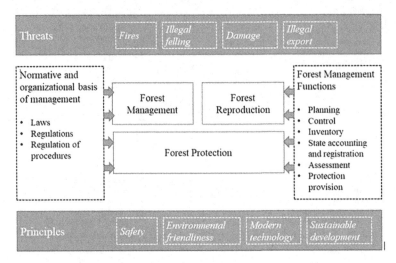

5.   Information for environmental control;
6.   Information about the enterprises of logging and timber processing industries;
7.   Information about forestries;
8.   Information on the reproduction of forest reserves;
9.   Information on violations of forest legislation and others.

The classification of forest resources in many cases can be multilevel. For example, forests are divided according to the land on which they are located, into forests on the lands of the forest fund and forests on lands of other categories. According to Article 10 of the Forest Code of the Russian Federation, forests located on the lands of the forest fund, for their intended purpose, are in turn divided into protective, operational and reserve forests.

The UAIS will allow receiving, processing, storing and using information on the state of forests, their quantitative and qualitative characteristics, on their use, protection, protection and reproduction, which will improve the quality of decisions made in the field of forest use, the effectiveness of planning and forecasting measures for forest use, protection and reproduction of forests.

Figure 3. Tasks of platform solutions based on the UAIS in relation to the Federal Forestry Agency (FFA)

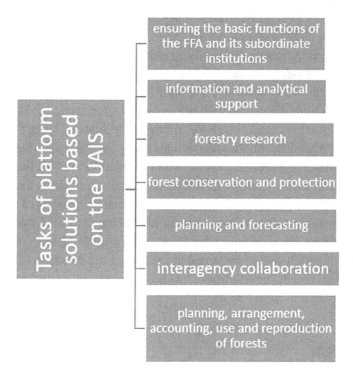

The turnover of UAIS information in terms of the effectiveness of various types of state control by the executive authorities in relation to forest users and other entities of forest relations is of great importance. This turnover is as well valuable for the efficient interagency interaction between various federal executive bodies and other persons involved in system of forest management, reproduction, conservation and protection of forests.

The translation of all the data necessary for the successful functioning (the volumes of which allow us to talk about big data) into a digital format will allow us to talk about the formation of a digital platform in the field of forest management, conservation, protection and reproduction of the forest. The platform solutions generated by the system being created are able to optimize the current state of the forest processing sector of the national economy, make it not only economically profitable, but also provide the necessary level of security in the forest sector, and preserve the national forest potential.

UAIS is called upon to provide, on the one hand, the necessary level of centralization of existing information systems in the field of forestry, and, on the other, to classify large data on forest resources (their quantitative and qualitative assessment) into blocks depending on the direction of managerial impact.

In relation to the Federal Forestry Agency, the tasks of platform solutions based on the UAIS will include several vectors, schematically depicted in Figure 3.

As part of the improvement of the forest management system, the current forest legislation of the Russian Federation is regularly updated. So, the latest changes to the Forest Code of the Russian Federation were related to improving the legal regulation of relations connected with preservation of forests on lands of the forest fund and lands of other categories (Federal Law of December 27, 2018 N 538-ФЗ).

In addition, a significant advance in addressing the issue of streamlining the use of forests, including reducing illegal wood circulation, was the introduction of amendments to the Forest Code of the Russian Federation, providing for control over the implementation of logging, the origin of wood and its turnover. The main tool for the implementation of these requirements has become a unified state automated information system for accounting for wood and transactions with it, the further development of which should be aimed at expanding the database of participants in forest relations and the possibilities of its use by interested parties and extending the scope to urban and rural forests.

CONCLUSION

The use of information aggregates based on data-centric and process approaches will allow obtaining a number of effects:

- transition "from documents to data": the collection, processing and organization of all necessary data is ensured, data protection, their storage and archiving, responsibility for data correctness (based on the concept of data lake);
- due to the maximum possible disclosure of data and the introduction of automated technologies, all decisions made are transparent, which ensures the necessary level of trust in the public administration system;
- decisions are made on the basis of real-time data;
- optimized costs for the state apparatus by eliminating unnecessary processes, functions, staffing units of public servants.

The information platform will simplify the management process through the use of dashboards, where all the necessary information is collected, that is, in essence, dashboards are "smart" control panels that display data in real time, which makes it possible to always see the final goal and motivates to achieve it.

As a result of digital transformation, a fundamentally new key opportunity appears in the system of targeted government administration, expressed in high speed.

In the case of state forest management based on the MTP, the dashboard will be an information management tool for monitoring the achievement of the stated goals through key indicators.

Based on the goals, dashboards should be classified into: analytical, strategic, operational, tactical, etc.).

The operational dashboard aims to quickly provide critical information to users as they solve time-dependent tasks. The main objectives of the operational dashboard are to quickly and clearly present data on deviations, display current resources and their status. This is a digital dispatch point designed to help users be fast, proactive, and efficient. This dashboard may need a manager lower level.

Unlike the operating room, the analytical dashboard provides the user with information that is used for analysis and decision making. They are less sensitive to time and are not oriented to immediate actions.

The main goal is to help users to better assess data, analyze trends and make decisions. This dashboard may be needed by senior managers.

The architecture of the dashboard, as information support for the visual state management control taking into account the BSC, is reflected (Sydinai, 2019).

The lower basic level of architecture provides data for the purposes of SSP from heterogeneous sources: structured and unstructured.

This is a set of physical and logical data storages organized in accordance with the concept of data lake, where large volumes of data from multiple sources are centrally aggregated, and their primary processing (if necessary) is carried out (for example, verification, cleaning) for further use. These bodies themselves are designed in accordance with a unified metamodel, which provides a unified approach to their interpretation and use. A single storage model combines data from various sources - such as government data (open and limited access), data from socio-economic statistics, industry data, scientific data, etc.

Based on the basic level data, the average level of services and platforms is based, which, in turn, can be divided into state and non-state, that is, these are fairly universal system technological solutions that are configured for specific goals and objectives. Thus, at the data processing stage, "monitoring points" are identified for the achievement of key indicators of the BSC.

At the upper level of the dashboard architecture, reports are generated that give a visual representation of the scenario fork in the BSC in the context of not only the administrative control loop, but also the strategic one.

To date, the architecture of dashboard panels is the best tool for monitoring and analyzing information about the effectiveness of managerial processes. This is not just a set of graphs and tables, but a complete information system that can integrate data from ERP systems and conduct analysis. Data can remain scattered across various accounting systems, be informal, and even based on subjective assessments, which must be regularly collected from experts.

If the process of collecting, calculating and storing indicators is not automated, then information about the performance of processes, departments and employees will not be collected promptly, and as a result, it may become outdated and meaningless from the point of view of decision-making. Application of dashboards of indicators allows this problem to be solved. Dashboard panels perform several basic functions. During the monitoring process, indicators that measure the effectiveness of processes in the information panel are presented in a generalized, enlarged form. By presenting information in graphical form in the form of charts, graphs and tables, the application allows you to instantly identify critical information based on relevant and relevant data, to issue warning signals in case of potential problems. The dashboard can display indicators related to the fulfillment of planned indicators, the current level of operating costs, etc. The monitoring of indicators in dynamics, carried out by the dashboard, helps managers at various levels in assessing the situation and making informed and informed decisions. Actual information is available in real time. Through flexible settings, the manager can independently collect on one screen information on the effectiveness and efficiency of various processes on the MTP (on the competencies of civil servants, internal forestry processes, economic and financial indicators and forest users).

At the same time, he himself chooses a convenient way to display information: in the form of a table, graph, chart or text, taking into accounts the dynamics and state of the indicator. Using the color design of the data, it is possible to focus on target indicators that are in critical areas (for example, red indicates the critical zone in which the indicator value is located, yellow indicates an acceptable level, green indicates the planned indicator value has been reached).

To obtain detailed information, you can interactively switch ("fail") to another information layer in which to analyze data by analyst, and also go to the level of primary documents (transactions).

In the process of analysis, the application used for these purposes allows one to conduct research and analysis of data on efficiency in various dimensions and with varying degrees of detail, to identify patterns and cause-effect relationships between various factors affecting the efficiency of the process. When conducting such an analysis, the user himself determines the parameters and measurements of the generated reports, he can go from the upper level grouping (aggregation) of data to the lowest level - a document (transaction) for a better understanding of the situation (Drill Down technique). For example, using this tool, you can evaluate the dynamics of logging with a certain characteristic in the selected region, build a schedule for loading warehouse space taking into account seasonality, etc.

The dashboard information aggregate uses multidimensional data analysis as a tool, which helps to reduce the time needed to obtain the necessary information due to the fact that the construction of reports takes place in "one touch". This analysis makes it possible to set up to 6 analytic sections for each target indicator (one predefined and 5 user-configurable). As practice has shown, such a number of cuts in analytics is quite enough to provide a deep immersion in the analysis of cause-effect relationships, while maintaining an acceptable system performance. As analytical sections, any accounting data can be used. The analytical system allows you to present data, both in the static idea (on a specific date) and in dynamics (for any periods); in the form of structured tabular reports, and in the form of charts and graphs. This helps to improve the quality of the analysis, and as a result, it has a positive effect on the effectiveness of decisions.

Along with the foregoing, the dashboard has the tools to determine the performance of employees, departments and departments responsible for the performance of the MTP.

Using this tool, it is possible to link strategic goals and current (operational) activities. The software product allows you to create performance matrices (MBO-matrices) for each position and unit. On the one hand, through this matrix, the responsibility of employees for achieving certain indicators is distributed, and on the other hand, it becomes possible to monitor the degree of effectiveness and efficiency of an employee or manager in this position. Such a matrix includes key performance indicators (KPI), and allows you to "digitize" the performance of an employee or unit - presenting it as a number. For each indicator, you can determine its priority by setting the weight in the general list of indicators.

Using the planned targets in the calculation, it is possible to translate the assessment of the effectiveness of the implementation of certain groups of delegated powers in the field of forest management into an objective plane. It should be noted that the planned values for each indicator of the effectiveness of the implementation of powers in the field of forest management are mini-tasks that managers are required to monitor monthly or quarterly to achieve the targets of state forest management. Such an approach allows further monitoring of the effectiveness of the implementation of powers in the field of forest management and clearly demonstrates the contribution of a specific employee to the results. Thus, an interactive analytics in the form of a dashboard is necessary for the concept of MTP, as it ensures the visibility of the results in the field of state forest management, taking into account economic, environmental and social goals for each of the processes of forestry production and forest management.

Working at the interface of complexity theory, quantitative sociology and Big Data-driven risk and knowledge management, the author advocates the establishment of new participatory systems in our digital society to enhance coordination, reduce

Figure 4. The system of priorities for effective forest management using platform solutions

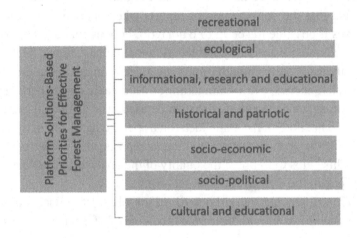

Figure 5. Data processing for forest management based on platform solutions

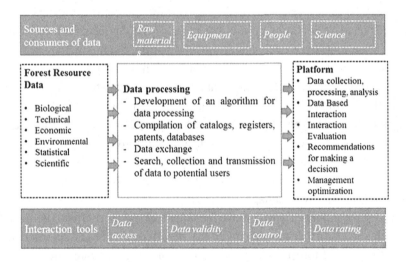

conflict and, above all, reduce the "tragedies of the commons," resulting from the methods now used in political, economic and management decision-making (Helbing, 2015).

Figure 6. Forest use indicators using platform solutions

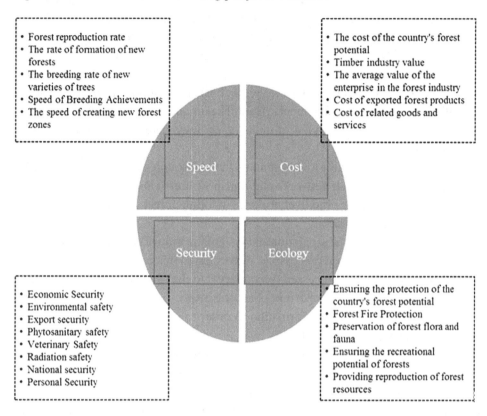

Scientists also suggest industrial methods that can be used either independently or in hybrid systems through various methods to provide the best performance in terms of optimal design and computational efficiency (Parmee and Hajela, 2002).

In recent years, based on system analysis in forestry, methods such as optimization and simulation, decision support systems, alternative planning methods, and spatial analysis have been actively developed. All of these methods are applicable for working with quantitative methods in forestry (Arthaud and Barrett, 2003).

The complexity of efficient forest management using platform solutions is confirmed by the system of priorities for efficient forest management using platform solutions. These priorities may be of greater or lesser significance in a certain period of time and depend on a number of factors: the environmental situation, natural disasters, military conflicts, the natural environment, historical and socio-economic mentality, the cultural level of the population of a particular territory, the economic development of the territory, the level of digitalization economics.

The basis of platform solutions in forest management is information, which is a collection of data structured, processed and analyzed using digital technology. Such processed information is in demand for a number of subjects of forest use and protection of forest resources. It serves as the basis for several actions, procedures, algorithms in the forest management system. The unique totality of such information is valuable from the point of view of industry, ecology, nature management, safety, and recreation.

In addition, it is advisable to differentiate forest resources data by thematic areas, for example, fire and fuel; networks and transport; forest and landscape planning; environmental modeling, biodiversity and wildlife; forest resource applications (Arthaud and Barrett, 2003).

Another criterion for the separation and systematization of data on forest resources is the degree of information processing. According to this criterion, the data can be divided into primary and processed (secondary). At the same time, the consumer of this information may be interested in obtaining a specific data package containing both primary and derivative information in order to effectively realize their goals in the forest management system.

Thus, the platform solutions method in forest management will allow more efficient modeling and analysis of the options and consequences of alternative management approaches for all components of forest ecosystems. UAIS, combining the digital capabilities of several information systems, is designed to ultimately help stakeholders and decision-makers come to reasonable decisions leading to the optimization of forest management system.

FUTURE RESEARCH DIRECTIONS

The direction of further research, we see the development of new forest management tools (similar to the proposed dashboard), based on the achievements of the digital economy.

ACKNOWLEDGMENT

The reported study was funded by RFBR according to the projects: N° 19-29-07545-мк, 20-010-00326-a.

REFERENCES

Akhtari, S., & Sowlati, T. (2015). Hybrid simulation and optimization approaches to tackle supply chain complexities – A review with a focus on forest products supply chains. *The Journal of Science and Technology for Forest Products and Processes. Special Issue on Value Chain Optimization, 5*(5), 26–39.

Alayet, C., Lehoux, N., Lebel, L., & Bouchard, M. (2018). Centralized supply chain planning model for multiple forest companies. Forestry Applications, 3–23. doi:10.1201/9781351269964-2

Anderson, J. R., Hardy, E. E., Roach, J. T., & Witmer, R. E. (1976). *A land use and land cover classification system for use with remote sensor data*. Professional Paper; doi:10.3133/pp964

Andersson, G., Flisberg, P., Lidén, B., & Ronnqvist, M. (2007). *RuttOpt - A Decision Support System for Routing of Logging Trucks*. SSRN Electronic Journal; doi:10.2139srn.1020628

Arthaud, G. J., & Barrett, T. M. (Eds.). (2003). *Systems Analysis in Forest Resources*. Managing Forest Ecosystems; doi:10.1007/978-94-017-0307-9

Barrett, R. H., & Salwasser, H. (1982). Adaptive management of timber and wildlife habitat using DYNAST and wildlife-habitat relationship models. *Western Association of Fish and Wildlife Agencies Proceedings, 62*, 350–365.

Bartsits, I. N. (2008). Reforma gosudarstvennogo upravleniya v Rossii: pravovoj aspect [*Reform of public administration in Russia: the legal aspect*]. Moscow, Russia: The formula of law.

Boyce, S. G. (1977). Management of eastern hardwood forests for multiple benefits (DYNAST-MB). *US Department of Agriculture, Forest Service, Southeastern Forest Experiment Station*, Asherville, North Carolina, Research Paper SE-168.

Boyce, S. G. (1978). Management of forest for timber and related benefits (DYNAST-TM). US Department of Agriculture, Forest Service, Southeastern Forest Experiment Station, Research Paper SE-184, *Asheville, North Carolina*.

Boyce, S. G. (1980). Management of forests for optimal benefits (DYNAST-OB). US Department of Agriculture, Southeastern Forest Experiment Station, Research Paper NC-204, *Asheville, North Carolina*.

Bykovsky, V. K. (2016). The legal and organizational basis of state forest management: A Textbook and practical Course for the SVE. 3rd ed., Revised and supplemented. Jurait Publishing House.

Corona, P., Köhl, M., & Marchetti, M. (Eds.). (2003). Advances in Forest Inventory for Sustainable Forest Management and Biodiversity Monitoring. Springer Netherlands. XVII. doi:10.1007/978-94-017-0649-0

Cortner, H. J., & Moote, M. A. (1994). Trends and issues in land and water resources management: Setting the agenda for change. *Environmental Management, 18*(2), 167–173. doi:10.1007/BF02393759

De Moraes Gonçalves, J. L., Silva, L. D., Behling, M., & Alvares, C. A. (2014). *Management of Industrial Forest Plantations. Managing Forest Ecosystems, 33.* Dordrecht, The Netherlands: Springer; doi:10.1007/978-94-017-8899-1

Federal Law of December 27, 2018 N 538-ФЗ "On Amendments to the Forest Code of the Russian Federation and Certain Legislative Acts of the Russian Federation Regarding Improving Legal Regulation of Relations Connected with Ensuring the Preservation of Forests on Forest Lands and Lands of Other Categories" // Official Internet Legal Information Portal http://www.pravo.gov.ru, 12/28/2018.

Fisenko, S. B. (2013). Implementation of the project management mechanism at the enterprises of the forest industry. *Transport Business in Russia*, 1, 222-225.

Forest Code of the Russian Federation dated 12/04/2006 N 200-ФЗ (as amended on 12/27/2018) // "Rossiyskaya Gazeta", N 277, 08/08/2006.

Hasenauer, H. (Ed.). (2006). *Sustainable Forest Management. Growth Models for Europe. Springer-Verlag Berlin Heidelberg.* XIX.

Helbing, D. (2015). *Thinking Ahead - Essays on Big Data, Digital Revolution, and Participatory Market Society.* Springer. doi:10.1007/978-3-319-15078-9

Isaev, A. S., & Korovin, G. N. (2009). *Actual problems of the national forest policy. M.: Institute for Sustainable Development.* Moscow, Russia: Center for Environmental Policy of Russia.

Köhl, M., & Marchetti, M. (2016). Objectives and Planning of Forest Inventories. Tropical Forestry Handbook, 749–776. doi:10.1007/978-3-642-54601-3_70

Kolesnik, V. G., & Sinyatullina, L. H. (2017). The Forest Complex State Management System: The current situation and main challenges. *Issues of State and Municipal Management, 1,* 129–148.

Konijnendijk, C. C. (2018). *The Forest and the City.* Future City; doi:10.1007/978-3-319-75076-7

Order of the Government of the Russian Federation of September 20, 2018 N 1989-r (as amended on February 28, 2019) "On Approving the Strategy for the Development of the Forestry Complex of the Russian Federation until 2030". Official Internet portal of legal information. Retrieved from http://www.pravo.gov.ru

Parmee, I. C., & Hajela, P. (Eds.). (2002). *Optimization in Industry.*, doi:10.1007/978-1-4471-0675-3

Reynolds, K. M., Twery, M., Lexer, M. J., Vacik, H., Ray, D., Shao, G., & Borges, J. G. (2008). Decision Support Systems in Forest Management. *Handbook on Decision Support Systems*, *2*, 499–533. doi:10.1007/978-3-540-48716-6_24

Roesch-McNally, G. E., Rabotyagov, S., Tyndall, J. C., Ettl, G., & Tóth, S. F. (2016). Auctioning the Forest: A Qualitative Approach to Exploring Stakeholder Responses to Bidding on Forest Ecosystem Services. *Small-scale Forestry*, *15*(3), 321–333. doi:10.100711842-016-9327-0

Rönnqvist, M. (2003). Optimization in forestry. *Mathematical Programming*, *97*(1), 267–284. doi:10.100710107-003-0444-0

Scholz, J., De Meyer, A., Marques, A. S., Pinho, T. M., Boaventura-Cunha, J., Van Orshoven, J., ... Nummila, K. (2018). Digital Technologies for Forest Supply Chain Optimization: Existing Solutions and Future Trends. *Environmental Management*, *62*(6), 1108–1133. doi:10.100700267-018-1095-5 PMID:30128584

Shpakovsky, Yu. G. (2018). Contemporary Problems of Legal Regulation of Forest Fire Protection. (2018). LEX RUSSICA (РУССКИЙ ЗАКОН). doi:10.17803/1729-5920.2018.134.1.043-056

Talapina, E. V. (2015). Gosudarstvennoe upravlenie v informacionnom obshchestve (pravovoj aspekt) [State management in the information society (legal aspect)]. Moscow.

Unified plan to achieve the national development goals of the Russian Federation for the period until 2024. Retrieved from http://static.government.ru as of May 13, 2019.

Von Gadow, K., Pukkala, T., & Tomé, M. (Eds.). (2000). *Sustainable Forest Management*. Managing Forest Ecosystems; doi:10.1007/978-94-010-9819-9

Zhavoronkova, N. G., & Vypkhanova, G. V. (2018). Legal Problems and Directions of Public Administration Improvement in the Field of Forest Relations. (2018). [РУССКИЙ ЗАКОН]. *LEX RUSSICA*, 2, 78–93. doi:10.17803/1729-5920.2018.135.2.078-093

KEY TERMS AND DEFINITIONS

The System of Forest Management Entities: A set of participants in public relations for the creation, use and protection of forest resources, interacting within the framework of socio-economic, environmental and other interests and united by common goals and principles of effective forest management.

Efficient Forest Management: Forest resources management, which includes two interconnected units: forestry and forestry complex.

Forest Management: Use of forest resources, their protection and reproduction of forests

Priorities for Effective Forest Management Using Platform Solutions: Target installations in forest management, taking into account the use of platform solutions, to ensure economic, environmental and other goals of sustainable forest management and protection of forest resources.

Forest Management Efficiency Indicators Using Platform Solutions: Criteria for assessing forest management effectiveness, which allow to measure and evaluate the results of forest use and protection of forest resources based on the digitalization of subjects' interaction and data exchange between them, taking into account the costs incurred to manage forest potential.

Chapter 10
New Perspectives on Cluster Model of Enterprise Development in the Context of Risk Management

Yulia Vertakova
ⓘ https://orcid.org/0000-0002-1685-2625
Financial University, Government of the Russian Federation, Russia

Galina Surovitskaya
Penza State University, Russia

Lubov Semerkova
Penza State University, Russia

Eugene Leontyev
ⓘ https://orcid.org/0000-0003-2269-4165
Southwest State University, Russia

Irina Izmalkova
Financial University Under the Government of the Russian Federation, Lipetsk Branch, Russia

Potapova Irina
Astrakhan SAS University, Russia

Maksim Kireev
K. G. Razumovsky Moscow State University of Technologies and Management (FCU), Russia

DOI: 10.4018/978-1-7998-1581-5.ch010

ABSTRACT

This chapter presents the author's views about new perspectives on cluster model of enterprise development in the context of risk management. Ensuring the efficiency and risk tolerance of enterprises is possible through the use of network organizational structures. Modern business conditions have created a significant variety of network forms, due to the peculiarities of the functioning of the industries and territories where they are used, the level of availability of information and communication technologies, the development of market infrastructure and social environment. One of the traditional and common forms of networks is the integration of enterprises into a cluster.

INTRODUCTION

Overcoming crisis phenomena in the country's region's economy and further developing market relations requires increasing the level of stability of the economic system as a whole and its most important elements - enterprises.

A negative factor that reduces the level of stability of any economic system is the risk, the study of management tools which is today an urgent scientific task.

In a market environment that operates on the principles of freedom of choice and competition, the effective operation of an enterprise is impossible without systemic risk management aimed at finding ways to rationally use favorable opportunities and achieve desired goals in conditions of total instability and dynamically growing threats of the modern economic era.

The need to adapt economic entities to the new realities of doing business actualizes the feasibility of substantiating theoretical and methodological provisions for the formation of effective organizational and economic support for the risk management process of their activities. That is why in recent years there has been an increase in interest in risk management among both scientists and managers at various levels of management.

The world economic science considers cluster associations in regions as an effective tool to increase the effectiveness and sustainability of individual enterprises. The formation of region's clusters in order to distribute risks among the participants in a cluster association seems to be an effective risk management tool. At the same time, the effectiveness of combining enterprises into a cluster is also associated with high uncertainty and risks. Incomplete assessment and, as a result, ineffective risk management lead to the failure of cluster projects and large financial losses for participants. Thus, the development of theoretical approaches and methodological tools for effective region's enterprise risk management in a cluster environment is an urgent scientific task.

BACKGROUND

The implementation of Industry 4.0 technologies into the regional economy leads to the emergence of not only new opportunities, but also new risks (Gamidullaeva, et al., 2019). The development of the digital economy is associated with technological, political, economic, social, psychological risks (Chernyakova, 2018). The level and scale of risks of industrial enterprises have changed significantly in the conditions of Industry 4.0. New risk factors due to digitalization processes significantly affect the efficiency and effectiveness of enterprises (Kuznetsova, 2018).

According to experts, at the present stage, the digital development niche is occupied by federal players who are not yet ready to invest in such promising projects for the development of the digital economy in the regions as smart cities, as well as projects on the digitization of housing and communal services and transport. It should be noted that the digitalization of local systems of the regional Russian economy was and is in the general global trend and is a specific traditionally innovative form of its development. It is an objective need and the need for the associated interaction of local systems of the regional Russian economy. At the same time, the proposed digitalization strategies of local systems of the regional Russian economy entail institutional traps (Postalyuk and Postalyuk, 2018).

The digital transformation of industrial enterprises has its positive aspects and possible risks. The latter include dependence on borrowed imported technologies, the degradation of their own competencies, the possibility of hidden "bookmarks" in hardware and software, uncertainty in the legal sphere, the growth of fraud, ethical problems, social stratification and other risks (Amelin and Schetinina, 2018).

The transition of the Digital Economy of the Russian Federation program to the national project format requires taking into account the relationship of the digital economy with the real one (Lenchuk and Vlaskin, 2018), and, on the other hand, makes regions more fully involved in digitalization processes.

For the regions and the country as a whole at the present stage, the introduction of effective risk management systems for national projects and their federal and regional projects is relevant. An analysis of the passports of regional projects within the framework of the national project "Digital Economy" showed the absence of a description of risks and risk management mechanisms in them. The solution to these problems is based on modern risk management approaches enshrined in international ones, for example, in the ISO 9001: 2015 standard (Kachalov, 2016).

The use of international standards in the field of quality management will also ensure effective risk management of digitalization of the quality management systems of industrial enterprises (Levchenko, 2018). At the same time, it is important to take into account the characteristics of such a source of risk as the environment of the enterprise quality management system processes (Popova, 2017).

According to experts, the mechanisms of public-private partnership have great potential in the implementation of strategic directions for the development of the digital economy in the regions (Tupchenko, 2018). This, in turn, determines the advisability of developing risk management mechanisms at enterprises in the region.

The activities of modern enterprises are associated with many risks, the impact of which has become especially noticeable in the conditions of developed market relations, namely, in the situation of growing uncertainty of economic phenomena and processes, the manifestation of which, in turn, is associated with both losses and profit.

In general, it is customary to define risk as the probability of the onset of some adverse event, entailing various kinds of losses.

The economic and legal culture of a business is expressed in a certain relation to risk. Risk aversion essentially means the cessation of any activity. At the same time, the ability to take risks into account in a timely manner increases the efficiency of enterprises and stimulates them to innovate.

Thus, the absence of actions or incorrect actions to manage risk are determined by a decrease in probable income, loss of profit or occurrence of losses.

When managing an enterprise, it is necessary not to avoid risk at all, but to evaluate the risk, try to anticipate, and minimize its negative impact on economic activity, through its management. By the beginning of the 18th century, mathematicians had developed almost all risk measurement tools that are still in use:

statistical sampling and the level of statistical significance, the principles of probability theory in different fields of science, and concepts such as normal distribution and standard deviation were first defined.

Fundamental risk theories include:

- classical (as a threat of an adverse event outcome);
- neoclassical (as the probability of deviation from the planned result).

The classical theory of risk belongs to the English philosopher and economist John Stuart Mill (1806-1873). In his work "Principles of Political Economy", J. Mill considers profit as the sum of the capitalist's "salary", share (percentage) of invested capital and risk fees. Under the risk payment, J. Mill understood the compensation for possible damage associated with the danger of loss of capital as a result of entrepreneurial activity.

An important contribution to the development of risk theory was made by J. von Thünen. He examined the essence of innovative risks. His conclusion was the first to outline the differences between a risk situation and a situation of uncertainty.

According to J. von Tyunen, "innovative activity is associated with unpredictable results, that is, reflects the conditions of uncertainty, therefore, the entrepreneur who carries it out is the only contender for this unpredictable risk income." At the beginning of the 20th century, English scientists Alfred Marshall (1842- 1924) and Arthur Pigou (1877-1959) proposed a neoclassical theory of economic risk. The essence of this theory is that in a market economy, an enterprise operates in conditions of uncertainty, therefore, profit is random and variable, hence the entrepreneur is interested not only in the amount of profit, but also in the range of its possible fluctuations.

The continuation of the neoclassical theory of risk was continued in the studies of the Hungarian economists T. Bachkai, D. Messen. In their opinion, risk should be understood as the possibility of deviation of the actual result from the set goal for which a decision was made. "

Another representative of the neoclassical risk theory is Joseph Schumpeter, who pointed out that "if risks are not foreseen in advance or, in any case, are not taken into account in the economic plan, then they become a source of losses, on the one hand, and profits on the other. The latter occurs when these potential losses for the enterprise do not occur at all or when - this circumstance is valid for other enterprises - due to an accident due to a temporary or long-term retirement, the victim's offer lags - and only temporarily - from demand at the usual price. "

In 1921, the American economist F. Knight, in his book "Risk, Uncertainty, and Profit," developed the theory of J. von Tyunen about the differences between countable and uncountable economic risk. F. Knight wrote that "practice has a great influence on scientific disciplines; the careless use of terms in everyday life leads to serious terminological confusion." This implies the need for separation of concepts: risk and uncertainty: "Measurable uncertainty is risk; immeasurable uncertainty is essentially uncertainty. "

Reisberg B.A. considers risk as a danger of unforeseen loss of profit, income or property, cash in comparison with the expected values due to accidental changes in the conditions of economic activity, adverse circumstances.

Another approach to the concept of "risk" was formulated by V. A. Oygenzikht. The author understands the risk as "the mental attitude of subjects to the result of objectively random events, which was expressed in the conscious assumption of negative property consequences". He attributed risk along with guilt to the category of subjective grounds of responsibility, explaining the possibility of the existence of cases of blaming responsibility without fault, i.e. when the entity suffers losses as a result of actions that are objectively lawful.

MAIN FOCUS OF THE CHAPTER

Issues, Controversies, Problems

In reality, the risk factors presented in this classification can interact and "overlap" each other.

For example, political and economic factors are closely interconnected and their interaction leads to a synergistic effect, significantly enhancing each other's influence. In such cases, it is necessary to consider as many areas of risk factors as possible.

Of course, it is impossible to take into account all risk factors, but it is quite possible to single out the main ones according to the results of impact on a particular type of economic activity of economic entities, while each type of risk has its own unique set of factors affecting it.

Evaluation of factors allows you to analyze the "risk" itself, pinpointing its cause. At the same time, to assess the factors themselves, their identification is necessary, which ultimately entails the adoption of the necessary risk management decisions.

Ultimately, the risk is due to the uncertainty of the conditions of the enterprise, the impossibility of a complete and comprehensive analysis of all factors affecting not the result of specific actions. In turn, uncertainty gives rise to a situation where several possible results are expected, but the available data are not enough to determine exactly which event will occur.

Thus, when studying various approaches to the classification of risks, we can say that the most optimal is the binding of "risk" to the factors within which it manifests itself.

Solutions and Recommendations

To increase the effectiveness of risk management in the implementation of regional projects in the digital economy, it is critical to create an effective risk management mechanism taking into account key trends in project management. It is advisable to include the section "Project Risk Management" in the passports of regional projects, which will reflect the really working risk management mechanisms.

In the context of risk management, a central place in the activities of the enterprise is the analysis and forecasting of possible loss of funds: unwanted, accidental, but permissible arising from the deviation from the intended course of action.

If an accidental event has a double effect on the final result, has adverse and favorable consequences, then when evaluating the risk, one and the other should be taken into account equally. In other words, when determining the total possible losses, the accompanying gain should be subtracted from the estimated losses.

In the activities of the enterprise there may be losses that can be divided into material, labor, financial, time and money losses. Material types of losses are expressed in direct losses of non-current and current assets or various unforeseen additional costs.

Labor losses are losses of the labor period, initiated by erratic, sudden factors.

Losses of time come in the event that the course of production and trading work is slower than planned.

Financial losses are formed as direct financial harm, interconnected with unforeseen payments, payment of fines, taxes, loss of funds placed on settlement and foreign currency accounts and securities.

Special types of financial harm are associated with stagnation of the economy: inflation, change in the ruble exchange rate, additional tax exemption to the local budget.

The danger of such losses is represented by risks allocated to a special group of financial risks, which play the most significant role in the overall "risk portfolio" of the enterprise.

It is generally accepted that financial risk is understood as the probability of unforeseen financial losses (decrease in profits, incomes, loss of capital, etc.) in a situation of uncertainty in the conditions of financial activity of the enterprise.

An increase in the degree of influence of financial risks on the results of the enterprise's activity is associated with the rapid variability of the economic situation in the country and market conditions, the expansion of the sphere of relations, the emergence of new technologies and tools, and a number of other factors. The types of financial risks are quite diverse.

The most common in the activities of the enterprise include production and commercial risks.

Production risk is associated with the enterprise's failure to fulfill its plans and obligations for the production of products, goods, services, and other types of production activities as a result of the adverse effects of the external environment, as well as the inadequate use of new equipment and technologies, fixed and circulating assets, raw materials, and working hours.

Commercial risk arises in the process of selling goods (services). The causes of commercial risk are: a decrease in sales due to changes in market conditions or other circumstances, an increase in the purchase price of goods, loss of goods in the process of circulation, an increase in distribution costs.

The top management of the organization should be able to establish the acceptable risk of the decision being made, and since these decisions are of an alternative form, it is necessary to calculate the degree of risk for all options of the decisions provided in order to choose the most optimal option. To calculate the degree of risk, it is necessary to assess the risk zone depending on the type and magnitude of losses.

The size of losses is formed using a qualitative and quantitative assessment. In the process of a qualitative assessment, they are limited to identifying possible risk zones.

The area in which losses are not expected is designated as a risk-free zone: there are zero or negative losses (excess profits).

The zone of acceptable risk means the sphere within which a certain type of work leaves its own financial rationality. Its border corresponds to the degree of loss equal to the estimated profit.

The following risk zone is called dangerous or critical: it is characterized by the possibility of losses in excess of the expected profit, up to the total estimated revenue.

The catastrophic risk zone is a loss that, in terms of volume, exceeds a critical level and at peak may reach a value equal to the entire state of the property of the enterprise.

Catastrophic should be attributed, regardless of property or monetary damage, to the risk associated with a direct danger to people's lives or the occurrence of environmental disasters that could lead to the collapse, bankruptcy of business entities, their closure and sale of property.

The probabilities of certain loss levels are important indicators that allow us to make a judgment about the level of expected risk and its acceptability, and to form a system of measures to manage them.

It is advisable to take the share of assets of the enterprise that it loses as a result of its activities as the basis for establishing the risk area.

The relationship between certain sizes of losses and the probability of their occurrence is expressed in the curve of probability of occurrence of a certain level of loss, which underlies the assessment of risk zones. To construct a probability curve for a certain level of losses (risk curve), various methods are used: statistical; cost-benefit analysis; expert evaluations; analytical; method of analogies.

Three methods are most commonly used:

- statistical;
- expert evaluations;
- analytical.

The main thing in the statistical method is the study of the statistics of losses and profits that took place in this or a similar production, the size and frequency of obtaining any economic effect is established, and the most adequate forecast for the future is made. The main tools are - variation, variance and standard deviation.

The risk level, in this case, can be measured by two criteria: the average and expected value and the variability (variability) of the possible result.

This method has been tested in practice by many enterprises. However, its use is characteristic of large firms and companies.

Small and medium-sized enterprises do not have the ability to use it.

The method of expert assessments is usually implemented by processing the opinions of experienced entrepreneurs and specialists (experts). It differs from the statistical only in the method of collecting information to build a risk curve.

This method involves the collection and study of estimates made by different experts (of the given enterprise or experts from outside) regarding the probabilities of occurrence of losses at various levels.

Estimates are based on taking into account all circumstances of financial risk, as well as statistical information.

The implementation of the method of expert assessments is greatly complicated if the total number of evaluated indicators is small.

The construction of a risk curve using the analytical method is a very complex process, since the components of the "game theory" underlying it can be accessed only by a small number of experts.

In practice, a subspecies of the analytical technique is more often used - an expert analysis of the sensitivity of the model.

The sensitivity analysis of the model consists of the following steps:

- selection of the standard value of the indicator, against which the sensitivity assessment is carried out (internal rate of return, net income, etc.);
- the choice of influencing parameters (inflation rate, height of the state of industrial policy, etc.);
- calculation of the indicator at various stages of the enterprise (procurement of raw materials, creation and sale, transportation, investments in non-current assets, etc.).

When using this method, charts are built that reflect the dependence of the selected indicator on changes in input parameters. Comparing the data obtained among them, the main indicators are determined that mainly affect the assessment of business profitability.

With effective management, the company is obliged to immediately, and most importantly, productively respond to external changes in the environment. For this, it is necessary to use well-prepared options for transformations that can change the situation for the better (lead to positive dynamics).

It is also important to note that effective management is based on a process of constant and consistent innovation in all levels and areas of the enterprise's activity, mandatory consideration of the total risks, as well as the possibility of introducing such management and financial mechanisms that allow you to get out of difficulties with the least losses for the enterprise.

FUTURE RESEARCH DIRECTIONS

In our studies of new approaches to improving the efficiency of enterprises, in our opinion, we should consider in more detail the use of such a risk management tool as diversification.One of the effective methods of risk prevention is diversification. However, even when it is introduced, risk situations may arise, which is a complex problem that arises when resolving the issue and deciding on the diversification of the enterprise. Prediction of economic risks in each specific situation is carried out taking into account the specifics of the implementation of a particular project or the implementation of a specific transaction.

The concept of "diversification" is interpreted as a process of expanding the range of products produced by individual firms and associations. In the second half of the twentieth century, many enterprises were characterized not by specialization in the manufacture of one type of product, but by diversification - the production of several goods.

CONCLUSION

The main goal of effective management is to quickly resume solvency and restore an adequate level of financial stability of the enterprise, and above all, to prevent its bankruptcy.

Ensuring effective management with a high level of uncertainty and risks involves a number of stages:

1. a periodic study of the financial condition of the enterprise, with the aim of early detection of signs of an increase in the level of risks of its crisis state, potentiating a possible threat of bankruptcy;
2. determination of the extent of the crisis state of the enterprise;
3. the study of the main factors that caused an increase in the degree of risk of the enterprise;
4. the formation of goals and the selection of the main mechanisms for the effective management of the enterprise in case of bankruptcy;
5. the introduction of internal mechanisms for financial stabilization of the enterprise;
6. the choice of effective forms of reorganization of the enterprise;
7. financial support for liquidation procedures in the event of bankruptcy of an enterprise.

With effective management, several risk management tools can be used:

- risk avoidance as the most effective way to prevent them, consisting in the development of measures that completely exclude a specific type of financial risk;
- insurance (internal and external). It consists in the transfer of responsibility to another organization (insurance), for the consequences of risk, with assigned remuneration;
- limitation, which is characterized by the establishment of a system of restrictions on the size of the transaction (restriction on the maximum size of inventory, the maximum amount of credit provided to customers);
- diversification, risk sharing of the enterprise in carrying out activities.

In order to study new approaches to improving the efficiency of enterprises, in our opinion, we should consider in more detail the use of such a risk management tool as diversification.

ACKNOWLEDGMENT

The reported study was funded by RFBR according to the projects: N° 18-010-00204-a, 19-29-07545-мк, 20-010-00326-a.

REFERENCES

Amelin, S. V., & Shchetinina, I. V. (2018). Organization of production in the digital economy. *Production Organizer.*, *26*(4), 7–18.

Chernyakova, M. M. (2018). Innovative diversification risks in the digital economy. Herald of the Eurasian Science. No. 6. Retrieved from https://esj.today/PDF/16ECVN618.pdf

Gamidullaeva, L., Vasin, S., Shkarupeta, E., Tolstykh, T., Finogeev, A., Surovirskaya, G., & Kanarev, S. (2019). Emergence of Industry 4.0 Technologies. Leapfrogging Opportunity for the Russian Federation. In U. G. Benna (Ed.), Industrial and Urban Growth Policies at the Sub-National, National, and Global Levels. Hershey, PA: IGI Global; doi:10.4018/978-1-5225-7625-9

Gumbus, A. (2005). Introducing the Balanced Scorecard: Creating Metrics to Measure Performance. *Journal of Management Education*, *29*(4), 617–630. doi:10.1177/1052562905276278

Kachalov, V. A. (2016). "Risks" and "Opportunities" in the ISO 9001: 2015 standard: separately or together? Methods of quality management. No. 7-8. - S. 1-10.

Kuznetsova, M. O. (2018). Risks of Industry 4.0 and their impact on industrial organizations. University Herald. No. 11. - P. 115-122.

Levchenko, E. V. (2018). Influence of digitalization on the development of a quality management system. Bulletin of the Saratov Socio-Economic University. No. 4 (73). - P. 9-14.

Popova, L. F. (2017). *Implementation of risk management in the enterprise quality management system.* Bulletin of the Saratov Socio-Economic University. - 2017. - No. 5 (69). pp. 104-109.

Postalyuk, M. P., & Postalyuk, T. M. (2018). Digitalization of local systems of the regional Russian economy: needs, opportunities and risks. Problems of the modern economy. No. 2 (66). pp. 174-177.

Tupchienko, V. A. (Ed.). (2018). Digital lifecycle management platforms for integrated systems. Moscow, Russia: Scientific Consultant.

Zhao, M., Heinsch, F. A., Nemani, R. R., & Running, S. W. (2005). Improvements of the MODIS terrestrial gross and net primary production global data set. *Remote Sensing of Environment*, *95*(2), 164–176. doi:10.1016/j.rse.2004.12.011

ADDITIONAL READING

Mkrttchian, V. (2013). Training of Avatar Moderator in Sliding Mode Control Environment for Virtual Project Management. In *Enterprise Resource Planning: Concepts, Methodologies, Tools, and Applications. IRMA* (pp. 1376–1405). IGI Global. doi:10.4018/978-1-4666-4153-2.ch074

Mkrttchian, V. (2015). Modeling using of Triple H-Avatar Technology in online Multi-Cloud Platform Lab. In *Encyclopedia of Information Science and Technology* (pp. 4162–4170). Hershey, PA: IGI Global; doi:10.4018/978-1-4666-5888-2.ch409

Mkrttchian, V., & Belyanina, L. (Eds.). (2018). *Handbook of Research on Students' Research Competence in Modern Educational Contexts*. Hershey, PA: IGI Global; doi:10.4018/978-1-5225-3485-3

Mkrttchian, V., Bershadsky, A., Bozhday, A., Kataev, M., & Kataev, S. (Eds.). (2016). *Handbook of Research on Estimation and Control Techniques in E-Learning Systems*. Hershey, PA, USA: IGI Global; doi:10.4018/978-1-4666-9489-7

Vertakova, Y., Plotnikov, V., & Leontyev, E. (2016). Methods of assessment the effectiveness of small business management in the telecommunications industry // *Proceedings of the 28th International Business Information Management Association Conference* - Vision 2020: Innovation Management, Development Sustainability, and Competitive Economic Growth. 2016. P. 1391-1399.

KEY TERMS AND DEFINITIONS

Avatar-Based Management: Is new management technology in Digital Economy introduced in 2018 from Professor Vardan Mkrttchian.

Digital Transformation: Is the process of using digital technologies to create new — or modify existing - business processes, culture, and customer experiences to meet changing business and market requirements.

Industry 4.0: The subset of the fourth industrial revolution that concerns industry. The fourth industrial revolution encompasses areas which are not normally classified as industry, such as smart cities for instance. Industry 4.0 is the trend towards automation and data exchange in manufacturing technologies and processes which include cyber-physical systems (CPS), the internet of things (IoT), industrial internet of things (IIOT), cloud computing, cognitive computing and artificial intelligence.

Chapter 11
Avatar–Based and Automated Testing System for Quality Control of Student Training:
Using Neuron Natural and Artificial Technology Platform Triple H

Mikhail Kataev
Tomsk State University of Control Systems and Radioelectronics, Russia

Vardan Mkrttchian
ⓘD https://orcid.org/0000-0003-4871-5956
HHH University, Australia

Larisa Bulysheva
Old Dominion University, USA

Anatoly Korikov
Tomsk State University of Control Systems and Radioelectronics, Russia

ABSTRACT

The chapter covers avatar-based control for neuron natural and artificial technology platform used in automated testing system for quality control of student training. The chapter proposes the concept of creating an automated software system for monitoring student knowledge in the learning process. It is proven that for successful students to learn remotely, it is necessary to develop a knowledge assessment system that takes into account various learning features, as well as the individual characteristics of the student. The block structure of an automated software system is presented and its elements are discussed in relation to the educational process. The role of the teacher in the virtual learning system is discussed and an algorithm of the learning process in this system is presented.

DOI: 10.4018/978-1-7998-1581-5.ch011

INTRODUCTION

The process of globalization makes new demands on the quality of school and especially higher education, as well as on the professional qualities of a specialist (both undergraduate and graduate). Although many leading universities in the United States already understand that four years for education at universities is no longer enough, and that it is necessary to move on to compulsory five years of education, especially in engineering, technical and physical-mathematical disciplines, but this will take time for the adoption of relevant laws on educational system. This naturally requires changes related to the modernization not of the education system itself, but of its elements related to the control of the learning process (Krasilnikova V.A., 2002).

In a situation of new requirements for the results of training specialists in the system of professional (competency-based) education, the following problems come to the fore (Korikov A.M., 2012):

1.   definition of common approaches to the formulation of diagnostic parameters of the educational process, understandable to students, employers and employees of educational institutions (universities);
2.   the unwillingness of educational institutions to evaluate the educational process, which involves students at an automated level;
3.   the lack of readiness of educational institutions to assess grades, the level of training and competence of students arising during the educational process;
4.   changes in the methodology of conducting the educational process, entailing corresponding changes not so much in the characteristics of teaching disciplines as in control and evaluation activities.

Consideration of all the identified problems highlights a feature related to the quality control of training, which leads to the need to develop quality assessment systems for training specialists at a new level (Mkrttchian V.S., 2012). This article discusses one of the possible solutions to this problem, namely the creation of an automated software knowledge control system based on an analysis of student's educational and test information assessments in the learning process.

Actuality of the Problem

Among the problems that modern society has to solve, one can single out one of the most important, related to the training of qualified specialists with higher education (bachelors and undergraduates) who meet the requirements of world standards. This is due to the fact that the speed of scientific and technological progress is constantly increasing and this requires the emergence of new qualities from graduates. Many leading universities in the United States already understand that four years for education at universities is no longer enough and that it is necessary to move on to compulsory at least five years of study, especially in engineering, technical and physical-mathematical disciplines, but this will take time for the adoption of relevant laws on educational system.

For example, we can cite the requirements for programmers who have changed significantly over the past 20 years. Previously, a programmer could master not only coding methods, but also the necessary approaches to algorithmization in all elements of software development (interface, modules, technical equipment, etc.). Currently, the number of specializations and their provision with various programming languages in the development of programs has grown significantly, which makes it impossible for one person to study them. This leads to the need for a more individual approach to the training process of such a specialist. This applies not only to the direction of software development, but also to many other areas of professional activity (Kataev M. Yu., Korikov A. M., Mkrttchian V. S., 2013).

An important condition for increasing the efficiency of the educational process, the quality of training of specialists and their competitiveness is the introduction of innovative technologies not only for training, but also for monitoring the quality of training. Quality control of training is necessary for the student to navigate the labor market, and for the employer, who need to know the competencies that a graduate of the university owns. At the same time, we note that only a change in teaching methods and methodological materials does not allow changes in the knowledge (competencies) of the graduate, it is necessary to introduce modern information technologies that allow quantitative measurement of students' knowledge before taking the course, after graduation and during training.

High competition for qualified personnel requires the employer to make responsible decisions about hiring graduates, on which both business efficiency and the psychological climate in the organization's team will depend on it. When applying for a job, professional qualities are very important that characterize the level of qualification of the graduate (competencies obtained at the university) and his personal, psychological qualities or "fit" to the company environment and culture, and so called "soft" skills are important. An error in admitting a graduate who does not meet the expected requirements entails negative consequences in the form of unjustified material costs (Kataev, M. Yu., Kataev, S. G., 2014).

Therefore, the preparation of a university graduate for future work is an essential part of the learning process, where the quality control system for education becomes central. The learning process can be viewed from the side of the management process in a complex technical system, where not only students but also educators, carriers of professional and personal knowledge (competencies) act as objects. To automate the management process in such a system, it is extremely difficult to develop a universal formalized model of the management system for the entire learning process. The difficulty lies in the specific requirements for the student, both from the educational organization itself and from various organizations acting as employers.

One of the possible forms of improving the management of the educational process is the possibility of creating an information system, the basis of which will be the results of monitoring the educational process, specifically for each student (Kataev, M. Yu., S. G. Kataev, Korikov A. M., 2014). Monitoring of the educational process implies the use of techniques based on the use of quantitative parameters of the educational process, which allow determining the values of indicators characterizing the level of knowledge of each student.

The existing experience of universities around the world shows that the use of modern information technologies in the activities of the university has a positive effect on the quality of education. The general requirements for automation are reflected in the ISO 9000 standards, directives of the European Association for Quality Assurance in Higher Education (ENQA). The development of the educational information environment of the university and the use of modern information technologies is the basis for ensuring the quality of education. Note that the individualization of the educational process leads to a change in the structure of the educational process, the emergence of new relationships between participants (between student and teacher).

In addition, this form of organization of the educational process leads to an increase in the flow and dimensionality of data that must be transmitted, received, processed and analyzed in an automated mode. This, in turn, leads to the need for a comprehensive analysis procedure and various aggregation of educational process indicators. Thus, the important and urgent is the task of a comprehensive analysis of the information arising in the framework of the educational process to ensure quality control of students of the university (Harasim, L., 2012).

Formulation of the Problem

The planning of the educational process in the framework of the curriculum development is one of the responsible, complex, time-consuming and poorly formalized tasks at the university. When planning, there is a desire to provide a high quality level of educational, scientific and educational work. It also involves the so-called "continuous improvement" process, based on the results accumulated in previous years of study and relying on data collected on the competencies formulated for each course in the discipline. However, with this approach, the individual qualities of each student are not taken into account, and they can be determined by the level of preparation at school, the psychological state, level of health, motivation, or other conditions.

Of course, this option will determine the increased complexity and complexity of solving the task of planning the work of teachers. Therefore, we propose to pay attention to, at the first stage, not to solve the entire problem at once, but to change only one part of the educational process associated with monitoring indicators of the educational process for each student. Moreover, some of the indicators are measured during the educational process in many universities (for example, attendance and academic performance), but are not used for a comprehensive and individual analysis for each student.

Any educational process in Russian and American universities begins with planning, which requires the preparation of educational material corresponding to the disciplines. In leading American universities, each department submits for approval by a special committee to develop new courses and disciplines at the school level, and then the entire university, new courses, new disciplines with full financial and scientific justification and justification of resources for this program or specialty. If a significant change is proposed to existing university majors, then the decision of the university committee to develop new courses or directions goes to the Senate for a vote. During the implementation of the educational process, conducting classes of all forms, knowledge is monitored in a qualitative and quantitative form (indicators in the form of grades or rating points).

The educational process indicators are accumulated in the database and analyzed by the teacher, as well as by the services of the university faculty. State requirements for changes in the educational process, emerging situations and long-term analysis of indicators lead to the need to change curricula, as well as modifications to educational material. The process presented in fig. 1 is repeated from year to year or depending on the requirements of higher organizations for the university. Note that in this structure the student is a generator of indicators and cannot change the structure of the educational process.

Figure 1. The structure of the model educational process of the university

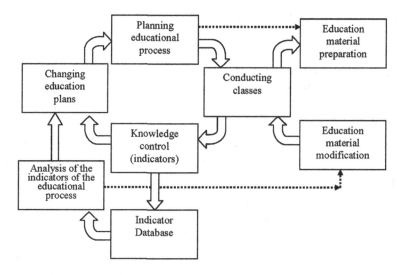

Consider the structure of the educational process, presented in Figure 1.

The modern direction of research and innovation in the educational process is the development and implementation of individual educational routes. This direction is known, but not systematized to date. However, it is not necessarily the best, due to various reasons. For example, in the USA this approach has been applied for more than 20 years, but it must be emphasized how this is achieved. Firstly, students must enroll in all compulsory classes in their specialty. These classes usually have a certain sequence, since each higher level class has requirements for the corresponding lower level class. Secondly, students, in order to gain the necessary number of credit (contact) hours for obtaining their diploma, must take a certain number of "optional courses" from a very limited and well-known set of courses. Moreover, if the number of students enrolling in such an optional class is less than 12-15, then the class will not take place due to financial restrictions.

And thus, students will be forced to enroll not where they want, but wherever there is an opportunity. And the opportunity may be to choose the most interesting class or useful, the easiest class, the easiest teacher in terms of easy grades. Sometimes, teachers agree to take one or two students and teach them in person, for example, to give them the opportunity to graduate. But this is done very rarely and only as an exception, since this work is not paid. Thus, an individual training route is such only theoretically, in practice, the choice is very limited.

It is also worth noting that there is a lack of well-known learning management systems (LMS) and training material (LCMS), which is associated with the lack of coherence between the use of training material, the form of training and verification of the quality of mastering the material. Many educational institutions in the United States make extensive use of the so-called Blackboard learning environment. It is used as a platform for distance learning and for regular classes. Blackboard provides an opportunity not only to store the entire course on the site, as for distance students, but also allows students to send their homework to the teacher, and also allows you to collect statistics about each course and class performance in general (how many excellent students, etc.), analyze the results of exams, report on questions that are poorly formulated by the teacher or missed by students.

The system will show an average score for each question and give recommendations for improving the exam text. In addition, at any time, the teacher can look at what question the student is on during the exam and what mistakes were made. They mainly use only the explanatory method of teaching through the provision of educational material of some forms of testing. In this case, the analysis of the quality of assimilation of educational material in a specific subject area is outside the scope of the information system.

Traditional forms of presentation of educational and methodological materials impose on the student the main work in highlighting and conveying to the students the semantic content of knowledge in the studied discipline. The teacher independently, within the framework of his experience and competence, distributes the time allotted within the framework of the educational process between the classroom and independent form of training. Recently, time preference has been given in favor of an independent form of training (for example, such a situation can be realized when classroom 40% and independent 60% of the total time). At the same time, it becomes difficult to find a compromise between the amount of information that the student can learn within the framework of both forms of training. It is clear that his further professional activity depends on the quality of assimilation of knowledge by a student.

In the mode when the process of controlling the knowledge acquired during the learning process is automated, numerous approaches are implemented, one of the most frequently encountered is testing (teacher tests, self-monitoring, repetition of the material passed, etc.). At the same time, it becomes possible to standardize when in the educational system you can use not only educational materials in electronic form, but also test materials. At the same time, test materials are necessary to control all stages of the learning process (lectures and laboratory, practical exercises). Such a software environment as Blackboard [https://www.blackboard.com] (and many others, for example, WEBCT [http://www.webct.ru], Moodle [https://moodle.org], Angel, RESPONDUS, etc.) allows automatic testing and automatic assessment of tests, immediately after completion of its implementation by the student.

ASSESSMENT OF THE QUALITY OF LEARNING OUTCOMES

Monitoring in the educational process is understood as controlling the learner's knowledge in various forms: qualitative (praise, nomination for a competition, etc.) or quantitative (assessment, scores, etc.). Without monitoring, it is impossible to effectively manage the educational process, to achieve the results determined by the learning objectives. In general, monitoring allows you to test the knowledge and skills of students, but after analyzing the data for a certain period, identify trends (stable, decreasing or increasing, or risk factors) and the dynamics of changes. The results of the analysis, the identification of dynamics, the determination of trends allows us to predict the further development of the learning process.

The basis for assessing the student's progress is the results of control on lecture material, term paper, laboratory work, etc. The evaluation function is not only limited to a statement of the student's knowledge, but also stimulates and motivates the further development of efforts to further gain knowledge. Note that the current system for assessing knowledge and skills requires a review in view of a certain subjectivity of its formation. Therefore, the formation of an independent, automated system for assessing knowledge allows you to get a new diagnostic significance and objectivity.

The most important principles for monitoring student performance in the disciplines under study are objectivity, systematic and visibility. Objectivity lies in the scientifically based content of tests (tasks, questions, examples, templates), logically accessible testing procedures, the possibility of equal choice of tests for all students, type of standardized exams, which are accurate, according to established criteria, assessment of knowledge and skills. When fulfilling this requirement, the student's grades are close to each other regardless of control methods.

The systematic requirement is related to the need for control at all stages of the educational process, from the initial stage of knowledge acquisition to the practical implementation of knowledge. Systematic requires regular monitoring of the knowledge of all students for the entire stay in the university, with such a frequency as to obtain a reliable assessment. This principle is difficult for analysis, since it leads to obtaining related assessments of knowledge, for example, knowledge of programming requires knowledge of the mathematical skills required in compiling algorithms, etc. Such a dependence excludes the universality of the applied methods for assessing knowledge. The visibility of the knowledge assessment consists in conducting test tasks available to all students and assessing knowledge according to the same criteria.

The quality of assimilation by students of the studied material in the discipline, their experience in the process of practical work can be characterized by several levels of assimilation. At the first level, acquaintance and getting some idea of the material being studied takes place. At this level, the ability to recognize, distinguish and relate objects and processes discussed in the academic discipline appears. The second level implies a more complex aspect of training associated with the reproduction of information given on the discipline, the ability to solve typical problems. A higher third level is associated with the acquisition of skills, when a student has the ability to perform, even template actions, knows the general methods and algorithm for solving problems. At this level, students are usually divided into two groups, when some perform actions for a sufficiently long time, while others perform actions automatically. These aspects must be considered when assessing student knowledge. The fourth level is the most difficult to assess, but the most interesting for the teacher, when the student performs actions with elements of creativity.

Intuitively, you can notice that according to the above levels, it is necessary to enter some weighting factors that would allow students to be divided into groups according to the level of assimilation. It is clear that students come to a university with different preparedness and psychological aspects, which affects the degree and time of mastering the material of a particular discipline. Most importantly, the state of the educational process (the time allotted for the discipline, the frequency of classes, the control method, etc.) and the amount of knowledge gained are, as you know, relative. It is difficult for a teacher to assess knowledge only in individual classes, and some tools are needed with which you can objectively evaluate the results of obtaining knowledge during classes. This will allow students to be divided into groups that differ in their level of knowledge, which in fact determines the methodology for managing the learning process. Such a tool is required to determine not only local sections (current), but also an understanding of the dynamics of the assessment information for each student individually.

The natural practice of teaching at the university is associated with a wide variety of qualitative and quantitative criteria for evaluating the educational activities of students. We must not forget about the educational functions of the teacher, but they are difficult to evaluate. In the opinion of the authors of the article, only the future work of a graduate can show an assessment of the effectiveness of the means and methods of individual educational impact on the student. The level of knowledge of the material in a particular discipline, the scientific and pedagogical experience of the teacher is directly related to the educational process and is determined by the

Figure 2. The structure of the developed information system for students' knowledge control in the learning process

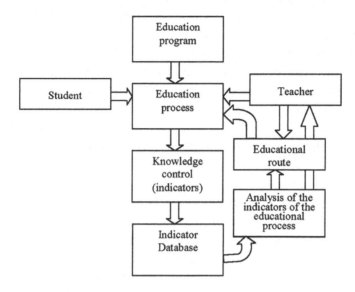

quality of test tasks, quizzes, tutorials, manuals, textbooks material, cases, examples discussed, team projects or individual homework and classwork assignments, and criteria for assessing students' knowledge. Sometimes, we could hear that students said that they learn nothing in the class, or they can't tell in 30 seconds so called an" elevator speech" what course or class is about. However, nevertheless, the personality of the teacher introduces some subjectivity and some independent model of student knowledge assessment is required.

Proposed Model

The development of the concept of information support for the learning process to increase its effectiveness is associated with the use of testing elements and appropriate decision-making approaches. As an object of management, educational material is considered as a set of educational objects structured in a special way and allowing approaching the individualization of education (Korikov A.M., 2002). The developed information system, which is part of the structure shown in Fig. 1, is presented in Fig. 2.

In the information system being developed, the tasks of managing educational material in the learning process are considered, which imply monitoring of knowledge in the form of tests. If the material is absorbed at a sufficient level of quality, then changes in the educational path are not required. A situation arises when the assimilation of the material is difficult, then it is necessary to solve the problem of managing the material of a particular discipline in the form of repeated tasks, assigning lighter material, etc. Of course, at the first stage, preparing the material from the teacher requires more effort than in the typical preparation format, however, in the future, most of the learning process falls on the shoulders of the information system, and for the teacher it is necessary to carry out only control.

The learning management process is associated with the decision-making process, in which the choice of the way to continue learning depends on the student's learning history and current performance. The information system, based on the available indicators that arose during the control of knowledge, allows these results to determine what knowledge is insufficient or incorrect and return the student to the appropriate section of theory or practice, or to provide additional clarifications. Moreover, to solve this problem, an appropriate educational trajectory is formed.

Naturally, in the field of knowledge, students will be divided among themselves according to the time of assimilation of a particular material in the studied discipline. In this regard, there is a need to search for approaches to motivating lagging students to accelerate the process of learning at a given level. These issues have been debatable for a long time and are not the subject of this article. The task that the authors pose in this article is to find a solution that allows automation of students' knowledge control in the learning process.

It is assumed that the student performs sequences of exercises (studying theoretical and practical material), while assessing his knowledge (ideally, competencies), the results of the assessment are submitted to the information system and the teacher with recommendations for making decisions, based on which the curriculum changes, errors are analyzed and work is done on the errors. (Rastrigin L.A., 1988) The concept can be applied both in the case of developing a new training course, and to expand the possibilities of using existing courses. The proposed concept is the basis for the development of mathematical, informational and algorithmic support for information systems working in the learning process.

ASSESSMENT OF THE QUALITY OF EDUCATION AT THE UNIVERSITY

Students studying at the university, according to the developed educational programs, after graduation enter the labor market. Therefore, the quality of education is the most important indicator that determines the success of the university and teachers (Bordovskaya I.V., 2004)). To assess the quality of training, various models, parameters and standards are used, for example, the Balanced Scorecard Model (BSC), Systems based on ISO standards, the European Excellence Model EFQM Excellence Model, CIPP Assessment Model, ESG ENQA, TQM, CATS, etc.

The balanced scorecard is a multi-level planning and management of activities and is widely used in industrial, state and non-profit organizations. This approach allows, on the basis of the analysis of the entered and measured indicators, to achieve improvement of activity, to reasonably build the internal and external relations of the organization, to monitor labor productivity in a clear dependence on strategic goals. ISO standards (ISO 9000) are sets of recognized standards at the international level and describe the requirements for the quality management system of organizations and enterprises. The organization's activity is presented in the form of interconnected processes that should be documented, those responsible for managing the process and performing its functions are introduced. During the process, regular monitoring of the main parameters of the process is carried out, their analysis is carried out, on the basis of which options for improving activities are sought. The analysis evaluates the effectiveness and efficiency of the process compared to the plan.

The European Excellence Model EFQM Excellence Model is designed to study the organization's management system based on a set of indicators that are evaluated according to several basic and particular criteria with respect to the previously thought out "Ideal" organization. The CIPP model allows you to evaluate the process and its outcome in the context of the chosen goal and possible alternatives to the strategic plan. The quality of the activity is related to how well the developed action plan is being implemented or already implemented. The idea of the Total Quality Management (TQM) model is that the organization must work not only on the quality of activities, but also on the quality of process control, which, with continuous monitoring of set parameters, leads to continuous improvement of activities.

The CATS quality assessment methodology, associated with the credit accumulation and credit system, is aimed at assessing learning outcomes and determining effectiveness for the concept of lifelong learning (Life Long Learning). In this methodology, the main goal of quality assessment is associated with the control of students' educational activities in conjunction with the desired competencies.

An analysis of the above methods for assessing quality in general allows us to conclude that they are successfully applied in the higher education system (Bolotov V.A., Efremov N.F., 2007). However, these techniques, reflecting the general points necessary for quality assessment, do not provide algorithms for their application in various educational institutions (humanitarian, technical, etc.). The objective of such a technique, in our opinion, is to build such a system in which the learning process for students from their passive role as a recipient of information turns into its active recipient to achieve a high level of knowledge and professional competence. The last condition requires the development of an information system that is embedded in the educational process of the university, where there is a receipt and analysis of all forms of assessment of student educational activity (Bolotov, V. A., Kovaleva, G. S., 2011). The results of such an information system should not only be accessible to students and teachers, but may also be available to future employers.

Description of the Mathematical Model of Decision Making

Currently, as mentioned above, the student's grades (indicators) are analyzed only point by point, at the current time from the occurrence or at the average level for a certain period. The various situations that arise in the learning process are resolved as they arise (Vasiliev V. I., Krasilnikov, V. V., Plaksiy, S. I., Tyagunov, T. N., 2005). We propose the development of a learning process management system by collecting current information about the educational activities of each student, its accumulation and analysis. The results of the analysis should show each student and those involved in the management process both the current situation about educational activities and their development trends and can show the risk of this student and predict the timing of graduation (Vasilieva, E. Yu., 2012).

In the learning process, according to the current academic performance R, the student's knowledge level Z is formed. Thus, the management of the learning process, through calculated control actions Y, which, through some function F, depend on current performance and factors, can be represented as:

$$Y=F(X,R)\rightarrow max(Z). \tag{1}$$

From formula (1) it can be seen that the level of knowledge (respectively, and the quality of training) of a student substantially depends on many factors that must be taken into account when teaching each student. Currently, the requirements for each student, regardless of factors, are unified and only rarely are taken into account in the learning process management system.

We propose an approach that is based on the fact that the results of the learning process are current academic performance R, time spent T (attending lectures, absences, consultations, additional classes, etc.) and V student activity. Thus, it is proposed to build a learning process management system on a time interval t based on a generalized criterion:

$$K=\alpha R+\beta T+\gamma V, \tag{2}$$

here α, β, γ are weight coefficients, t is a time slice that shows a moment in time from the entire training cycle (for example, week or month number).

One of the options for the numerical assessment of the weight coefficients can be associated with the theoretically possible maximum value, for example, $\alpha=Ro=5$ (maximum average grade), $\beta=To$ (training time per semester according to the curriculum) and $\gamma=Vo=5$ (average activity rating). Another option is related to the weight of each factor in the criterion, for example, $\alpha=0.5$, $\beta=0.3$, $\gamma=02$.

We consider separately all the components of the criterion. Current performance can be estimated from the expression:

$$R = \frac{1}{N}\sum_{i=1}^{N}\frac{1}{Ti}\sum_{j=1}^{Ti}R_{ij}, \tag{3}$$

where N is the number of subjects, Ti is the time allotted for each subject according to the curriculum, Rij is the grade obtained for the i-th subject in the j-th lesson.

Student time spent on training:

$$T = \frac{1}{N}\left(\sum_{i=1}^{N}\sum_{j=1}^{Ti}\varepsilon_{j}\cdot T_{ij}\right)+Tk+Td, \tag{4}$$

here ε_{j} is a factor of 1 in the presence of the student in the lesson and 0 in his absence, Tij is the time for the i-th subject in the j-th lesson, Tk is the time spent on consultations, and Td is the time for additional training.

Considering the learning process of a particular discipline of the educational process to be linear (i.e. structured in the order when each lecture $i=1,...,I$, consists of a certain set of topics $i=1,...,Ji$), we can assume that when testing after studying each topic, the total time will be determined by the expression (4). In expression (4), we assume that when testing the j-th topic of the i-th lecture, test questions belong to different levels of complexity.

With the introduction of testing, after each element of the educational process (lectures, laboratory work, etc.), the total value of the correct answers Z can be calculated:

$$Z = \sum_{i=1}^{I} Z_i = \sum_{i=1}^{I} \sum_{j=1}^{Ji} Z_{ij} , \qquad (5)$$

here Z_i is the total value of the correct answers for the *i*-th block of material and Z_{ij} is the total value of the correct answers for the *j* test of the *i*-th block of material.

$$Z = \sum_{i=1}^{I} \sum_{j=1}^{Ji} \delta_{ij} \omega_{ij} \sum_{k=1}^{Kij} \sum_{m=1}^{Mij} z_{ijm} , \qquad (6)$$

where z_{ijm} is the estimate (1 is the correct answer and 0 is incorrect) for the answer to the time *Tt* of the mth question for the *j* test of the *i*-th block of material, δij - shows in which test *j* for the *i*-th block of material, how time is used preparation for the answer, ωij - shows the difficulty level of test *j* for the *i*-th block of material (for example, ω can take values 1, 2 or 3), $k = 1, ..., Kij$ - the number of repetitions when passing the test *j* for the *i*-th block material, $m = 1, ..., Mij$ is the number of questions in test *j* for the *i*-th block of material.

The coefficient δ is calculated by the following formula:

$$\delta = \begin{cases} 1, & Tt \leq Tn \\ 1 - \dfrac{Tt - Tn}{T\max - Tn}, & Tn < Tt < T\max , \\ 0, & Tt > T\max \end{cases} \qquad (7)$$

here *Tn* is the time stipulated by the standard for the answer (for example, 3 minutes) and *Tmax* is the time, which is the maximum limit on the answer (for example, 5 minutes).

Thus, using two indicators of student learning *T* and Z, it becomes possible to automatically control the quality of student learning in the disciplines taught at the university, according to the student's chosen specialty. Obviously, one can distinguish at least four student states when the learning time is minimal and the grade is maximum, as well as the opposite event, when the learning time is maximal and the grade is minimal.

It is clear that there are two other events when the training time is minimal and the grade is minimal, and the training time is maximum and the grade is maximum (Ignatiev, E. Yu., 2014)). Note that the results of using this information depend on the teaching methodology. However, the possession of this information is a significant help for the teacher when choosing a teaching methodology, assessing the quality of educational material. For students, this information is the basis for self-esteem and an incentive for development, the search for solutions to move from one state to another, higher. For employers, this is also important information, as it allows you to see the qualities of a potential employee and his capabilities.

CONCLUSION

The chapter presents the methodology and structure of an automated software system for assessing the quality of student learning at a university. The methodology is based on the fact that a student attending classes, spending more time studying and leading an active lifestyle, is more successful in future work. This information is necessary not only for managing the educational process, but also for the students themselves and, most importantly, for potential employers.

ACKNOWLEDGMENT

The reported study was funded by RFBR according to the projects: N° 18-010-00204-a, 19-29-07545-мк, 20-010-00326-a.

REFERENCES

Bolotov, V. A., & Efremov, N. F. (2007) Education quality assessment systems. Moscow, Russia. University book.

Bolotov, V. A., & Kovaleva, G. S. (2011) Russian experience in the field of assessment of educational achievements of schoolchildren. Innovative projects and programs in education. No 4. pp. 39–45.

Bordovskaya, I. V. (2004) The quality management system of education at a university. Assessment of the quality of education at Russian universities. Experience and challenges. St. Petersburg. pp. 16–25.

Harasim, L. (2012). *Learning Theory and Online Technologies*. New York, NY: Routledge. doi:10.4324/9780203846933

Ignatiev, E. Yu. (2014) Means for assessing the learning outcomes of university students: method. Recommendations. Novgorod State University. Veliky Novgorod.

Kataev, M. Yu., & Kataev, S. G. (2014). An approach to knowledge control in a virtual educational environment. *Tomsk State Pedagogical University Journal, 5*(146), 41–44.

Kataev, M. Yu., Kataev, S. G., & Korikov, A. M. (2014). On the application of avatar technology in physical and technical electronic education. *Tomsk State Pedagogical University Journal, 11*(152), 187–192.

Kataev, M. Yu., Korikov, A. M., & Mkrttchian, V. S. (2013). The concept of electronic education based on Avatar technology. *Doklady TUSUR, 2*(28), 95–100.

Korikov, A. M. (2002). *Fundamentals of control theory: textbook. allowance*. Tomsk, Russia: NTL Publishing House.

Korikov, A. M. (2012) Education paradigms and the role of management theory in the creation of educational technologies. Modern education: problems of ensuring the quality of specialist training in the context of the transition to a multi-level system of higher education: international materials. scientific method. conf., February 2–3, 2012, Russia, Tomsk: TUSUR, pp. 127–128.

Krasilnikova, V. A. (2002). *The formation and development of computer technology training. OSU, Orenburg*. Moscow, Russia: IIO RAO.

Mkrttchian, V. S. (2012). *Avatar manager and student reflective conversations as the base for describing meta-communication model. Meta-communication for reflective online conversations: Models for distance education* (pp. 75–101). Hershey, PA: IGI Global.

Rastrigin, L. A. (1988). *Adaptive learning with learner model.* Riga, Latvia: Zinante.

Vasiliev, V. I., Krasilnikov, V. V., Plaksiy, S. I., & Tyagunov, T. N. (2005). *Assessment of the quality of the educational institution.* Moscow, Russia: IKAR.

Vasilieva, E. Yu. (2012) Development and implementation of standards for quality control of education at the university. University Management: Practice and Analysis, April. No. 1.

ADDITIONAL READING

Mkrttchian, V. (2013). Training of Avatar Moderator in Sliding Mode Control Environment for Virtual Project Management. In *Enterprise Resource Planning: Concepts, Methodologies, Tools, and Applications. IRMA* (pp. 1376–1405). IGI Global. doi:10.4018/978-1-4666-4153-2.ch074

Mkrttchian, V. (2015). Modeling using of Triple H-Avatar Technology in online Multi-Cloud Platform Lab. In *Encyclopedia of Information Science and Technology* (pp. 4162–4170). Hershey, PA: IGI Global; doi:10.4018/978-1-4666-5888-2.ch409

Mkrttchian, V., & Aleshina, E. (2017). *Sliding Mode in Intellectual Control and Communication: Emerging Research and Opportunities.* Hershey, PA, USA: IGI Global; doi:10.4018/978-1-5225-2292-8

Mkrttchian, V., & Belyanina, L. (Eds.). (2018). *Handbook of Research on Students' Research Competence in Modern Educational Contexts.* Hershey, PA: IGI Global; doi:10.4018/978-1-5225-3485-3

Mkrttchian, V., Bershadsky, A., Bozhday, A., Kataev, M., & Kataev, S. (Eds.). (2016). *Handbook of Research on Estimation and Control Techniques in E-Learning Systems.* Hershey, PA, USA: IGI Global; doi:10.4018/978-1-4666-9489-7

Mkrttchian, V., Gamidullaeva, L., & Aleshina, E. (Eds.). (2019). *Avatar-Based Models, Tools, and Innovation in the Digital Economy.* Hershey, PA: IGI Global; doi:10.4018/978-1-7998-1104-6

KEY TERMS AND DEFINITIONS

Avatar-Based Management: Is innovation management technique for human intellectual control.

Avatar Model of High Technology: Is new model with natural intelligent for Avatar introduced in 2011 from Professor Vardan Mkrttchian.

Big Data Analytics: Is the mathematical and software techniques for examining large and varied data sets to uncover hidden patterns, unknown correlations, market trends, customer preferences and other useful information that can help organizations make more-informed business decisions.

Entrepreneurs to Real Using Emerging Tools: Is entrepreneurs for the real use of new tools is a new approach to the concept of entrepreneurial phenomenon in a regional digital economy that can be used both at the national and national levels introduced in 2018 from Professor Vardan Mkrttchian.

Help and Control System: Is the system of reference and control is a new system based on knowledge and used for entrepreneurial in a digital economy introduced in 2018 from Professor Vardan Mkrttchian.

Intelligent Visualization Techniques: Is the process of presenting data in the form of an image in order to maximize the convenience of understanding them; giving a visible form to any conceivable object, subject, process, and so on.

Response to Intervention (RTI): Is a multi-tier approach to the early identification and support of students with learning and behavior needs; service for management educational process for corrections.

Sharing Digital Resource: Is exchanged of the digital resource is a new type of cooperation between enterprises in the digital economy in the form of knowledge obtained from digital avatars introduced in 2018 from Professor Vardan Mkrttchian.

Chapter 12

Avatar–Based Control and Development of Neuron Multi–Functional Platforms for Transformation Processes in the Digital Economy

Vardan Mkrttchian
iD https://orcid.org/0000-0003-4871-5956
HHH University, Australia

Serge Chernyshenko
iD https://orcid.org/0000-0002-2852-6878
Open University for the Humanities and Economics, Russia

Ekaterina Aleshina
Penza State University, Russia

ABSTRACT

The diverse sectors of the economy are subject to transformational processes in the digital economy. The reason for the rapid digital progress based on a functioning mechanism and the great attention to this transformation are the only economic reasons for reducing the costs of the transformation elements that are present in every product and, along with the transformation, affect mainly all sectors of the economy. For example, in the European Union there is a Permanent Forum on the digital teaching of environmental disciplines. In authors' opinion, the existing transformation models are extremely useful in connection with the decision of Russia and the EAEU member countries on the transformation of Digital Economy. This chapter sets the task of managing on the basis of avatars and developing neural multifunctional technological platforms for transformation processes in Digital Economy as based on the analysis of world experience in the use of digital technologies in teaching environmental disciplines and Triple H Avatar.

DOI: 10.4018/978-1-7998-1581-5.ch012

INTRODUCTION AND BACKGROUND

Extensive literature is devoted to the use of digital technologies in the teaching of environmental disciplines. Consider some relevant publications of scientists from different countries on this topic. First of all, we note that the focus is not on teaching ecology as a scientific discipline, but rather on teaching the fundamentals of ecological culture to a wide audience, including primary and secondary school students, university students of various profiles, trainees, retraining courses, etc. In addition, it is often a question of including elements of environmental education in courses that are not directly related to ecology or biology. It can be such objects as cultural studies, physical education, music, foreign languages, etc. Moreover, since ecology is considered as an element of general culture, in many cases we are talking about taking into account national or local characteristics of the students' culture, into which they should be "embedded" elements of environmental culture.

Here are some examples of such "nationally-oriented" methodologies. So, in an article (Bartasson, & Saito, 2015), the authors consider ways of teaching the basics of biodiversity to students in the 6th grade of a comprehensive school in Brazil. A special computer program (PROBIO-EE) is described, with the help of which students build special "conceptual maps", which helps them to understand the importance of preserving the diversity of nature - which, of course, is very important for Brazil with its very rich and unique, but at the same time the time is very fragile tropical flora and fauna, despite the fact that local folk culture is more inherent in the idea of exploiting natural objects, rather than protecting them.

In the paper (Debes & Oznacar, 2018), also devoted to the problems of education in the Amazon, the situation is considered in a more general perspective: how can digitalization improve the level of education of the population of the region? It is emphasized that no financial injections into the equipment of local schools will give the desired result without a systematic approach to the use of computer technology, without competent management of the educational process that specifically takes into account the new opportunities introduced by digital technologies.

The article (Fish & Syed, 2018) contains suggestions for revising the structure of educational programs for US Indians. The educational program is proposed to be based on some ecosystem models (expressed in the form of specially designed information environments) that reflect, to a large extent, the traditional attitude of these ethnic groups.

Environmental education in Mozambique in conditions of high migration activity of the population (associated with both rapid social changes and urban growth, and with the remaining nomadic traditions of a part of the population) is considered in the article (Tumbo, 2018). It is shown that the latest digital technologies open up fundamentally new opportunities, in particular, thanks to effective telecommunication facilities, and, naturally, contribute to a new outbreak of interest in various forms of distance education.

Nepal's unique experience in developing digital environmental education is described in (Tapa & Sein, 2018). It is shown how the national program "to every student - a laptop" works in a mountainous landscape with significant territorial and cultural isolation of certain regions of the country. It is noted that for developing countries, even a very modest improvement in the material and methodological support of schools can lead to a noticeable increase in the level of education.

The work (Findlow & Challenging 2019) deals with the development of environmental education in developing countries as a whole (such regions as Latin America, South Africa, and the Arab world are mentioned). The thesis is put forward that environmental education in countries with a weak economy and an underdeveloped political structure in any discourse (didactic, information-digital, organizational) should integrate the idea of political equality of people (national, gender, etc.), since sustainable development is impossible without ensuring such equality. Similar provisions are developed in the article (Peters & Jandric, 2017), where the close connection of the political structure of society on the one hand, and the level and style of education (in particular, its "environmental friendliness") on the other, is considered not so much from a geographical perspective as from a temporary perspective . Trends in the development of education over the past hundred years are shown, and special emphasis is placed on the features of the modern, "digital" era, with its rapidly growing technological capabilities.

The publication (Fuit, & Urbaniak, 2019) examines the inevitability of developing environmental teaching methods that integrate the experience of a wide variety of local cultures. It is emphasized that environmental problems are planetary in nature and their solution is impossible without universal involvement in the process. This should be reflected in environmental education; at the same time, digital technologies that make possible a wide international exchange of information and ideas are a key element in the formation of a new style of environmental education.

Development Trends of Digitalization of Environmental Education in Certain Countries

A number of articles contain a description of the level and trends in the development of digitalization of environmental education in various countries, but without reference to the local characteristics of the educational environment and the needs of society. When considering national systems, the question naturally arises of the degree and nature of state regulation in the field of education. As already mentioned, the most active topic of introducing digital technologies into education is developed by Russian and Chinese researchers, so we will give several articles on the state of affairs in these countries, supplementing them with an example of the relationship of the problem in such a developed country as the United States.

In the article (Bogoviz, et all, 2018), the authors talk mainly about the needs of higher education. In their opinion, digital technologies in Russia are well implemented at the level of individual advanced higher educational institutions, and they are also quite effectively used by individual teachers in planning and conducting classes. At the same time, at the global level of digitalization, there is a lack of consistency, both the assessment of the activities of individual educational institutions and their interaction with management structures and with each other are poorly formalized. The authors believe that a single effective state system for regulating the digitalization process should be developed, which is based on its adequate model. The article suggests some basic elements of such a model.

An article is also devoted to the Russian experience in the field of state educational management (Nekrasov, 2018). The main idea of this work is that digitalization should not be regarded as a mechanical process, but in each case creatively understood. The current tendency to "translate everything into a digital system" and build formal management schemes based on these figures is quite dangerous for the national educational and scientific system. Reducing the assessment of the activities of universities in the number of publications and their citation indices does not contribute to an increase in the quality of education. According to the author, while Russia has begun to understand this problem, and formal quantitative methods have begun to give way, to some extent, to such deeper methods as external examination of the achievements of scientific schools, the development of the peer-review institute, and the return to the use of informative reports that complement the filling out of formal questionnaires.

An example of a successful state system for assessing the quality of environmental education is the system that has developed in China (Ping, et all, 2018). This approach also includes many quantitative indicators, but is largely based on a system of expert assessments, taking into account the views of the widest range of stakeholders - students, employers, government employees, and members of the public. The problems of state regulation in the field of education in such an advanced digital country as the United States are considered in (Fujishiro et al., 2017). The article is devoted to the study of "socio-environmental" aspects of the impact of digitalization on the health and mental state of not only students, but also teachers. By analyzing statistics on 7836 teachers, it was shown that educational reforms in a significant part of teachers lead to sleep disturbances and problems with well-being. The thesis is put forward that radical changes in the style and volume of teaching should be accompanied by a deep legal study of the situation and corresponding changes in the rules of work of teachers, taking into account all medical and environmental factors.

MAIN FOCUS OF THE CHAPTER

Issues, Controversies, Problems

Another, no less important area in which environmental education is developing is its adaptation to various education profiles of students. Within the framework of this review, works devoted to various aspects of the environmental training of specialists in the field of ICT, mathematics, and physics are of particular interest. It is important to note here that environmental education for representatives of the exact sciences is not only the development of the foundations of ecological culture. Mathematical modeling and computer simulation of ecological systems are part of the classics of the systems approach, which is one of the cornerstones of modern scientific thinking. When using mathematical models, a mathematician or physicist can understand the specifics of environmental processes no worse than an ecologist, and this should be taken into account when forming appropriate training programs. So, the work(Abrahamson & Sanchez-Garcia, (2016), describes the advantages of using environmental dynamic computer models in mathematical education that work in real time and are focused on the use of touch screens.

The idea of using environmental concepts and models in the study of computer science was proposed in (Harlow, et all, 2018), and it is argued that this method can be effective even for primary and secondary school students. It is believed that the systems approach, which is the basis for object-oriented programming, will be better understood when using analogies with environmental systems. In particular, the software environment is considered as some analogue of the natural environment.

A similar approach to the study of ICT is proposed in article (van den Beemt, & Diepstraten, 2016), but already in relation to teacher training. Under the "ecological environment" is understood the whole range of conditions for study, including individual "populations" - software and hardware, as well as training sessions. In this case, it is believed that teachers initially have a certain environmental culture and knowledge, and this baggage helps them to master new knowledge in the field of digital technologies.

In (Yan, 2019), the concept of the "ecological environment" is proposed to be used in the formation of curricula in the preparation of physicists. At the same time, ecological models should complement the classical physical models.

The work (Bluteau et al., 2017), is devoted to the "interprofessional" (but, quite professional enough) study of the fundamentals of the theory of ecological systems. Again, it is proposed to expand the concept of "ecosystem" into non-biological objects (in this case, the social structure, as well as the organization of the educational process). An online course is offered using a fairly wide range of interactive and multimedia technologies.

Articles (Bushkova, 2019 and Bushkova & Matochenko, 2019) are devoted to the use of modern technologies in the training of environmentalists. The focus is on the library site RNPLS & T, dedicated to the global environmental problems of our time (such as climate change) as part of the teachings of V. I. Vernadsky on the biosphere and no sphere. It is shown how the resources of the site allow improving educational programs, conducting master classes, etc.

In (Mormul, et al., 2017), ways of informational support of the process of introducing scientific achievements in the field of biodiversity into the practice of training professional ecologists (using the example of studying amphibian populations) are discussed. It is shown that the existing representation of scientific information on the Internet does not always contribute to the widespread use of scientific achievements in educational activities. A proposed step is to improve the situation.

Another aspect of the informatization of applied zoology was considered in (Yoshioka & Yaegashi, 2017). Here we are talking about the application, for educational and practical purposes, of serious mathematical models of "stochastic optimization" that describe fish farming. A computer implementation of the model was applied for the case of breeding Plecoglossus actively in Japan.

The use of advanced mathematical and computer techniques in teaching landscape architecture is the subject of (Carlsson, 2017). Rightly emphasizing that when transforming the landscape, it is necessary to take into account all the complex relationships both within ecosystems and the human factor, the authors propose non-trivial mathematical models suitable for use both in the process of learning and in practical activities. The technique was tested during a special "educational experiment", and its first results were discussed in the article.

SOLUTIONS AND RECOMMENDATIONS

The use of modern technologies in environmental education of students studying ordinary architecture is considered in the article (Gulec & Turan, 2017). Cases are offered, when working with which students independently design computer models in the Ecotect v5.20 environment, which describe the relationship of architectural solutions with environmental environmental conditions. It is important to note that the study included an empirical test of the effectiveness of the educational methodology using several groups of students who used cases to different degrees. The article convincingly shows that the use of the proposed tools really enhances the professional level of architects. In addition to the publications cited above, which advocate the use of digital technologies in environmental education of representatives of the exact sciences, it was emphasized in (Kim et al., 2017), that during such education a part of traditional non-digital environmental knowledge should continue to be used as an important part of universal human culture and history thoughts.

A number of interesting publications are devoted to the use of digital technologies in teaching the fundamentals of the ecology of medical students. As in several works cited above, the article (Ellaway et al., 2017) emphasizes the importance of studying the theory of ecological systems for students to understand the basics of a systems approach in their professional activities. As applied to medical education, such important concepts as "biotic and abiotic factors", "system stability", "adaptability", "homeostasis" and many others are considered ". It is emphasized that for the development of the approach it is necessary to use special software.

In (Mundi, et al., 2015), a special digital application for a computer or smartphone is described, which allows the user to assess how healthy a lifestyle he leads, taking into account environmental factors, diet, etc. It is proposed to use the application both for educational purposes and for use during treatment of a certain group of patients, in particular, obese. The group of patients shows the effectiveness of the technique.

Provides (Mores et al., 2019) an example of developing a distance course for healthcare workers in the province of Mato Grosso, Brazil. The course is focused on teaching the basics of statistical data analysis, in particular, identifying statistically significant trends in changing environmental conditions, as well as in the spread and development of certain diseases. The positive effect of the use of digital statistical methods on the organization of health care in the region is shown.

An interesting aspect of the development of digitalization in medical education was considered in (Mueller et al., 2018), using the example of the situation in Bavaria. The main thesis is that for the successful implementation of new digital technologies in everyday teaching practice, of course, the active participation of teachers is necessary, while the latter are loaded with everyday teaching and have neither the ability nor the desire to have an additional unpaid load. This is especially true for medical education with its load on various types of practical exercises. The authors see the solution in the legal plane, by revising some normative indicators of teachers' activities.

A computer model for education in the field of ecotourism was proposed in (Wei et al., 2015). It is possible to change a number of model parameters (the intensity of the flow of tourists into the protected area, the level of their environmental education, etc.) and observe what impact this process leads to on nature. The program is aimed at future specialists in this field, but can also be used in practical environmental activities.

Publication (Melnik & Teplyashina. 2019), is devoted to the digitalization of higher education in journalism. Naturally, the emphasis is on the use of multimedia technologies for this area, but it is emphasized that the introduction of new technologies is impossible without a serious didactic study and revision of the course. It is indicated that digital technologies should be taught not only in terms of the direct presentation of journalistic materials, but also to support other business processes that are included in modern journalism: information management, marketing, safe storage of information, etc.

A narrower profile of philological education was considered in (Ashton & Conor, 2016). It is shown that the use of modern digital information resources and ecological systemic thinking makes it possible to train screenwriters much more efficiently.

Ways of digitalization of higher education in the field of teaching foreign languages for agricultural students are considered in (Bogdanova & Zharkova, 2018). It is shown that the use of distance education elements, for the implementation of which special Internet resources have been prepared, provides a number of advantages compared to traditional methods, developing students' skills in working with information resources and allowing them to adapt to the needs of their specialty, improving vocabulary in the field of science about nature.

The experience of China in the field of environmental education for student translators from English, using modern information technology, is the subject of an article (Wei, 2019). It is emphasized that for linguists whose profession involves understanding the cultural characteristics of speakers of different languages, environmental education should be cross-cultural in nature, taking into account the peculiarities of the ecological culture of different countries.

Chinese experience in the combined use of information approaches and elements of environmental thinking in teaching students studying in the field of art is also interesting. So, in (Liu, & Chen, 2018), there are curious data obtained during observations of a group of 257 students of art. It is shown that the systematic approach that students comprehend during environmental lessons contributes to the development of their skills in effectively solving creative problems, although at the same time they do not contribute to the simple accumulation of knowledge. The article (Liu, 2019), describes a similar study of 316 music students. The positive impact of "musical-ecological" education has been statistically confirmed both on students' interest in learning and on the level of their learning outcomes.

Finally, we turn to a review of publications containing a synthesis of world experience in building digital environmental education. We note that two categories of works can be distinguished: those devoted to the modernization of environmental education itself; and promoting the "greening" of modern education in general.

In a number of works devoted to the digitalization of environmental education, emphasis is placed on the argumentation of the importance of such education in the present conditions for all mankind, on the critical need to form a universal environmental culture. The named thought is central in the article (Apanasyuk et al., 2019), which further emphasizes that, in accordance with the concept of the noosphere, man cannot be separated from nature, he has become an important environmental factor, and the future of the Earth depends on his rational behavior. The article proposes a methodology for developing courses in ecology and environmental pedagogy, which are based on the latest technology and are focused on a wide variety of categories of students. A similar theme is developed in (Danylova & Salata, 2018), but from more philosophical and psychological positions. It is noted that when designing environmental education, one should delve deeper into the specifics of "human nature", skillfully combining global vision, which is absolutely necessary when considering environmental problems that are global in nature, and local (national, cultural) perception of environmental problems by individuals.

In a more constructive way, the general ideas for updating environmental education on a global scale are considered in a fairly fundamental publication (Klemow et al., 2019). Firstly, the ideas presented in it form the basis of the activities of the broad international environmental association ESA. Secondly, a clear "four-dimensional framework for environmental education" (4DEE) is formulated with four priority areas of teaching identified: key environmental concepts; environmental research practices; human-nature interaction; "Ck

FUTURE RESEARCH DIRECTIONS

Several articles devoted to the "greening" of education are based on the importance of using environmental approaches not only in teaching ecology, but also in organizing the educational process as a whole. This approach is most fundamentally presented in (Mackenzie et all, 2016), where an analogy is consistently drawn between purely ecological concepts (such as an individual, population, ecological niche, etc.) and subjects of the educational process. So it is possible to say (and it is often said) that various educational institutions occupy different "ecological niches" in the educational "ecological environment". Separate disciplines or technological approaches (such as the use of digital statistical methods) can be considered as separate physiological functions that, in general, ensure the functioning of an individual - an educational program. According to the authors, such a look at the organization of the educational system gives it dynamism and consistency. Note that in general, thanks to the work of A. Lotka, V. Volterra, V. Vernadsky, L. background Bertalanffy and many others, ecology, as a science, has become a model of a systematic approach, and its study is considered as an important contribution to the development of an individual's systemic thinking. This approach is used in [20], which emphasizes that the ecological (systemic) approach is very important in the student's self-education, which will be much more successful if he can identify elements of the educational process; to cover the information environment that must be mastered to understand the course; identify learning objectives. Naturally, the study of ecology as such should instill the skills of systemic thinking. A similar view, but deeper, develops in (Campbell, 2018). The very concept of learning is interpreted as adaptation to environmental conditions, and in this sense is considered to be inherent in all living things, and not just people. The environment, according to the author, is a continual object, and adaptation to it is processes that cannot be completed or even have a clear plan. The author, in the end, suggests making the education process much more flexible than is now accepted, and the information capabilities of the digital era may well make it possible. Finally, work (Herrera & De Ona Cots, 2016), also postulates the crucial importance of the "ecological environment", the social and cultural environment of the student, for the consideration, construction, and progress of the educational process. All other elements of the system - goals, content, and methodology - must be adjusted to the environmental conditions.

CONCLUSION

- The review showed that the topic of environmental education in the digital era has attracted the attention of researchers. Naturally, most often we find works devoted to a narrow topic - the development of environmental education in a particular region of a country (and often a single educational institution), in the preparation of specialists of a certain profile, or in the teaching of a particular discipline or group of disciplines. Describing the practical experience gained by a group of specialists, such publications cannot be of interest to their colleagues. I would especially like to note as a positive fact that in many works the conclusions and recommendations are based not on the speculative constructions and intuition of the authors, but on competently constructed statistical experiments, when experimental and control groups of students are selected, data about them is collected, which are then processed by standard analysis methods data.

- In addition to the specific results mentioned, many works contain important methodological generalizations, up to philosophical ones. We note one feature already noted above, which in some cases can lead to a misunderstanding of the author's approach. In many works, "environmental education" refers not only to biological topics, or to the topic of environmental protection in an arbitrarily broad sense, but is used as a synonym for "systematic" or "systemically organized" education. As a rule, in such works it is also implied that the teacher must have an "ecological" approach, and the student should be trained in it, i.e. The importance of the ecological in the usual narrow sense of the word is also noted.

- Since all the publications reviewed are concerned with the development of environmental education, its adaptation to new and constantly updated conditions of the current day, the issues of the effective use of modern digital technologies (and the inevitable changes in the educational process associated with this) are somehow addressed. In some cases, this is a very general discussion, but in many works very specific recommendations are given, supported by the practical experience of the authors, which means of digitalization are especially effective in certain cases. Moreover, the range of information technology considered is very wide: from the simple use of Internet information resources to complex mathematical models and methods.

ACKNOWLEDGMENT

The reported study was funded by RFBR according to the projects: N° 18-010-00204-a, 19-29-07545-мк, 20-010-00326-a.

REFERENCES

Abrahamson, D., & Sanchez-Garcia, R. (2016). Learning Is Moving in New Ways: The Ecological Dynamics of Mathematics Education. *Journal of the Learning Sciences*, *25*(2), 203–239. doi:10.1080/10508406.2016.1143370

Apanasyuk, L. A., Lisitzina, T. B., & Zakirova, C. S. (2019). Factors and Conditions of Student Environmental Culture Forming in the System of Ecological Education. *EKOLOJI*, *28*(107), 191–198.

Ashton, D., & Conor, B. (2016). Screenwriting, higher education and digital ecologies of expertise. *New Writing - The International Journal for the Practice and Theory of Creative Writing*, *13*(1), 98–108.

Bartasson, L. A., & Saito, C. H. (2015). The understanding of ecological concepts in Basic Education: Evaluation by concept maps. *COMUNICACOES*, *22*(2), 165–190.

Bluteau, P., Clouder, L., & Cureton, D. (2017). Developing interprofessional education online: An ecological systems theory analysis. *Journal of Interprofessional Care*, *31*(4), 420–428. doi:10.1080/13561820.2017.1307170 PMID:28471258

Bogdanova, Y. Z., & Zharkova, M. A. (2018). On The Digitalization of a University Education and The Possibility of Distance Foreign Language Teaching of Students of Agrarian University. *Modern Journal of Language Teaching Methods*, *8*(12), 186–192.

Bogoviz, A. V., Gimelshteyn, A. V., & Shvakov, E. E. (2018). Digitalization of the Russian education system: opportunities and perspectives. *Quality-Access to Success*, *19*(2), 27–32.

Bychkova, E. (2019). The conference on the global ecological problems held on the occasion of the 155th anniversary of Vladimir Vernadsky within the framework of the Fourth World Professional Forum "The book. Culture. Education. Innovations" // Scientific and Technical Libraries, 2019, No. 1. pp. 102-118.

Bychkova, E., & Matochenko, A. (2019). Education programs at RNPLS&T Ecological Information Research & Consultation Department. "Climate change" master class and research & practical workshop. Scientific and Technical Libraries, 2019, No. 1. pp. 97-105.

Campbell, C. (2018). Returning 'learning' to education: Toward an ecological conception of learning and teaching. *Sign Systems Studies*, *46*(4), 538–568. doi:10.12697/SSS.2018.46.4.07

Carlsson, M. K. (2017). Environmental Design, Systems Thinking, and Human Agency: McHarg's Ecological Method and Steinitz and Rogers's Interdisciplinary Education Experiment. *Landscape Journal*, *36*(2), 37–52. doi:10.3368/lj.36.2.37 PMID:30034076

Challenging, F. S. (2019). Bias in Ecological Education Discourses: Emancipatory 'Development Education' in Developing Countries. *Ecological Economics*, *157*, 373–381. doi:10.1016/j.ecolecon.2018.11.020

Danylova, T., & Salata, G. (2018). The ecological imperative and human nature: A new perspective on ecological education. Interdisciplinary Studies of Complex Systems, 2018, No. 12. pp. 17-24.

Debes, G., & Oznacar, B. (2018). Evaluation of the opinions of the manager, teacher, employees (secretary and servants) about school management of the digitalization and management processes of the system engineering model in education. *Amazonia Investiga*, *7*(16), 243–253.

Ellaway, R. H., Bates, J., & Teunissen, P. W. (2017). Ecological theories of systems and contextual change in medical education. *Medical Education*, *51*(12), 1250–1259. doi:10.1111/medu.13406 PMID:28857233

Fish, J., & Syed, M. (2018). Native Americans in Higher Education: An Ecological Systems Perspective. *Journal of College Student Development*, *59*(4), 387–403. doi:10.1353/csd.2018.0038

Fiut, I. S., & Urbaniak, M. (2019). Education in Defense of Biodiversity. Will the Ecological and Ethical Footprint Counteract Environmental Changes? *Environmental Studies*, *14*(1), 73–78.

Fujishiro, K., Farley, A. N., Kellemen, M., & Swoboda, C. M. (2017). Exploring associations between state education initiatives and teachers' sleep: A social-ecological approach. *Social Science & Medicine*, *191*, 151–159. doi:10.1016/j.socscimed.2017.09.019 PMID:28923520

Gong, R., & Yu, K. (2018). Key Success Factors in Using Virtual Reality for Ecological Education. *Ekoloji*, *27*(106), 257–262.

Gulec, O. D.; & Turan B. O. (2017), Ecological Architectural Design Education Practices Via Case Studies. Megaron, 2015, 10(2). pp. 113-129.

Harlow, D. B., Dwyer, H. A., Hansen, A. K., Iveland, A. O., & Franklin, D. M. (2018). Ecological Design-Based Research for Computer Science Education: Affordances and Effectivities for Elementary School Students. *Cognition and Instruction*, *36*(3), 224–246. doi:10.1080/07370008.2018.1475390

Herrera, P. D., & De Ona Cots, J. M. (2016). The relevance of the learning environment. Ecological education in a detention centre. *Revista Fuentes*, *18*(1), 77–90.

Kim, E.-J. A., Asghar, A., & Jordan, S. (2017). A Critical Review of Traditional Ecological Knowledge (TEK) in Science Education. *Canadian Journal of Science Mathematics and Technology Education*, *17*(4), 258–270. doi:10.1080/14926156 .2017.1380866

Klemow, K., Berkowitz, A., Cid, C., & Middendorf, G. (2019). Improving ecological education through a four-dimensional framework. *Frontiers in Ecology and the Environment*, *17*(2), 71–71. doi:10.1002/fee.2013

Liu, Y. (2019). Effects of Information Technology Integrated Music Ecological Education on Learning Interest and Performance. *Ekoloji*, *28*(107), 3441–3448.

Liu, Y., & Chen, M. (2018). From the Aspect of STEM to Discuss the Effect of Ecological Art Education on Knowledge Integration and Problem-Solving Capability. *Ekoloji*, *27*(106), 1705–1711.

Mackenzie, H., Tolley, H., Croft, T., Grove, M., & Lawson, D. (2016). Senior management perspectives of mathematics and statistics support in higher education: Moving to an 'ecological' approach. *Journal of Higher Education Policy and Management*, *38*(5), 550–561. doi:10.1080/1360080X.2016.1196932

Melnik, G. S., & Teplyashina, A. N. (2019). The Impact of Digitalization of Network Space on Journalism Education. Media Education, 2019, No. 1. pp. 86-92.

Moraes dos Santos, M. L., Zafalon, E. J., Bomfim, R., Kodjaoglanian, V. L., Mendonça de Moraes, S. H., do Nascimento, D. D. G., ... De-Carli, A. D. (2019). Impact of distance education on primary health care indicators in central Brazil: An ecological study with time trend analysis. *PLoS One*, *14*(3). doi:10.1371/journal. pone.0214485 PMID:30913272

Mormul, R. P., Mormul, T. D. S., Santos, G. M. B., & Santana, A. R. A. (2017). Looking for attitudes related to amphibian species decline: How are peer-reviewed publications of education activities compared to ecological research? *Anais da Academia Brasileira de Ciências*, *89*(1), 491–496. doi:10.1590/0001-3765201720160463 PMID:28562826

Mueller, Ch., Fuengerlings, S., & Tolks, D. (2018). Teaching load - a barrier to digitalisation in higher education? A position paper on the framework surrounding higher education medical teaching in the digital age using Bavaria, Germany as an example. *GMS Journal for Medical Education*, *35*(3). PMID:30186944

Mundi, M. S., Lorentz, P. A., Grothe, K., Kellogg, T. A., & Collazo-Clavell, M. L. (2015). Feasibility of Smartphone-Based Education Modules and Ecological Momentary Assessment/Intervention in Pre-bariatric Surgery Patients. *Obesity Surgery*, *25*(10), 1875–1881. doi:10.100711695-015-1617-7 PMID:25702141

Nekrasov, S. I. (2018). Interrelated processes of digitalization of the modern Russian science and education. *Education in Science*, *20*(2), 162–179.

Peters, M. A., & Jandric, P. (2017). Dewey's Democracy and Education in the age of digital reason: The global, ecological and digital turns. *OPEN REVIEW OF EDUCATIONAL RESEARCH*, *4*(1), 205–218. doi:10.1080/23265507.2017.1395290

Ping, R., Liu, X., & Liu, J. (2018). Research on construction of indicator system for evaluation of the ecological civilization education in Chinese universities. *Cognitive Systems Research*, *52*, 747–755. doi:10.1016/j.cogsys.2018.08.025

Thapa, D., & Sein, M. K. (2018). An ecological model of bridging the digital divide in education: A case study of OLPC deployment in Nepal. *The Electronic Journal on Information Systems in Developing Countries*, *84*(2), e12018. doi:10.1002/isd2.12018

Tumbo, D. L. (2018). Digital technologies in higher education in distance: Mapping and use by the tutors at the Pedagogical University of Mozambique. *CADERNOS EDUCACAO TECNOLOGIA E SOCIEDADE*, *11*(4), 613–623.

van den Beemt, A., & Diepstraten, I. (2016). Teacher perspectives on ICT: A learning ecology approach. *Computers & Education*, *92-93*, 161–170. doi:10.1016/j.compedu.2015.10.017

Wei, D., Zheng, Q., & Wen, Sh. (2015). Multiparameter Stochastic Dynamics of Ecological Tourism System with Continuous Visitor Education Interventions. *Mathematical Problems in Engineering*, *2015*, 968365. doi:10.1155/2015/968365

Wei, X. (2019). Research on the Development Strategy of Cross-cultural Ecological Education in English Translation Teaching at Colleges. *EKOLOJI*, *28*(107), 1665–1669.

Yan, L. (2019). On the Innovation of Physical Education Model: Based on the View of Ecological Environment. *EKOLOJI*, *28*(107), 3255–3261.

Yoshioka, H., & Yaegashi, Y. (2017), Stochastic optimization model of aqua cultured fish for sale and ecological education. JOURNAL OF MATHEMATICS IN INDUSTRY, 2017, 7, 8.

ADDITIONAL READING

Bychkova, E. (2019), The conference on the global ecological problems held on the occasion of the 155-th anniversary of Vladimir Vernadsky within the framework of the Fourth World Professional Forum "The book. Culture. Education. Innovations" // SCIENTIFIC AND TECHNICAL LIBRARIES, 2019, No. 1. P. 102-118.

Gonzalez-Sanmamed, M., Sangra, A., & Souto-Seijo, A. (2018). Learning ecologies in the digital age: Challenges for higher education. *REVISTA PUBLICACIONES*, *48*(1), 11–38.

Hohl, M. (2015). Living in cybernetics: Polynesian voyaging and ecological literacy as models for design education. *Kybernetes*, *44*(8-9), 1262–1273. doi:10.1108/K-11-2014-0236

KEY TERMS AND DEFINITIONS

Application of Blockchain Technology: Is application multifunctional and multilevel information technology designed to reliably record various assets in Digital Economy for help the technological challenges and created tools.

Avatar-Based Management: Is innovation management technique for human intellectual control.

Avatar Model of High Technology: Is new model with natural intelligent for Avatar introduced in 2011 from Professor Vardan Mkrttchian.

Big Data Analytics: Is the mathematical and software techniques for examining large and varied data sets to uncover hidden patterns, unknown correlations, market trends, customer preferences and other useful information that can help organizations make more-informed business decisions.

Blockchain Technology: Is a multifunctional and multilevel information technology, designed to reliably record various assets in digital economy.

Entrepreneurs to Real Using Emerging Tools: Is entrepreneurs for the real use of new tools is a new approach to the concept of entrepreneurial phenomenon in a regional digital economy that can be used both at the national and national levels introduced in 2018 from Professor Vardan Mkrttchian.

Help and Control System: Is the system of reference and control is a new system based on knowledge and used for entrepreneurial in a digital economy introduced in 2018 from Professor Vardan Mkrttchian.

Intelligent Visualization Techniques: Is the process of presenting data in the form of an image in order to maximize the convenience of understanding them; giving a visible form to any conceivable object, subject, process, and so on.

Response to Intervention (RTI): Is a multi-tier approach to the early identification and support of students with learning and behavior needs; service for management educational process for corrections.

Sharing Digital Resource: Is exchanged of the digital resource is a new type of cooperation between enterprises in the digital economy in the form of knowledge obtained from digital avatars introduced in 2018 from Professor Vardan Mkrttchian.

State-owned Corporation (SOE): Is a business enterprise where the state has significant control through full, majority, or significant minority ownership.

Chapter 13

Intellectual Property Institute as a Means of Regional Economic Integration in the Digital Framework:
Searching for Ways to Increase Efficiency

Leyla Gamidullaeva
 https://orcid.org/0000-0003-3042-7550
Penza State University, Russia

Saniyat Agamagomedova
Penza State University, Russia

Oleg Koshevoy
Penza State University, Russia

Valentina Smagina
Derzhavin Tambov State University, Russia

Natalia Rasskazova
 https://orcid.org/0000-0001-8369-9061
Penza State University, Russia

ABSTRACT

The effectiveness of intellectual property management in the context of Eurasian economic integration is positioned as a factor in reducing business costs in the EAEU. One of the basic conditions for effective economic development is competition in the field of intellectual property. In the context of globalization and digital transformation,

DOI: 10.4018/978-1-7998-1581-5.ch013

intellectual property management reaches a qualitatively new level of organizational and legal regulation and determines the freedom of movement of goods and services in the single economic territory of interstate integration entities. The authors of the chapter concluded that an effective intellectual property management mechanism in the EAEU is a factor of reducing the costs of foreign trade business. Inequality in the protection of intellectual property in the EAEU impedes the formation and development of competitive relations, and impedes the freedom of movement of goods as the basic goal of economic integration of the EAEU states.

INTRODUCTION

Intellectual property is an interdisciplinary institution, which is quite specifically positioned in various fields of scientific knowledge. Many studies of philosophers, legal scholars, economists, historians, sociologists, political scientists, psychologists, as well as representatives of technical sciences are devoted to the various aspects of intellectual property.

In this case, the most developed can be considered legal and economic issues of intellectual property. So, in the framework of legal science, intellectual property is considered as:

- the results of intellectual activity and equivalent means of individualization, which are granted with legal protection;
- sub-sectors (institutes) of civil law;
- a set of rights arising in relation to a few intangible objects;
- integrated legal institution;
- theoretical and legal category.

As the leading representatives of legal science, considering intellectual property issues, following can be noted: I. A. Bliznets (Bliznets, 2010; Bliznets, 2018), E. P. Gavrilov (Gavrilov, 2010; Gavrilov, 2014; Gavrilov, 2018), A. P. Sergeev (Sergeev, 2004; Sergeev, 2016), I. A. Zenin (Zenin, 2015), O. A. Gorodov (Gorodov, 1999; Gorodov, 2018), D. Yu. Shestakov (Shestakov, 2000), V. I. Eremenko (Eremenko, 2015; Eremenko, 2016), L. A. Trachtengerts (Trachtengerts, 2016).

Economists view intellectual property as:

- institute of market economy;

- factor and criterion for the development of "intellectual nature", "intellectual genesis";
- subject of intelligence;
- intangible assets;
- a structural element of human capital;
- a structural element of the intellectual capital of an individual, enterprise, industry, country.

The issues of managing intellectual assets and intellectual property are the work of a number of scientists, among which B. B. Leontyev (Leontyev, 2008, Leontyev, 2017; Leontyev, 2018).

Bautin V. M., Kostin V. D., Dashchyan, M. are developing a methodology for trust management of intellectual property (Bautin and Kostin, 2006; Dashyan, 2006), issues of information support for such management were developed by Kolodyazhnaya, O. A., Rudem, S. N. (Kolodyazhnaya, 2018; Rud, 2014), regional aspects of intellectual property management are considered by Salitskaya, E. A. (Salitskaya, 2017). Some scholars study the managerial foundations of intellectual property taking into account the globalization factor (Sevryukov, 2015).

Scientists use various approaches to managing intellectual property: systemic (Iskhakova, 2011), process-oriented (Semenova, 2015), and institutional (Leontyev, 2008).

The specifics of intellectual property management at an industrial enterprise as a component of the innovation activity management system are distinguished by Kolodko, G. N., Kalinkin, V. I. (Kolodko and Kalinkin, 2014); Ezzeddine, S., Hammami, M. S. (Ezzeddine and Hammami, 2018). Some authors consider the costs of research and development (R&D) as a factor in stimulating innovation (Cieślik et al., 2018).

Intellectual property is positioned as a structural element of human capital, intellectual capital, organizational capital and innovative capital as well. An assessment of intangible assets based on the concept of intellectual capital is contained in the works of Tkachenko E., Rogova E., Kokha V., Bodrunova S. (Tkachenko, et al., 2018).

Intellectual property-based innovation policies are considered by modern scholars in the context of economic integration, for example, within the framework of the European Union (Chesbrough and Vanhaverbeke, 2018; Jones-Evans, et al., 2018).

Most of the scientists who studied human and intellectual capital, one way or another touched on intellectual property as a structural component of these categories at the level of the individual, enterprise, industry, national economy in general. A number of experts attribute intellectual property to organizational capital (Juneja and Amar, 2018).

Today, scientists have ascertained the fact that various forms of capital contribute to the creation of a firm's value (Beretta, et al., 2019; Kreus and Saukkonen, 2018); build a relationship between human capital, intellectual property rights and production productivity (Habib, et al., 2019); link human capital to patent protection (Demir and Cergibozan, 2018).

It should be noted that the features of the functioning of the intellectual property institution as an organizational-legal and socio-economic institution in the context of integration processes have not been practically studied by scientists. At the same time, taking into account the peculiarities of using intellectual property in the conditions of economic unification of states, the formation of regional interstate entities with a single economic space will increase the effectiveness of such use in the context of globalization processes.

A relevant aspect in modern conditions requiring development is the management (including use and protection) of intellectual property in the context of Eurasian economic integration. Separate works of V.N. Lopatin are devoted to this. (Lopatin, 2016; Lopatin, 2017; Lopatin, 2018a; Lopatin, 2018b), Agamagomedova S.A. (Agamagomedova, 2013; Agamagomedova, 2015; Agamagomedova and Belousova, 2019). In most works, scientists recognize the existence of the Eurasian market of intellectual property, highlight the problems of its formation, determine the patterns and prospects of its development, but at the same time, issues of the effectiveness of intellectual property management in the context of integration are not resolved. In our opinion, the solution of such issues lies in the plane of economic and legal approaches in the management of intellectual property. The interdisciplinarity of the institution of intellectual property as a social institution determines the interdisciplinarity and complexity of its analysis and evaluation approaches.

Certain aspects of the integration features of intellectual property management were addressed in the works of V.I. Eremenko and Gavrilova E.P. The work of Abdullin A.I. is devoted to issues of legal protection and protection of rights to intellectual property in the European Union, the processes of harmonization and unification of mechanisms for managing intellectual property in the territory of a single European space, the role of integration courts in protecting intellectual property in the EU (Abdullin, 2006; Abdullin, 2012; Abdullin, 2013).

At the same time, it should be recognized that there is a lack of systematic comprehensive research on the institution of intellectual property in the context of integration processes in order to optimize its management. This work is called ⋅ upon to fill this gap.

Improving the mechanisms for creating, using and protecting intellectual property is designed to provide the basic goals of integration processes within the framework of the Eurasian Economic Union, which include freedom of movement of goods, services, capital and labor. Intellectual property provides economic relations, serves them to a certain extent, contributes to their positive development, and advocates the development of competition among business entities in the emerging single economic territory (Agamagomedova, et al., 2019).

Problem Statement

1. *The registration procedure for common trademarks, service marks and appellations of origin of EAEU goods has not been approved.* The Council of the Eurasian Economic Commission (ECE) has signed the Treaty on Trademarks, Service Marks and Appellations of Origin of Goods of the Eurasian Economic Union, but its entry into force is planned after 2020.
2. *The regulation for maintaining a Unified Customs Register of Intellectual Property of the Member States of the Eurasian Economic Union has not entered into force.* Currently, there are no registered intellectual property objects in the Unified Customs Register of Intellectual Property. The reasons for the fact that a single TROIS in the EAEU is not valid, although it was proclaimed back in 2010, is the problem of "former Soviet" trademarks, when identifiers are registered for the copyright holder in various EAEU states that are former republics of the USSR.
3. *Differences in the protection of the exclusive rights of copyright holders by violators and third parties at the territory of the EAEU* (different list of protected IP objects in the EAEU member states, different occupancy of TROIS, different measures of responsibility for IP violations).
4. *Problems of protection in case of abuse of rights by copyright holders*, incl. with parallel imports under the sanctions regime and non-use of intellectual property.

In 2018, there has been a new surge in interest in parallel imports. It was reflected in the Resolution of the Constitutional Court No. 8-P of February 13, 2018 in the case

Figure 1. Dynamics of the inclusion of intellectual property in the customs registers of the EAEU Member States in 2016-2018 (unit)

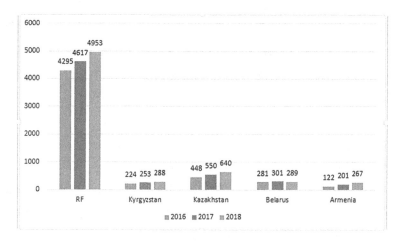

on the verification of the constitutionality of the provisions of paragraph 4 of Article 1252, Article 1487, paragraphs 1, 2 and 4 of Article 1515 of the Civil Code of the Russian Federation, in which the Constitutional Court of the Russian Federation expressed its attitude to the parallel import and banned the application of the same sanctions for the parallel import and sale of counterfeit products. According to the Constitutional Court of the Russian Federation, the globalization of world trade, the introduction of economic sanctions against our country once again made urgent the problem of exhausting the exclusive rights of the copyright holder in relation to a trademark, which is a legal restriction on the legal monopoly on the use of the exclusive right to a trademark.

Recognizing that the national principle of exclusive rights' exhaustion, enshrined in the Civil Code of the Russian Federation, does not contradict the Constitution of the Russian Federation, the court nevertheless does not exclude the possibility of the copyright holder to unfairly use the exclusive right to a trademark and restrict the introduction of goods marked with a trademark into the Russian national market. The Constitutional Court of the Russian Federation rightly recognized the potential danger of such actions within the framework of the sanctions policy pursued in relation to Russia in the current period.

The constitutional and legal interpretation of the disputed norms of the Civil Code of the Russian Federation represents the possibility of using, in cases of unfair

Figure 2. Dynamics of filing applications and registration of trademarks in the EAEU Member States in 2014-2018 (unit)

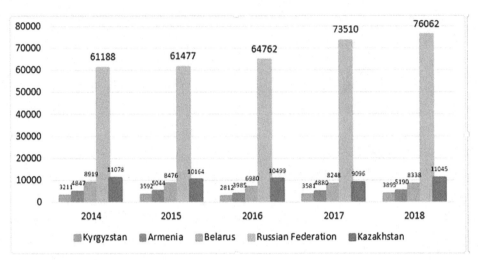

behavior of the copyright holder of a trademark, civil-law means of combating abuse of law. The court may refuse the right holder the claim in whole or in part, if the fulfillment of its requirements may create a threat to constitutionally significant values.

5.   ***Low activity of copyright holders*** (in comparison with the EU). There is practically no judicial practice at the EAEU level, as business entities do not file claims with the EAEU Court (in the EU, decisions of the EU court influenced the activities of the European Commission in the field of intellectual property).

We should separately highlight the problem of different register occupancy in the EAEU member states (volume and dynamics of occupancy).

Given the deferred action of the unified TROIS of the EAEU member states, such differences in the number of registered intellectual property objects at the national level (Figure 1) entail a different level of legal protection for copyright holders in the EAEU countries, which contradicts the basic goals of Eurasian economic integration (Fig. 1).

Moreover, an analysis of the statistical data of submitted applications and registered trademarks in the EAEU member states over the past 5 years indicates a steady dynamic of their growth (Fig. 2). Growth is more significant than the increase in the number of intellectual property objects included in the national customs registers of states.

Thus, the following data are indicators of intellectual activity in the EAEU member states:

- the number of applications for registration of a trademark;
- the number of registered trademarks in the EAEU Member States;
- the number of OIPs entered in the national customs registers of the EAEU Member States.

Their analysis indicates a different level of intellectual activity in the EAEU member states and, as a result, the level of protection of intellectual rights in the integration member states.

It can be said that differences in intellectual activity in the EAEU member states determine differences in the level of protection of intellectual rights in the EAEU unified economic territory, which ultimately impedes the freedom of movement of goods as a basic goal of economic integration.

This section of the study is devoted to the practical aspects of the innovation activity influence on indicators of economic development in the region. Due to the lack of detailed data for all EAEU countries, the analysis was carried out by regions of the Russian Federation, which allows us to test the hypothesis about the positive effect of the number of applications for trademark registration on the level of economic development of the region.

It is proposed to use the gross regional product ("GRP") as a comprehensive indicator of the level of economic development of the regions, which reflects various aspects of the economic life of the region. From a formal point of view, the following hypotheses will be tested in the work:

Hypothesis I. The number of applications for trademark registration filed in a particular region positively affects the gross regional product.

Hypothesis II. Regions with a high coefficient of inventive activity have a higher gross regional product.

Next, it is necessary to provide a description of the methodology used and the data by which the hypotheses of the study will be tested (Agamagomedova, et al., 2019).

MAIN FOCUS OF THE CHAPTER

Issues, Controversies, Problems

To assess the impact of patent and other innovative activities on the level of regional GRP, it is necessary to select a qualitative model that describes the dynamics of the GRP. As such a model, it is proposed to use the following equation:

$$g\,gdp_{it} = const + \beta * X_{it} + \gamma * g\,tm_{it} + \delta * patent_{it} + \varepsilon_{it} \tag{2}$$

where:

- $g\,gdp_{it}$ – the index of the physical volume of GRP of region i at time t (at constant prices; in percent to the previous year).
- X_{it} – a set of exogenous factors that have a potential impact on the region's GRP (a full list is given later in the text).
- $g\,tm_{it}$ – increase in the number of applications for trademark registration filed in region i in the period of time t.
- $patent_{it}$ – coefficient of inventive activity in region i at time t. That is the number of applications filed for the grant of patents for inventions and utility models per 10,000 people.
- $const, \beta, \gamma, \delta$ – the parameters that will be estimated by the least squares' method in the course of further analysis.
- ε_{it} – the stochastic component of the model. The specific nature of the error will be determined later in the work.

As can be seen from the model's details above, to evaluate it is necessary to use methods of analysis of panel data. This allows one to take into account both the spatial and temporal components of the considered dependence. Panel data allows you to control variables that are unobservable, as well as variables that change over time but differ by region. Such data make it possible to more accurately consider the individual heterogeneity of the sample. To work with panel data, there are two generally accepted methods (Anatolyev, 2003) that allow you to evaluate the coefficients of models:

- Fixed Effect Model (FE);
- Random Effect Model (RE).

According to Wooldridge (2010), the FE model is designed to study the causes of changes within a specific object, in our case a separate region. Thus, the FE model can eliminate the influence of time-invariant characteristics on the estimate, which allows us to study only the complex effect of exogenous variables on the dependent variable.

Another assumption of this method is that time-independent parameters are unique to the region and should not be correlated with other individual parameters. Each element of the data set is different from the other, so the model error should not correlate with other parameters. Therefore, if errors are correlated, then this FE method cannot be used.

Unlike the FE model, the RE model assumes that differences between regions are not related to the predictor or independent variables and, of course, are random. In other words, if we find evidence that differences between regions affect the dependent variable, then we use the RE model.

The Hausman test is used for a reasoned choice between FE and RE. As we have already said, in the panel data model, the "region effect" can be modeled as fixed or random effects using the following rule:

- if the influence of the region correlates with other independent variables, FE is consistent and RE is insolvent;
- if the effect of the region does not correlate with other independent variables, both methods are consistent, but RE is effective.

Therefore, since both methods are consistent in the absence of correlation, we must evaluate the difference between them and choose RE if this difference is relatively small, since RE is more effective in this case. As a result, to evaluate the difference, we can apply the Hausman criterion, which is based on this difference:

- the difference between the two estimates is insignificant (errors are not correlated) - we use RE;
- the difference between the two estimates is significant (errors are correlated) - we use FE.

After describing the main technical details of the methodology, it is necessary to proceed to the determination of a set of exogenous variables. According to the classical concepts of gross product and output in the economy (King, 2000):

Table 1. Evaluation of the fixed effects model

Variables	(FE) g_gdp	(FE) g_gdp
g_income	0.143***	0.144***
	(0.0210)	(0.0249)
g_invest	0.0870***	0.0921***
	(0.00999)	(0.00998)
innovation	0.0797	-0.00321
	(0.0543)	(0.0683)
g_tm	-0.0378	
	(0.247)	
patent	0.132	0.282
	(0.220)	(0.278)
L.g_tm		0.263*
		(0.157)
Constant	78.14***	77.55***
	(2.103)	(2.396)
Observations	554	477
R-squared	0.324	0.344
Number of region	81	81

Robust standard errors in parentheses
*** $p<0.01$, ** $p<0.05$, * $p<0.1$
Source: authors' calculations

$$GRP = Consumption + Investment + Gov. Expenditures + Net Export$$

$$(3)$$

Due to the limitation of consumption data, it is proposed to use the level of population income growth in a certain region as an explanatory variable for consumption. The dependence of consumption on income is also noted in Friedman (2018). The relationship between gross domestic product and population income is noted in the works of Kohli (2004), Feldstein (2017). Based on the conclusions of classical economic theory, we expect a significant positive dependence of the gross regional product on the income level of the population.

Table 2. Evaluation of the random effects model

Variables	(RE) g_gdp	(RE) g_gdp
g_income	0.162***	0.160***
	(0.0208)	(0.0251)
g_invest	0.0859***	0.0911***
	(0.0103)	(0.0105)
innovation	0.0717**	0.0545
	(0.0345)	(0.0379)
g_tm	-0.0361	
	(0.216)	
patent	-0.0383	-0.0143
	(0.113)	(0.129)
L.g_tm		0.194
		(0.126)
Constant	76.70***	76.10***
	(1.935)	(2.300)
Observations	554	477
R-squared	0.323	0.340
Number of region	81	81

Robust standard errors in parentheses
*** p<0.01, ** p<0.05, * p<0.1
Source: authors' calculations

It is proposed to use the index of physical volume of investments in fixed assets in comparable prices in the form of percentage to the previous year as a proxy for investments. The presence of an investment component in the model is confirmed, inter alia, by the works of Looney, Frederiksen (1981), Banister, Berechman (2001), Ouyang, Fu (2012).

Government expenditures and net export are outside the scope of this study due to its regional focus. Since a significant part of government spending is represented by the federal budget, the use of the regional component is debatable. The absence of an export-import component in the model is justified by the absence of any administrative barriers between the regions of the Russian Federation.

To consider the entire spectrum of innovative development of the region, an additional exogenous variable is included in the model - the innovative activity of the region, calculated as the proportion of organizations implementing technological, marketing and organizational innovations, in the total number of organizations examined; in percentage (Agamagomedova, et al., 2019)..

Research Data

After the methodology of analysis is described in the work, it is necessary to proceed to a detailed description of the data and sources used. The main sources of data for work are:

- Federal State Statistics Service
- Federal Service for Intellectual Property.

The time horizon of the data used covers the period from 2010 to 2016. The frequency of data is annual. Despite the availability of relevant data on the number of applications for trademark registration (up to 2018 inclusive), the use of data for 2017–2018 is limited due to the lack of relevant data on GRP in the official publications of the State Statistics Committee.

Using the data described above in the framework of the considered methodology allowed us to assess the effect of innovation activity on the economic development of the regions of the Russian Federation. Evaluation of the model with fixed effects is shown in the Table 1.

As can be seen from the table above, household incomes and the size of investments significantly positively affect the region's GRP. Moreover, in the framework of the basic model, no significant effect on the gross product was found either created by the number of applications for registration of a trademark or by the patent activity. In this regard, an assumption was made that there is a time lag between the growth of innovative activity and the growth of output (second column in the table above). In this case, we see a significant positive effect of the number of applications for trademark registration on GRP. Next, we proceed to the evaluation of models with random effects (Table 2).

The above calculation results confirm the hypothesis that household incomes and investments positively affect output. However, the model with random effects does not confirm the significant influence of patent activity and the number of applications for trademark registration on the level of economic development of the regions of the Russian Federation.

At this stage, you need to choose between two types of models. According to the Hausman test (p-value = 0.0013), a model with fixed effects is preferable.

Solutions and Recommendations

From a formal point of view, testing of the set hypotheses led to the following results:

- Hypothesis I. The number of applications for registration of trademarks filed in a particular region positively affects the gross regional product. - It is confirmed statistically.
- Hypothesis II. Regions with a high coefficient of inventive activity have a higher gross regional product. - no significant dependence was found on the data used.

The following aspects can be distinguished as the main results of the study:

- The region's GRP growth rate is significantly positively dependent on the growth of household incomes and the size of investments in fixed assets.
- An increase in the number of applications for trademark registration in a certain period in the region by 1% leads to an increase in GRP of this region in the next period of time by 0.263%.

CONCLUSION

The effectiveness of intellectual property management in the context of Eurasian economic integration is positioned as a factor in reducing business costs in the EAEU.

One of the basic conditions for effective innovative development is competition in the field of intellectual property. In the context of globalization, intellectual property management reaches a qualitatively new level of organizational and legal regulation and determines the freedom of movement of goods and services in the single economic territory of interstate integration entities.

IP management involves several stages: stimulating the creation of IP, creating (registering) IP, using, commercializing, protecting IP. The latter provides for two aspects: protection in the domestic national market and in the cross-border movement of goods (customs protection).

Currently, within the framework of the Eurasian Economic Union, mechanisms for unification of two of these stages are provided: creation in the form of registration and protection during the cross-border movement of goods.

1. Registration of a single trademark (service mark, appellation of origin) of the EAEU
2. The Unified Customs Register of Intellectual Property of the EAEU Member States.

Both designs involve a reduction in the costs of the foreign trade business. However, the analysis indicates the problems of the functioning of these mechanisms.

Experts propose introducing the practice of antitrust regulation and assessing the integrity of intellectual property market entities in the EAEU countries through the competition index (ratio of the number of patents and the share of patent sales) (Agamagomedova, et al., 2019).

Our suggestions:

- IP business education;
- stimulation of intellectual activity and commercialization of IP;
- formation of an active competitive position of copyright holders in the field of IP protection;
- reduction of administrative barriers when including IPOs in national TRIOS (currently, when including IPOs in TROIS, the insured amount or the amount of security for the fulfillment of an obligation should be equivalent to at least 10 thousand euros, which acts as a barrier for a number of copyright holders (small and medium-sized businesses))

The main research findings are:

1. an effective IP management mechanism in the EAEU is a factor in reducing the costs of foreign trade business
2. inequality in the protection of IP in the EAEU impedes the formation and development of competitive relations, impedes the freedom of movement of goods as the basic goal of economic integration of the EAEU states.

The main results of this paper were presented at the 34th International Business Information Management Association Conference, IBIMA 2019. Seville; Spain; 13 November 2019 - 14 November 2019 (Agamagomedova, et al., 2019).

ACKNOWLEDGMENT

The reported study was funded by RFBR according to the projects: N° 18-010-00204-a, 19-29-07545-мк, 20-010-00326-a.

REFERENCES

Abdullin, A. I. (2006), Intellectual property right in the European Union: genesis, unification, development prospects: dissertation for the degree of Doctor of Law, Moscow.

Abdullin, A. I. (2012). 'Interaction mechanism of the EU court and national courts of member states in the field of legal protection of intellectual property,' *Bulletin of Economics, Law, and Sociology, 2,* 97–101.

Abdullin, A. I. (2013). Some problems of formation and formation of legal protection of trademarks in the European Union. *Eurasian Law Journal, 6*(61), 71–74.

Agamagomedova, S., Gamidullaeva, L., & Taktarova, S. (2019). Economic and legal aspects of increasing the efficiency of intellectual property management in the Eurasian Economic Union. *Proceedings of the 34th International Business Information Management Association Conference,* IBIMA 2019. Seville; Spain; 13 November 2019 - 14 November 2019.

Agamagomedova, S. A. (2013). The interaction of international and national law in the field of cross-border protection of intellectual property rights. *Journal of Russian Law, 12,* 122–129. doi:10.12737/1555

Agamagomedova, S. A. (2015). Supranational Institute of Administrative Legal Regulation of the Protection of Intellectual Property Rights in the Framework of Eurasian Integration. *Bulletin of the Eurasian Academy of Administrative Sciences, 2*(31), 28–35.

Agamagomedova, S. A., & Belousova, D. V. (2019), 'The Institute of Intellectual Property in the Context of Economic Integration: Transformation Vector' In the Proceedings: *Actual problems of foreign economic activity and customs affairs materials of the IX International Scientific and Practical Conference,* 18-22.

Bautin, V. M., & Kostin, V. D. (2006). Trust management of rights to intellectual property objects, *Achievements of science and technology of the agro-industrial complex, 8,* 43-44.

Beretta, V., Demartini, C., & Trucco, S. (2019). Does environmental, social and governance performance influence intellectual capital disclosure tone in integrated reporting. *Journal of Intellectual Capital, 20*(1), 100–124. doi:10.1108/JIC-02-2018-0049

Bliznets, I. A. (2010). *Intellectual Property Law: A Textbook*. Moscow, Russia.

Bliznets, I. A. (2018). *Intellectual property law: international legal regulation*. Moscow, Russia.

Chesbrough, H. W., & Vanhaverbeke, W. (2018). Open innovation and public policy in the EU with implications for SMEs (Book Chapter). *Researching Open Innovation In SMEs*, 455-492.

Cieślik, A., Qu, Y., & Qu, T. (2018). Innovations and export performance: Firm level evidence from China. *Entrepreneurial Business and Economics Review, 6*(4), 27–47. doi:10.15678/EBER.2018.060402

Commentary on the Civil Code of the Russian Federation. Part four. (article by article). In 2 volumes. Ed. L. A. Trachtengerts. Moscow, Russia: Infra-M, 2016.

Commentary on the Civil Code of the Russian Federation. Part four: Educational-practical commentary. Ed. A. P. Sergeeva. Moscow, Russia: Prospect, 2016.

Dashyan, M. (2006). Intellectual property trust management: opportunities and trends, Intellectual property. *Industrial property, 12,* 11-16.

Demir, C., & Cergibozan, R. (2018). Determinants of Patent Protection Regimes: A Self-Organizing Map Approach. *Review of Economic Perspectives, 18*(3), 261–283. doi:10.2478/revecp-2018-0013

Eremenko, V. I. (2015). Improving legislation in the field of intellectual property protection in information and telecommunication networks. *Legislation and Economics, 8,* 19–28.

Eremenko, V. I. (2016). On the reform of the single trademark system of the European Union. *Intellectual Property Exchange, 15*(8), 1–10.

Ezzeddine, S., & Hammami, M. S. (2018). Nonlinear effects of intellectual property rights on technological innovation. *Journal of Economic Integration, 33*(2), 1337–1362. doi:10.11130/jei.2018.33.2.1337

Gavrilov, E. P. (2010). Legal protection of trademarks and copyright: Problems of differentiation. Law. *Journal of the Higher School of Economics, 2,* 36–46.

Gavrilov, E. P. (2014). Patents for inventions in the countries of the Customs Union in the aspect of private international law, *Patents and licenses. Intellectual rights 1,* 24.

Gavrilov, E. P. (2018). Intellectual Property Law of the Russian Federation: Legislation and Doctrine, *Patents and Licenses. Intellectual rights, 8,* 14-19.

Gorodov, O. A. (1999). Intellectual Property: Legal Aspects of Commercial Use: Diss. ... doctor. Legal Sciences, S.-P.

Gorodov, O. A. (2018). About new forms of using the results of intellectual activity, *Patents and Licenses. Intellectual rights 10,* 14-20.

Habib, M., Abbas, J., & Noman, R. (2019). Are human capital, intellectual property rights, and research and development expenditures really important for total factor productivity? An empirical analysis. *International Journal of Social Economics, 46*(6), 756–774. doi:10.1108/IJSE-09-2018-0472

Iskhakova, E. I. (2011). System approach to intellectual property management at the enterprise, *Innovations and investments 3,* 164-168.

Jones-Evans, D., Gkikas, A., Rhisiart, M., & MacKenzie, N. G. (2018). Measuring open innovation in SMEs (Book Chapter), *Researching Open Innovation in SMEs,* 399-427.

Juneja, J. A., & Amar, A. D. (2018). An organizational capital decision model for knowledge-intensive organizations. *IEEE Transactions on Engineering Management, 65*(3), 417–433. doi:10.1109/TEM.2018.2790898

Kolodko, G. N., & Kalinkin, V. I. (2014). Intellectual property management at an industrial enterprise as a component of the innovation activity management system. *Innovations, 4*(186), 115–119.

Kolodyazhnaya, O. A. (2018). Intellectual property management system development information: essence, organization, management, *Management of Economic Systems: Electronic Scientific Journal, 9* (115), 26.

Kreus, P., & Saukkonen, J. (2018). 'The role of intellectual property rights in growth aspiring SMEs,' *Proceedings of the European Conference on Knowledge Management,* ECKM, 423-429.

Leontiev, B. B. (2008). Functions of intellectual property: institutional approach to management of high-technology business, *Management and business administration,* 1, 11-31.

Leontiev, B. B. (2017). 'Is the foreign experience of commercializing intellectual property useful to Russia,' *Intellectual property. Industrial property, 3*, 4.

Leontiev, B. B. (2018). Intellectology - the integration science of the future, *Intellectual property. Industrial property, 3,* 41-50.

Lopatin, V. N. (2016). Problems and prospects of the Eurasian intellectual property market in the EAEU and CIS. *Intellectual Property Law, 3*, 29–44.

Lopatin, V. N. (2017). Intellectual property as an investment resource: Tatarstan's experience for the EAEU and CIS. *Intellectual Property Law, 3*, 46–48.

Lopatin, V. N. (2018). Eurasian intellectual property market in the EAEU and CIS in 2017 and its development priorities up to 2025. *Intellectual Property Law, 2*, 7–18.

Lopatin, V. N. (2018). Legal risks of intellectual property at transition to digital economy in EAEU. *Law, 6*(56), 64–70.

Rud, S. N. (2014). Application of information technologies in the management of intellectual property objects, In *Proceedings: Science and Education in the 21st Century, a collection of scientific papers based on the materials of the International Scientific and Practical Conference: in 17 parts,* 120-122.

Salitskaya, E. A. (2017). Modern approaches to intellectual property management: Regional aspect. *Bulletin of the Russian Academy of Sciences, 87*(11), 1026–1034.

Semenova, V. G. (2015). Process-oriented approach to management of intellectual property of enterprises, *Technological audit and production reserves, 5*(23), 45-50.

Sergeev, A. P. (2004). *Intellectual Property Law in the Russian Federation: Textbook. Moscow, Russia: TK Velby.* Prospect Publishing House.

Sevryukov, I. Yu. (2015). Intellectual property market: Approaches to management, formation of brands, influence of globalization. *Bulletin of the Trans-Baikal State University, 3*(118), 174–178.

Shestakov, D. Y. (2000). Intellectual Property in the Russian Federation: Theoretical and Legal Analysis. (Doctoral dissertation). Legal Sciences, Moscow, Russia.

Tkachenko, E., Rogova, E., Kokh, V., & Bodrunov, S. (2018). The valuation of intangible assets based on the intellectual capital leverages concept. *Proceedings of the International Conference on Intellectual Capital, Knowledge Management, and Organizational Learning, ICICKM,* 2018-November, pp. 319-329.

Zenin, I. A. (2015). *Problems of Russian intellectual property law (selected works). Moscow, Russia:* Statute.

KEY TERMS AND DEFINITIONS

Intellectual Property (IP): creations of the mind, such as inventions; literary and artistic works; designs; and symbols, names and images used in commerce.

The Eurasian Economic Union (EAEU): is an economic union of states located in central and northern Asia and Eastern Europe.

Chapter 14
Emerging Perspectives on Using Avatar-Based Management Techniques for Internet User Investigations:
Social Media as an Information Source

Leyla Gamidullaeva
iD https://orcid.org/0000-0003-3042-7550
Penza State University, Russia

Sergey Vasin
Penza State University, Russia

Nadezhda Chernetsova
Penza State University, Russia

Elena Shkarupeta
iD https://orcid.org/0000-0003-3644-4239
Voronezh State Technical University, Russia

Dina Kharicheva
Moscow Pedagogical State University, Russia

Maria Gerasimenko
K. G. Razumovsky Moscow State University of Technologies and Management, Russia

ABSTRACT

This chapter shows that statistics collection methods are the same for various types of websites. Often, a simple "counter" is used for both unique visitors to the site and the total number of hits to the site from unique and previously registered users. Speaking

DOI: 10.4018/978-1-7998-1581-5.ch014

of a "digital" or "smart" economy, authors distinguish different categories (levels) of development: analysis, content of business intelligence, large data warehouses. Business analytics can be divided into a number of parts: modeling and analysis of system dynamics, expert systems and databases; knowledge and technology; geographic information (geo location); system analysis and design. The various methods and forms of information (statistical models) used to identify non-trivial patterns and propose solutions are often associated today with the concept of data mining. Intelligent data analysis involves the use of knowledge from a complex of data (databases). According to experts, data mining is one of the elements that is part of the process (database management system), which includes the analysis and cleaning of data.

INTRODUCTION

The "digital economy" can be called the "global economy", the purpose of which is to include almost all transactions in the Internet space. Management, monitoring and analysis of all the main business processes of the company on the Internet, collective bargaining, accounting and organizing transaction registration processes, procurement, hiring and training personnel, monitoring relationships with partners and customers, technical support and much more are all basic elements digital economy. In addition to the technical component, the importance of introducing a digital culture into the company should be mentioned. This is necessary in order to gain a competitive advantage over companies and countries that do not own these technologies. An important point is the awareness of the need to change the mentality of company employees to provide digital services, training, work with new technologies, the introduction of which is necessary for business development, so that employees can clearly imagine the preferences that digital technologies carry, both for business and for personal development in general.

Unfortunately, in Russia, the digitalization of business is still in its infancy, it is not ubiquitous, but fragmentary. Changes are the most difficult task precisely for domestic companies, as this requires a complete restructuring of the corporate culture and business as a whole. The Russian economy, as you know, is heavily dependent on raw materials and markets, therefore, at the moment, it is difficult for our country to compete with more technologically advanced countries. In the IT sector, there is still an acute shortage of qualified personnel. This problem should be solved at the level of educational institutions (training courses at schools and universities) and for business (companies), as well as at the state level (education and training in this area). In addition to the above, a low level of venture business development should be noted, due to low predictability and high risk of investing in venture projects. A venture project is a project with a high degree of risk of investment in innovative developments, but, despite the high risk, if successful, high profitability is possible. Examples of successful venture projects include Facebook, Google, VKontakte, Telegram and many others). So, in 2015 due to the worsening macroeconomic situation, the Russian venture capital market decreased by 2 times compared to 2014. Although Russia has a fairly effective mechanism for supporting projects in the early stages, these projects, in many respects, start with the support of Russian private business. As a result, even a successfully growing company as part of a venture project does not always have enough government support, which the giants of the IT industry in other countries certainly use.

BACKGROUND

As the digital economy develops new categories enter the scientific revolution, including the term "digital maturity of the population". We propose to understand by this term the level of digital susceptibility of society, due to many factors, including the historical features of the processes of digitalization, socio-cultural attitudes of the population (for example, with the level of interpersonal trust and trust in the authorities). A large role in increasing the digital maturity of the population, and as a result, in accelerating the digitalization of the economy, is undoubtedly played by social networks that contribute to the development of digital interaction by linking the user profile with images (avatars) of other individuals or groups. Social networks include a huge amount of online resources, each of which has unique features, such as social networks, blogs, microblogging, social news, social bookmarking and media sharing (Manzoor, 2008).

In practice, the concepts of "social media" and "social networks" are often synonymous, which is incorrect (Obar and Wildman, 2015). The authors L. Safko and D. Break (2009) suggest that social media "refers to activities, practices, and behaviors among communities of people who gather online to share information, knowledge, and opinions using conversational media" (p. 6). The authors draw attention to the discrepancy between these categories, introducing the concept of an ecosystem of social network media. They propose to understand this ecosystem as a complex set of elements that interact intensively with each other. Each unit of an organism and collective populations of organisms represent themselves as one of the components of the system. Some organisms collaborate with or complement each other, while others compete for resources necessary for survival. The same principles apply when considering the interconnectedness and interdependence of tools and applications that exist, grow and compete in social networks. Some compete with each other, while others work together and are happy with it. In addition, the authors propose to consider social media as a generic term for social networks along with other types of social media, such as social news (e.g. Digg, Sphinn and others), social sharing (e.g. Flick, Snapfish and others) and social bookmarks (e.g. Delicious, Stumble Upon, and others). Social forms of communication through the Internet represent a historically new form of communication (Tang, et al., 2012). The work of business consultants is to communicate with potential consumers who are involved in the promotion of the product when each reader / subscriber of the blog can act as an author, teacher, reporter, photo correspondent, editor, marketer, trader, manufacturer, buyer, designer, etc. A social network, in fact, provides planetary user interaction through rapidly evolving electronic communication, which allows billions of people to communicate at the speed of light for various purposes. The concept of a "global village", in fact, allows you to implement those strategies that previously simply could not be represented. The authors suggest to understand by social media "a group of Internet applications on one or another ideological and technological basis of Web 2.0, which allows members of a social network to create content in the process of exchange (user-generated content)" (Kaplan and Haenlein, 2010). At the same time, one cannot ignore the trend towards strengthening state control in the field of social media due to the administration's access to many user accounts, and, accordingly, to their personal information. To date, a number of social networks has more than 100 million users at its disposal, for example: Facebook, Google +, VK, Instagram, Twitter, YouTube. According to some statements, unlike traditional media, social networks evoke a sense of belonging to a particular community, social class (for example, Instagram). The American scientist B. Solis (2007) gives the following definition of social media: "... is the detection, reading and commenting on news and information materials. This is a fusion of social management, high technology, which turn a monologue (one to many) into dialogue (many to many)".

There are many different types of social networks, including blogs, business networks, general-purpose social networks, dating sites, geosocial services, forums, micro blogging, photo hosting, review sites, social bookmarking, social games, video hosting and virtual game networks. Social networks make communication easier (Kadushin, 2002; Sailer and McCulloh, 2012; Foster and Charles, 2017, et al.). Research at the Pew Research Center claims that more than half of Internet users (52%) use one or more social networks (Facebook, Twitter, Instagram, and Interest) to chat with family or friends. Television and the press have always been an essential part of the formation of American collective memory over the past decades, but this trend has changed dramatically. During the last two presidential elections, the use of social networks such as Facebook and Twitter made it possible to predict future election results (Kirkpatrick, 2011).

Social media is a significant source of information for the economic development. Quality information is needed to clear decision-making about what products develop, for what customers, at what cost, through which distribution channels, reducing the uncertainty that a new product service development always brings with it (Kotler, et al., 1999; Mohr, et al., 2010, et al.).

As Sundar (2008) suggests, "[m]ore complex examples of autogenerated cues appear in the form of navigational aids offered by algorithms used in search-engine and aggregator. These appear as part of—or surrounding—the central content of the site, and emit "information scent" helpful in making quick decisions about the quality of the information available for consumption" (p. 78).

Social media analytics tools are becoming a huge business and can be divided into two broad categories: comprehensive platforms and specific solutions focused on one particular feature, like social monitoring, sentiment analysis (Ducange and Fazzolari, 2017), community responsiveness, content analysis, competitive benchmarking, and similar (Gašpar and Mabić, 2019). Many works are devoted to the study of social media monitoring and analytic techniques (Kelsey, 2017; Mukesh and Rao, 2017; Ceyp and Scupin, 2012; Liu, 2016, et al.).

MAIN FOCUS OF THE CHAPTER

Issues, Controversies, Problems

In general, it can be argued that the audience of the social network provides the main audience of the Internet (the number of users registered on the social network and having received or written at least one message to someone). Due to the audience data, we can talk about the popularity of a particular social network. The methods for collecting statistics are the same as for other types of websites. Often, a simple "counter" is used for both unique visitors to the site and the total number of visits to the site from unique and previously registered users. Speaking of a "digital" or "smart" economy, we can distinguish four categories (levels) of development: analysis, content of business analytics, large data warehouses. Business analytics can be divided into a number of parts: modeling and analysis of system dynamics, expert systems and databases; knowledge and technology; geographical information (geolocation); system analysis and design. Various methods and forms of information (statistical models) used to identify non-trivial patterns and propose solutions are often associated today with the concept of data mining. Data mining involves the use of knowledge from a complex of data (databases). According to experts, data mining is one of the elements that is part of the DBMS (database management system) process, which includes analysis and data cleaning. The purpose of big data analysis is to extract the necessary information from a common stream. For example, the model predicts what the client can pay attention to, selects exactly the information that is useful for the company (as the Pareto rule says - this information is not more than 20% of the total flow). Predictive mathematical models help improve research aimed at collecting statistics, preferences, and so on. Big data analysis creates and develops projects aimed at improving operations such as marketing, domestic sales, production optimization, logistics, management, planning.

SOLUTIONS AND RECOMMENDATIONS

There are evolutionary tools for understanding the development of technological developments in the industrial sphere. Decision trees and other management methods differ only in the ways of solving the same problem. As can be seen from the table, each method has its own strengths and weaknesses. It is clear that none of the methods presented above claims to be universal. However, it is possible to provide a solution to all types of tasks using data mining. This requires the correct configuration of the program and the use of professional analysts who will select one or another method to solve a specific economic problem. The combination of complementary analytical methods in business analytics can improve the quality of decisions. The difference between the actual situation and the planned indicators means that the current version of the program simply cannot make a more accurate forecast. For this, control by professionals is needed to correct the program at any of the selected stages, or to cancel the forecast of the program.

The benefits of the digital approach in economics are. The concept of "digital" emphasizes the difference between the approach and classical production and business processes. The digital approach allows the company to engage in its traditional activities more efficiently, quickly and at the lowest cost. Under the current conditions, digital technologies blur the boundaries between markets in the search for new business models. The world is entering an era of digital business that demonstrates an unprecedented level of convergence of technology and processes, communications, artificial intelligence and "smart materials". The transition to the digital business creates waves of breakthrough radical innovations in many industries. The term "digital enterprise" is described in the book of the director of the Massachusetts Institute of Technology N. Negroponte media laboratory.

There are some examples of digital enterprises and projects in Russian Federation. Representatives of the banking sector can be mentioned as an example of enterprises that have embarked on the path of "digital transformation": Sberbank has announced the creation of a new digital product - its own messenger, which will allow customers to communicate not only with each other, but also with employees connected to the network of commercial companies receive the necessary advice and order goods and services. Directly in the messenger integrated with the Sberbank Online system, you can pay for the goods and send a money transfer. One of the most important advantages of the messenger will be the so-called smart search, which will be able to select the most suitable options for the client for each request, taking into account its location, preferences and "transaction data". For business travelers, the messenger must provide a new tool for serving customer requests. Alfa-Bank introduced ABBYY Cloud technologies for SDK recognition and developed a service that allows you to recognize accounts, as well as to generate payment orders for clients of the small and medium-sized business segment in Alfa-Business Mobile. The client photographs the account or downloads the file, and after a few seconds sees the completed form on the screen of his mobile device.

Financial Services and e-Commerce for Enhancing of Digital Maturity of the Population

"Globality" in internet is fully exposed to trading platforms in all countries. The cross-border trade is one of the main drivers for the growth of e-commerce around the world. Local giants go to foreign markets, steadily being transformed in the global players, looking for business opportunities in new regions. While the buyers are motivated with the opportunity to is guaranteed to obtain a high-quality product at the right price from anywhere in the world, internet retailers cross-border electronic commerce provides tremendous opportunities for the expansion of the market for their products and attracting new clients. The number of online purchases at foreign websites will increase from year to year. Consumers from different countries are looking at foreign sites goods unavailable in their region or price and quality which are more attractive (Gamidullaeva, et al., 2019).

Trade in the Internet is gradually becoming an integral part of the world economy. However, the development of a new direction in theaters is different pace. Asian region is situated in the absolute leaders in segment, almost twice as overtaking North America on drug Internet commerce (mainly at the expense of China). This trend is due to the strong economic growth in developing Asian countries and informatization.

However, the new market is less true and transparent in comparison with traditional retail due to the specifics of existing virtual technologies. In some cases, the emerging commodity-money relations is already becoming difficult to regulate the rules in force in the territory of one country (in particular, allowed to sell goods - for example, medicines, and ways of delivery), it becomes evident that the necessity of regulation of the internal and cross-border Internet-trade on the basis of uniform principles, regardless of jurisdiction, is needed.

However, the common practice for regulation at this point has not happened yet. While there was a clear trend related to the popularization of protectionist measures (except for the United States and several other countries where taken on the course of market self-regulation) in most developed and developing countries in the world in order to stimulate the national Internet retailers and manufacturers. The commodity structure of the e-commerce market includes a lot of various categories - from the spare parts for cars, hazard appliances to perfumes and art objects (practically all that is presented in a traditional retail).

The trend of e-commerce will be the mobile commerce. Now more and more users prefer to make purchases on their way in a convenient for them at the appropriate time. Retailers constantly improve applications for customers convenience and easy to execute orders through smartphones.

The ability to directly buy goods on social platforms, a growing number of bots and services artificial intelligence, the popularity of instant messengers and IoT devices with voice operated control will promote the development of mobile commerce. Consumers prefer to use different devices when making a purchase - to search for goods and read reviews about it with smartphones, and execute the order with the desktop. It is important to monitor the sale, committed with different devices and make the transition from one to another smooth and integrated. The ability to identify the buyer allows companies to have recourse to it personally at the right time, bearing in mind the preferences and needs. The technology of the cross-tracking device can help you to explore user behavior and to understand its "path" to purchase, as well as to develop client-oriented marketing strategy at different devices (Gamidullaeva, et al., 2019).

Thus, each customer will be able to receive individual recommendations and will see the ads, based on his past purchases and preferences, geolocation and the trends of the market.

According to the consulting and auditing firm PwC, for 50% of the respondents social networks are the main platform, enabling them to make purchases. According to a study conducted by the company, BrightLocal specializing in CEO, 85% of users' degree of confidence to online reviews as great as to personal recommendations from friends and acquaintances. Influencers generate traffic, drawing on the target page visitors. More than 40% of the companies represented online, have the significant increase in traffic from social media.

A new stage in the development of financial technologies is based on cloud computing technology, which gives much more opportunities for critical infrastructure changes, and the functioning of the financial sector of the economy. The widespread introduction of artificial intelligence in the area of financial technologies is having the place. Among them there are the chat bots for customer service, robotic players on the stock market, machine learning and big data for decision on the loan for the client (Gamidullaeva, et al., 2019).

FUTURE RESEARCH DIRECTIONS

The technology of a digital company is needed in order to fill the concept with real content, to create a specific methodology. Over the years of the digital industry, experts have identified four main trends: social, mobile, and analytical and cloud. Each of these trends, taken separately, is only a technical method, but together they represent a powerful tool for digital control (synergy effect). This quartet made the first "shot" in the consumer market (B2C), and then established itself in the business market (B2B) to become the basis of digital transformation. This is the Internet, the Internet of things (internet of things), which provides the ability to collect analytical data for the system from almost anywhere - with built-in sensors and smart products in various control systems. We believe that the fourth industrial revolution manifests itself as a series of digital waves: a consumer who has more interactive and personal experience using this technology (social, mobile, and analytical and cloud technologies), a digital project uses technology to reduce costs, in order to increase performance. The main labels of the new digital era are artificial intelligence, robotics, cognitive computing and the Internet of things. Finance and accounting as drivers of digital transformation are consulting company calls ERP systems digital conversion drivers. But it will be a new generation of ERP that meets the design principles for digital technology. The purpose of such a restructuring is to respond as quickly as possible to the needs of consumers and bring the product to the market, that is, production should become flexible, adaptive and practically personal - because the requests of each client are individual. This can be achieved using a technology stack in developing an ERP platform system. Big data and analytics are Business Intelligence. Big data provides fuel for digital transformation, opening up new opportunities, new customers, markets. Business intelligence has become a decision-making tool that is used not only by experienced professionals, but also by business leaders at various levels. The transition to a digital enterprise also means an increase in the volume of data - now the control loop includes information from social networks, various external sources and, mainly, various sensors, since production also goes to the digital format. Due to the increase in the volume and complexity of data, semantic analysis and artificial intelligence systems will be in demand.

CONCLUSION

The authors attempted to analyze existing trends in the field of digitalization of the economy. The main approaches to the consideration of digital activity and digital maturity of the population as key indicators reflecting the level of digital transformation of the country's economy are highlighted. It is proposed to use social media monitoring to assess digital maturity and population activity. The article argues that the level of digital development of society is directly dependent on the development of the country's economy. It is concluded that in modern conditions, to increase the global competitiveness of the state's economy, it is advisable to focus on increasing the digital activity of the country's population. It is necessary to more actively involve society in the processes of digitalization of the economy and the social sphere. The study also showed that most enterprises (those that can survive in a competitive environment) will soon become digital. Among the leading sectors in the future digital industry will be high-tech industry, financial sector enterprises (banks, exchanges, auctions, etc.), retail sector companies (retailers). Companies need to think about changing the business model and add new management methods if they want to stay afloat in the near future. Among conservatives who do not yet want to switch to digital technologies, insurance companies, as well as energy and utility companies, are often found. The general assessment of the digital maturity of society and companies is such that at the moment we are witnessing a rare phenomenon - the emergence of a new (sixth) technological structure, and, possibly, the transition to a new "digital" historical formation.

ACKNOWLEDGMENT

The reported study was funded by RFBR according to the research project No. 18-010-00204-a.

REFERENCES

Ceyp, M., & Scupin, J.-P. (2012). Social Media Monitoring. Erfolgreiches Social Media Marketing, 189–196. doi:10.1007/978-3-658-00035-6_10

Foster, K. A., & Charles, V. A. (2017). Social Networks. Encyclopedia of Social Work. doi:10.1093/acrefore/9780199975839.013.103

Gamidullaeva, L. A., Merkulova, N. S., Kryachkova, L. I., Kondratieva, Z. A., Efimova, Y. A., & Matukin, S. V. (2019). Emerging Trends and Opportunities for Industry Development at the Sub-National Level in Russia. In U. Benna (Ed.), *Industrial and Urban Growth Policies at the Sub-National, National, and Global Levels* (pp. 342–363). Hershey, PA: IGI Global; doi:10.4018/978-1-5225-7625-9.ch017

Gašpar, D., & Mabić, M. (2019). Strengths and Limitations of Social Media Analytics Tools. In I. Management Association (Ed.), Social Entrepreneurship: Concepts, Methodologies, Tools, and Applications (pp. 595-615). Hershey, PA: IGI Global. doi:10.4018/978-1-5225-8182-6.ch031

Kadushin, C. (2002). The motivational foundation of social networks. *Social Networks*, *24*(1), 77–91. doi:10.1016/S0378-8733(01)00052-1

Kaplan, A. M., & Haenlein, M. (2010). Users of the world, unite! The challenges and opportunities of social media. *Business Horizons*, *53*(1), 59–68. doi:10.1016/j.bushor.2009.09.003

Kelsey, T. (2017). Social Media Monitoring and Analytics. Introduction to Social Media Marketing, 123–148. doi:10.1007/978-1-4842-2854-8_8

Kirkpatrick, D. (2011). *The Facebook effect: the real inside story of Mark Zuckerberg and the world's fastest-growing company.* London, UK: Virgin.

Kotler, P., Armstrong, G., Saunders, J., & Wong, V. (2001). Principles of Marketing, 2nd ed. Corporate Communications: An International Journal, 6(3), 164–165. doi:10.1108/ccij.2001.6.3.164.1

Liu, Y. (2016). Social Media Monitoring. Social Media in China, 185–193. doi:10.1007/978-3-658-11231-8_10

Manzoor, A. (2018). Using Social Media Marketing for Competitive Advantage. In I. Management Association (Ed.), Social Media Marketing: Breakthroughs in Research and Practice (pp. 21-38). Hershey, PA: IGI Global. doi:10.4018/978-1-5225-5637-4.ch002

Moe, W. W., & Schweidel, D. A. (n.d.). Moving from Social Media Monitoring to Social Media Intelligence. Social Media Intelligence, 180–186. doi:10.1017/cbo9781139381338.016

Mohr, J. J., Sengupta, S., & Slater, S. (n.d.). Toward a Theory of Technology Marketing: Review and Suggestions for Future Research. Handbook of Business-to-Business Marketing. doi:10.4337/9781781002445.00042

Mukesh, M., & Rao, A. (2017). Social media measurement and monitoring. Contemporary Issues in Social Media Marketing, 184–205. doi:10.4324/9781315563312-14

Negroponte, N. (1995). Being Digital. Knopf. (Paperback edition, 1996, Vintage Books).

Obar, J. A., & Wildman, S. (2015). Social media definition and the governance challenge: An introduction to the special issue. *Telecommunications Policy, 39*(9), 745–750. doi:10.1016/j.telpol.2015.07.014

Safk, L., & Brake, D. (2009). *The social media bible: tactics, tools, and strategies for business success*. Hoboken, N. J.: John Wiley & Sons.

Sailer, K., & McCulloh, I. (2012). Social networks and spatial configuration—How office layouts drive social interaction. *Social Networks, 34*(1), 47–58. doi:10.1016/j.socnet.2011.05.005

Solis, B. (2007). Defining Social Media. Retrieved from http://www.briansolis.com/2007/06/defining-social-media/

Sundar, S. S. (2008). The MAIN model: A heuristic approach to understanding technology effects on credibility. In M. J. Metzger, & A. J. Flanagin (Eds.), *Digital media, youth, and credibility* (pp. 73–100). Cambridge, MA: The MIT Press.

Tang, Q., Gu, B., & Whinston, A. (2012). Content Contribution for Revenue Sharing and Reputation in Social Media: A Dynamic Structural Model. *Journal of Management Information Systems, 29*(2), 41–75. doi:10.2753/MIS0742-1222290203

ADDITIONAL READING SECTION

Ducange, P., & Fazzolari, M. (2017). Social sensing and sentiment analysis: Using social media as useful information source. *2017 International Conference on Smart Systems and Technologies (SST)*. doi:10.1109st.2017.8188714

Management Association. I. (2018). Social Media Marketing: Breakthroughs in Research and Practice (2 Volumes) (pp. 1-1572). Hershey, PA: IGI Global. doi:10.4018/978-1-5225-5637-4

Raisinghani, M. S. (Ed.). (2004). *Business Intelligence in the Digital Economy.*, doi:10.4018/978-1-59140-206-0

Raisinghani, M. S. (Ed.). (2008). *Handbook of Research on Global Information Technology Management in the Digital Economy.*, doi:10.4018/978-1-59904-875-8

Social media monitoring for market intelligence. (2014). An Introduction to Social Media Marketing, 76–87. doi:10.4324/9780203727836-7

KEY TERMS AND DEFINITIONS

Digital Maturity: Is the process of the company learning how to respond appropriately to the emerging digital competitive environment.

Social Media: Are interactive computer-mediated technologies that facilitate the creation and sharing of information, ideas, career interests and other forms of expression via virtual communities and networks. The variety of stand-alone and built-in social media services currently available introduces challenges of definition; however, there are some common features.

Social Network: Is a social structure made up of a set of social actors (such as individuals or organizations), sets of dyadic ties, and other social interactions between actors. The social network perspective provides a set of methods for analyzing the structure of whole social entities as well as a variety of theories explaining the patterns observed in these structures.

Chapter 15
Math Model of Neuron and Nervous System Research Based on AI Constructor Creating Virtual Neural Circuits

Rinat Galiautdinov
https://orcid.org/0000-0001-9557-5250
Independent Researcher, Italy

Vardan Mkrttchian
https://orcid.org/0000-0003-4871-5956
HHH University, Australia

ABSTRACT

The research describes the mathematical modeling of a neuron and the possibility of its technical implementation. Unlike existing technical devices for implementing a neuron based on classical nodes oriented to binary processing, the proposed path is based on bit-parallel processing of numerical data (synapses) for obtaining result. The proposed approach of implementing a neuron can serve as a new elementary basis for the construction of neuron-based computers with a higher processing speed of biological information and good survivability. The research demonstrates the developed nervous circuit constructor and its usage in building of the nervous circuits of biological creatures and simulation of their work.

DOI: 10.4018/978-1-7998-1581-5.ch015

INTRODUCTION

Nowadays the development of the new computer technologies is a must and we can see it on a daily basis. The development of technologies led to computer modeling of different processes and systems. Modeling is one of the most effective ways of research.

A model approach to research allows us to overcome the limitations and difficulties that arise when setting up a laboratory experiment, due to the possibility of conducting so-called numerical experiments, and to study the response of the system under study to changes in its parameters and initial conditions.

In this regard, computer simulation is widely used in all natural sciences. Neuroscience or the science of the brain, whose task is to study the functioning of the brain and nervous system, was no exception. The brain is a complex object consisting of a large number of different types of cells, including the main signal cells - neurons (cells that generate and transmit electrical impulses that can form networks through contacts called synapses), glial cells that regulate metabolism, blood vessel cells, etc. Modeling such systems, complex in internal connections and large in the number of elements, using modern personal computers is extremely difficult, due to the large th computing capacity derived models.

However, the use of supercomputer technologies allows the use of more diverse modeling methods. One of such the methods is called large-scale modeling. Large-scale modeling is one of the directions in supercomputer modeling. This method is intended for the development and conduct of numerical experiments with global computer models of multidimensional systems in which macro and micro models that simulate the interconnected functioning of multilevel systems are integrated. This direction arose relatively recently due to significant progress in the technology of manufacturing microcircuits, parallel computing, and the increased processing power of supercomputer systems, which became available with the advent of specialized software. Large-scale modeling is based on the principle of hierarchical reduction, which assumes that any complex system consists of hierarchically subordinate subsystems (levels of organization). A high-level organization system consists of lower-level systems, and a combination of low-level organization systems forms a higher-level system (Lee, et al., 2012). Application of this principle to modeling in neuroscience allows us to represent the brain in the form of several 4 interacting independently described subsystems. The hierarchy of the model allows you to achieve the level of detail required by research, by increasing or decreasing the number of organization levels considered. However, with an increase in the number of levels of organization, the number of parameters describing the system increases, which greatly complicates the task of creating a realistic model that reproduces the phenomena observed in a laboratory experiment. An increase in the number of model parameters leads to an increase in the amount of input data required to determine them, data that are difficult to measure and often do not have a sufficient degree of accuracy. In this regard, abstraction is used when creating models - an approach that allows you to discard parameters that are unimportant for research in the framework of the task, with the aim of solving which the model was developed. Thus, the task of abstracting is to preserve only what is important for the construction and analysis of models at different levels of the organization without losing the convenience of manipulation. The considered modeling method provided researchers with a set of neural network simulators that can greatly simplify research in the field of neuroscience.

Additionally to that it's very important to have the ability of virtual construction of neural circuit both for researching goals and the applied ones in the sphere of AI. As a result the author describes the major features of such the neural constructor and represents it, showing how it was applied in simulation of the neural circuit of Aplysia(the mollusk) and Planarian(Tricladida).

ARTIFICIAL NEURON

The artificial or programming neuron used in Computer Science partially simulates the biological neuron. Such the artificial neuron receives the number of the signals as the input data and each of these signals is in fact the output of another neuron. Each input gets multiplied by the appropriate weight(simulating the synaptic strength) then we can sum all the values and define the level of neuron activation. The final result of this operation would be either 0 or 1.

There are different kind of the neural networks but all of them are based on the above described configuration. There are multiple input signals for the artificial neuron: x_1, x_2,...,x_n . These input signals correspond to the input signal in the synapses of biological neurons. Each signal gets multiplied by the appropriate weight w_1,w_2,..,w_n, and then all they gets redirected to the summation block marked with a symbol $\sum$. Each weight corresponds to the power of a single biological synapse. The summation block which corresponds to the body of the biological element, arithmetically sums the inputs and creates the output R.

Such the description can be defined with the following formula:

$$R = \sum_{i=1}^{n} W_i X_i + W_0$$

Figure 1. Illustrates the artificial neuron

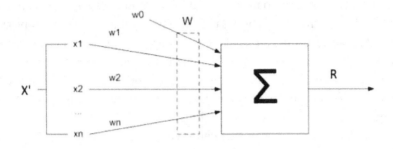

Figure 2. Illustrates the artificial neuron with the activation function

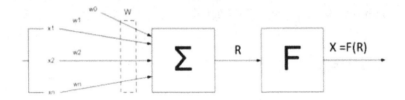

Where:

W_0 – is a bias
W_i – is the weight of the ith neuron
x_i – is the exit of the ith neuron
n – is the number of the neurons, which serve as the input for the processing neuron

The signal W_0 which has a name "bias" represents the shift limit function (Abbott & Kepler, 1990). This signal allows you to shift the origin of the activation function, which subsequently leads to an increase in the learning speed. This signal is added to each neuron, it learns like all other scales, and its feature is that it connects to the +1 signal, and not to the output of the previous neuron. The received signal R gets processed by the activation function and returns the output signal X (Figure 2)

In the case if the activation function narrows the range of variation X the way so that for each value of R the value of X belongs to some range – the final interval, then the function F is called a function which narrows. For this it's usually used logistic function. This function can be described in the following way:

Figure 3. Type of logistic/sigmoidal activation function

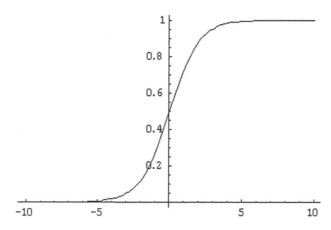

The major advantage of such the function is that it has a simple derivative and differentiates along the abscissa. The graph of the function looks in the following way: (Figure 3)

The function increases the weak signals and reduces "too strong" signals.

Another function that is also often used is hyperbolic tangent. It resembles a sigmoid in shape and is often used by biologists as a mathematical model of nerve cell activation. It looks in the following way:

Like the logistic function, the hyperbolic tangent is S-shaped, but it is symmetrical with respect to the origin, and at the point of R = 0 the value of the output signal X = 0

The graph shows that this function unlike logistic one accepts the values of the different signs, what could be a beneficial for a certain type of neural networks (Figure 4).

The considered model of an artificial neuron ignores many properties of a biological neuron. For example, it does not take into account time delays that affect the dynamics of the system. Input signals immediately generate the source. But despite this, artificial neural networks composed of the considered neurons reveal the properties that are inherent in the biological system (Figure 5).

Figure 4. The graph shows that this function unlike logistic one accepts the values of the different signs

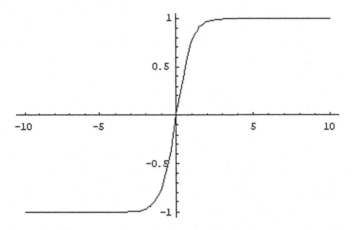

Figure 5. Artificial neural networks composed of the considered neurons reveal the properties that are inherent in the biological system

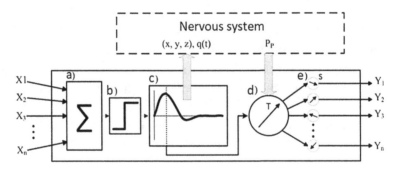

MATHEMATICAL MODEL OF BIOLOGICAL NEURON

Imagine the beginning vector, which is located in the center of the active stand, and the end is directed to the pattern point defined for a given neuron. Denote as the vector of the preferred direction of propagation of the excitation (T, trend). In the biological neuron, the vector T can manifest itself in the structure of the neuroplasm itself, perhaps these are the channels for the movement of ions into the body of the cell, or other changes in the structure of the neuron. A neuron has the property of memory; it can memorize the vector T, the direction of this vector, can change and overwrite depending on external factors. The degree to which the vector T can undergo changes is called neuroplasticity (Migliore, et al., 2006).

This vector, in turn, affects the functioning of the neuron synapses. For each synapse, we define the vector S beginning, which is located in the center of the cell, and the end is directed to the center of the target neuron with which the synapse is connected. Now the degree of influence for each synapse can be determined as follows: the smaller the angle between the vector T and S is, the more the synapse will be amplified; the smaller the angle, the stronger the synapse will weaken and may possibly stop the transmission of excitation. Each synapse has an independent memory property; it remembers the meaning of its strength. The indicated values change with each activation of the neuron, under the influence of the vector T, they either increase or decrease by a certain value.

The input signals $(x_1, x_2, \ldots x_n)$ of the neuron are real numbers that characterize the strength of the synapses of the neurons that affect the neuron.

A positive value of the input means a stimulating effect on the neuron, and a negative value means an inhibitory effect.

For a biological neuron, it does not matter where the signal exciting it came from, the result of its activity will be identical. A neuron will be activated when the sum of the effects on it exceeds a certain threshold value. Therefore, all signals pass through adder (a), and since neurons and the nervous system work in real time, therefore, the effect of the inputs should be evaluated in a short period of time, that is, the effect of the synapse is temporary. The result of the adder passes the threshold function (b), if the sum exceeds the threshold value, then this leads to neuron activity. When activated, a neuron signals its activity to the system, advanced information about its position in the space of the nervous system and the charge that changes over time (c). After a certain time, after activation, the neuron transmits excitation along all the available synapses, previously recounting their strength. The entire activation period of the neuron ceases to respond to external stimuli, that is, all the effects of synapses of other neurons are ignored. The activation period also includes the recovery period of the neuron (Davison, et al., 2008).

The vector T (d) is adjusted taking into account the value of the pattern point Pp and the level of neuroplasticity. Next, there is a reassessment of the values of all synapse forces in the neuron (e).

Note that blocks (d) and (e) run in parallel with block (c).

The next simplification of the Hodgkin-Huxley model is the MorrisLecar model, proposed in 1981. This system of equations describes the complex relationship between the membrane potential and the activation of ion channels in the membrane. Mathematically, the model is written as follows (Figure 6):

Figure 6. Mathematically, the model

$$
\begin{cases}
C\dfrac{dV}{dt} = I - g_L(V - V_L) - g_{Ca}M_{ss}(V - V_{Ca}) - g_K N(V - V_K) \\[2mm]
\dfrac{dN}{dt} = \dfrac{N - N_{ss}}{\tau_N},
\end{cases}
$$

$$M_{ss} = 0.5(1 + \tanh[\frac{V - V_1}{V_2}]),$$

$$N_{ss} = 0.5(1 + \tanh[\frac{V - V_3}{V_4}]),$$

$$\tau_N = 1/(\phi\cosh[\frac{V - V_3}{2V_4}]),$$

Figure 7. Phase plane of the FitzHugh-Nagumo model with a threshold manifold

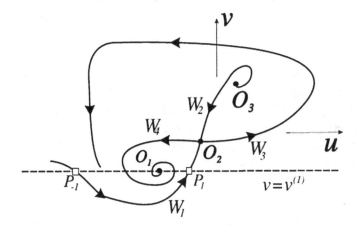

The open state probability functions, MSS (V) and WSS (V), are obtained from the assumption that in equilibrium the open and closed states of the channels are delimited, according to the Boltzmann distribution. Changes in the external current, I, are accompanied by a saddle-node bifurcation, leading to the birth of a limit cycle. In the field of theoretical modeling of neural oscillators the author as an independent researcher developed the number of new math models of neural dynamics.

Figure 8. Model of an excitable element with subthreshold oscillations. Functional diagram.

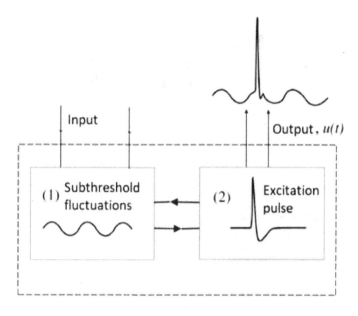

Figure 9. The dynamics of the model can be described by the following 4th-order system

Where:

the variables x and y describe the dynamics of the first block,

u, v – of the second one,

f(u) – nonlinear function of cubic form,

ε1, ε2 – small positive parameters

I – constant external stimulus

γ, β, l > 0, α < 0 – the parameters characterizing the dynamics of Van der Pol variables and the relationship between blocks.

$$\begin{cases} \varepsilon_1 \dot{u} = f(u) - v - y; \\ \dot{v} = \varepsilon_2(u + I), \\ \dot{x} = y, \\ \dot{y} = (\gamma(1 + \alpha I + \beta u) - lx^2)y - \omega_0^2 x, \end{cases}$$

One of the most interesting developments is the model of the modified FitzHugh-Nagumo generator, which is a simplified version of the Hodgkin-Huxley model. This model has a separatrix threshold manifold that separates signals into subthreshold oscillations and suprathreshold excitation pulses, which are further used for

Figure 10. The amplitude of subthreshold oscillations depends on the membrane potential u and external stimulus I

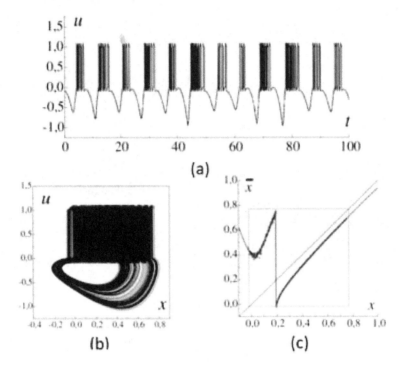

(a)

(b)   (c)

communication between neurons. In addition, the model simultaneously possesses the properties of an integrative response typical of threshold systems and resonance characteristics similar to oscillatory systems. In other words, there is a fundamental possibility of simultaneously performing both frequency and phase encoding and decoding of information (Figure 7).

Previously, the authors of the model of the modified FitzHugh-Nagumo generator proposed a model of a neuron with spontaneous periodic oscillations below the excitation threshold. Such neurons, in particular, play a crucial role in the problem of coordination of movements of the brain, setting the universal rhythm of muscle contractions. The model is based on well-known dynamic systems and is described by a system of fourth-order differential equations (Figure 8).

The first block describes subthreshold oscillations and can be implemented as a Van der Pol generator in a soft excitation mode. The second block is responsible for the formation of an impulse and is implemented as an excitable FitzHugh-Nagumo element. When introducing a nonlinear connection between the blocks, we obtain that the dynamics of the model can be described by the following 4th-order system (Figure 9).

Note that the dynamics of the variable u in model (5) qualitatively reflects the evolution of the membrane potential of a neuron, the variables x, y, and v show the dynamics of ion currents, parameter I determines the level of depolarization of the neuron. The introduction of two small parameters ε1, ε2 into system (5) is necessary for matching the characteristic time scales of blocks (pulse duration and period of subthreshold oscillations). Note that in model (5), two nonlinear systems interact with fundamentally different dynamic properties. Communication between the blocks is as follows. Oscillations close to harmonic from the first block (x, y) change the state of the second in the variable u. In turn, the change in the amplitude of subthreshold oscillations depends on the membrane potential u and external stimulus I (Figure 10).

Chaotic Burst Vibrations in a Model (5) I=-0.027. (a) Membrane potential evolution. (b) Phase trajectory in the projection onto the plane (x,u). (c) Poincare map corresponding to a chaotic attractor.

Note that for a certain ratio of the characteristic time scales of the model blocks, the oscillations are in the form of bursts, which can be both regular and chaotic. An example of a chaotic temporal realization and the Poincaré map corresponding to a chaotic attractor are presented in the Figure 10.

EXPERIMENTS

Programming Implementation and AI based Constructor's Experiments

The programming model of the artificial neuron which is based on the biological model (Abbott, & Kandel, 2012) contains the following key features:

- Each artificial biological neuron has generic list of the Queues for dendrites(input signals) and axons(output signals)
- Each synapse can generate the vesicles containing different type o neurotransmitters (in our research we used only 2 neurotransmitters: Glu, GAMA) (Jin, et al., 2012). The generation of the vesicles starts when the neuron receives the AP which can be instantiated based on the signals received from the Qeue(s) of dendrite(s). Such the signal is not constant and depends on the quantity of neurotransmitters caught by the synaptic membrane(for the case if summation process runs – Non-NMDA receptors were triggered) or it's constant enough even with the small quantity of neurotransmitters for the case when NMDA receptors were targeted and one of the initial signals was strong enough. The values of the signals and detailed work of the processes

were described of chapter authors. Each axon can have only one type of neurotransmitters.

- The programmable synapse can generate the calcium ions coming inside and simulate the process of interaction with the vesicles, which effects on simulation of moving of the vesicles towards the synaptic membrane and emission of neurotransmitters into the synaptic cleft which will effect on initiation of the signal in another neuron.

- The emitted neurotransmitters do not effect directly on another neuron, they effect on the synaptic membrane which is programmatically represented as an input object of the dendrite connected with another neuron. The emission result fully depends on the type of the receptors and the whether NMDA receptor(if this is a case) is "turned on"(what could be caused by the initial strong signal)

Such the approach was used by the author in creation of the neuron based constructor in the beginning of 2016. This neuron-constructor allows constructing the neural circuits including the virtual muscles and virtual sensors. The virtual sensors serve as a triggering mechanism effecting on the neural circuit and the virtual muscles serve as outcome. Each neuron and each synapse generate the logs, which includes the data of the APs, the number of emitted calcium ions, the number of instantiated vesicles with neurotransmitters, the number of emitted neurotransmitters, the type of the receptors and the data related to the newly generated signals. This constructor allows to move the experiments on biological objects (such as Aplysia – the mullusc) into the virtual sphere where no animal is necessary for exploring of the work of the nervous system. More important, it allows to construct extremely complex virtual neural circuits and research its behavior. Such the approach allows to simulate the nervous system even of the complex creatures. During the experiment, with the help of the author's neuro-constructor, the author virtually created the nervous system of Aplysia and Planarian(Tricladida) (Choi, et al, 2014). The generated neural circuit was able to simulate the work and behavior of the natural creatures.

It's also necessary to mention that it's possible to implement the mobile version, which would be fully independent, however in this case it makes sense to consider the usage of Nano scaled Electrodes in the frame of providing a power for such the mobile device.

CONCLUSION

In the research the authors described the math model of the biological neuron and suggested the new approach in Artificial Intelligence. The author described created by him the neuron-constructor and the received results of simulation of the work of the virtually created neural circuits of Aplysia(the mollusc) and Planarian(Tricladida).

REFERENCES

Davison, A. P., Brüderle, D., Eppler, J. M., Kremkow, J., Muller, E., Pecevski, D., ... Yger, P. (2008). A Common Interface for Neuronal Network Simulators. *Frontiers in Neuron Informatics*, *2*, 11–15. PMID:19194529

Abbott, L., & Kandel, E. (2012). A computational approach enhances learning in Aplysia. *Nature Neuroscience*, *15*(2), 178–189. doi:10.1038/nn.3030 PMID:22281713

Abbott, L., & Kepler, T. (1990). In L. Garrido (Ed.), *Model neurons: from hodgkin-huxley to hopfield. Statistical Mechanics of neural networks* (Vol. 18, pp. 5–18). Springer.

Choi, Y., Kadakkuzha, B., Liu, A., Akhmedov, K., Kandel, R., & Puthanveettil, S. (2014). Huntingtin is critical both pre- and postsynaptically for long-term learning-related synaptic plasticity in Aplysia. *PLoS One*, *9*(7), e103004. doi:10.1371/journal.pone.0103004 PMID:25054562

Choi, S., Lee, N., Lee, C., Bailey, C., Kandel, E., Jang, J., ... Kaang, B. (2012). Learning-related synaptic growth mediated by internalization of Aplysia cell adhesion molecule is controlled by membrane phosphatidylinositol 4,5-bisphosphate synthetic pathway, *The Journal of Neuroscience: the Official Journal of the Society For Neuroscience, 32,* pp. 296-305.

Jin, I., Udo, H., Rayman, J., Puthanveettil, S., Kandel, E., & Hawkins, R. (2012). Spontaneous transmitter release recruits postsynaptic mechanisms of long-term and intermediate-term facilitation in Aplysia. *Proceedings of the National Academy of Sciences of the United States of America*, *109*(23), 9137–9142. doi:10.1073/pnas.1206846109 PMID:22619333

Migliore, M., Cannia, C., Lytton, W. W., Markram, H., & Hines, M. L. (2006). Parallel network simulations with NEURON. *Journal of Computational Neuroscience*, *21*(2), 119–129. doi:10.100710827-006-7949-5 PMID:16732488

Chapter 16
Brain Machine Interface for Avatar Control and Estimation for Educational Purposes Based on Neural AI Plugs:
Theoretical and Methodological Aspects

Rinat Galiautdinov
iD https://orcid.org/0000-0001-9557-5250
Independent Researcher, Italy

Vardan Mkrttchian
iD https://orcid.org/0000-0003-4871-5956
HHH University, Australia

ABSTRACT

In the future education process where Avatar will be used, it is critically important to have a layer which is responsible for transferring the knowledge from a Student's Avatar to Student. In this research, authors show the method and high-level architecture of how it could be done. And although the suggested approach works, the current level of technology does not allow creating a mobile set which could implement this approach. The general high-level schema of the Avatar methodology used in the education process is enclosed in the following. There are 4 layers which interact with each other. On the first layer there is a professor, who is an expert in some domain. The professor transfers their knowledge to the second layer which is a computer program, performing the role of the Professor's Avatar. The knowledge gets transferred to a Student's Avatar, which is the 3rd layer, and eventually the Student's Avatar transfers the newly received knowledge to the Student, the 4th layer in this schema. So, the most difficult part here is to transfer the knowledge from machine to human.

DOI: 10.4018/978-1-7998-1581-5.ch016

INTRODUCTION

"I know Kung Fu", Neo.

"I know Kung Fu" is a famous phrase known to everyone. Many people dreamt of technology which could allow them to receive the new knowledge without actual learning. This research describes the high-level approach of this.

The general high-level schema of the Avatar methodology used in the education process is enclosed in the following: There are 4 layers which interact with each other. On the first layer we have a professor, who is an expert in some domain. He transfers his knowledge to the second layer which is a computer program, performing the role of the Professor's Avatar. After that the knowledge gets transferred to a Student's Avatar, which is the 3rd layer. And eventually the Student's Avatar transfers the newly received knowledge to the Student, who is the 4th layer in this schema. So the most difficult part here is to transfer the knowledge from machine to human (Mkrttchian, et. all, 2016, 2017, 2018, 2019a, 2019b).

Who Will Need the System and How it could be Applied

The system can be used in lots of spheres, such as but not limited to:

- Lazy students
- Necessity to possess some knowledge during extremely short interval of time
- People with Parkinson's/dementia/sclerosis disease
- Etc.

The Principal of Memory Work

In order to better understand how the memory works it's necessary to consider several mechanisms, such as Summation, Long Lasting Potentiation, Papez circle.

Summation, Long Lasting Potentiation, Papez Circle

One of the neural processes which describes the mechanism of memory's work is called summation. It was described in the details in the research of Rinat Galiautdinov (Rinat Galiautdinov, "Brain machine interface - the accurate interpretation of neurotransmitters' signals targeting the muscles"). The major key of the process is enclosed in the fact that weak but frequent enough signals can eventually make the signal "to jump" to another neuron in the neural circuit and the mechanism of this process is based on collection of calcium ions. The memory based on this mechanism does not last long and the information received through the usage of this mechanism disappears as soon as calcium ions "get disappeared".

Another very important neural process which is related to the memory mechanism is called Long Lasting Potentiation. The mechanism gets started in the case if there was a strong enough signal (~ -30mV) which makes the receptors "to spits out" the ion of Mg^{2+}.

Another example of how the memory works is Papez circle, which represents some kind of connected route of neural circuit in the brain and runs the signal in the circle.

Experimental Part

For the experimental part the authors took into consideration the visual area of the brain. The "output" of the visual transformation in the brain is a circuit of an object we see. Consequently every object can be decomposed into the smaller number of the primitive short lines having different angle. There are special neural cells in the visual area of the brain which are responsible for each of such the smaller lines of different angle or for the smaller lines moving according to some particular direction. As an example, there is a neural cell which reacts on a signal corresponding to the vertical line (90^0), but at the same time the neighbors of the cell have slightly different behavior: one of them would react on a signal corresponding to the vertical line with the angle of 91^0, etc. Consequently each visible object gets decomposed into such the lines and these lines effect on the appropriate neural cells in the visual area of the brain.

For the experiment the authors used a piece of cheese and a mouse. Obviously the piece of cheese can be recognized not only by its form but also with the help of smell, etc.

During the initial phase of the experiment the authors put the piece of cheese into the closed area where the mouse could not feel the smell of cheese. But the mouse already knew that the piece which is looking this way is a piece of cheese, so the mouse wanted to get to the closed area.

During the next phase of the experiment the authors formed the cheese in the form of an abstract but simple figure: the triangle and put it into the closed area so that the mouse could not feel the smell of the cheese. Such the form of cheese was unknown to the mouse and the mouse did not react.

Then the authors let the mouse to get to the cheese to eat it. So the mouse received the new knowledge that such the thing could be the cheese.

In the final stage of the experiment 3 electrodes were connected to the appropriate areas of the visual area of the brain, where such the areas were responsible for recognition of the smaller lines. The combination of these 3 lines allows to geometrically build a triangle. Then the authors effected on the neural cells sending the series of the APs equal to -50mV and the mouse tried to get to the "cheese area" although there was no cheese inside.

The experiment showed that the new knowledge can be established in the brain even without a physical representation of such the object and that the brain would react on such the object because it received the number of decomposed signals which all together build the "picture" of such the object. This "picture" is not limited with only neural cells corresponding to the different types of the lines. The visual representation of an object is just one part of the whole "picture". And the more sensors are included, the better "picture" the brain receives.

Modeling of the Experimental Part

During the modeling stage, the authors used the software "Neural circuit Constructor" of Rinat Galiautdinov, which allows to model and build the neural circuits and model neural behavior based on simulation of biological neurons, synapses, muscles.

The initially constructed model included:

- 9 visual sensor neuron, each of them reacted on a particular line having its own angle.
- Visual receptor connected to 9 visual sensor neurons.
- 3 inter neurons, each of them connected with 3 visual sensor neuron and were able to react on a primitive figure containing the combination of 3 appropriate lines.
- 3 taste sensor neurons, responsible for its own taste (sour, sweet, protein)
- 1 "pleasure" inter-neuron having the axons with Glu (neuromediator)
- 1 "displeasure" inter-neuron having the axon with GAMA
- Analyzer module connected with the defined preference list
- One motor-neuron connected to the muscle
- The muscle

No other neuromediators/hormons were used in the modeling process, although it was possible to extend the "pleasure" center adding the additional neurons and construct the model which could include serotonin, endorphin, etc.

Figure 1. Illustrates the final schema of the neural construction (for simplicity sake it shows only the synaptic contacts leading to the expected behavior)

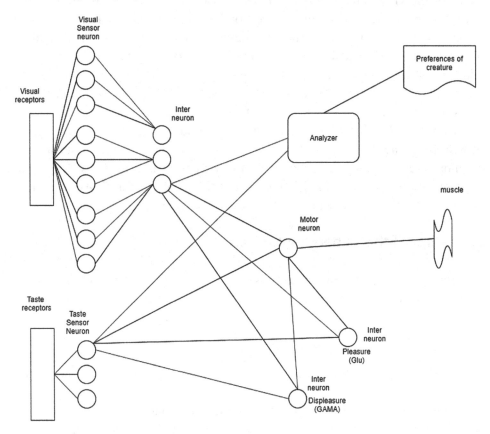

During the first phase of the experiment the analyzer detected, that only the signals from the 3rd inter-neuron(connected with 3 appropriate visual sensor neurons) and the signal from 1 taste sensor neuron correspond to the favorable defined parameters which should react to the signal related to the predefined behavior reflecting on the work of the muscle. After that the "Neural circuit Constructor" automatically established the synaptic contacts between the motor neuron and the inter-neurons causing the corresponding signal.

After that the system automatically activated the muscle every time the authors sent the appropriate signals to the visual and taste sensors.

In the schema it's obvious that if visual sensors detected that the object corresponds to the expected object but instead of the neuron responsible for protein detection we have activated neuron for sweet taste detection than the inter-neuron called "displeasure" will send GAMA and consequently the muscle will not be activated.

Experiment to Effect on the Certain Neurons to Effect some Action

The idea of the experiment was to effect on the sensor neuron of Aplysia(the mollusk) so that it could interpret the signal as if it was a signal from the gills and as a result it would go to the motor neuron effecting on the muscle leading to muscle contraction.

In this experiment a sensor neuron of Aplysia (the mollusk) was connected with a device sending the Action Potential (AP) in the range of -30mV to 30mV. There was no effect on the gills of the mollusk caused by a stream of water, Then the authors sent the series of APs in the range of -30: 30mV which caused the sensor neuron to send a signal to the motor neuron which effected on the muscle.

GENERAL APPROACH

Based on the experiments it's obvious that transfer of the knowledge consists of 2 parts:

1. Gathering the info about the neurons and synapses responsible for a certain quantum of knowledge
2. Sending the signal effecting on those neurons, so that it could either create or enhance the synaptic contacts.

Effecting on the neuron can be done in several ways:

- Using Action Potential (AP)
- Injecting the neurotransmitters into the synaptic cleft
- Opening artificially made calcium channels

Let's consider each of the options:

Effecting on the Neurons Using AP

One of the ways to effect on the neuron so that it could send a signal is simply sending the AP (Action Potential). However, there are some important rules which are necessary to take into consideration:

- The electrode must effect only on a particular neuron, avoiding a contact with the other neurons and/or synapses. It means that the size of the electrode must be extremely small and it also must be isolated from the other sides: for this goal the best decision is to use glia (imitating the glial cells), however they must leave a spot on the electrode for a direct contact with a neuron we are effecting on.
- The level of the AP must differ depending on the type of the signal which could correspond either to a summation process or long-lasting potentiation.

Effecting on the Neurons Injecting the Neurotransmitters into the Synaptic Cleft

This approach was described in the research of Rinat Galiautdinov (Brain machine interface - the accurate interpretation of neurotransmitters' signals targeting the muscles) and it's based on extremely small devices (either having the size of 5nm or bigger but in this case used as a polysynaptic membrane of another neuron) which are responsible both for analyses of the caught neurotransmitters and emitting of one of the following neurotransmitters(Glu, GABA). These 2 neurotransmitters are used in ~80% of the cases, so for the initial stage it's enough to limit the ability of the device to operate with only these 2 types of the neurotransmitters. However, it's not limited and in the future the number of the used neurotransmitters could be increased to 20+.

Emission of the neurotransmitters(for example: Glu) will target the polysynaptic membrane and initiate the AP on the following neuron in the neural circuit.

Effecting on the Neurons Opening Artificially Made Calcium Channels

This approach is based on the artificial made calcium channels of the synapse. Such the channels could be the additional ones to the natural channels and operate (having 2 operations: Open, Close) based on the wireless signals of special devices. The goal of such the channels would be to allow the calcium ions to get inside of the synapse – which corresponds to the Open command. The Close command could just close the channel avoiding the entrance of the calcium ions.

Figure 2. Illustrates the general architecture of the solution

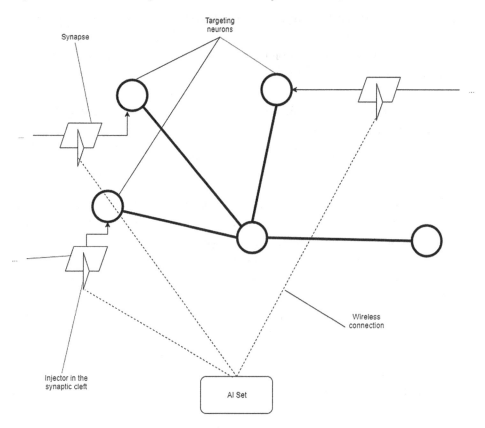

General Architecture

The general architecture would look in the following way (Figure 2)

The major task here is to effect on the properly selected synapses. The Figure 1 shows the selected synapses which are necessary to activate in order to trigger the target neuron(s). Each selected synapse contains a special device which acts in either of the proposed ways described above:

- Using Action Potential (AP)
- Injecting the neurotransmitters into the synaptic cleft
- Opening artificially made calcium channels

This effects on the target neuron(s).

In order to effect on the target neuron we need to start from initiating the summation process, which we can achieve in one of the following ways (in both considered cases we do not effect on the neurons by electrode, instead we emit the Glu on the polysynaptic membrane):

- Send the series of weak signals so that the synaptic ending could collect enough number of calcium ions
- Send a single signal emitting the quantity of Glu corresponding to the AP of -50mV

For more details on how to effect on synapses with neurotransmitters instead of using the electrodes read Rinat Galiautdinov (Brain machine interface - the accurate interpretation of neurotransmitters' signals targeting the muscles)

After that the system sends a strong enough signal corresponding to the converted value in the range of (-30, 30)mV. This signal will make the receptor(s) "to spits out" the ion of Mg^{2+}.

At the next stage the system will initiate constant weak enough signals with the interval of 10ms. The Converted value of the AP depends on the interval but the final result should keep the value in the interval of ~(-60,-50)mV

The whole duration of such the work will depend on the goals:

If the goal is to get/remember the new knowledge during short period of time then the whole work of the system would last only for the duration of the "mission", and in the case if the length of the mission is not more than a day, then for the system it's enough to work during either several minutes or several hours because this would run Long Lasting Potentiation mechanism.

In the case if the goal is to get/remember the new knowledge during very long period of time (longer than several days) then the system must work during several minutes/hours per day but the duration of the work should be at least a week, so that the signals could biologically establish strong synaptic contacts in the neural circuit which is responsible for the knowledge of some particular subject. The speed of creation the new synaptic contacts depends on many factors, such as: age, daily food ration, etc.

The Figure 2 also illustrates the AI Set which is a central managing component in the system. The goal of the component is to control the work of the devices effecting on the synapses using wireless connection.

The approaches used in the software of the AI Set are described below.

Artificial Intelligence in Data Gathering

As discussed earlier one of the major challenges will be to gather the info regarding the used neurons and neural circuit related to the particular pieces of retrieving of the knowledge. As an example, the most trivial task could be image recognition. Probably the best way to resolve such the task would be the usage of Convolutional neural network.

Convolutional Neural Network

Convolutional neural network (CNN) is a special architecture of the neural networks and is especially effective in the sphere of deep learning. The major idea in this architecture is the usage of convolution layers and subsampling ones. For learning the neural network uses backpropagation. The network architecture got its name because of the convolution operation, the essence of which is that each image fragment is multiplied by the matrix (core) of the convolution element by element, and the result is summed and written to the same position in the output image.

The operation of a convolutional neural network is usually interpreted as a transition from specific features of the image to more abstract details, and then to even more abstract details, up to highlighting concepts of a high level. At the same time, the network self-adjusts and generates the necessary hierarchy of abstract features (sequence of feature maps), filtering unimportant details and highlighting the essential.

General Principal of Work

In a conventional perceptron, which is a fully connected neural network, each neuron is connected to all the neurons of the previous layer, and each connection has its own personal weight coefficient. In the convolutional neural network, the convolution operation uses only a limited matrix of small-sized weights that are "moved" throughout the processed layer, forming an activation signal for the next layer neuron with a similar position after each shift. In the other words, for different neurons of the output layer, the same weight matrix is used, which is also called the convolution core. It is interpreted as graphic coding of a feature, for example, the presence of an inclined line at a certain angle. Then the next layer, resulting from the convolution operation by such a weight matrix, shows the presence of this feature in the layer being processed and its coordinates, forming the so-called feature map. In a convolutional neural network, the set of weights is not one, but a whole gamma encoding image elements. Moreover, such convolution kernels are not laid in advance by the researcher, but are formed independently by training the network

Figure 3. The general architecture of convolutional neural network

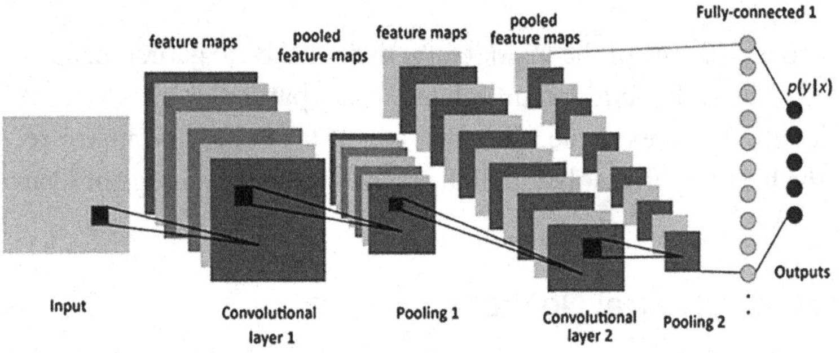

with the classical method of back propagation of error. The passage with each set of weights forms its own instance of the feature map, making the neural network multi-channel. It should also be noted that when sorting a layer with a weight matrix, it is usually moved not by a full step (the size of this matrix), but by a small distance.

We can consider the typical structure of the convolutional neural network in more detail. A network consists of a large number of layers. After the initial layer, the signal passes through a series of convolutional layers, in which the convolution itself and alternating downsampling (pooling) alternate. Alternating layers allows you to create "feature maps" from feature maps; on each subsequent layer, the map decreases in size, but the number of channels increases. In practice, this means the ability to recognize complex feature hierarchies. Usually, after passing through several layers, a feature map degenerates into a vector or even a scalar, but there are hundreds of feature maps. At the output of the convolutional layers of the network, several layers of a fully connected neural network (perceptron) are additionally installed, to the input of which terminal cards of signs are fed.

The general architecture of convolutional neural network is represented in Figure 3.

Convolutional Layer

The convolution layer is the main unit of the convolutional neural network. The convolution layer includes for each channel its own filter, the convolution core of which processes the previous layer by fragments. The weighting coefficients of the convolution kernel (small matrix) are unknown and are established in the learning process.

Activation Layer

The scalar result of each convolution falls on the activation function, which is a certain non-linear function. The activation layer is usually logically combined with the convolution layer. The nonlinearity function can be any one of the researcher's choice, traditionally for this purpose functions like the hyperbolic tangent were used

$f(x) = \tanh(x), f(x) = |\tanh(x)|)$

or sigmoid

$$f\left(x\right) = \left(1 + e - x\right)^{-1}$$

However, there is another activation function called ReLU, which is more effective from the viewpoint of the speed of the learning process and is more simple from the viewpoint of calculations.

$f(x) = \max(0, x)$

This is the operation of cutting off the negative part of a scalar quantity. There are the bunch of modifications of this function, some of them are: Noisy ReLU, Leaky ReLU, etc.

Pooling

The pooling layer is a nonlinear compaction of the feature map, while a group of pixels (usually 2×2 in size) is compressed to one pixel, undergoing a nonlinear transformation. The maximum function is most commonly used. Transformations affect disjoint rectangles or squares, each of which is squeezed into one pixel, and the pixel with the maximum value is selected. The pooling operation can significantly reduce the spatial volume of the image. The pooling is interpreted as follows: if some signs were already detected in the previous convolution operation, then such a detailed image is no longer needed for further processing, and it is compressed to a less detailed one. In addition, filtering already unnecessary parts helps not to retrain. The pooling layer is usually inserted after the convolution layer before the next convolution layer.

In addition to pooling with a maximum function, you can use other functions - for example, the average value or L2-normalization. However, practice has shown the advantages of precisely pooling with a maximum function, which is included in standard systems.

In order to more aggressively reduce the size of the resulting views, the idea of using smaller filters or a complete rejection of pooling layers is increasingly found.

Fully Connected Neural Network

After several passes of image convolution and compaction using pooling, the system is rebuilt from a specific grid of pixels with high resolution to more abstract feature maps, as a rule, the number of channels increases on each next layer and the image dimension in each channel decreases. In the end, there remains a large set of channels that store a small amount of data (even one parameter), which are interpreted as the most abstract concepts identified from the original image.

This data is combined and transmitted into a regular fully connected neural network, which can also consist of several layers. In this case, fully-connected layers already lose the spatial structure of pixels and have a relatively small dimension.

Learning

The simplest and most popular way of teaching is the method of teaching with a teacher (on labeled data) - the method of back propagation of error and its modification. But there are also a number of techniques for teaching a convolutional network without a teacher. For example, convolution operation filters can be trained separately and autonomously, applying randomly cut pieces of the source images of the training set to them and applying any known learning algorithm without a teacher for them (for example, an auto-associator or even the k-means method) - this technique is known as patch -based training. Accordingly, the next layer of network folding will be trained in pieces from the already trained first layer of the network. You can also combine a convolutional neural network with other deep learning technologies. For example, to make a convolutional auto-associator, a convolutional version of cascading limited Boltzmann machines, learning from the probabilistic mathematical apparatus, a convolutional version of sparse coding, called deconvolutional networks ("deploying" networks).

To improve the network, increase its stability and prevent retraining, the exception (dropout) is also used - a method of training a subnet with the throwing of random single neurons.

Algorithm of Back Propagation

To train the described neural network, the backpropagation algorithm is frequently used. This method of training a multilayer neural network is called a generalized delta rule. This algorithm is the first and main practically applicable for training multilayer neural networks.

For the output layer, the adjustment of the weights is intuitive, but for hidden layers the algorithm was not known for a long time. The weights of the hidden neuron should vary in direct proportion to the error of those neurons with which the given neuron is associated. That is why the back propagation of these errors through the network allows you to correctly configure the weights of the bonds between all layers. In this case, the magnitude of the error function decreases and the network learns.

The main relations of the back propagation method of error are obtained with the following notation:

E_p – error function value for image p

t_{pj} – desired output of neuron j for image p

y_{pj} – activated neuron output j for image p

s_{pj} – the weighted sum of the outputs of the connected neurons of the previous layer on the weight of the connection, in another way is also referred to as the inactive state of the neuron j for the image p

w_{pj} – weight between i and j neurons

The error value is determined by the formula (I1):

$$Ep = \frac{1}{2}\sum_{j}\left(tpj - ypj\right)^2$$

The output of each neuron j is the value of the activation function f_j, which puts the neuron in an activated state. As the activation function, any continuously differentiable monotonic function can be used. The activated state of a neuron is calculated by the formula:

$$y_{pj} = f_j(s_{pj})$$

Figure 4. Gradient descent method

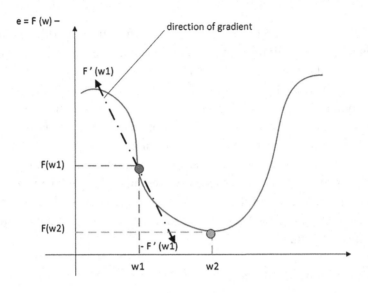

Where:

y_{pj} – activated state of neuron j for image p
f_j – activation function
s_{pj} – non-activated state of neuron j for image p

The gradient descent method is used as a method of error minimization; the essence of this method is reduced to finding the minimum (or maximum) of a function due to movement along the gradient vector. To find the minimum, the movement should be in the direction of the anti-gradient. Gradient descent method as shown in Figure 4

The gradient of the loss function is a partial derivative vector calculated by the formula:

$$\Delta E\left(W\right) = \left[\frac{dE}{dw_1},...,\frac{dE}{dw_n}\right]$$

Where

$\Delta E(W)$ – gradient of the loss function from the weight matrix
dE/dw_1 – partial derivative of neuron weight error function
n – total number of network weights

The derivative of the error function in a specific image can be written according to the chain rule:

$$dE/dw_{ij} = dE/dy_j * dy_j/ds_j * ds_j/dw_{ij}$$

where

dE/dy_j - value of the derivative of the weight error function w_{ij} between i and j neurons
dE/dw_{ij} - the error of j neuron
dy_j/ds_j - the value of the derivative of the activation function with respect to its argument for neuron j
ds_j/dw_{ij} - the output of neuron i of the previous layer

The dE/dy_j neuron error is usually written as the symbol δ (delta). For the output layer, the error is defined explicitly, if we take the derivative of the formula (I1), we get t minus y, that is, the difference between the desired and the resulting output. But how to calculate the error for hidden layers? To solve this problem, the back propagation algorithm of the error was just invented. Its essence is to sequentially calculate the errors of hidden layers using the error values of the output layer, i.e. error values propagate across the network in the opposite direction from output to input.
The error δ for the hidden layer is calculated by the formula (I2):

$$\delta_i = \frac{dy_i}{ds_i} \sum_j \delta_j * w_{ij}$$

Figure 5. The error back propagation algorithm in a multilayer perceptron

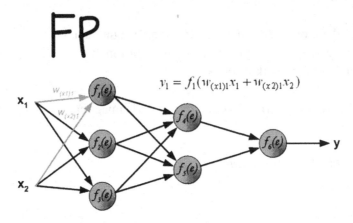

Where

$\dfrac{dy_i}{ds_i}$ - the value of the derivative of the activation function with respect to its argument

for neuron j

δ_i – the error of hidden layer's neuron i

δ_j – the error of neuron j of the next layer

w_{ij} – the weight of the connection between the neuron i of the current (hidden) layer and the neuron j of the output or hidden layer

The error propagation algorithm is reduced to the following steps:

- direct signal propagation through the network, calculation of the state of neurons;
- calculation of the error δ for the output layer;
- backpropagation: sequentially from the end to the beginning for all hidden layers we calculate δ by the formula (I2);
- updating the network weights to the previously calculated δ errors.

The error back propagation algorithm in a multilayer perceptron is shown below (Figure 5.):

Up to this point, cases of error propagation through the perceptron layers, that is, along the output and hidden, but besides them, in the convolutional neural network there are subsample and convolutional ones, have been considered.

Figure 6. Illustrates interpretation of the convolution operation in a multilayer form, where relations with the same color have the same weight. The subsample map is indicated in blue, the synaptic core in multicolored, and the resulting convolution in orange.

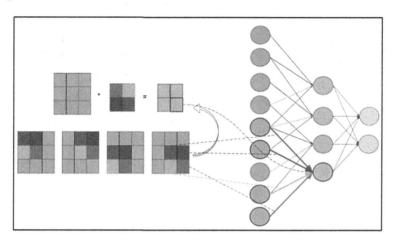

Figure 7. Illustrates calculation of δ subsample layer due to δ convolutional layer and core

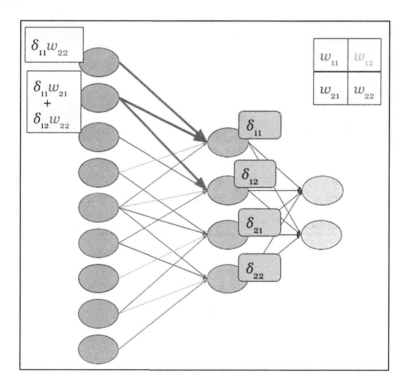

Figure 8. Illustrates the result of the reverse convolution operation

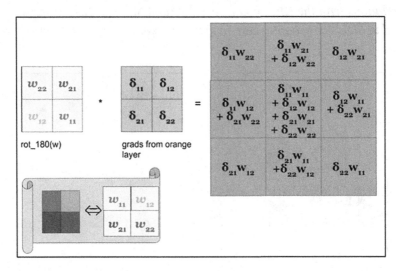

Figure 9. Illustrates the rotated core scans the convolution card 180 degrees

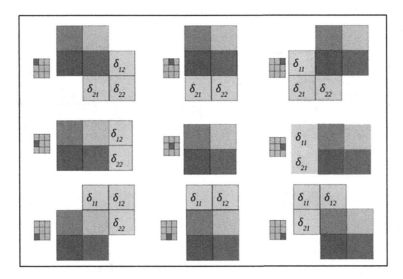

Calculation of Error on the Subsample Layer

The calculation of errors in the subsample layer is presented in several ways. The first case, when the subsample layer is in front of a fully connected layer, then it has neurons and connections of the same type as in a fully connected layer, respectively, the calculation of the δ error is no different from the calculation of the δ hidden layer. The second case, when the subsample layer is in front of the convolutional layer, the calculation of δ occurs by reverse convolution. To understand the convolution back, you must first understand the usual convolution and the fact that a sliding window on a feature map (during direct signal propagation) can be interpreted as a regular hidden layer with connections between neurons, but the main difference is that these connections are separable. that is, several pairs of neurons, and not just one, can have one connection with a specific weight value. Interpretation of the convolution operation in the usual multilayer form in accordance with shown in Figure 6.

Now that the convolution operation is presented in the usual multi-layer form, it is possible to intuitively understand that the calculation of deltas occurs in the same way as in a hidden layer of a fully connected network. Accordingly, having previously convolutional deltas of the convolutional layer, it is possible to calculate the deltas of the subsample according to Figure 7

Reverse convolution is the same way of calculating deltas, only in a slightly tricky way, which consists in rotating the core 180 degrees and the sliding process of scanning a convolutional map of deltas with modified edge effects. In simple words, we need to take the core of the convolutional card (following the subsample layer) to rotate it 180 degrees and make a normal convolution using the previously calculated convolutional deltas, but so that the scan window extends beyond the map. The result of the reverse convolution operation in accordance with Figure 8, the loopback pass cycle in accordance with Figure 9.

Convolution Error Calculation

Usually, the leading layer after a convolutional layer is a subsample, so our task is to calculate the deltas of the current layer (convolutional) due to the knowledge about the deltas of the subsample layer. In fact, the delta error is not calculated, but copied. With direct signal propagation, subsample layer neurons were formed due to a non-overlapping scan window along the convolutional layer, during which neurons with the maximum value were selected, with back propagation, we return the error delta to the previously selected maximum neuron, while the rest receive zero error delta.

Advantages

- Compared to a fully connected neural network, there are much fewer customizable weights, since one core of the weights is used entirely for the entire image, instead of having its own personal weighting factors for each pixel of the input image. This encourages the neural network during training to generalize the information displayed, rather than per-pixel memory of each image shown in the myriad of weighting factors, as the perceptron does.
- Convenient parallelization of calculations, and therefore, the ability to implement work algorithms and network training on GPUs.
- Relative resistance to rotation and shift of the recognized image.
- Training using the classical method of back propagation of error.

Disadvantages

- Too many variable network parameters; it is not clear for what task and computing power what settings are needed. Thus, the following parameters can be classified as variable: the number of layers, the dimension of the convolution core for each layer, the number of cores for each layer, the step of the core shift when processing the layer, the need for sub-sampling layers, the degree of dimension reduction, the function to reduce the dimension, the transfer function of neurons, the presence and parameters of an output fully connected neural network at the output of a convolutional one. All these parameters significantly affect the result, but are selected empirically by the researchers. There are several verified and perfectly working network configurations, but there are not enough recommendations on which to build a network for a new task.

Major Challenges

There are two major challenges in the system, both of them are caused by the small sizes of the objects required to interaction and the huge number of the synaptic contacts between the neurons. Each neuron has in average from 10,000 to 1,000,000 synapses and the total number of the neurons in the brain of a human being varies from ~80,000,000,000- to ~150,000,000,000+ (this number depends on the size of brain which, according to the statistics, depends on gender and ethnicity: according to the statistics the Turkic and Mongolian ethnic groups possess the biggest brains on the planet, in average it's weight is around 1600gm)

So at the initial stage the solution requires the map of the neural system and identification of the neurons' synapses responsible for different associations.

The next stage will require the ability of creation a small device which would be able to effect on the polysynaptic membrane of the selected synapse emitting either of two (at the initial stage) neurotransmitters: Glu, GAMA.

CONCLUSION

In this research the authors described the methodology of transferring the knowledge to people/animals via brain neuron interface. The authors described the principals of how the brain works during the learning process and how the memory works. The authors demonstrated the experiments proving the suggested concept and delivered the working model constructed with the help of Rinat Galiautdinov's software "Neural circuit constructor".

REFERENCES

David, H. (1988). *Hubel, Eye, Brain, and Vision*. Scientific American Library.

Galiautdinov, R. (2020). Brain machine interface: The accurate interpretation of neurotransmitters' signals targeting the muscles [IJARB]. *International Journal of Applied Research in Bioinformatics, 0102*. doi:10.4018/IJARB.2020

Hubel, D. H., & Wiesel, T. N. (2004). Brain and Visual Perception: The Story of a 25-Year Collaboration, 2004. Oxford University Press.

Jain, V., & Seung, S. H. (2008). Natural image denoising with convolutional networks. In Advances in Neural Information Processing Systems (pp. 769-776).

Lee, H., Grosse, R., Ranganath, R., & Ng, A. Y. (2009a). Convolutional deep belief networks for scalable unsupervised learning of hierarchical representations. In ICML'2009. doi:10.1145/1553374.1553453

Mkrttchian, V., & Aleshina, E. (2017). *Sliding Mode in Intellectual Control and Communication: Emerging Research and Opportunities* (pp. 1–128). Hershey, PA: IGI Global; doi:10.4018/978-1-5225-2292-8

Mkrttchian, V., & Belyanina, L. (2018). *Handbook of Research on Students' Research Competence in Modern Educational Contexts* (pp. 1–518). Hershey, PA: IGI Global; doi:10.4018/978-1-5225-3485-3

Mkrttchian, V., Bershadsky, A., Bozhday, A., Kataev, M., & Kataev, S. (2016). *Handbook of Research on Estimation and Control Techniques in E-Learning Systems* (pp. 1–679). Hershey, PA: IGI Global; doi:10.4018/978-1-4666-9489-7

Mkrttchian, V., Krevskiy, I., Bershadsky, A., Glotova, T., Gamidullaeva, L., & Vasin, S. (2019a). Web-Based Learning and Development of University's Electronic Informational Educational Environment. [IJWLTT]. *International Journal of Web-Based Learning and Teaching Technologies*, *14*(1), 32–53. doi:10.4018/IJWLTT.2019010103

Mkrttchian, V., Palatkin, I., Gamidullaeva, L. A., & Panasenko, S. (2019b). About Digital Avatars for Control Systems Using Big Data and Knowledge Sharing in Virtual Industries. In A. Gyamfi, & I. Williams (Eds.), *Big Data and Knowledge Sharing in Virtual Organizations* (pp. 103–116). Hershey, PA: IGI Global; doi:10.4018/978-1-5225-7519-1.ch004

Zeiler, M., Krishnan, D., Taylor, G., & Fergus, R. (2010). Deconvolutional networks. In CVPR'2010. doi:10.1109/CVPR.2010.5539957

Compilation of References

Abbott, L., & Kandel, E. (2012). A computational approach enhances learning in Aplysia. *Nature Neuroscience*, *15*(2), 178–189. doi:10.1038/nn.3030 PMID:22281713

Abbott, L., & Kepler, T. (1990). In L. Garrido (Ed.), *Model neurons: from hodgkin-huxley to hopfield. Statistical Mechanics of neural networks* (Vol. 18, pp. 5–18). Springer.

Abdullin, A. I. (2006), Intellectual property right in the European Union: genesis, unification, development prospects: dissertation for the degree of Doctor of Law, Moscow.

Abdullin, A. I. (2012). 'Interaction mechanism of the EU court and national courts of member states in the field of legal protection of intellectual property,' *Bulletin of Economics, Law, and Sociology*, 2, 97–101.

Abdullin, A. I. (2013). Some problems of formation and formation of legal protection of trademarks in the European Union. *Eurasian Law Journal*, *6*(61), 71–74.

Abrahamson, D., & Sanchez-Garcia, R. (2016). Learning Is Moving in New Ways: The Ecological Dynamics of Mathematics Education. *Journal of the Learning Sciences*, *25*(2), 203–239. doi:10.1080/10508406.2016.1143370

Acorn, A. G. (1981). Alternative learning curves for cost estimating. *Aeronautical Journal*, *844*, 194–205.

Agamagomedova, S. A., & Belousova, D. V. (2019), 'The Institute of Intellectual Property in the Context of Economic Integration: Transformation Vector' In the Proceedings: *Actual problems of foreign economic activity and customs affairs materials of the IX International Scientific and Practical Conference,* 18-22.

Agamagomedova, S., Gamidullaeva, L., & Taktarova, S. (2019). Economic and legal aspects of increasing the efficiency of intellectual property management in the Eurasian Economic Union. *Proceedings of the 34th International Business Information Management Association Conference*, IBIMA 2019. Seville; Spain; 13 November 2019 - 14 November 2019.

Agamagomedova, S. A. (2013). The interaction of international and national law in the field of cross-border protection of intellectual property rights. *Journal of Russian Law*, *12*, 122–129. doi:10.12737/1555

Agamagomedova, S. A. (2015). Supranational Institute of Administrative Legal Regulation of the Protection of Intellectual Property Rights in the Framework of Eurasian Integration. *Bulletin of the Eurasian Academy of Administrative Sciences, 2*(31), 28–35.

Aggarwal, C. C. (2018). *Neural networks and deep learning.* Springer. doi:10.1007/978-3-319-94463-0

Ahn, A., & Haugh, M. (2015). Linear programming and the control of diffusion processes. *INFORMS Journal on Computing, 27*(4), 646–657. doi:10.1287/ijoc.2015.0651

Akhtari, S., & Sowlati, T. (2015). Hybrid simulation and optimization approaches to tackle supply chain complexities – A review with a focus on forest products supply chains. *The Journal of Science and Technology for Forest Products and Processes. Special Issue on Value Chain Optimization, 5*(5), 26–39.

Alayet, C., Lehoux, N., Lebel, L., & Bouchard, M. (2018). Centralized supply chain planning model for multiple forest companies. Forestry Applications, 3–23. doi:10.1201/9781351269964-2

Al-Chalabi, A., Calvo, A., Chio, A., Colville, A., & Pearce, N. (2014) Analysis of amyotrophic lateral sclerosis as a multistep process: a population-based modelling study. In The Lancet Neurology, pp. 1108-1113. doi:10.1016/S1474-4422(14)70219-4

Alqezweeni, M. M., Gorbachenko, V. I. (2017). Improvement of the learning algorithms in radial basis functions networks for solving the approximation tasks. *Models, systems, networks in economics, technology, nature and society, 3*(23), 123–138 (in Russian).

Alqezweeni, M. M., Gorbachenko, V. I., Zhukov, M. V., & Jaafar, M. S. (2018). Efficient solving of boundary value problems using radial basis function networks learned by trust region method. *Hindawi. International Journal of Mathematics and Mathematical Sciences,* 9457578.

Amelin, S. V., & Shchetinina, I. V. (2018). Organization of production in the digital economy. *Production Organizer., 26*(4), 7–18.

Anderson, J. R., Hardy, E. E., Roach, J. T., & Witmer, R. E. (1976). *A land use and land cover classification system for use with remote sensor data.* Professional Paper; doi:10.3133/pp964

Andersson, G., Flisberg, P., Lidén, B., & Ronnqvist, M. (2007). *RuttOpt - A Decision Support System for Routing of Logging Trucks.* SSRN Electronic Journal; doi:10.2139srn.1020628

Anfimov, A. M. (1961) Zemel'naya arenda v Rossii v nachale 20 veka. Moskva: Izdatel'stvo Akademii nauk USSR.

Apanasyuk, L. A., Lisitzina, T. B., & Zakirova, C. S. (2019). Factors and Conditions of Student Environmental Culture Forming in the System of Ecological Education. *EKOLOJI, 28*(107), 191–198.

Arakaki, T., Barello, G., & Ahmadian, Y. (2017). Capturing the diversity of biological tuning curves using generative adversarial networks, [Electronic resource] Retrieved from (access date: 21.10.2018). doi:10.1101/167916

Arévalo, A., Niño, J., Hernández, G., & Sandoval, J. (2016). High-frequency trading strategy based on deep neural networks. *Lecture Notes in Computer Science*, *9773*, 424–436. doi:10.1007/978-3-319-42297-8_40

Arifovic, J., Dawid, H., Deissenberg, C., & Kostyshyna, O. (2010). Learning Benevolent Leadership in a Heterogenous Avatars Economy. *Journal of Economic Dynamics & Control*, *34*(9), 1768–1790. doi:10.1016/j.jedc.2010.06.023

Arjovsky, M., & Bottou, L. (2017). Towards Principled Methods for Training Generative Adversarial Networks. *arXiv*.

Arora, S., Ge, R., Liang, Y., Ma, T., & Zhang, Y. (2017). Generalization and Equilibrium in Generative Adversarial Nets (GANs). *arXiv*.

Arthaud, G. J., & Barrett, T. M. (Eds.). (2003). *Systems Analysis in Forest Resources*. Managing Forest Ecosystems; doi:10.1007/978-94-017-0307-9

Ashton, D., & Conor, B. (2016). Screenwriting, higher education and digital ecologies of expertise. *New Writing - The International Journal for the Practice and Theory of Creative Writing*, *13*(1), 98–108.

Atsalakis, G. S., & Valavanis, K. P. (2009). Forecasting stock market short-term trends using a neuro-fuzzy based methodology. *Expert Systems with Applications*, *36*(7), 10696–10707. doi:10.1016/j.eswa.2009.02.043

Atsalakis, G. S., & Valavanis, K. P. (2009). Surveying stock market forecasting techniques – Part II: Soft computing methods. *Expert Systems with Applications*, *36*(3), 5932–5941. doi:10.1016/j.eswa.2008.07.006

Australia's first Open Government National Action Plan 2016-18. [Electronic resource] // URL: https://ogpau.pmc.gov.au/australias-first-open-government-national-action-plan-2016-18

Bakti, N., Hussain, A., & El-Hassani, S. (2011). A rare complication of acute appendicitis: Superior mesenteric vein thrombosis. *International Journal of Surgery Case Reports*, *2*(8), 250–252. doi:10.1016/j.ijscr.2011.08.003 PMID:22096743

Barrett, R. H., & Salwasser, H. (1982). Adaptive management of timber and wildlife habitat using DYNAST and wildlife-habitat relationship models. *Western Association of Fish and Wildlife Agencies Proceedings*, *62*, 350–365.

Bartasson, L. A., & Saito, C. H. (2015). The understanding of ecological concepts in Basic Education: Evaluation by concept maps. *COMUNICACOES*, *22*(2), 165–190.

Bartsits, I. N. (2008). Reforma gosudarstvennogo upravleniya v Rossii: pravovoj aspect [*Reform of public administration in Russia: the legal aspect*]. Moscow, Russia: The formula of law.

Basu, S. (1977). The investment performance of common stocks in relation to their price-earnings ratios: A test of the efficient market hypothesis. *The Journal of Finance*, *32*(3), 663–682. doi:10.1111/j.1540-6261.1977.tb01979.x

Bautin, V. M., & Kostin, V. D. (2006). Trust management of rights to intellectual property objects, *Achievements of science and technology of the agro-industrial complex*, 8, 43-44.

Beltrami, E. (1993). *Mathematical models in the social and biological sciences*. Boston, MA: Jones & Bartlett.

Belytschko, T., Krongauz, Y., Organ, D., Fleming, M., & Krysl, P. (1996). Meshless methods: An overview and recent developments. Computers Methods in Applied Mechanics and Engineering, 139(1–4). pp. 3–47.

Beretta, V., Demartini, C., & Trucco, S. (2019). Does environmental, social and governance performance influence intellectual capital disclosure tone in integrated reporting. *Journal of Intellectual Capital, 20*(1), 100–124. doi:10.1108/JIC-02-2018-0049

Bernal, F. (2016). Trust-region methods for nonlinear elliptic equations with radial basis functions. *Computers & Mathematics with Applications (Oxford, England), 72*(7), 1743–1763. doi:10.1016/j.camwa.2016.07.014

Bertalanffy, L. (1973). *General system theory (foundation, development, application)*. New York: Brazillier.

Bliznets, I. A. (2010). *Intellectual Property Law: A Textbook*. Moscow, Russia.

Bliznets, I. A. (2018). *Intellectual property law: international legal regulation*. Moscow, Russia.

Bluteau, P., Clouder, L., & Cureton, D. (2017). Developing interprofessional education online: An ecological systems theory analysis. *Journal of Interprofessional Care, 31*(4), 420–428. doi:10.1080/13561820.2017.1307170 PMID:28471258

Bogdanova, Y. Z., & Zharkova, M. A. (2018). On The Digitalization of a University Education and The Possibility of Distance Foreign Language Teaching of Students of Agrarian University. *Modern Journal of Language Teaching Methods, 8*(12), 186–192.

Bogoviz, A. V., Gimelshteyn, A. V., & Shvakov, E. E. (2018). Digitalization of the Russian education system: opportunities and perspectives. *Quality-Access to Success, 19*(2), 27–32.

Bolotov, V. A., & Efremov, N. F. (2007) Education quality assessment systems. Moscow, Russia. University book.

Bolotov, V. A., & Kovaleva, G. S. (2011) Russian experience in the field of assessment of educational achievements of schoolchildren. Innovative projects and programs in education. No 4. pp. 39–45.

Bordovskaya, I. V. (2004) The quality management system of education at a university. Assessment of the quality of education at Russian universities. Experience and challenges. St. Petersburg. pp. 16–25.

Bossel, H. (1994). *Modelling and simulation*. Wellesley, MA: A. K. Peters.

320

Boyce, S. G. (1977). Management of eastern hardwood forests for multiple benefits (DYNAST-MB). *US Department of Agriculture, Forest Service, Southeastern Forest Experiment Station*, Asherville, North Carolina, Research Paper SE-168.

Boyce, S. G. (1978). Management of forest for timber and related benefits (DYNAST-TM). US Department of Agriculture, Forest Service, Southeastern Forest Experiment Station, Research Paper SE-184, *Asheville, North Carolina.*

Boyce, S. G. (1980). Management of forests for optimal benefits (DYNAST-OB). US Department of Agriculture, Southeastern Forest Experiment Station, Research Paper NC-204, *Asheville, North Carolina.*

Brigham, K. L., & Johns, M. M. E. (2012). *Predictive health: How we can reinvent medicine to extend our best years.* Basic Books.

Brownlee, J. (2017). *Why One-Hot encode data in machine learning?* Retrieved from https://machinelearningmastery.com/why-one-hot-encode-data-in-machine-learning/

Bruce, P., & Bruce, F. (2017). *Practical statistics for data scientists: 50 essential concepts.* O'Reilly.

Buhmann, M. D. (2004). *Radial basis functions: theory and implementations.* Cambridge University Press.

Buslenko, N. P. (1978). *Modeling complex systems.* Moscow, USSR: Science.

Bychkova, E. (2019). The conference on the global ecological problems held on the occasion of the 155th anniversary of Vladimir Vernadsky within the framework of the Fourth World Professional Forum "The book. Culture. Education. Innovations" // Scientific and Technical Libraries, 2019, No. 1. pp. 102-118.

Bychkova, E., & Matochenko, A. (2019). Education programs at RNPLS&T Ecological Information Research & Consultation Department. "Climate change" master class and research & practical workshop. Scientific and Technical Libraries, 2019, No. 1. pp. 97-105.

Bykovsky, V. K. (2016). The legal and organizational basis of state forest management: A Textbook and practical Course for the SVE. 3rd ed., Revised and supplemented. Jurait Publishing House.

Campbell, C. (2018). Returning 'learning' to education: Toward an ecological conception of learning and teaching. *Sign Systems Studies, 46*(4), 538–568. doi:10.12697/SSS.2018.46.4.07

Campbell, J. (1987). Stock returns and the term structure. *Journal of Financial Economics, 18*(2), 373–399. doi:10.1016/0304-405X(87)90045-6

Carlsson, M. K. (2017). Environmental Design, Systems Thinking, and Human Agency: McHarg's Ecological Method and Steinitz and Rogers's Interdisciplinary Education Experiment. *Landscape Journal, 36*(2), 37–52. doi:10.3368/lj.36.2.37 PMID:30034076

Casti, J. L. (1979). *Connectivity, complexity, and catastrophe in large-scale systems.* Chichester, UK: Wiley.

Cegarra, J., Soto-Acosta, P., & Wensley, A. (2015). Structured knowledge processes and firm performance: The role of organizational agility. *Journal of Business Research, 69.*. doi:10.1016/j.jbusres.2015.10.014

Cervello-Royo, R., Guijarro, F., & Michniuk, K. (2015). Stock market trading rule based on pattern recognition and technical analysis: Forecasting the djia index with intraday data. *Expert Systems with Applications, 42*(14), 5963–5975. doi:10.1016/j.eswa.2015.03.017

Ceyp, M., & Scupin, J.-P. (2012). Social Media Monitoring. Erfolgreiches Social Media Marketing, 189–196. doi:10.1007/978-3-658-00035-6_10

Challenging, F. S. (2019). Bias in Ecological Education Discourses: Emancipatory 'Development Education' in Developing Countries. *Ecological Economics, 157*, 373–381. doi:10.1016/j.ecolecon.2018.11.020

Chandrashekar, G., & Sahin, F. (2014). A survey on feature selection methods. *Computers & Electrical Engineering, 40*(1), 16–28. doi:10.1016/j.compeleceng.2013.11.024

Che, Z., Cheng, Y., Zhai, S., Sun, Z., & Liu, Y. (2017). Boosting Deep Learning Risk Prediction with Generative Adversarial Networks for Electronic Health Records. In *Proceedings IEEE International Conference on Data Mining (ICDM)*. Piscataway, NJ: IEEE. pp. 787–792.

Chen, X., Duan, Y., Houthooft, R., Schulman, J., Sutskever, I., & Abbeel, P. (2016). InfoGAN: Interpretable Representation Learning by Information Maximizing Generative Adversarial Nets. *Advances in Neural Information Processing Systems. arXiv.*

Chen, Zh., Rose, A., Prager, F., & Chatterjee, S. (2017) Economic consequences of aviation system disruptions: A reduced-form computable general equilibrium analysis. In Transportation Research Part A: Policy and Practice, pp. 207-226. Doi:10.1016/j.tra.2016.09.027

Cheng, W., Su, L., Chen, Sh., Li, T., & Lin, H. (2014) Economic Burden of Diabetes Mellitus on Patients with Respiratory Failure Requiring Mechanical Ventilation during Hospitalizations. In Value in Health Regional Issues, pp. 33-38. Doi:10.1016/j.vhri.2014.02.003

Chen, H., Kong, L., & Leng, W. (2011). Numerical solution of PDEs via integrated radial basis function networks with adaptive learning algorithm. *Applied Soft Computing, 11*(1), 855–860. doi:10.1016/j.asoc.2010.01.005

Chen, T., & Chen, F.-Y. (2016). An intelligent pattern recognition model for supporting investment decisions in stock market. *Information Sciences, 346*, 261–274. doi:10.1016/j.ins.2016.01.079

Chen, W., & Fu, Z.-J. (2014). *Recent advances in radial basis function collocation methods.* Springer. doi:10.1007/978-3-642-39572-7

Chernousenko, V. M., Chernyshenko, S. V., & Chernenko, I. V. (1988). *Analysis of nonlinear models of distributed learning system.* Nonlinear and turbulent processes in physics. In *Proc. of the 3rd Intern. Workshop.* Kiev, Ukraine: Naukova Dumka. Vol. 1. pp. 239-243.

Chernyakova, M. M. (2018). Innovative diversification risks in the digital economy. Herald of the Eurasian Science. No. 6. Retrieved from https://esj.today/PDF/16ECVN618.pdf

Chernyshenko, S. V. (1997). Discrete effects in dynamical differential models. Social Science Microsimulation: Tools for Modelling, Parameter Optimisation, and Sensitivity Analysis. Seminar report, Dagstuhl, Germany. pp. 29-30.

Chernyshenko, S. V. (2005). Monograph.

Chesbrough, H. W., & Vanhaverbeke, W. (2018). Open innovation and public policy in the EU with implications for SMEs (Book Chapter). *Researching Open Innovation In SMEs*, 455-492.

Chiang, W.-C., Enke, D., Wu, T., & Wang, R. (2016). An adaptive stock index trading decision support system. *Expert Systems with Applications*, *59*, 195–207. doi:10.1016/j.eswa.2016.04.025

Choi, S., Lee, N., Lee, C., Bailey, C., Kandel, E., Jang, J., … Kaang, B. (2012). Learning-related synaptic growth mediated by internalization of Aplysia cell adhesion molecule is controlled by membrane phosphatidylinositol 4,5-bisphosphate synthetic pathway, *The Journal of Neuroscience: the Official Journal of the Society For Neuroscience, 32,* pp. 296-305.

Choi, Y., Kadakkuzha, B., Liu, A., Akhmedov, K., Kandel, R., & Puthanveettil, S. (2014). Huntingtin is critical both pre- and postsynaptically for long-term learning-related synaptic plasticity in Aplysia. *PLoS One, 9*(7), e103004. doi:10.1371/journal.pone.0103004 PMID:25054562

Chollet, F. (2017). *Deep learning with Python.* Manning Publications.

Chong, E., Han, C., & Park, F. C. (2017). Deep Learning Networks for Stock Market Analysis and Prediction: Methodology, Data Representations, and Case Studies. *Expert Systems with Applications, 83,* 187–205. doi:10.1016/j.eswa.2017.04.030

Cieślik, A., Qu, Y., & Qu, T. (2018). Innovations and export performance: Firm level evidence from China. *Entrepreneurial Business and Economics Review, 6*(4), 27–47. doi:10.15678/EBER.2018.060402

Commentary on the Civil Code of the Russian Federation. Part four. (article by article). In 2 volumes. Ed. L. A. Trachtengerts. Moscow, Russia: Infra-M, 2016.

Commentary on the Civil Code of the Russian Federation. Part four: Educational-practical commentary. Ed. A. P. Sergeeva. Moscow, Russia: Prospect, 2016.

Conn, A. R., Gould, N. I. M., & Toint, P. L. (1987). *Trust-region methods.* MPS-SIAM.

Corona, P., Köhl, M., & Marchetti, M. (Eds.). (2003). Advances in Forest Inventory for Sustainable Forest Management and Biodiversity Monitoring. Springer Netherlands. XVII. doi:10.1007/978-94-017-0649-0

Cortner, H. J., & Moote, M. A. (1994). Trends and issues in land and water resources management: Setting the agenda for change. *Environmental Management, 18*(2), 167–173. doi:10.1007/BF02393759

Cover, T. M. (1965). Geometrical and statistical properties of systems of linear inequalities with applications in pattern recognition. *IEEE Transactions on Electronic Computers, EC-14*(3), 326–334. doi:10.1109/PGEC.1965.264137

Creswell, A., White, T., Dumoulin, V., Arulkumaran, K., Sengupta, B., & Bharath, A. A. (2018). Generative Adversarial Networks: An Overview. *IEEE Signal Processing Magazine, 35*(1), 53–65. doi:10.1109/MSP.2017.2765202

Da Costa, T. R. C. C., Nazario, R. T., Bergo, G. S. C., Sobreiro, V. A., & Kumura, H. (2015). Trading system based on the use of technical analysis: A computational experiment. *Journal of Behavioral and Experimental Finance, 6,* 42–55. doi:10.1016/j.jbef.2015.03.003

Danylova, T., & Salata, G. (2018). The ecological imperative and human nature: A new perspective on ecological education. Interdisciplinary Studies of Complex Systems, 2018, No. 12. pp. 17-24.

Dashyan, M. (2006). Intellectual property trust management: opportunities and trends, Intellectual property. *Industrial property, 12,* 11-16.

David, H. (1988). *Hubel, Eye, Brain, and Vision.* Scientific American Library.

Davies, P. (1988). A new science of complexity. *New Scientist, 120,* 48–50.

Davison, A. P., Brüderle, D., Eppler, J. M., Kremkow, J., Muller, E., Pecevski, D., ... Yger, P. (2008). A Common Interface for Neuronal Network Simulators. *Frontiers in Neuron Informatics, 2,* 11–15. PMID:19194529

Dawid, H., & Fagiolo, G. (2008). Avatar-based models for economic policy design: Introduction to the special issue. *Journal of Economic Behavior & Organization, 67*(2), pp. 351–354. doi:10.1016/j.jebo.2007.06.009

De Moraes Gonçalves, J. L., Silva, L. D., Behling, M., & Alvares, C. A. (2014). *Management of Industrial Forest Plantations. Managing Forest Ecosystems, 33.* Dordrecht, The Netherlands: Springer; doi:10.1007/978-94-017-8899-1

Debes, G., & Oznacar, B. (2018). Evaluation of the opinions of the manager, teacher, employees (secretary and servants) about school management of the digitalization and management processes of the system engineering model in education. *Amazonia Investiga, 7*(16), 243–253.

Decree of the President of the Republic of Kazakhstan No. 1471 dated November 10, 2004 "On the State Program of Forming an "Electronic Government" in the Republic of Kazakhstan for 2005-2007". It became invalid by the Decree of the President of the Republic of Kazakhstan No. 829 dated June 18, 2009. Retrieved from http://adilet.zan.kz/rus/docs/U040001471_

Decree of the President of the Republic of Kazakhstan No. 464 dated January 8, 2013 "On the State Program" Information Kazakhstan - 2020 "and amending the Decree of the President of the Republic of Kazakhstan dated March 19, 2010 No. 957" On Approval of the List of State Programs". Retrieved from http://adilet.zan.kz/rus/docs/U1300000464

Decree of the President of the Republic of Kazakhstan No. 840 of June 17, 2014 "On Amendments to the Decrees of the President of the Republic of Kazakhstan of June 18, 2009 No. 827" On the System of State Planning in the Republic of Kazakhstan "and on March 4, 2010 No. 931" On Some Issues further functioning of the State Planning System in the Republic of Kazakhstan". Retrieved from http://adilet.zan.kz/rus/docs/U1400000840

Demir, C., & Cergibozan, R. (2018). Determinants of Patent Protection Regimes: A Self-Organizing Map Approach. *Review of Economic Perspectives*, *18*(3), 261–283. doi:10.2478/revecp-2018-0013

DeNardis, L. E-governance policies for interoperability and open standards // Policy & Internet. 2010. N°2 (3). [Electronic resource] // URL: URL: http://psocommons.org/vol2/iss3/art6

Doesken, B., Abraham, A., Thomas, J., & Paprzycki, M. (2005) Real stock trading using soft computing models // International Conference on Information Technology: Coding and Computing (ITCC 05), vol. 2, pp. 162–167.

Donahue, J., Krähenbühl, P., & Darrell, T. (2016). Adversarial Feature Learning. *arXiv*.

Dourra, H., & Siy, P. (2002). Investment using technical analysis and fuzzy logic. *Fuzzy Sets and Systems*, *127*(2), 221–240. doi:10.1016/S0165-0114(01)00169-5

Dumoulin, V., Belghazi, I., Poole, B., Mastropietro, O., Lamb, A., Arjovsky, M., & Courville, A. (2016). Adversarially Learned Inference. *arXiv*.

Edwards, R., Magee, J., & Bassetti, W. H. C. (2013). *Technical Analysis of Stock Trends*. Boca Raton, FL: CRC Press.

EEU digital agenda. [Electronic resource] // Retrieved from http://www.eurasiancommission.org/ru/act/dmi/workgroup/Pages/default.aspx

Elisov, L. N., Gorbachenko, V. I., & Zhukov, M. V. (2018). Learning radial basis function networks with the trust region method for boundary problems. *Automation and Remote Control*, *79*(9), 1621–1629. doi:10.1134/S0005117918090072

Elizarov, M., Ivanyuk, V., Soloviev, V., & Tsvirkun, A. (2017) Identification of high-frequency traders using fuzzy logic methods // 2017 Tenth International Conference Management of Large-Scale System Development (MLSD). Piscataway, NJ: IEEE. pp. 1-4.

Ellaway, R. H., Bates, J., & Teunissen, P. W. (2017). Ecological theories of systems and contextual change in medical education. *Medical Education*, *51*(12), 1250–1259. doi:10.1111/medu.13406 PMID:28857233

Enke, D., & Mehdiyev, N. (2013). Stock market prediction using a combination of stepwise regression analysis, differential evolution-based fuzzy clustering, and a fuzzy inference neural network. *Intelligent Automation and Soft Computing*, *19*(4), 636–648. doi:10.1080/10798587.2013.839287

Epps, T. W., & Epps, M. (1976). The stochastic dependence of security price changes and transactions volumes: Implications for the mixture of distribution hypothesis. *Econometrica*, *44*(2), 305–321. doi:10.2307/1912726

Eremenko, V. I. (2015). Improving legislation in the field of intellectual property protection in information and telecommunication networks. *Legislation and Economics*, *8*, 19–28.

Eremenko, V. I. (2016). On the reform of the single trademark system of the European Union. *Intellectual Property Exchange*, *15*(8), 1–10.

Erickson, Z., Chernova, S., & Kemp, C. C. (2017). Semi-Supervised Haptic Material Recognition for Robots using Generative Adversarial Networks. *arXiv.*

Escobar, A., Moreno, J., & Munera, S. (2013). A technical analysis indicator. *Electronic Notes in Theoretical Computer Science*, *292*, 27–37. doi:10.1016/j.entcs.2013.02.003

Esteban, C., Hyland, S. L., & Rätsch, G. (2017). Real-valued (Medical) Time Series Generation with Recurrent Conditional GANs. *arXiv.*

Ezzeddine, S., & Hammami, M. S. (2018). Nonlinear effects of intellectual property rights on technological innovation. *Journal of Economic Integration*, *33*(2), 1337–1362. doi:10.11130/jei.2018.33.2.1337

Fadeev, V. P. (2001) Fermerskoe hozyajstvo: problemy stanovleniya i razvitiya. Saratov: Saratovskij gosudarstvennyj universitet im. N.I. Vavilova

Fama, E. F. (1965). The behavior of stock market price. *The Journal of Business*, *38*(1), 34–105. doi:10.1086/294743

Fama, E. F. (1991). Efficient capital markets. *The Journal of Finance*, *46*(5), 1575–1617. doi:10.1111/j.1540-6261.1991.tb04636.x

Fama, E. F., & French, K. (1998). Dividend yields and expected stock returns. *Journal of Financial Economics*, *22*(1), 3–25. doi:10.1016/0304-405X(88)90020-7

Fama, E. F., & French, K. (1998). Permanent and temporary components of stock prices. *Journal of Political Economy*, *96*(2), 246–273. doi:10.1086/261535

Fama, E. F., & Schwert, W. (1977). Asset returns and inflation. *Journal of Financial Economics*, *5*(2), 115–146. doi:10.1016/0304-405X(77)90014-9

Fang, J., Qin, Y., & Jacobsen, B. (2014). Technical market indicators: An overview. *Journal of Behavioral and Experimental Finance*, *4*, 25–56. doi:10.1016/j.jbef.2014.09.001

Farlow, S. J. (1993). *Partial differential equations for scientists and engineers.* Dover Publications.

Fasshauer, G. E. (2002). Newton iteration with multiquadrics for the solution of nonlinear PDEs. *Computers & Mathematics with Applications (Oxford, England)*, *43*(3–5), 423–438. doi:10.1016/S0898-1221(01)00296-6

Fasshauer, G. E. (2007). *Meshfree approximation methods with MATLAB.* World Scientific Publishing Company. doi:10.1142/6437

Fasshauer, G., & Zhang, J. (2007). On choosing "optimal" shape parameters for RBF approximation. *Numerical Algorithms, 45*(1–4), 345–368. doi:10.100711075-007-9072-8

Federal Law of December 27, 2018 N 538-ФЗ "On Amendments to the Forest Code of the Russian Federation and Certain Legislative Acts of the Russian Federation Regarding Improving Legal Regulation of Relations Connected with Ensuring the Preservation of Forests on Forest Lands and Lands of Other Categories" // Official Internet Legal Information Portal http://www.pravo.gov.ru, 12/28/2018.

Ferber, J. (1999). *Multi-Agent Systems.* Addison-Wesley.

Fernandez-Rodriguez, F., Gonzalez-Martel, C., & Sosvilla-Rivebo, S. (2000). On the profitability of technical trading rules based on artificial neural networks: Evidence from the Madrid stock market. *Economics Letters, 69*(1), 89–94. doi:10.1016/S0165-1765(00)00270-6

Fisenko, S. B. (2013). Implementation of the project management mechanism at the enterprises of the forest industry. *Transport Business in Russia, 1,* 222-225.

Fish, J., & Syed, M. (2018). Native Americans in Higher Education: An Ecological Systems Perspective. *Journal of College Student Development, 59*(4), 387–403. doi:10.1353/csd.2018.0038

Fiut, I. S., & Urbaniak, M. (2019). Education in Defense of Biodiversity. Will the Ecological and Ethical Footprint Counteract Environmental Changes? *Environmental Studies, 14*(1), 73–78.

Fletcher, R., & Reeves, C. M. (1964). Function minimization by conjugate gradients. *The Computer Journal, 7*(2), 149–154. doi:10.1093/comjnl/7.2.149

Forest Code of the Russian Federation dated 12/04/2006 N 200-ФЗ (as amended on 12/27/2018) // "Rossiyskaya Gazeta", N 277, 08/08/2006.

Foster, K. A., & Charles, V. A. (2017). Social Networks. Encyclopedia of Social Work. doi:10.1093/acrefore/9780199975839.013.103

Franke, R. (1982). Scattered data Interpolation: Tests of some Methods. *Mathematics of Computation, 38*(157), 181–200.

Fujishiro, K., Farley, A. N., Kellemen, M., & Swoboda, C. M. (2017). Exploring associations between state education initiatives and teachers' sleep: A social-ecological approach. *Social Science & Medicine, 191,* 151–159. doi:10.1016/j.socscimed.2017.09.019 PMID:28923520

Galiautdinov, R. (2020). Brain machine interface: The accurate interpretation of neurotransmitters' signals targeting the muscles [IJARB]. *International Journal of Applied Research in Bioinformatics, 0102.* doi:10.4018/IJARB.2020

Gambal, M., Kotlarsky, J., & Asatiani, A. (2018). Enabling Strategic Technological Innovations in IS Outsourcing Relationships: Towards an Innovation-melding Framework. New York.

Gamidullaeva, L., Vasin, S., Shkarupeta, E., Tolstykh, T., Finogeev, A., Surovirskaya, G., & Kanarev, S. (2019). Emergence of Industry 4.0 Technologies. Leapfrogging Opportunity for the Russian Federation. In U. G. Benna (Ed.), Industrial and Urban Growth Policies at the Sub-National, National, and Global Levels. Hershey, PA: IGI Global; doi:10.4018/978-1-5225-7625-9

Gamidullaeva, L. A., Merkulova, N. S., Kryachkova, L. I., Kondratieva, Z. A., Efimova, Y. A., & Matukin, S. V. (2019). Emerging Trends and Opportunities for Industry Development at the Sub-National Level in Russia. In U. Benna (Ed.), *Industrial and Urban Growth Policies at the Sub-National, National, and Global Levels* (pp. 342–363). Hershey, PA: IGI Global; doi:10.4018/978-1-5225-7625-9.ch017

Gašpar, D., & Mabić, M. (2019). Strengths and Limitations of Social Media Analytics Tools. In I. Management Association (Ed.), Social Entrepreneurship: Concepts, Methodologies, Tools, and Applications (pp. 595-615). Hershey, PA: IGI Global. doi:10.4018/978-1-5225-8182-6.ch031

Gavrilov, E. P. (2014). Patents for inventions in the countries of the Customs Union in the aspect of private international law, *Patents and licenses. Intellectual rights 1,* 24.

Gavrilov, E. P. (2018). Intellectual Property Law of the Russian Federation: Legislation and Doctrine, *Patents and Licenses. Intellectual rights, 8,* 14-19.

Gavrilov, E. P. (2010). Legal protection of trademarks and copyright: Problems of differentiation. Law. *Journal of the Higher School of Economics, 2,* 36–46.

Geiger, C., & von Lucke, J. Open Government and (Linked) (Open) (Government) (Data) // JeDEM – eJournal of eDemocracy and Open Government. 2012. Nº4 (2). Retrieved from https://www.researchgate.net/publication/271325963_Open_Government_and_Linked_Open_Government_Data

General assessment of the promotion of standards of effective public administration in the Republic of Kazakhstan on the example of implementation and development of the principles of the "Open Government" - Almaty, 2017 - 37 p.

Geron, A. (2017). *Hands-on machine learning with Scikit-Learn and TensorFlow: Concepts, tools, and techniques to build intelligent systems.* O'Reilly.

Gigler, S., Custer, S., & Rahemtulla. Realizing the vision of open government data, 2011, [Electronic resource] // Retrieved from https://www.researchgate.net/publication/314237022_Realizing_the_Vision_of_Open_Government_Data_Opportunities_Challenges_and_Pitfalls

Gilbert, N., & Troitzsch, K. G. (2005). *Simulation for the Social Scientist* (2nd ed.). Open University Press.

Gill, P. E., Murray, W., & Wright, M. H. (1982). *Practical optimization.* Emerald Group.

Gishko, V. Ya., Kovalenko, A. S., & Pridyba, O. V. (2015). The "Open Government" Strategy and Some Aspects of Ensuring the Information Security of Russian Society // State and Municipal Management. Scientific notes of SKAGS, 2015, N°3. Retrieved from http://cyberleninka.ru/article/n/strategiya-otkrytogo-pravitelstva-i-nekotorye-aspekty-obespecheniya-informatsionnoy-bezopasnosti-rossiyskogo-obschestva

Glaziev, S. Yu., Nizhegorodtsev, R. M., Kupryashin, G. L., Makogonova, N. V., Sidorov, A. V., & Sukharev, O. S. (2017). Managing the Development of the National Economy at the Federal Level, 2017. N°60 // Public administration. [Electronic resource] // Retrieved from http://cyberleninka.ru/article/n/upravlenie-razvitiem-natsionalnoy-ekonomiki-na-federalnom-urovne-materialy-kruglogo-stola-26-10-2016

Glorot, X., & Bengio, Y. (2010). Understanding the difficulty of training deep feedforward neural networks. *International conference on artificial intelligence and statistics*, 249–256.

Glorot, X., Bordes, A., & Bengio, Y. (2011). Deep sparse rectifier neural networks. *Proceedings of the 14th International Conference on Artificial Intelligence and Statistics*, Vol. 15, 315–323.

Gong, R., & Yu, K. (2018). Key Success Factors in Using Virtual Reality for Ecological Education. *Ekoloji*, 27(106), 257–262.

Goodfellow, I. J., Pouget-Abadie, J., Mirza, M., Xu, B., Warde-Farley, D., Ozair, Sh., . . . Bengio, Y. (2014). Generative Adversarial Nets. *arXiv*.

Goodfellow, I., Bengio, Y., & Courville, A. (2016). *Deep learning*. MIT Press.

Gorbachenko, V. I., & Artyukhina, E. V. (2010). Mesh-free methods and their implementation with radial basis neural networks. *Neirokomp'yutory: Razrabotka, Primentnine*, No. 11, 4–10 (in Russian).

Gorbachenko, V. I., Lazovskaya, T. V., Tarkhov, D. A., Vasiljev, A. N., & Zhukov, M. V. (2016). *Neural network technique in some inverse problems of mathematical physics. Advances in Neural Networks - ISNN 2016: 13th International Symposium on Neural Networks, ISNN 2016, St. Petersburg, Russia, July 6-8*. Springer, 310–316. 10.1007/978-3-319-40663-3_36

Gorbachenko, V. I., Alqezweeni, M. M., & Jaafar, M. S. (2017). Application of parametric identification method and radial basis function networks for solution of inverse boundary value problems. *2017 Annual Conference on New Trends in Information and Communications Technology Applications, NTICT 2017; Baghdad; Iraq*, 18–21. 10.1109/NTICT.2017.7976151

Gorbachenko, V. I., & Zhukov, M. V. (2017). Solving boundary value problems of mathematical physics using radial basis function networks. *Computational Mathematics and Mathematical Physics*, 57(1), 145–155. doi:10.1134/S0965542517010079

Gorodov, O. A. (1999). Intellectual Property: Legal Aspects of Commercial Use: Diss. ... doctor. Legal Sciences, S.-P.

Gorodov, O. A. (2018). About new forms of using the results of intellectual activity, *Patents and Licenses. Intellectual rights 10,* 14-20.

Griebel, M., & Schweitzer, M. A. (2008). *Meshfree methods for partial differential equations IV*. Springer. doi:10.1007/978-3-540-79994-8

Grieves, M. (2014). Digital Twin: manufacturing excellence through virtual factory replication. *White Paper*, 1–7.

Gulec, O. D.; & Turan B. O. (2017), Ecological Architectural Design Education Practices Via Case Studies. Megaron, 2015, 10(2). pp. 113-129.

Gulli, A., & Pal, S. (2017). *Deep learning with Keras: Implementing deep learning models and neural networks with the power of Python*. Packt Publishing.

Gumbus, A. (2005). Introducing the Balanced Scorecard: Creating Metrics to Measure Performance. *Journal of Management Education*, *29*(4), 617–630. doi:10.1177/1052562905276278

Habib, M., Abbas, J., & Noman, R. (2019). Are human capital, intellectual property rights, and research and development expenditures really important for total factor productivity? An empirical analysis. *International Journal of Social Economics*, *46*(6), 756–774. doi:10.1108/IJSE-09-2018-0472

Halonen, A. (2012). Being open about data. Analysis of the UK open data policies and applicability of data. 2012. [Electronic resource] // Retrieved from http://finnishinstitute.org.uk/images/stories/pdf2012/being%20open%20about%20data.pdf

Harasim, L. (2012). *Learning Theory and Online Technologies*. New York, NY: Routledge. doi:10.4324/9780203846933

Harlow, D. B., Dwyer, H. A., Hansen, A. K., Iveland, A. O., & Franklin, D. M. (2018). Ecological Design-Based Research for Computer Science Education: Affordances and Effectivities for Elementary School Students. *Cognition and Instruction*, *36*(3), 224–246. doi:10.1080/07370008.2018.1475390

Hasenauer, H. (Ed.). (2006). *Sustainable Forest Management. Growth Models for Europe. Springer-Verlag Berlin Heidelberg*. XIX.

Hawawini, G., & Keim, D. (1995) On the predictability of common stock returns: Worldwide evidence // Handbooks in Operations Research and Management Science, Vol. 9 (Finance) / eds. R. Jarrow et al. Amsterdam: Elsevier Science, pp. 497–544.

Haykin, S. O. (2008). *Neural networks and learning machines*. Pearson. Retrieved from http://ieeexplore.ieee.org/document/7976151/authors. http://www.scottsarra.org/math/papers/mqMonographSarraKansa.pdf

Haykin, S. O. (2008). *Neural networks and learning machines*. Pearson.

Helbing, D. (2015). *Thinking Ahead - Essays on Big Data, Digital Revolution, and Participatory Market Society*. Springer. doi:10.1007/978-3-319-15078-9

Herrera, P. D., & De Ona Cots, J. M. (2016). The relevance of the learning environment. Ecological education in a detention centre. *Revista Fuentes, 18*(1), 77–90.

Hesamzadeh, M. R., Galland, O., & Biggar, D. R. (2014). Short-run economic dispatch with mathematical modelling of the adjustment cost. In *International Journal of Electrical Power* (pp. 9–18). Energy Systems; doi:10.1016/j.ijepes.2013.12.020

Heydt, M. (2017). *Learning pandas: High performance data manipulation and analysis using Python*. Packt Publishing.

Hinton, G. E., Srivastava, N., Krizhevsky, A., Sutskever, I., & Salakhutdinov, R. (2012). *Improving neural networks by preventing co-adaptation of feature detectors*. Retrieved from https://arxiv.org/abs/1207.0580

Hinton, G. E., & Salakhutdinov, R. R. (2006). Reducing the dimensionality of data with neural networks. *Science, 313*(5786), 504–507. doi:10.1126cience.1127647 PMID:16873662

Huang, C.-Y., & Lin, P. K. P. (2014). Application of integrated data mining techniques in stock market forecasting. *Cogent Economics and Finance, 2*(1), 92905–92921. doi:10.1080/23322039.2014.929505

Hubel, D. H., & Wiesel, T. N. (2004). Brain and Visual Perception: The Story of a 25-Year Collaboration, 2004. Oxford University Press.

Hunter, M. G., & Tan, F. B. (2007). *Strategic use of information technology for global organizations*. Hershey, PA: IGI Global. doi:10.4018/978-1-59904-292-3

Ignatiev, E. Yu. (2014) Means for assessing the learning outcomes of university students: method. Recommendations. Novgorod State University. Veliky Novgorod.

Isaev, A. S., & Korovin, G. N. (2009). *Actual problems of the national forest policy. M.: Institute for Sustainable Development*. Moscow, Russia: Center for Environmental Policy of Russia.

Iskhakova, E. I. (2011). System approach to intellectual property management at the enterprise, *Innovations and investments 3,* 164-168.

Isola, P., Zhu, J.-Y., Zhou, T., & Efros, A. A. (2016). Image-to-Image Translation with Conditional Adversarial Networks. *arXiv.*

Jain, V., & Seung, S. H. (2008). Natural image denoising with convolutional networks. In Advances in Neural Information Processing Systems (pp. 769-776).

Janssen, M., Charalabidis, Y., & Zuiderwijk, A. (2012). Benefits, Adoption Barriers and Myths of Open Data and Open Government [ISM]. *Information Systems Management, 29*(4), 258–268. doi:10.1080/10580530.2012.716740

Jianyu, L., Siwei, L., Yingjian, Q., & Yaping, H. (2003). Numerical solution of elliptic partial differential equation by growing radial basis function neural networks. *Neural Networks, 16*(5–6), 729–734. doi:10.1016/S0893-6080(03)00083-2 PMID:12850028

Jia, W., Zhao, D., Shen, T., Su, C., Hu, C., & Zhao, Y. (2014). *A New optimized GA-RBF neural network algorithm* (p. 982045). Article, ID: Computational Intelligence and Neuroscience.

Jin, I., Udo, H., Rayman, J., Puthanveettil, S., Kandel, E., & Hawkins, R. (2012). Spontaneous transmitter release recruits postsynaptic mechanisms of long-term and intermediate-term facilitation in Aplysia. *Proceedings of the National Academy of Sciences of the United States of America*, *109*(23), 9137–9142. doi:10.1073/pnas.1206846109 PMID:22619333

Jo, L. M., Esteve, A., & Wareham, J. D. (2014). Open Data & Civic Apps: 1st Generation Failures – 2nd Generation Improvements // ESADE Business School Research Paper. 2014. N°256. [Electronic resource] // Retrieved from https://ssrn.com/abstract=2508358

Jones-Evans, D., Gkikas, A., Rhisiart, M., & MacKenzie, N. G. (2018). Measuring open innovation in SMEs (Book Chapter), *Researching Open Innovation in SMEs*, 399-427.

Joskowicz, L. (2017). Computer-aided surgery meets predictive, preventive, and personalized medicine. *The EPMA Journal*, *8*(8), 1–4. doi:10.100713167-017-0084-8 PMID:28670350

Jost, Z. Overview of GANs (Generative Adversarial Networks) – Part I, 2017 [Electronic resourse]. Retrieved from https://www.kdnuggets.com/2017/11/overview-gans-generative-adversarial-networks-part1.html (access date: 21.10.2018).

Juneja, J. A., & Amar, A. D. (2018). An organizational capital decision model for knowledge-intensive organizations. *IEEE Transactions on Engineering Management*, *65*(3), 417–433. doi:10.1109/TEM.2018.2790898

Kachalov, V. A. (2016). "Risks" and "Opportunities" in the ISO 9001: 2015 standard: separately or together? Methods of quality management. No. 7-8. - S. 1-10.

Kadushin, C. (2002). The motivational foundation of social networks. *Social Networks*, *24*(1), 77–91. doi:10.1016/S0378-8733(01)00052-1

Kamalova, G. (2017). Public policy in the field of open data: analysis of practices // Economics and Management: A Scientific and Practical Journal, 2017, N°3. [Electronic resource] // Retrieved from https://elibrary.ru/download/elibrary_29969774_73911263.pdf

Kamalova, G. R. (2014). Open state management: Russian and foreign experience // State and municipal management. Scientific notes of SKAGS, 2014, N°1. [Electronic resource] // Retrieved from http://cyberleninka.ru/article/n/otkrytoe-gosudarstvennoe-upravlenie-rossiyskiy-i-zarubezhnyy-opyt

Kansa, E. J. (1990a). Multiquadrics — A scattered data approximation scheme with applications to computational fluid-dynamics — I surface approximations and partial derivative estimates. *Comput. Math. Appl.*, *19*(8–9), 127–145.

Kansa, E. J. (1990b). Multiquadrics — A scattered data approximation scheme with applications to computational fluid-dynamics — II solutions to parabolic, hyperbolic and elliptic partial differential equations. *Comput. Math. Appl.*, *19*(8–9), 147–161.

Kansa, E. J. (1999) *Motivation for using radial basis function to solve PDEs*. Retrieved from http://www.cityu.edu.hk/rbf-pde/files/overview-pdf.pdf

Kaplan, A. M., & Haenlein, M. (2010). Users of the world, unite! The challenges and opportunities of social media. *Business Horizons, 53*(1), 59–68. doi:10.1016/j.bushor.2009.09.003

Karras, T., Aila, T., Laine, S., & Lehtinen, J. (2017). Progressive Growing of GANs for Improved Quality, Stability, and Variation. *arXiv*.

Kataev, M. Yu., & Kataev, S. G. (2014). An approach to knowledge control in a virtual educational environment. *Tomsk State Pedagogical University Journal, 5*(146), 41–44.

Kataev, M. Yu., Kataev, S. G., & Korikov, A. M. (2014). On the application of avatar technology in physical and technical electronic education. *Tomsk State Pedagogical University Journal, 11*(152), 187–192.

Kataev, M. Yu., Korikov, A. M., & Mkrttchian, V. S. (2013). The concept of electronic education based on Avatar technology. *Doklady TUSUR, 2*(28), 95–100.

Kelsey, T. (2017). Social Media Monitoring and Analytics. Introduction to Social Media Marketing, 123–148. doi:10.1007/978-1-4842-2854-8_8

Kemeny, J., & Snell, J. (1970). *Cybernetic Modeling*. New York: Some Applications.

Keras: The Python deep learning library. Usage of callbacks. (2019). Retrieved from https://keras.io/callbacks/

Kharkovyna, O. (2019). *Top 10 best deep learning frameworks in 2019*. Retrieved from https://towardsdatascience.com/top-10-best-deep-learning-frameworks-in-2019-5ccb90ea6de

Kim, E.-J. A., Asghar, A., & Jordan, S. (2017). A Critical Review of Traditional Ecological Knowledge (TEK) in Science Education. *Canadian Journal of Science Mathematics and Technology Education, 17*(4), 258–270. doi:10.1080/14926156.2017.1380866

Kingma, D. P., & Ba, J. (2014). *Adam: A method for stochastic optimization*. Retrieved from https://arxiv.org/abs/1412.6980

Kirkpatrick, D. (2011). *The Facebook effect: the real inside story of Mark Zuckerberg and the world's fastest-growing company*. London, UK: Virgin.

Klemow, K., Berkowitz, A., Cid, C., & Middendorf, G. (2019). Improving ecological education through a four-dimensional framework. *Frontiers in Ecology and the Environment, 17*(2), 71–71. doi:10.1002/fee.2013

Köhl, M., & Marchetti, M. (2016). Objectives and Planning of Forest Inventories. Tropical Forestry Handbook, 749–776. doi:10.1007/978-3-642-54601-3_70

Kolesnik, V. G., & Sinyatullina, L. H. (2017). The Forest Complex State Management System: The current situation and main challenges. *Issues of State and Municipal Management, 1*, 129–148.

Kolmogorov, A. N. (1946). Justification of least squares method. In Advances in Mathematical Science. pp. 57–70.

Kolodko, G. N., & Kalinkin, V. I. (2014). Intellectual property management at an industrial enterprise as a component of the innovation activity management system. *Innovations, 4*(186), 115–119.

Kolodyazhnaya, O. A. (2018). Intellectual property management system development information: essence, organization, management, *Management of Economic Systems: Electronic Scientific Journal, 9* (115), 26.

Konijnendijk, C. C. (2018). *The Forest and the City*. Future City; doi:10.1007/978-3-319-75076-7

Korikov, A. M. (2012) Education paradigms and the role of management theory in the creation of educational technologies. Modern education: problems of ensuring the quality of specialist training in the context of the transition to a multi-level system of higher education: international materials. scientific method. conf., February 2–3, 2012, Russia, Tomsk: TUSUR, pp. 127–128.

Korikov, A. M. (2002). *Fundamentals of control theory: textbook. allowance*. Tomsk, Russia: NTL Publishing House.

Kotler, P., Armstrong, G., Saunders, J., & Wong, V. (2001). Principles of Marketing, 2nd ed. Corporate Communications: An International Journal, 6(3), 164–165. doi:10.1108/ccij.2001.6.3.164.1

Krasilnikova, V. A. (2002). *The formation and development of computer technology training. OSU, Orenburg*. Moscow, Russia: IIO RAO.

Kreus, P., & Saukkonen, J. (2018). 'The role of intellectual property rights in growth aspiring SMEs,' *Proceedings of the European Conference on Knowledge Management*, ECKM, 423-429.

Krishna, S. (1992). *Introduction to Database and Knowledge-base Systems*. Singapore: World Scientific Publishing. doi:10.1142/1374

Kudaykulova, H. Sh. (2007). Electronic government in the Republic of Kazakhstan // State administration, 2007. [Electronic resource] // Retrieved from http://cyberleninka.ru/article/n/elektronnoe-pravitelstvo-v-respublike-kazahstan

Kumar, M., & Yadav, N. (2011). Multilayer perceptions and radial basis function neural network methods for the solution of differential equations: A survey. *Computers & Mathematics with Applications (Oxford, England), 62*(10), 3796–3811. doi:10.1016/j.camwa.2011.09.028

Kusherov, N. S. (2015). The development of "e-government" in Kazakhstan // Law and modern states, 2015, N°2. [Electronic resource] // Retrieved from http://cyberleninka.ru/article/n/razvitie-elektronnogo-pravitelstva-v-kazahstane

Kuzmin, A. V., & Razvozzhaev, D. G. (2017). The development of legal regulation of the processes of openness in the activities of public authorities // Research papers Tambov RuSMU branch. 2017. N°8. [Electronic resource] // Retrieved from http://cyberleninka.ru/article/n/razvitie-normativno-pravovogo-regulirovaniya-protsessov-otkrytosti-v-deyatelnosti-organov-gosudarstvennoy-vlasti

Kuznetsova, M. O. (2018). Risks of Industry 4.0 and their impact on industrial organizations. University Herald. No. 11. - P. 115-122.

Lagace, M. (2010). Data.gov: Matching government data with rapid innovation // Harvard Business School Working Knowledge. 2010. [Electronic resource] // URL: http://hbswk.hbs.edu/item/6423.html

Lamarino, A. P. M., Juliano, Y., Rosa, O. M., Novo, N. F., Favaro, M. L., & Ribeiro, M. A. F. (2017). Risk factors associated with complications of acute appendicitis. *Journal of Brazilian College of Surgeons, 44*(6), 560–566. PMID:29267552

Law of the Republic of Kazakhstan dated November 16, 2015 No. 401-V ZRK "On Access to Information". Retrieved from http://adilet.zan.kz/rus/docs/Z1500000401

Law of the Republic of Kazakhstan dated November 24, 2015 No. 418-V ZRK "On informatization". Retrieved from http://adilet.zan.kz/rus/docs/Z1500000418

Le Baron, B., & Winker, P. (2008). Introduction to the Special Issue on Avatar-Based Models for Economic Policy Advice. *Journal of Economics and Statistics, 228.*

Ledig, C., Theis, L., Huszar, F., Caballero, J., Cunningham, A., Acosta, A., . . . Shi, W. (2016). Photo-Realistic Single Image Super-Resolution Using a Generative Adversarial Network. *arXiv.*

Lee, H., Grosse, R., Ranganath, R., & Ng, A. Y. (2009a). Convolutional deep belief networks for scalable unsupervised learning of hierarchical representations. In ICML'2009. doi:10.1145/1553374.1553453

Lee, J. D., Simchowitz, M., Jordan, M. I., & Recht, B. (2016). Gradient Descent Converges to Minimizers. *arXiv.*

Leontiev, B. B. (2008). Functions of intellectual property: institutional approach to management of high-technology business, *Management and business administration, 1*, 11-31.

Leontiev, B. B. (2017). 'Is the foreign experience of commercializing intellectual property useful to Russia,' *Intellectual property. Industrial property, 3,* 4.

Leontiev, B. B. (2018). Intellectology - the integration science of the future, *Intellectual property. Industrial property, 3,* 41-50.

Levchenko, E. V. (2018). Influence of digitalization on the development of a quality management system. Bulletin of the Saratov Socio-Economic University. No. 4 (73). - P. 9-14.

Li, C., Liu, H., Chen, C., Pu, Y., Chen, L., Henao, R., & Carin, L. (2017). ALICE: Towards Understanding Adversarial Learning for Joint Distribution Matching. *Advances in Neural Information Processing Systems. arXiv.*

Li, J. C., Hon, Y. C. (2004). Domain decomposition for radial basis meshless methods. *Numeric Methods Partial Differ. Eq., 20*(3), 450–462.

Liesen, J. (2015). *Krylov subspace methods: principles and analysis.* Oxford University Press.

Ling, L., & Kansa, E. J. (2005). A least-squares preconditioner for radial basis functions collocation methods. *Advances in Computational Mathematics, 23*(1-2), 31–54. doi:10.100710444-004-1809-5

Liu, G. R. (20013). *Mesh free methods: moving beyond the finite element method.* Boca Raton, FL: CRC Press.

Liu, Y. (2016). Social Media Monitoring. Social Media in China, 185–193. doi:10.1007/978-3-658-11231-8_10

Liu, Y. (2019). Effects of Information Technology Integrated Music Ecological Education on Learning Interest and Performance. *Ekoloji, 28*(107), 3441–3448.

Liu, Y., & Chen, M. (2018). From the Aspect of STEM to Discuss the Effect of Ecological Art Education on Knowledge Integration and Problem-Solving Capability. *Ekoloji, 27*(106), 1705–1711.

Lopatin, V. N. (2016). Problems and prospects of the Eurasian intellectual property market in the EAEU and CIS. *Intellectual Property Law, 3*, 29–44.

Lopatin, V. N. (2017). Intellectual property as an investment resource: Tatarstan's experience for the EAEU and CIS. *Intellectual Property Law, 3*, 46–48.

Lopatin, V. N. (2018). Eurasian intellectual property market in the EAEU and CIS in 2017 and its development priorities up to 2025. *Intellectual Property Law, 2*, 7–18.

Lopatin, V. N. (2018). Legal risks of intellectual property at transition to digital economy in EAEU. *Law, 6*(56), 64–70.

Lotka, A. G. (1925). *Elements of physical biology.* Baltimore, MD: Williams and Wilkens.

Luc, P., Couprie, C., Chintala, S., & Verbeek, J. (2016). Semantic Segmentation using Adversarial Networks. *arXiv.*

Mackenzie, H., Tolley, H., Croft, T., Grove, M., & Lawson, D. (2016). Senior management perspectives of mathematics and statistics support in higher education: Moving to an 'ecological' approach. *Journal of Higher Education Policy and Management, 38*(5), 550–561. doi:10.1080/1360080X.2016.1196932

Madni, A. M., Madni, C. C., & Lucero, S. D. (2019). Leveraging digital twin technology in model-based systems engineering. *Systems, 7*(1). *Article-Number, 7.* doi:10.3390ystems7010007

Mai-Duy, N., & Tran-Cong, T. (2005). Solving high order ordinary differential equations with radial basis function networks. *International Journal for Numerical Methods in Engineering, 62*(6), 824–852. doi:10.1002/nme.1220

Maiyya, S., Zakhary, V., Agrawal, D., & El Abbadi, A. (2018). Database and distributed computing fundamentals for scalable, fault-tolerant, and consistent maintenance of blockchains. *Proceedings of the VLDB Endowment, 11*. pp. 2098-2101. 10.14778/3229863.3229877

Manyika, J., Chui, M., Farrell, D., Van Kuiken, S., Groves, P., Van Kuiken, S., & Doshi, E. A. Open data: Unlocking innovation and performance with liquid information. (McKinsey Global Institute, Ed.). [Electronic resource] // Retrieved from http://www.mckinsey.com/insights/business_technology/open_data_unlocking_innovation_and_performance_with_liquid_information?cid=other-eml-alt-mgi-mck-oth-2910)

Manzoor, A. (2018). Using Social Media Marketing for Competitive Advantage. In I. Management Association (Ed.), Social Media Marketing: Breakthroughs in Research and Practice (pp. 21-38). Hershey, PA: IGI Global. doi:10.4018/978-1-5225-5637-4.ch002

Markopoulos, A. P., Georgiopoulos, S., & Manolakos, D. E. (2016). On the Use of Back Propagation and Radial Basis Function Neural Networks in Surface Roughness Prediction. *Journal of Industrial Engineering International, 12*(3), 389–400. doi:10.100740092-016-0146-x

Marquardt, D. W. (1963). An algorithm for least-squares estimation of nonlinear parameters. *Journal of the Society for Industrial and Applied Mathematics, 11*(2), 431–441. doi:10.1137/0111030

Maynard Smith, J. (1974). *Models in ecology*. Cambridge, MA: Cambridge University Press.

Mazumder, S. (2015). *Numerical methods for partial differential equations: finite difference and finite volume methods*. Academic Press.

Melnik, G. S., & Teplyashina, A. N. (2019). The Impact of Digitalization of Network Space on Journalism Education. Media Education, 2019, No. 1. pp. 86-92.

Mescheder, L., Nowozin, S., & Geiger, A. (2017). Adversarial Variational Bayes: Unifying Variational Autoencoders and Generative Adversarial Networks. *arXiv*.

Migliore, M., Cannia, C., Lytton, W. W., Markram, H., & Hines, M. L. (2006). Parallel network simulations with NEURON. *Journal of Computational Neuroscience, 21*(2), 119–129. doi:10.100710827-006-7949-5 PMID:16732488

Miner, L., Bolding, P., Hilbe, J., Goldstein, M., Hill, T., Nisbet, R., ... Miner, G. (2014). *Practical predictive analytics and decisioning systems for medicine: Informatics accuracy and cost-effectiveness for healthcare administration and delivery including medical research*. Academic Press.

Mirza, M., & Osindero, S. (2014). Conditional Generative Adversarial Nets. *arXiv*.

Mkrttchian, V. (2013). Training of Avatar Moderator in Sliding Mode Control Environment for Virtual Project Management. In Enterprise Resource Planning: Concepts, Methodologies, Tools, and Applications. IRMA (pp. 1376–1405). Hershey, PA: IGI Global. doi:10.4018/978-1-4666-4153-2.ch074

Mkrttchian, V. (2015). Modeling using of Triple H-Avatar Technology in online Multi-Cloud Platform Lab. In *Encyclopedia of Information Science and Technology* (pp. 4162–4170). Hershey, PA: IGI Global; doi:10.4018/978-1-4666-5888-2.ch409

Mkrttchian, V. S. (2012). *Avatar manager and student reflective conversations as the base for describing meta-communication model. Meta-communication for reflective online conversations: Models for distance education* (pp. 75–101). Hershey, PA: IGI Global.

Mkrttchian, V., & Aleshina, E. (2017). *Sliding Mode in Intellectual Control and Communication: Emerging Research and Opportunities*. Hershey, PA: IGI Global; doi:10.4018/978-1-5225-2292-8

Mkrttchian, V., & Belyanina, L. (2018). *Handbook of Research on Students' Research Competence in Modern Educational Contexts* (pp. 1–518). Hershey, PA: IGI Global; doi:10.4018/978-1-5225-3485-3

Mkrttchian, V., Bershadsky, A., Bozhday, A., Kataev, M., & Kataev, S. (Eds.). (2016). *Handbook of Research on Estimation and Control Techniques in E-Learning systems*. Hershey, PA: IGI Global; doi:10.4018/978-1-4666-9489-7

Mkrttchian, V., Krevskiy, I., Bershadsky, A., Glotova, T., Gamidullaeva, L., & Vasin, S. (2019a). Web-Based Learning and Development of University's Electronic Informational Educational Environment. [IJWLTT]. *International Journal of Web-Based Learning and Teaching Technologies*, *14*(1), 32–53. doi:10.4018/IJWLTT.2019010103

Mkrttchian, V., Palatkin, I., Gamidullaeva, L. A., & Panasenko, S. (2019b). About Digital Avatars for Control Systems Using Big Data and Knowledge Sharing in Virtual Industries. In A. Gyamfi, & I. Williams (Eds.), *Big Data and Knowledge Sharing in Virtual Organizations* (pp. 103–116). Hershey, PA: IGI Global; doi:10.4018/978-1-5225-7519-1.ch004

Mkrttchian, V., Veretekhina, S., Gavrilova, O., Ioffe, A., Markosyan, S., & Chernyshenko, S. (2019). *The Cross-Cultural Analysis of Australia and Russia: Cultures, Small Businesses, and Crossing the Barriers // Industrial and Urban Growth Policies at the Sub-National, National, and Global Levels* (pp. 229–249). Hershey, PA: IGI Global; doi:10.4018/978-1-5225-7625-9.ch012

Moe, W. W., & Schweidel, D. A. (n.d.). Moving from Social Media Monitoring to Social Media Intelligence. Social Media Intelligence, 180–186. doi:10.1017/cbo9781139381338.016

Mohan, C. (2017). Tutorial: blockchains and databases. In *Proceedings of the VLDB Endowment*, 10. pp. 2000-2011. 10.14778/3137765.3137830

Mohr, J. J., Sengupta, S., & Slater, S. (n.d.). Toward a Theory of Technology Marketing: Review and Suggestions for Future Research. Handbook of Business-to-Business Marketing. doi:10.4337/9781781002445.00042

Moraes dos Santos, M. L., Zafalon, E. J., Bomfim, R., Kodjaoglanian, V. L., Mendonça de Moraes, S. H., do Nascimento, D. D. G., ... De-Carli, A. D. (2019). Impact of distance education on primary health care indicators in central Brazil: An ecological study with time trend analysis. *PLoS One*, *14*(3). doi:10.1371/journal.pone.0214485 PMID:30913272

Mormul, R. P., Mormul, T. D. S., Santos, G. M. B., & Santana, A. R. A. (2017). Looking for attitudes related to amphibian species decline: How are peer- reviewed publications of education activities compared to ecological research? *Anais da Academia Brasileira de Ciências*, *89*(1), 491–496. doi:10.1590/0001-3765201720160463 PMID:28562826

Mueller, Ch., Fuengerlings, S., & Tolks, D. (2018). Teaching load - a barrier to digitalisation in higher education? A position paper on the framework surrounding higher education medical teaching in the digital age using Bavaria, Germany as an example. *GMS Journal for Medical Education*, *35*(3). PMID:30186944

Mukesh, M., & Rao, A. (2017). Social media measurement and monitoring. Contemporary Issues in Social Media Marketing, 184–205. doi:10.4324/9781315563312-14

Mundi, M. S., Lorentz, P. A., Grothe, K., Kellogg, T. A., & Collazo-Clavell, M. L. (2015). Feasibility of Smartphone-Based Education Modules and Ecological Momentary Assessment/Intervention in Pre-bariatric Surgery Patients. *Obesity Surgery*, *25*(10), 1875–1881. doi:10.100711695-015-1617-7 PMID:25702141

Muratova, G. K., & Baisalykova, Sh. A. (2017). E-government in Kazakhstan // Science and education: a new time, 2017, N°1. [Electronic resource] // Retrieved from https://elibrary.ru/download/elibrary_28779613_94050576.pdf

Nadarajah, S., & Secomandi, N. (2017) Relationship between least squares Monte Carlo and approximate linear programming. In Operations Research Letters, pp. 409-414. doi:10.1016/j.orl.2017.05.010

Nair, B. B., Mohandas, V. P., & Sakthivel, N. R. (2010). A Genetic Algorithm Optimized Decision TreeSVM based Stock Market Trend Prediction System. *International Journal on Computer Science and Engineering*, *2*(9), 2981–2988.

Natalicchio, A., Ardito, L., Savino, T., & Albino, V. (2017). Managing knowledge assets for open innovation: A systematic literature review. *Journal of Knowledge Management, 21.* . doi:10.1108/JKM-11-2016-0516

Negroponte, N. (1995). Being Digital. Knopf. (Paperback edition, 1996, Vintage Books).

Nekrasov, S. I. (2018). Interrelated processes of digitalization of the modern Russian science and education. *Education in Science*, *20*(2), 162–179.

Neural network models (supervised) . (2019). Retrieved from https://scikitlearn.org/stable/modules/neural_networks_supervised.html

Niaki, S. T. A., & Hoseinzade, S. (2013). Forecasting S&P 500 index using artificial neural networks and design of experiments. *Journal of Industrial Engineering International, 9*(1), 1–9. doi:10.1186/2251-712X-9-1

Niyogi, P., & Girosi, F. (1996). On the relationship between generalization error, hypothesis complexity, and sample complexity for radial basis functions. *Neural Computation, 8*(4), 819–842. doi:10.1162/neco.1996.8.4.819

Nizhegorodtsev, R. M. (2014). Stimulation of research and innovation in Russia under the conditions of growth of external threats. Materials of the international scientific-practical conference Innovation management - 2014. pp. 7-14.

Nizhegorodtsev, R. M. (2016). Import substitution of institutions: the key task of ensuring national security // News of USUE, 2016, N°4 (66). [Electronic resource] // Retrieved from http://cyberleninka.ru/article/n/importozameschenie-institutov-klyuchevaya-zadacha-obespecheniya-natsionalnoy-bezopasnosti

Noor, H., & Van Den Broek, T. (2011). Open Data: An International Comparison of Strategies. *European Journal of ePractice., 12*(1), 4–16. Retrieved from http://unpan1.un.org/intradoc/groups/public/documents/UN-DPADM/UNPAN046727.pdf

Obar, J. A., & Wildman, S. (2015). Social media definition and the governance challenge: An introduction to the special issue. *Telecommunications Policy, 39*(9), 745–750. doi:10.1016/j.telpol.2015.07.014

Okolesnova, O. A. Open data as an innovative mechanism for disclosing information // State audit. right. Economy, 2017, N°2. [Electronic resource] // Retrieved from https://elibrary.ru/download/elibrary_29869433_87777383.pdf

Open Government III Action Plan 2017–2019. [Electronic resource] // Retrieved from http://vm.fi/documents/10623/4505456/Open+Government+III+Action+Plan+2017–2019+Finland.pdf/21c926e6-b86b-435f-8d76-d4e9871ef45e

Order of the Government of the Russian Federation of September 20, 2018 N 1989-r (as amended on February 28, 2019) "On Approving the Strategy for the Development of the Forestry Complex of the Russian Federation until 2030". Official Internet portal of legal information. Retrieved from http://www.pravo.gov.ru

Palazzo, S., Spampinato, C., Kavasidis, I., Giordano, D., & Shah, M. (2017). Generative Adversarial Networks Conditioned by Brain Signals, [electronic resource]. Retrieved from http://openaccess.thecvf.com/content_ICCV_2017/papers/ Palazzo_Generative_Adversarial_Networks_ICCV_2017_paper.pdf (access date: 21.10.2018).

Park, S. Y., & Kim, S. M. (2015). Acute appendicitis diagnosis using artificial neural networks. *Technology and Health Care, 23*(s2), S559–S565. doi:10.3233/THC-150994 PMID:26410524

Parmee, I. C., & Hajela, P. (Eds.). (2002). *Optimization in Industry.*, doi:10.1007/978-1-4471-0675-3

Patel, J., Shah, S., Thakkar, P., & Kotecha, K. (2015). Predicting stock market index using fusion of machine learning techniques. *Expert Systems with Applications*, 42(4), 2162–2172. doi:10.1016/j.eswa.2014.10.031

Pattanayak, S. (2017). *Pro deep learning with tensorflow: A mathematical approach to advanced artificial intelligence in Python*. Apress. doi:10.1007/978-1-4842-3096-1

Peters, M. A., & Jandric, P. (2017). Dewey's Democracy and Education in the age of digital reason: The global, ecological and digital turns. *OPEN REVIEW OF EDUCATIONAL RESEARCH*, 4(1), 205–218. doi:10.1080/23265507.2017.1395290

Ping, R., Liu, X., & Liu, J. (2018). Research on construction of indicator system for evaluation of the ecological civilization education in Chinese universities. *Cognitive Systems Research*, 52, 747–755. doi:10.1016/j.cogsys.2018.08.025

Plummer, T. (1990). *Forecasting Financial Markets: Technical Analysis and the Dynamics of Price*. New York: Wiley.

Polak, E., & Ribiére, G. (1969). Note sur la convergence de méthodes de directions conjuguées. *Revue française d'informatique et de recherche opérationnelle*, série rouge, Tome 3, n° 1, 35–43.

Polyak, B. T. (1964). Some methods of speeding up the convergence of iteration methods. *U.S.S.R. Computational Mathematics and Mathematical Physics*, 4(5), 1–17. doi:10.1016/0041-5553(64)90137-5

Popov, A. V. (2019). Business Process Optimization in the Digitalization Era of Production. In Strategic Decisions and Risk Management. pp. 28–35. Doi:10.17747/2618-947X-2019-1-28-35

Popova, L. F. (2017). *Implementation of risk management in the enterprise quality management system*. Bulletin of the Saratov Socio-Economic University. - 2017. - No. 5 (69). pp. 104-109.

Postalyuk, M. P., & Postalyuk, T. M. (2018). Digitalization of local systems of the regional Russian economy: needs, opportunities and risks. Problems of the modern economy. No. 2 (66). pp. 174-177.

Prabhudesai, S. G., Gould, S., Rekhraj, S., Tekkis, P. P., Glazer, G., & Ziprin, P. (2008). Artificial neural networks: Useful aid in diagnosing acute appendicitis. *World Journal of Surgery*, 32(2), 305–309. doi:10.100700268-007-9298-6 PMID:18043966

Putko, B. A., Didenko, A. S., & Dubovikov, M. M. (2014). The volatility model of the RUB / USD exchange rate, built on the basis of the fractal characteristics of the financial series [in Russian]. *Applied Econometrics, No.*, 36(4), 79–87.

Qiu, M., Song, Y., & Akagi, F. (2016). Application of artificial neural network for the prediction of stock market returns: The case of the Japanese stock market. *Chaos, Solitons, and Fractals*, 85, 1–7. doi:10.1016/j.chaos.2016.01.004

Radford, A., Metz, L., & Chintala, S. (2015). Unsupervised Representation Learning with Deep Convolutional Generative Adversarial Networks. *arXiv*.

341

Radosteva, M., Soloviev, V., Ivanyuk, V., & Tsvirkun, A. (2018). Use of neural network models in market risk management. *Advances in Systems Science and Applications*, *18*(2), 53–58.

Rastrigin, L. A. (1988). *Adaptive learning with learner model*. Riga, Latvia: Zinante.

Reed, S., Akata, Z., Yan, X., Logeswaran, L., Schiele, B., & Lee, H. (2016). Generative adversarial text to image synthesis. *arXiv.*

Ren, S., He, K., Girshick, R., & Sun, J. (2015). Faster R-CNN: Towards Real-Time Object Detection with Region Proposal Networks. Advances in Neural Information Processing Systems. *arXiv.*

Reynolds, K. M., Twery, M., Lexer, M. J., Vacik, H., Ray, D., Shao, G., & Borges, J. G. (2008). Decision Support Systems in Forest Management. *Handbook on Decision Support Systems*, *2*, 499–533. doi:10.1007/978-3-540-48716-6_24

Roesch-McNally, G. E., Rabotyagov, S., Tyndall, J. C., Ettl, G., & Tóth, S. F. (2016). Auctioning the Forest: A Qualitative Approach to Exploring Stakeholder Responses to Bidding on Forest Ecosystem Services. *Small-scale Forestry*, *15*(3), 321–333. doi:10.100711842-016-9327-0

Rönnqvist, M. (2003). Optimization in forestry. *Mathematical Programming*, *97*(1), 267–284. doi:10.100710107-003-0444-0

Rud, S. N. (2014). Application of information technologies in the management of intellectual property objects, In *Proceedings: Science and Education in the 21st Century, a collection of scientific papers based on the materials of the International Scientific and Practical Conference: in 17 parts,* 120-122.

Saad, Y. (2003). *Iterative methods for sparse linear systems*. SIAM. doi:10.1137/1.9780898718003

Safk, L., & Brake, D. (2009). *The social media bible: tactics, tools, and strategies for business success*. Hoboken, N. J.: John Wiley & Sons.

Sailer, K., & McCulloh, I. (2012). Social networks and spatial configuration—How office layouts drive social interaction. *Social Networks*, *34*(1), 47–58. doi:10.1016/j.socnet.2011.05.005

Salitskaya, E. A. (2017). Modern approaches to intellectual property management: Regional aspect. *Bulletin of the Russian Academy of Sciences*, *87*(11), 1026–1034.

Santonja, F.-J., Sánchez, E., Rubio, M., & Morera, J.-L. (2010) Alcohol consumption in Spain and its economic cost: A mathematical modeling approach. In Mathematical and Computer Modelling, pp. 999-1003. doi:10.1016/j.mcm.2010.02.029

Sarra, S. A., & Kansa, E. J. (2009). Multiquadric radial basis function approximation methods for the numerical solution of partial differential equations. *Advances in Computational Mechanics, 2*(2).

Sarra, S. (2005). Adaptive radial basis function methods for time dependent partial differential equations. *Applied Numerical Mathematics*, *54*(1), 79–94. doi:10.1016/j.apnum.2004.07.004

Scholz, J., De Meyer, A., Marques, A. S., Pinho, T. M., Boaventura-Cunha, J., Van Orshoven, J., ... Nummila, K. (2018). Digital Technologies for Forest Supply Chain Optimization: Existing Solutions and Future Trends. *Environmental Management, 62*(6), 1108–1133. doi:10.100700267-018-1095-5 PMID:30128584

Scikit-Learn. Machine learning in Python. (2019). Retrieved from https://scikit-learn.org/stable/

Semenova, V. G. (2015). Process-oriented approach to management of intellectual property of enterprises, *Technological audit and production reserves, 5*(23), 45-50.

Sergeev, A. P. (2004). *Intellectual Property Law in the Russian Federation: Textbook. Moscow, Russia: TK Velby.* Prospect Publishing House.

Sevryukov, I. Yu. (2015). Intellectual property market: Approaches to management, formation of brands, influence of globalization. *Bulletin of the Trans-Baikal State University, 3*(118), 174–178.

Shahjahan, H. (2011). Bhuiyan. Trajectories of E-Government Implementation for Public Sector Service Delivery in Kazakhstan. *International Journal of Public Administration*, (34), 9.

Shannon, C. (1948). A mathematical theory of communication. *The Bell System Technical Journal, 27*(4), 379–423. doi:10.1002/j.1538-7305.1948.tb01338.x

Sheryazdanova, G., & Butterfield, J. (2017). E-government as an anti-corruption strategy in Kazakhstan. *Journal of Information Technology & Politics, 14*(1), 83–94. doi:10.1080/1933168 1.2016.1275998

Sheskin, D. J. (2003). *Handbook of parametric and nonparametric statistical procedure.* Chapman and Hall. doi:10.1201/9781420036268

Shestakov, D. Y. (2000). Intellectual Property in the Russian Federation: Theoretical and Legal Analysis. (Doctoral dissertation). Legal Sciences, Moscow, Russia.

Shpakovsky, Yu. G. (2018). Contemporary Problems of Legal Regulation of Forest Fire Protection. (2018). LEX RUSSICA (РУССКИЙ ЗАКОН). doi:10.17803/1729-5920.2018.134.1.043-056

Sjödin, D., Frishammar, J., & Thorgren, S. (2018). How Individuals Engage in the Absorption of New External Knowledge: A Process Model of Absorptive Capacity. *Journal of Product Innovation Management, 10.* 1111/jpim.12482.

Sklearn.neural_network. MLPClassifier. (2019). Retrieved from https://scikit-learn.org/stable/modules/generated/sklearn.neural_network.MLPClassifier.html/

Smirlock, M., & Starks, L. (1990). An empirical analysis of the stock price-volume relationship. *Journal of Banking & Finance, 12*(1), 31–42. doi:10.1016/0378-4266(88)90048-9

Solis, B. (2007). Defining Social Media. Retrieved from http://www.briansolis.com/2007/06/defining-social-media/

Soloviev, V. (2017). Forecasting stock market turnovers with boosted decision trees // 2017 11th International Conference on Application of Information and Communication Technologies (AICT). Piscataway, NJ: IEEE, pp. 140–143.

Spender, J.-C., Corvello, V., Grimaldi, M. & Rippa, P. (2017). Startups and open innovation: a review of the literature. *European Journal of Innovation Management, 20*. pp. 4-30. . doi:10.1108/EJIM-12-2015-0131

Srivastava, N., Hinton, G., Krizhevsky, A., Sutskever, I. R., & Salakhutdinov, R. (2014). Dropout: A simple way to prevent neural networks from overfitting. *Journal of Machine Learning Research, 15*(1), 1929–1958.

Staihaug, T. (1983). The conjugate gradient method and trust region in large scale optimization. *SIAM Journal on Numerical Analysis, 20*(3), 626–637. doi:10.1137/0720042

Starfield, A. M., Smith, K. A., & Bleloch, A. L. (1990). *How to model it: Problem solving for the computer age*. New York: McGraw-Hill.

Strategic Plan of the Ministry of Information and Communications of the Republic of Kazakhstan for 2017 - 2021, approved. by order of the Minister of Information and Communications of the Republic of Kazakhstan No. 310 of December 28, 2016.

Sulimin, A. N. Features of the implementation of the principles of open (electronic) regional management in the Astrakhan region // Bulletin of the expert council, 2015, N°3. [Electronic resource] // Retrieved from http://cyberleninka.ru/article/n/osobennosti-realizatsii-printsipov-otkrytogo-elektronnogo-regionalnogo-upravleniya-v-astrahanskoy-oblasti

Sundar, S. S. (2008). The MAIN model: A heuristic approach to understanding technology effects on credibility. In M. J. Metzger, & A. J. Flanagin (Eds.), *Digital media, youth, and credibility* (pp. 73–100). Cambridge, MA: The MIT Press.

Sutskever, I., Martens, J., Dahl, G., & Hinton, G. (2013). On the importance of initialization and momentum in deep learning. *ICML'13 Proceedings of the 30th International Conference on International Conference on Machine Learning*, Vol. 28, III-1139-III-1147.

Svirezhev, Yu. M. (2001). *Thermodynamics and ecological modelling*. Berlin, Germany: Springer.

Takeuchi, Y. (1996). *Global dynamical properties of Lotka-Volterra systems*. Singapore: World Scientific. doi:10.1142/2942

Talapina, E. V. (2015). Gosudarstvennoe upravlenie v informacionnom obshchestve (pravovoj aspekt) [State management in the information society (legal aspect)]. Moscow.

Tang, Q., Gu, B., & Whinston, A. (2012). Content Contribution for Revenue Sharing and Reputation in Social Media: A Dynamic Structural Model. *Journal of Management Information Systems, 29*(2), 41–75. doi:10.2753/MIS0742-1222290203

Tarkhov, D. A. (2014). *Neural network models and algorithms. Reference book*. Radiotekhnika. (in Russian)

Thapa, D., & Sein, M. K. (2018). An ecological model of bridging the digital divide in education: A case study of OLPC deployment in Nepal. *The Electronic Journal on Information Systems in Developing Countries*, *84*(2), e12018. doi:10.1002/isd2.12018

Theis, L., van den Oord, A., & Bethge, M. (2015). A note on the evaluation of generative models. *arXiv*.

Thom, R. (1972). *Structural stability and morphogenesis*. New York.

Tkachenko, E., Rogova, E., Kokh, V., & Bodrunov, S. (2018). The valuation of intangible assets based on the intellectual capital leverages concept. *Proceedings of the International Conference on Intellectual Capital, Knowledge Management, and Organizational Learning, ICICKM*, 2018-November, pp. 319-329.

Towards an Open Government in Kazakhstan. (2017). Paris, France: OECD Publishing; doi:10.1787/9789264279384-

Treynor, J., & Ferguson, R. (1985). In defense of technical analysis. *The Journal of Finance*, *40*(3), 757–773. doi:10.1111/j.1540-6261.1985.tb05000.x

Troitzsch, K. G. (1994). Modelling, simulation, and structuralism. *Poznan Studies in the Philosophy of the Science and the Humanities*, *42*, 159–177.

Tumbo, D. L. (2018). Digital technologies in higher education in distance: Mapping and use by the tutors at the Pedagogical University of Mozambique. *CADERNOS EDUCACAO TECNOLOGIA E SOCIEDADE*, *11*(4), 613–623.

Tuning the hyper-parameters of an estimator . (2019). Retrieved from https://scikit-learn.org/stable/modules/grid_search.html

Tupchienko, V. A. (Ed.). (2018). Digital lifecycle management platforms for integrated systems. Moscow, Russia: Scientific Consultant.

Uhlemann, T. H.-J., Schock, C., Lehmann, C., Freiberger, S., & Steinhilper, R. (2017). The digital twin: Demonstrating the potential of real time data acquisition in production systems. In *7th Conference on Learning Factories* Procedia Manufacturing, 9, 13–120.

UK Open Government National Action Plan 2016-18. [Electronic resource] // Retrieved from https://www.gov.uk/government/publications/uk-open-government-national-action-plan-2016-18/uk-open-government-national-action-plan-2016-18

Unified plan to achieve the national development goals of the Russian Federation for the period until 2024. Retrieved from http://static.government.ru as of May 13, 2019.

van den Beemt, A., & Diepstraten, I. (2016). Teacher perspectives on ICT: A learning ecology approach. *Computers & Education*, *92-93*, 161–170. doi:10.1016/j.compedu.2015.10.017

Vaschenko, P. A., Solomakha, A. A., Gorbachenko, V. I., Khazratov, A. A. (2014). *Clinical and laboratory parameters of patients with acute appendicitis*. Certificate of State Registration of Database No. 2014621431. Date of State Registration in the Register of Databases 10 October 2014 (in Russian).

Vasilieva, E. Yu. (2012) Development and implementation of standards for quality control of education at the university. University Management: Practice and Analysis, April. No. 1.

Vasiliev, A. N., & Tarkhov, D. A. (2009). *Neural network modeling: Principles. Algorithms. Applications*. St. Petersburg Polytechnic University Publishing House. (in Russian)

Vasiliev, V. I., Krasilnikov, V. V., Plaksiy, S. I., & Tyagunov, T. N. (2005). *Assessment of the quality of the educational institution*. Moscow, Russia: IKAR.

Vasilyev, A., Tarkhov, D., & Malykhina, G. (2018). Methods of creating digital twins based on neural network modeling. *Modern Information Technologies and IT-Education, 14*(3), 521–532.

Volkova, E. S., Gisin V. B., Soloviev V. I. (2017). Modern approaches to application of intelligent analysis methods for the credit scoring problem // Finances & Credit, 23(34), (754), pp. 2044–2060. (in Russian)

Volkova, E. S., Gisin, V. B., Soloviev, V. I. (2017). Data mining techniques: Modern approaches to application in credit scoring // Digest Finance, 22(4), (244), pp. 400–412.

Volkova, E. S., Gisin, V. B., Soloviev, V. I. (2017). Methods of the fuzzy sets theory in credit scoring // Finance and Credit, 23(35), (755), pp. 2088–2106. (in Russian)

Volterra, V. (1931). *Leçons sur la theorie mathématique de la lutte pour la vie*. Paris, France: Gauthier-Villars.

Von Gadow, K., Pukkala, T., & Tomé, M. (Eds.). (2000). *Sustainable Forest Management*. Managing Forest Ecosystems; doi:10.1007/978-94-010-9819-9

von Neumann J. (1951). The general and logical theory of automata. Cerebral mechanisms of behavior. *The Hixon Symposium*. pp. 1-31. New York.

Von Neumann, J., & Morgenstern, O. (1944). *Theory of Games and Economic Behavior*. Princeton University Press.

Wackerly, D., Mendenhall, W., & Scheaffer, R. L. (2008). *Mathematical statistics with applicationsition*. Thomson Brooks.

Wang, J., Dong, J., Wang, Y., He, J., & Changqi, O. (2011) The design of an optimal decision-making algorithm for fertilization. In Mathematical and Computer Modelling, pp. 1100-1106. doi:10.1016/j.mcm.2010.11.041

Wang, H., Qin, Q.-H., & Kang, Y. L. (2005). A new meshless method for steady-state heat conduction problems in anisotropic and inhomogeneous media. *Archive of Applied Mechanics, 74*(8), 563–579. doi:10.100700419-005-0375-8

Watkins, D. (2010). *Fundamentals of matrix computations*. Wiley.

Wei, D., Zheng, Q., & Wen, Sh. (2015). Multiparameter Stochastic Dynamics of Ecological Tourism System with Continuous Visitor Education Interventions. *Mathematical Problems in Engineering, 2015*, 968365. doi:10.1155/2015/968365

Wei, X. (2019). Research on the Development Strategy of Cross-cultural Ecological Education in English Translation Teaching at Colleges. *EKOLOJI, 28*(107), 1665–1669.

Wendland, H. (2010). *Scattered data approximation*. Cambridge University Press.

West, J., & Bogers, M. (2014). Leveraging external sources of innovation: A review of research on open innovation. *Journal of Product Innovation Management, 31*(4), 814–831. doi:10.1111/jpim.12125

Wild, S. M., Regis, R. G., & Shoemaker, C. A. (2008). ORBIT: Optimization by radial basis function interpolation in trust-regions. *SIAM Journal on Scientific Computing, 30*(6), 3197–3219. doi:10.1137/070691814

Xie, T., Yu, H., Hewlett, J., Rozycki, P., & Wilamowski, B. (2012). Fast and Efficient Second-Order Method for Learning Radial Basis Function Networks. *IEEE Transactions on Neural Networks and Learning Systems, 23*(4), 609–619. doi:10.1109/TNNLS.2012.2185059 PMID:24805044

Yadav, N., Yadav, A., & Kumar, M. (2015). *An introduction to neural network methods for differential equations*. Springer. doi:10.1007/978-94-017-9816-7

Yan, L. (2019). On the Innovation of Physical Education Model: Based on the View of Ecological Environment. *EKOLOJI, 28*(107), 3255–3261.

Yoshioka, H., & Yaegashi, Y. (2017), Stochastic optimization model of aqua cultured fish for sale and ecological education. JOURNAL OF MATHEMATICS IN INDUSTRY, 2017, 7, 8.

Yu, H., & Robinson, D. The New Ambiguity of "Open Government" // Princeton CITP//Yale ISP Working Paper. 2012. [Electronic resource] // Retrieved from http://papers.ssrn.com/sol3/papers.cfm?abstract_id=2012489

Zarrabi, N., Snaith, S., & Coakley, J. (2017). FX technical trading rules can be profitable sometimes! *International Review of Financial Analysis, 49*, 113–127. doi:10.1016/j.irfa.2016.12.010

Zeiler, M. D. (2012). *ADADELTA: An adaptive learning rate method*. Retrieved from Shttps://arxiv.org/abs/1212.5701

Zeiler, M., Krishnan, D., Taylor, G., & Fergus, R. (2010). Deconvolutional networks. In CVPR'2010. doi:10.1109/CVPR.2010.5539957

Zenin, I. A. (2015). *Problems of Russian intellectual property law (selected works). Moscow, Russia:* Statute.

Zhang, L., Li, K., & Wang, W. (2012). An improved conjugate gradient algorithm for radial basis function (RBF) networks modelling. In *Proceedings of 2012 UKACC International Conference on Control.* pp. 19–23.

Zhang, L., Li, K., He, H., & Irwin, G. W. (2013, November). A New Discrete-Continuous Algorithm for Radial Basis Function Networks Construction. *IEEE Transactions on Neural Networks and Learning Systems*, *24*(11), 1785–1798. doi:10.1109/TNNLS.2013.2264292 PMID:24808612

Zhao, M., Heinsch, F. A., Nemani, R. R., & Running, S. W. (2005). Improvements of the MODIS terrestrial gross and net primary production global data set. *Remote Sensing of Environment*, *95*(2), 164–176. doi:10.1016/j.rse.2004.12.011

Zhavoronkova, N. G., & Vypkhanova, G. V. (2018). Legal Problems and Directions of Public Administration Improvement in the Field of Forest Relations. (2018). [РУССКИЙ ЗАКОН]. *LEX RUSSICA*, *2*, 78–93. doi:10.17803/1729-5920.2018.135.2.078-093

Zheng, A., & Casari, A. (2018). *Feature engineering for machine learning: Principles and techniques for data scientists*. O'Reilly Media.

Zhong, X., & Enke, D. (2017). Forecasting daily stock market return using dimensionality reduction. *Expert Systems with Applications*, *67*, 126–139. doi:10.1016/j.eswa.2016.09.027

Zimmermann, H.-D., & Pucihar, A. Open Innovation, Open Data and New Business Models, 2015. [Electronic resource] // Retrieved from https://ssrn.com/abstract=2660692

Zohali, H., Naderi, B., & Mohammadi, M. (2019) The economic lot scheduling problem in limited-buffer flexible flow shops: Mathematical models and a discrete fruit fly algorithm. In Applied Soft Computing, pp. 904-919. Doi:10.1016/j.asoc.2019.03.054

About the Contributors

Vardan Mkrttchian graduated from State Engineering University of Armenia, the Faculty of Cybernetics as an Electronics Engineer & received his Doctorate of Sciences (Engineering) in Control Systems from Lomonosov Moscow State University (former USSR). Dr. Vardan Mkrttchian taught for undergraduate and graduate student's courses of control system, information sciences and technology, at the Astrakhan State University (Russian Federation), where he was is the Professor of the Information Systems (www.aspu.ru) six years. Now he is full professor CAD&Economy departments of Penza State University (www.pnzgu.ru). He is currently chief executive of HHH University, Australia and team leader of the international academics (www.hhhuniversity.com). He also serves as executive director of the HHH Technology Incorporation. Professor Vardan Mkrttchian has authored over 400 refereed publications. He is the author of over twenty books published of IGI Global, included ten books indexed of SCOPUS in IT, Control System, Digital Economy, and Education Technology, and 41 works in SCOPUS and 15 in WoS. He also is Editor-in-Chief of International Journal of Applied Research in Bioinformatics (IJARB).

Ekaterina Aleshina graduated from Penza State Pedagogical University, the Faculty of Foreign Languages with English as a major and German as a minor (Philology), getting qualifications of a teacher of English and German. E. Aleshina got her PhD in History from the above university in 2006 followed by the title of associate professor in 2008. In 2009-2010, E. Aleshina was doing Fulbright Faculty Development Program in Southern Connecticut State University (USA). While in the USA, she was invited as guest speaker to several universities and high schools. In 2010-2014, E. Aleshina was head of department of English and English Language Teaching Methodology at Penza State Pedagogical University, now she is head of department of Foreign Languages and FLT Methodology at Penza State University. Currently, E. Aleshina is doing her doctoral research in the specificity of political communication at Moscow Pedagogical State University. She has authored more than 80 publications featuring interdisciplinary issues and approaches.

Leyla Gamidullaeva graduated from Penza State University, the Faculty of Economics and Management, getting qualifications of an economist. L. Gamidullaeva got her PhD in Economics from Penza State University of Architecture and Construction in 2010 followed by the title of associate professor in 2018. Now she is associate professor at the department of management and economic security of Penza State University. Currently, L. Gamidullaeva is doing her doctoral research in the regional innovation system management at St Petersburg State University. She has authored more than 200 refereed publications and over ten books in innovation management, regional economic growth, networking and collaboration.

* * *

Saniyat Agamagomedova is a candidate of sociological sciences. She works as an associate professor at the Department of Management and Economic Security at Penza State University. Research interests: state control, public administration, intellectual property, administrative barriers, digitalization of management, customs control.

Serge Chernyshenko is involved in ecological researches since 1982, when he graduated from Dnepropetrovsk State University (former USSR) by the major of "Applied Mathematics". In 1986 he received his Doctorate of Sciences (Physics and Mathematics) in Mathematical Modeling from Shevchenko Kiev State University (former USSR) and the degree of Doctorate of Sciences (Biology) in Ecology from Dnepropetrovsk National University (Ukraine) in 2006. In his research, he is focused on mathematical modeling of forest ecosystems and has more than 100 publications in the field. During his scientific career he has the position of professor in several universities: Regional Moscow University, Sholokhov State University for the Humanities (Russia); Dnipropetrovsk National University, Khmelnitsky National University (Ukraine); Marie Curie-Sklodowska University (Poland), Koblenz-Landau University (Germany). Also he delivered lectures, as an invited professor, in universities of Italy, UK, Spain and Portugal. The main topics of his lectures are the following: Mathematical Modelling; Systems Analysis; General Systems Theory; Ecological Modelling; Data Mining; Mathematical Statistics and so on. He was a supervisor of about 20 international and national research and educational projects. He is the author of two monographs on mathematical ecology, over thirty books, more than 150 articles, published in various conference proceedings, books and journals in Mathematical Modelling, Ecology, IT, Control Theory, Education Technology.

Maria Gerasimenko is master student of information technologies at the department of applied and business at K.G. Razumovsky Moscow State University of technologies and management (the First Cossack University).

Irina Izmalkova is a Senior Lecturer of the Department "Accounting, Audit, Statistics" of Financial University under the Government of the Russian Federation, Lipetsk branch. Priority areas of scientific research: the study of theoretical and methodological foundations of risks in the activities of business entities in modern conditions; analysis and assessment of the competitiveness of the enterprise in a market economy; development of control and analytical support for managing business risk of an economic entity.

Mikhail Kataev Doctor of Sciences, Professor of Tomsk State University of Management Systems and radio electronics (TUSUR). In 1984 he graduated from Tomsk State University (TSU), in 1989 - graduate school at TSU. Full member of the International Academy of Higher Education Sciences. Academician International Academy of Informatization. from 1984 to 1995, senior researcher at the Institute of Optics Atmospheres SB RAS; from 1995 to the present - an employee of TUSUR. Head of Processing Laboratory Images ", Scientific Director of the Center for Space Monitoring of the Earth TUSUR. Author of about 250 scientific works, including two monographs. Research interests related to the development of processing methods and algorithms data, including multidimensional.

Dina Kharicheva is head of department the technological and information systems of Institute of Physics, Technology and Information Systems MPSU. Doctor of Technical Sciences. Specialist in the field of laser technology and technology, information technology and education. She is the author of more than 80 scientific and methodological works, has 2 monographs in the publishing house "Science", and patents for invention.

Anatoly Korikov is the Head of the Department of Automated Control Systems Tomsk State University of Control Systems and Radio Electronics (TUSUR). In 1966 he graduated from Tomsk State University (TSU), in 1970 - graduate school at TSU. Doctor of Technical Sciences, Professor, Full Member of the International Academy of Higher Education Sciences. From 1967 to 1972 - graduate student, assistant, and. about. Associate Professor, TSU, Junior Researcher, Senior Researcher at the Siberian Physical-Technical Institute (SIPT) at TSU; from 1972 to 1976 Senior Lecturer, Associate Professor of TUSUR; from 1976 to 1984 - Head of the Laboratory of Physics and Technology Institute at TSU; from 1984 to 1991 - professor, head of the department of automated control systems, Vice-Rector for Research TUSUR; Since 1991 - Head of the Department of Automated Systems TUSUR management. The author of about 250 scientific papers, including nine monographs. Honored Scientist of the Russian Federation (1998). Research interests related to the development of methods and algorithms management of complex objects.

Natalya Rasskazova received her PhD of History at Moscow Pedagogical State University. Currently she is an associate professor of the Department of Economic Theory and International Relations at Penza State University (Russian Federation). Associate professor Natalya Rasskazova teaches economic theory to PSU students. She is the author of more than 90 scientific works on the problems of sustainable development of social and economic system, small business, economic interests, etc.

Yulia Vertakova, Doctor of Economics, Professor, Head of the Department of Regional Economics and Management South-west State University. Yulia Vertakova graduated from Kursk State Technical University as a Manager & received her Doctorate of Sciences (Economics) in Economy and national economy management from Voronezh State Technical University. She is Professor, Director of Financial University under the Government of the Russian Federation, Kursk branch. She is the leading scientist of digital economy, industry development 4.0, indicative governance of sustainable development of regional economy, cluster initiatives in the region, structural transformation industrial complex regulation in terms of digitalization of economy, green economy, scaling business models, business planning, innovative management, strategic management, socio-economic systems, indicative planning, regional economics, socio-economic forecasting, proactive management, re-engineering of business processes. Professor Yulia Vertakova has authored over 300 refereed publications including 14 monographs, 26 textbooks, 28 works indexed of SCOPUS and 25 works indexed of Web of Science in Economics and IT, Digital Economy, and Education Technology. She is also has authored more than 200 articles published in various conference proceedings and journals.

Viktor Volodin is Doctor in Economics, Professor at the Department of Management and Economic Security, Head of the Institute of Economics and Management at Penza State University. Research interests: digital transformation of the economy, industrial development.

Ekaterina Zolotareva works at Financial University under the Government of the Russian Federation, a PhD in 'Mathematics in Economics'. Current research interest - the application of machine learning technologies in finance and banking. Previously worked as head of risk management unit within a major Russian banking group. An author of several scientific and professional publications, a participant of the machine learning project on behalf of a large investment company.

Index

A

B

C

D

E

F

G

H

I

Ensure Quality Research is Introduced to the Academic Community

Become an IGI Global Reviewer for Authored Book Projects

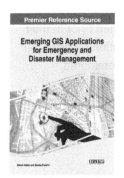

Premier Reference Source

Emerging GIS Applications for Emergency and Disaster Management

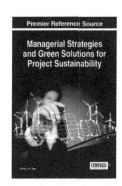

Premier Reference Source

Managerial Strategies and Green Solutions for Project Sustainability

Premier Reference Source

Comparative Approaches to Using R and Python for Statistical Data Analysis

Premier Reference Source

Solutions for High-Touch Communications in a High-Tech World

The overall success of an authored book project is dependent on quality and timely reviews.

In this competitive age of scholarly publishing, constructive and timely feedback significantly expedites the turnaround time of manuscripts from submission to acceptance, allowing the publication and discovery of forward-thinking research at a much more expeditious rate. Several IGI Global authored book projects are currently seeking highly-qualified experts in the field to fill vacancies on their respective editorial review boards:

Applications and Inquiries may be sent to:
development@igi-global.com

Applicants must have a doctorate (or an equivalent degree) as well as publishing and reviewing experience. Reviewers are asked to complete the open-ended evaluation questions with as much detail as possible in a timely, collegial, and constructive manner. All reviewers' tenures run for one-year terms on the editorial review boards and are expected to complete at least three reviews per term. Upon successful completion of this term, reviewers can be considered for an additional term.

If you have a colleague that may be interested in this opportunity, we encourage you to share this information with them.

Printed in the United States
By Bookmasters